'SOMETHING BETTER...'

AUTOBIOGRAPHICAL ESSAYS

SHAW CLIFTON

CREST BOOKS

Salvation Army National Headquarters
Alexandria, VA, USA

'SOMETHING BETTER...'
AUTOBIOGRAPHICAL ESSAYS

SHAW CLIFTON

Copyright © 2014
The Salvation Army

ISBN: 978-0-9913439-6-6
Library of Congress Control Number: 2014944818

Lt. Colonel Allen Satterlee, Editor in Chief and National Literary Secretary
Judith L. Brown, Crest Books Coordinator
Project Editors Paul Mortlock and Major John P. Murray
Cover Design by Berni Georges
Photo Section Design by Jooles Tostevin

Quotes from *The Song Book of The Salvation Army* (SASB)
are from the 1986 edition

Available from your nearest Salvation Army trade department:
Des Plaines, IL – (847)937-8896
West Nyack, NY – (888) 488-4882
Atlanta, GA – (800) 786-7372
Long Beach, CA – (847) 937-8896

Published by Crest Books
The Salvation Army National Headquarters
615 Slaters Lane
Alexandria, VA 22313
Phone: 703/684-5523
www.publications.salvationarmyusa.org

Printed in the United States of America

ALSO BY SHAW CLIFTON

What Does the Salvationist Say?
The Salvation Army, London, UK, 1977

Growing Together
(with Helen Clifton)
The Salvation Army, London, UK, 1984

Strong Doctrine, Strong Mercy
The Salvation Army, London, UK, 1985

Never the Same Again
Crest Books, Alexandria, USA, 1997

Who Are These Salvationists?
Crest Books, Alexandria, USA, 1999

New Love: Thinking Aloud About Practical Holiness
Flag Publications, Wellington, New Zealand, 2004

Selected Writings, Volumes 1 and 2
Salvation Books, London, UK, 2010

*From Her Heart – Selections from the Preaching
and Teaching of Helen Clifton*
Salvation Books, London, UK, 2012

CONTENTS

INTRODUCTION

I AM under no illusion. Had I not become the world leader of The Salvation Army, few if any would expect me to produce an autobiographical volume. However, in normal circumstances the Army has a right to anticipate some sort of life-account about or by its Generals. Hence this present offering compiled between March 2013 and January 2014.

When introducing *From Her Heart*, the 2012 volume of my wife's teaching and preaching, I made reference to the demotivating effect Helen's death had upon my (our) plans for an autobiography. Passing time and the generously warm encouragement of many have helped to revive gradually a readiness to put pen to paper, thus allowing me to enlarge considerably upon the data offered in my brief introductions to each entry in Helen's book.

The title

The title chosen for this autobiographical work will be recognised by many readers as a phrase from the fourth verse of General William Booth's stirring hymn, 'O boundless salvation', otherwise known around the Army world as 'The Founder's Song'. I have chosen it because it signals that we are never spiritually complete in this life. There is always something more, *something better*, God can do and is doing in us. That is my testimony.

Essay format

This book is simply a series of self-contained Essays of varied lengths, each one revealing – sometimes with a hint of candour – some aspect of my life's story. Readers can, I hope, take the Essays in any order and find a coherent account in each one.

I have intentionally not used a chronological approach. The sequence of the Essays is merely alphabetical by title. At an early stage I imposed upon myself the rather artificial structural discipline of using single words starting with 'S' as titles for each Essay. I found it worked pretty well, but I must seek the indulgence of readers for the title of Essay 8. It is the best I could do!

The Essays can be read in conjunction with my *Selected Writings – Volumes 1 and 2* released by Salvation Books in London and by Crest Books in Alexandria, USA in 2010 and also with the various introductory paragraphs included in Helen's 2012 book, mentioned above, from the same two publishers.

My Journal

Early in 1989 I fell into the habit of keeping a private Journal. Much of the content is far too personal, too sensitive to be made public, but after careful thought I have chosen to use extracts in several Essays. By this means I invite readers to share my journey with a greater sense of immediacy, intimacy and transparency.

I hope that those who do not know me well, and some who might mistakenly think they do, will come to understand me better by means of these insertions. Some are quite revealing and are included only after hesitation on my part.

Appreciation

Many deserve my lasting thanks for their help as these Essays have taken shape. General John Larsson (Rtd) has more than once been a knowledgeable sounding-board. So too has my friend and Army comrade, Peter Cooke. Lieut-Colonel Laurie Robertson, Paul Mortlock and Major John Murray of International Headquarters have been most welcome sources of encouragement and practical help. Sylvia Hawken, my sister, has shown a heartening and consistent interest as the work has taken shape. My children and children-in-law have allowed me freedom to write about them and the life of our family, and Matt has offered numerous perceptive suggestions leading to improvements.

Two people have played key roles. I owe them much. Major Richard Gaudion, previously my Private Secretary for seven years, has selflessly devoted endless hours of his personal time to the preparation of the manuscript, saving me from many an error of fact or style. Commissioner Birgitte Brekke, who recently assented to my becoming her husband, has been a ready source of affectionate affirmation. Her patient interest in the project has done much to revive a measure of self-confidence and a sense of motivation.

Songs and ranks

The numbers shown for Salvation Army songs are as used in the 1986 edition of the *Song Book* published by International Headquarters, London.

Ranks used for Army officers are those applicable at the time of the events related.

Finally

I alone remain responsible for any factual errors or omissions. Opinions expressed are entirely personal to me, unless stated to be formal Salvation Army policy.

I offer this book to God and to God's Army in the hope readers will sense that I am still, with them, pursuing his holy will by seeking after lasting purity, knowing that '*something better* most surely would be if once thy pure waters would roll over me.'

Shaw Clifton
General (Rtd)

London, June 2014

Come unto me,
all ye that labour and are heavy laden,
and I will give you rest.

Jesus of Nazareth

Now tossed with temptation, then haunted with fears,
My life has been joyless and useless for years;
I feel something better most surely would be
If once thy pure waters would roll over me.

General William Booth

Down at thy feet all my fears I let go,
Back on thy strength all my weakness I throw;
Lord, in my life thou shalt have thine own way,
Speak but the word, and thy child will obey...
Ask what thou wilt my devotion to test,
I will surrender the dearest and best.

Ruth Tracy

Cowardice asks the question, 'Is it safe?'
Expediency asks the question, 'Is it politic?'
Vanity asks the question, 'Is it popular?'
But conscience asks the question, 'Is it right?'

Dr Martin Luther King Jr

ESSAY 1

❧

SALVATION

ESSAY 1
SALVATION

IT IS unlikely that the small towns of Enniskillen in Northern Ireland and Goole in England's county of Yorkshire would ever claim much by way of affinity. So the love story I am about to tell was by human standards improbable, but by the standards of Heaven it carries the imprint of a divine hand. God can take the delicate threads of human lives and interweave them into something beautiful. That is what happened to Alice and Albert.

Alice and Albert

Alice Shaw was born in Enniskillen on 19 April 1912 (the year General William Booth was promoted to Glory) to Annie and Edward Shaw. Annie's maiden name was Fiddis and when she married Edward she was thirty-three, eight years his senior. Edward had been born to George and Margaret Shaw as the son of a watchmaker in the Shankill area of Belfast. The daughter of Samuel and Mary Jane Fiddis, Annie was born on 25 October 1878. Her father was a farm labourer. Annie and Edward had three children, all girls. When war broke out in 1914 Edward, who was by profession a gardener, responded to his country's call. He was shot dead by a sniper's bullet in France on 25 April 1915 at the second Battle of Ypres. So the three girls, Alice, Lily and Minnie never really knew their father.

Annie lived in a small, whitewashed, terraced house at 8 New Row, Enniskillen, with her three daughters. Alice, the eldest, was my mother. When Edward died in France, Alice's maternal grandfather, Samuel Fiddis, moved into the house with them and became their father-figure. Samuel had a full white beard and Alice was devoted to him. He would take the girls for countryside rambles and was a wonderful teller of stories. Often he would intervene to speak for the girls when their mother's patience grew thin. Also a loving and protective influence upon the young Alice and her sisters were their aunt and uncle, Thomas and Bella Fiddis, the residential caretakers of the local Working Men's Club. Uncle Thomas sometimes took his nieces fishing in a rowing boat on Lough Erne, not far from New Row.

As I write, Enniskillen's beautiful Lough Erne is suddenly much in the news for it is the venue for the 2013 Summit of the G8 powers (Canada, Japan, France, USA, United Kingdom, Germany, Italy and Russia).

Albert Clifton came into the world in Wakefield, Yorkshire, on 24 May 1916 some four years after Alice was born. The second son of Jessie Clifton (née Wood) and Ernest John Clifton who hailed from Somersham in Huntingdonshire (later renamed Cambridgeshire), he moved with his parents and elder brother, Donald, from Crowle, Lincolnshire, to live in Goole, first in Spencer Street and then at 32 Adeline Street, a small terraced house still standing today with a yard and a lane at the back. Albert's father ran a confectionery shop but the business failed and he later worked in the docks at Goole on the river Humber, eventually becoming a warehouse foreman there. He was a loving but strict father. Albert's maternal grandmother also lived in Goole and received frequent visits from her grandsons. His mother's sister, Mary, was there too and married Samuel King. Mary was a committed Roman Catholic while Sam became and remained a Salvation Army cornet player and served as the songster leader of Goole Town Corps. Mary went to church on Sunday mornings but attended the Army with Sam in the evenings.

The Army came to Enniskillen. Alice started to attend the meetings and at the age of 13 made a solid decision to follow Jesus Christ. In later years she would tell us about the day she went forward to kneel at the Mercy Seat. She knew about getting saved (salvation: forgiveness for the past) and also about living a holy and pure life (sanctification: grace for a pure life in the present). She told us, 'When I knelt as a young girl I gave the whole of myself to God. Nothing was held back. I was saved and sanctified all in that moment. Everything around me glowed with colour and I saw with new eyes.'

This decisive event in her early teens was to become the bedrock of all her remaining years. She put on the Army uniform and bonnet, but when she went home wearing it her mother took the bonnet from her head and threw it upon the blazing fire in the hearth. Within Alice this moment created an even more steely determination to live up to what she had promised in her Articles of War as a soldier in the Army. With the passing of time her mother's antipathy softened and she began to understand her eldest daughter's deep commitment to God.

Meanwhile, many miles away across the Irish Sea, the young Albert Clifton in Goole was about to receive a visitor. He was at home when a knock was heard on the front door and there his mother discovered Adjutant Tuffin, the local Salvation Army officer. 'I'm looking for 500 children to start a Salvation Army Sunday school,' he said. 'Do come in,' was the response. Albert, my father, was called into the room to meet the adjutant, his first encounter with the Army. Soon the uniformed visitor was suggesting that the whole family might come along to the Sunday meetings. He went on his way to knock on the many other doors in Adeline Street. A few moments later the Cliftons received a further visitor, this time at the back door. There stood the milkman saying with a grin, 'I too belong to the Army, so my son will come and collect your son and get him to the Sunday school.' Between them, the adjutant and the Army milkman had it all worked out!

Thus God's Army came into Albert's young life. He and his mother became regular attenders and soon his father followed, later to become the corps sergeant-major. My grandfather, Ernest, would head the march each Sunday night as the band returned to the hall after the open-air witness. The men he supervised in the docks would observe him from the public houses. 'They watch me more closely', he often remarked, 'than they do the local Anglican vicar. They want to see if my commitment to Christ and to the cause of the Army is real.'

Alice Shaw left home and went to London to become a cadet in the Torchbearers Session at the Army's William Booth Memorial Training College at Denmark Hill in 1933. She was 21. In her heart she wanted to help the poor. 'I wanted to do the work of a slum sister, going into the homes of the poor and helping to wash and cook for them.' It was not to be. They told her, to her puzzlement and dismay, she was far too bright for such work. When her session was commissioned, and because she had an attractive singing voice, she found herself assigned to the 'Musical Miriams', a group that toured England leading meetings both indoor and out as part of the energetic evangelical thrust of that time. Later, however, she was glad to be appointed to her native Northern Ireland where she served at Newtownards, Donaghadee, Armagh and Banbridge.

Albert too left home. A shy young man with delicate health, he had left school at 14 and worked as a delivery boy for a local greengrocer.

However, his hungry mind made him a reader and lover of books and he went to be a cadet in London with a well-stocked intellect. Childhood illness had not prevented him from developing the world of his thoughts. So it was that this reserved, courteous and intelligent young Salvationist became a cadet in the Guardians of the Covenant Session in 1936. He stood out and was appointed to be a cadet-sergeant, helping to train the next year's intake.

Not long afterwards, in 1938, he was appointed to take charge of Newry Corps in Northern Ireland. Writing of these years, my Dad records: 'During my time in Newry I had an experience which was to change my entire life. I believe it was under the hand of God. Officers in Ireland were then attached to what was known as the Ireland and Scotland Territory. We were taken to Glasgow by boat for officers' meetings. On one such journey I met an officer by the name of Captain Alice Shaw and discovered she was stationed only 13 miles from me. Alice proved to be very special and I fell deeply in love with her. It was easy to fall in love with her and just as easy to stay in love with her. Her devotion to God and his cause was so very genuine and her desire to become a Salvation Army officer in response to God's call was followed through in spite of opposition from home. Alice was an outstanding preacher of the Word, a caring pastor of her people, and a courageous witness for Christ. Her nature and disposition were gentle, forthright, caring, loving and in every way self-negating. In truth she was a valiant soldier for Christ. Her lovely presence filled the house and our home.'

So Alice and Albert at last met and were married. Their service together as officers took them and their three children from Ballymacarrett and Portadown in Northern Ireland to Southampton in England. Then it was on to Barnsley in Yorkshire, Parkhead in Glasgow, Edmonton in the north of London (where I met Helen), and later to appointments in Leicester, Lancaster, Doncaster, Preston and finally to International Headquarters (with their home in Ilford and later Hornchurch, Essex) where Albert served as the Under Secretary for Public Relations. They entered honourable retirement together in 1981. The Chief of the Staff, Commissioner Stanley Cottrill, presented their retirement certificates at a gathering at Sunbury Court where colleagues and loved ones came together to honour them.

Alice died of cancer on 12 June 1984. My sister, Sylvia, and I were with Dad at her bedside in Rush Green Hospital near Hornchurch when she breathed her last. He had nursed her at home during most of her final illness. She wanted her funeral to be for the benefit of her unsaved neighbours, so before the main funeral event at the South Essex Crematorium we held a short preliminary service in the house in Purbeck Road with neighbours and friends gathered closely around her coffin. Major John West led the funeral and spoke of Mum's longings and prayers to see her neighbours come to Christ.

Twenty-two years later on 30 May 2006 Albert died in Ilminster, Somerset, with my sisters, Sylvia and Mary, and Mary's husband, Nick, beside him at home. He had relished his life in this country town, sharing Sylvia's lovely cottage for many years. He died just a few weeks after I took office as the General. I led his funeral service in the Minster Church of St Mary, which stands visible only 100 metres from the cottage. Yeovil Corps Band, with Majors John and Ann Thomas, took part. So too did the Methodist minister, Ruth Goodland, and the vicar, the Reverend Prebendary Alastair Wallace. We had asked that, as the coffin left the Minster, the church bells would ring out, not with the customary doleful toll we associate with a death, but with a gloriously triumphant peal of celebration and rejoicing for a life's journey consummated in Christ. As Dad's coffin was placed in the hearse, the vicar's wife, Judy, was heard to say: 'I want those bells at my funeral too.' Later, Alastair told me this service was the most uplifting event he had seen in his church. What a gracious person, I thought, to say a lovely thing like that (see also my Journal extracts in Essay 12).

Sylvia, Mary and Shaw

Born in Belfast on 21 September 1945, I was the youngest of three and the only boy. This led to a combination of outcomes. Sometimes I was favoured but sometimes firmly rebuked lest I got above myself. My sisters were at first my playmates and later my protectors. From time to time they were also the victims of my pranks, for which they made me pay heavily. So all in all we were a pretty normal bunch and led a happy, noisy, active family life.

Our parents were unfailingly loving and even-handed toward all three of us. We knew where the behavioural boundaries had been set and that ignoring or defying them would bring consequences. The result was that we felt secure. At the heart of things was the obvious love and devotion which bonded our parents in covenantal union. We were beneficiaries of that incomparable factor which gives any child the best prospect of an effective childhood, namely being raised by a man and a woman openly committed to each other in the bonds of marriage. Moreover, this was a Christian marriage and as children we were given all the good that can flow from such a foundation.

Neither of our parents was for a single moment sanctimonious. They loved God as a completely natural response to his evident beneficence, they loved each other with a love that sprang from mutual respect as well as mutual attraction, and they loved their three children with a selfless devotion that allowed us to be ourselves and yet shaped and prepared us to respond to God if and when he might come calling.

Thus religion was a commonplace topic of conversation in our home. It was as natural as eating or sleeping, not reserved for special moments but instead interlaced with everyday life. We were encouraged to question everything, to think hard and to draw conclusions for ourselves. Significantly, we were encouraged to love and respect the Army. Our parents made no secret of their sacred callings and yet we were free to hear them air their own questions about Army methods, regulations, personnel and decisions. They told us explicitly that the Army was not perfect but would then go on to say that God had raised it up and wanted to use it in his plans for the salvation of the world.

So we knew full well the difference between God and God's Army. We were under no illusions. God was to be worshipped, adored and obeyed. The Army was merely his tool, imperfect but useful, at its best very impressive but at its worst deeply flawed, with the rest of the Body of Christ, the other churches, exactly like that too.

So as children our vocabulary included words like Jesus, God, Heaven, Saviour, eternity, holiness, others, purity, sin alongside words like food, bed, football, homework, band practice, school, pocket money, aniseed balls and chewing gum! Christianity was no mere add-on. It was part of the air we breathed and yet amid it all we were still allowed to come to faith for ourselves. The faith of the parent can be made part of the child's environment, but the child must in the end choose for himself.

Let me leap forward for a moment to the time of completing law degree studies in the summer of 1968 (see Essay 13). My mother wrote a letter to me in her own hand. Compiled in the month of August, it reveals the things that ruled her life and her heartfelt longings for her child:

> *My Dear Son,*
>
> *I am glad about any success that may come to you. I believe humility to be the most necessary grace to strive after and maybe the most elusive. So I have ever guarded against saying many lovely things to you, although I could have done so, in case it made you proud.*
>
> *You were a model boy, a gentle, lovable, trusting toddler, a reliable lad, trustworthy and obedient to your teachers and parents. As you grew into your teenage years you showed many signs of the makings of a man of God. I am not surprised at that because I took your coming to me as a mighty serious trust. If prayer is the greatest power in the universe then all your life that power has been your standby.*
>
> *Now all I desire for you is a continual growing further into the knowledge of God. I beg you to put all he has given you at his disposal. Consider him in all things and follow steadily what is good. Many times you will be tempted to meanness, greed, self. Wrong doctrine is rife so try to study God's Word. I assure you that pain and shame suffered for his sake is more to be desired than the praise of man.*
>
> *My heart's cry to you is 'Love him, the sinner's friend.' God bless you and dear Helen.*

My mother kept a notebook beside her bed because often she would wake in the small hours with words of Scripture running through her mind. She made a habit of writing these down, with other thoughts as well which would shape her preaching for subsequent occasions. I still have in my possession one of her notebooks and can find there night-time phrases and quotations which eventually grew into sermons I recall her preaching. Here are a few selected lines from one set of handwritten notes based on Matthew 22:42 and entitled 'What think ye of Christ?'

> *Before we dismiss Christ as a myth, an idealist, an agitator, a liar or a lunatic we must see what the Bible says…. He was not pretending to be human but was a genuine human being. He was not a man who resembled God. He was God (these words underlined three times!). Christ changes us through friendship with him, simply by us being with him and through his loving us with a love and a patience that will never let us go.*

From war-torn Belfast we moved to Sholing in Southampton where I first went to school (see Essay 13), then to Barnsley. Three years later we began life in Parkhead and from there the family ventured southward again to Edmonton. It was 1957 and by then I was 12. Like many of that age I was very open to God. I arrived in London having just undergone a strange, almost mystical experience in Parkhead.

I was walking home from school in the mid-afternoon. Passing the grassy spaces of the Tollcross Park on my left, I was about to turn right into Tennyson Drive and reach our house at number 64 when I heard a voice addressing me by my first name: 'Shaw, one day you will be a Salvation Army officer.' There was no other person near me. Somehow I knew I was not hearing with my ears but with some other faculty I could not then name. The words were as clear as a bell, the meaning unmistakeable. I felt neither troubled nor pleased. My boyish mind had been full of other things like homework and guessing what might be on our teatime plates. However, here was a simple, matter-of-fact yet other-worldly word to me. I do not recall even breaking my stride, but the moment lingered. Later I told my parents what had happened and they responded without fuss. 'God often speaks like that,' they said. Here again was the everyday normality of the divine.

Helen and Shaw

It was many years before I heard that voice speak again. By then Helen and I were married. We were attending the East London Division's annual Youth Councils meetings in Ilford Town Hall, a building now demolished but which then stood near to where our son, John, and his wife, Naomi, currently serve as lieutenants. We had discussed together the prospect of

Army officership but matters had not crystallised for us. It was Sunday 10 May 1970, I was 24, and we had been married for three years. I was seated just a few rows from the back of the auditorium with Helen to my left. We were both in our high-collared uniforms. During the final segment of the evening meeting and while prayer was taking place and many were responding at the Mercy Seat, the Lord's voice whispered clearly to me again. 'This is the time. Everything so far in your life has been preparatory. Now you are to make a decisive change of direction.' I recall moments of intense, silent dialogue. I sought reassurance. 'If I say "yes", will things be alright?' I scarcely knew what I was asking. 'Yes,' came the reply, 'you have seen officership and its sometimes harsh realities in your parent's lives, but now you must come. I will be with you.' Then again, 'Everything in your life thus far is but a making ready.'

The meeting ended. We drove our little maroon Mini car toward our tiny apartment in Muswell Hill, but first ascended the hilly roads to Alexandra Palace with its huge TV transmitter and sat in the parking area looking out over the lights of northern London. As best I could, I told Helen what had happened. She was unperturbed and, in some inexplicable way, prepared. 'Then we will do it together,' was her simple but immediate reply. I held her for a long time. Our tiny car was holy, even romantic, ground as we sealed and settled matters in our hearts.

My family had moved to Edmonton in 1957 when Helen was 10. Her parents were Donald and Betty Ashman (née Willis), the son and daughter respectively of Jack and Daisy Ashman and Eliza Willis who was widowed early in her marriage. Helen, like me, was one of three children but she was the eldest, a sister to Ruth and Kevin. By the time we were in our early teenage years we both knew we would one day be husband and wife. We married on Saturday 15 July 1967. Helen was 19, I was 22. My father officiated at Edmonton Citadel hall in Fore Street with Ruth as Helen's bridesmaid and my brother-in-law, Nick, as my best man. We were all in Army uniform.

Among the wedding vows was a promise not to let our marriage hinder our service for God. We promised this gladly for we felt that together we could serve better. Helen's impact upon me was profound. Above everything and everyone else I wanted *her* approval. This never faded through all the years. It meant everything to me. Did that sermon go alright? Is this article ready to send to the editor? Am I acting wisely? What would you do or say on this? Am I getting ahead of myself? In the end we could tell at a glance what the other was thinking.

Helen never once doubted that her place was in the Army. She was very clear-minded about that. Happy to wear her uniform whenever it was needed or useful, she immersed herself in everything we did as Salvationists. She affected me in every way, but especially in my soul. I knew she was inherently good, always ready to give time and attention to others, especially those sneered at by society. In this she was Christlike.

We raised our three children in the faith as we ourselves had been raised. When they were old enough to make choices for themselves it was a condition of living together that each of us went to a place of Christian worship at least once on Sundays. It did not have to be the Army. The children could choose. We hoped our children would be, as Dr Martin Luther King Jr puts it in his collection of sermons, *Strength to Love* (1970), tough-minded but tender-hearted, wise as serpents but innocent as doves. This is a balance we see in Jesus as he spoke truth fearlessly and yet was moved with compassion by the plight of those in need. We wanted our children also to know truth from falsehood, to recognise foolishness when they saw or heard it, to discern superstition from true religion, and yet be open to love, to friendship, to those in pain or experiencing problems, and to sense deep within themselves the place of the Saviour in all of this. We were very conscious too of our duty to let them see a similar balance in their parents' lives. Helen had a calmer, more even spirit than me which meant that if the children incurred her disapproval it stung all the more. She wanted each of them to be loving and selfless, but able also to think for themselves. They were the recipients of a very powerful, affirming, motherly love.

Why the Army?

Being a Salvationist was a natural outcome of my childhood, but maturity required that I did not simply drift passively or in some token manner into lifelong commitments. Meeting and marrying Helen cemented things. It was easier to serve with her than without her. Our personal documents file holds various commissions and other records evidencing God's way with us from when we were young.

My dedication certificate records that on Sunday 28 October 1945, some five weeks after my birth, I was dedicated by my parents to God at Mountpottinger Corps in Northern Ireland, Brigadier Arthur Ling conducting the ceremony.

A little cerise slip entitled 'Declaration of Salvation' and dated 21 February 1954 records my kneeling at the Mercy Seat in the young people's hall at Barnsley and publicly acknowledging Jesus as my Saviour. This was simply a formality for I had always known about Jesus from the moment I first heard his name and learned of him at my mother's knee. I cannot remember a time in my life when I did not know about Jesus or any time when I did not feel glad and pleased about that. So I have no dramatic or startling conversion story to tell. I can speak of later, decisive moments and of growing in grace but I was raised in the faith and am a child of the faith.

The Army moved our family from Barnsley to Scotland. Young People's Sergeant-Major Henry Bland of Parkhead Corps endorsed my junior soldier's pledge on 20 April 1954 when I was eight years old. In February 1955 I became a commissioned member of the singing company (see Essay 5) and a year later a member of the young people's band, playing a tenor horn. In April 1956 they gave me a certificate of merit for Bible knowledge learned in what was then known as the directory class, which met early on Sunday mornings. In July 1957 the notable Bandmaster Alex Thain from Edinburgh Gorgie Corps signed a certificate saying I had passed a test in music theory and instrumental practice at the Territorial Youth Music Camp, the certificate being countersigned by Lieut-Commissioner William Grottick, the Territorial Commander for Scotland and Ireland.

We moved to Edmonton, where the Army corps was quite large. In July 1959 they gave me a corps cadet certificate of merit, but it was labelled second class! A few years later I was commissioned as a senior bandsman on 25 February 1962, although in fact I had been playing in the large senior band for quite some time before that, having gained something of a reputation as a tenor horn player and fledgling soloist. Later, in August 1969, I was commissioned Assistant Corps Sergeant-

Major at the age of 23 and soon thereafter became Corps Sergeant-Major in October 1970.

Helen joined the Sunbeam brigade in October 1956 aged eight. The motto was 'Do right!' In April 1957 she signed her pledge to become a junior soldier. I still have the cards she signed from 1958 to 1961 on the yearly Junior Soldier's Day of Renewal. She became a singing company member and later a songster but I do not have the commissions for these steps. Neither do I have her commission as Corps Cadet Guardian at Edmonton, a position she was given in 1967 when she was only 19 and a university student.

We were happy to be Christians in the Army. Early childhood steps in service and involvement grew into more considered commitments as our faith grew. Adulthood and marriage brought us to a rounded, mature determination to go on serving God in the Army. We valued its freedom from ceremonial controversy, its boldness in witness, its esteeming of persons regardless of gender, its heart for the poor, and its global expression. It was a good fit for us.

ESSAY 2

⟨⟨

SANCTIFICATION

ESSAY 2
SANCTIFICATION

MANY factors have combined to keep me in The Salvation Army, prominent among them the Army's precious heritage as part of the holiness movement.

A sanctified life, a holy life, is at root a simple concept. Countless words have been written, preached or taught by Salvationists and others on this matter and I confess to having made my own faltering contribution from time to time. The idea of being holy is best expressed in straightforward language. Cecil Frances Alexander (1818-95) does this in her wonderful hymn 'There is a green hill'. The third verse says simply:

> 'He died that we might be *forgiven*,
> He died to make us *good*,
> That we might go at last to Heaven,
> Saved by his precious blood.'

The first line is about salvation, the second about sanctification. Jesus died at Calvary to make it possible for us to be both forgiven *and* good. You can be forgiven without going on to become good. You cannot become good (that is, grow in the holy life) unless first forgiven. Ideally, forgiveness sought and received will move on to goodness longed for and realised.

All this is caught by William Booth's wonderful song, 'O boundless salvation'. A phrase from the fourth verse forms this book's title:

> 'I feel *something better* most surely would be
> If once thy *pure* waters would roll over me.'

It is a longing for lasting purity, for something better than a repetitive cycle of sinning and repenting, sinning and repenting....

The train to Liverpool Street

In Essay 1 I record something of my spiritual beginnings. Now here I try to describe my walk of faith as I have grown older and grown in grace.

Essay 9 will touch further on spirituality and for continuity could well be read next after this one, but here let me write frankly about the early condition of my soul.

Spiritual things – the person of Jesus, the availability of grace, the life to come, the need to serve – were the common stuff of my upbringing. As a teenager I knew and felt a clear devotion to Christ and his cause. Undergirding the typical experiences of moving into early adulthood, my Christian roots in the Army provided a framework and a stability for which I was and am thankful. Reading included Christian literature, some of Army origin, some not. Knowledge of the Scriptures grew steadily. So too did my interest in the Army itself and how it functioned. I liked having contact with a number of fine but unheralded Salvation Army officers and saw in them something to be admired.

Marriage to Helen cemented much of this for she shared the same outlook and was relaxed and happy in her Christian walk. Eventually we found our way into Salvation Army officership and launched out in 1972 upon our first appointments, then to Africa and four years later back to London. Service at International Headquarters (IHQ) followed in 1982 with much overseas travel and a hectic workload, but it was stimulating and fulfilling. I saw all of this in deeply spiritual terms and held in my heart a clear focus on the person of Jesus and a desire to honour him in everything. Yet often I intuited there was 'something better'. I could not put it into words.

It was early in 1989 that I experienced a strange but special moment that felt decisive in many ways. It arose like this. An invitation reached us from Commissioner Roy Lovatt to travel to Australia to undertake teaching roles at a Brengle Holiness Institute to be held in Sydney (see Essay 7A). Neither of us had previously been involved in such an event either as a delegate or as a member of the teaching faculty. I had spoken at a Brengle Institute held at Sunbury Court near London in June 1988 but that was just a fleeting visit. The roles we were asked to fulfil in Sydney would immerse us in teaching and counselling throughout the event on a daily basis.

We started our preparation several months ahead of time for there was much to do. I began a systematic reading or rereading of everything I could find on the subject of holiness published by the Army going back to the Booths, Samuel Brengle, Frederick Coutts and others. I explored also the works of John Wesley, Martin Luther and Augustine. We read and analysed the many holiness songs in the *Song Book*. Our preparation was more than thorough.

This process had its own effect upon us and gently sensitised us still further to the beauty of our holiness heritage as Salvationists. In the course of my preparation I paid particular attention to the various editions of the *Handbook of Doctrine* which set out the primary tenets of Army beliefs and their basis in the Scriptures. One day I made plans to read the 1940 edition of the *Handbook* during the lengthy early morning commute from our home in Brentwood Road, Hornchurch, to IHQ in central London's Queen Victoria Street. Settling into my seat on the crowded train and dressed in full uniform and cap, I placed my briefcase (it often served as a travelling reading-desk) upon my knees and took out the 1940 book. It had belonged to my father. Turning to Chapter Ten entitled 'Entire Sanctification', I began to read. I do not know quite how to explain what happened next. I became so fully absorbed in its pages, almost mesmerised, that I was oblivious to those around me. As I read, the truths explained seemed to burn deeply into my soul. Although I had been reading holiness literature extensively for many weeks, here was something different. It had been written for a verdict. It was simple but profound. It was as clear as could be. I felt as though the pages were calling out to me, asking me to let their contents enfold and fill me. Silently my heart was responding with an unreserved assent.

The train rumbled on, stopping at station after station, the commuters boarding or alighting, but I noticed nothing of this so absorbed was I in the 24 pages of Chapter Ten. My mind was captivated, my soul stirred. It was as though all I knew of the holy life and of our teaching was now mystically affirmed and embedded anew in those recesses of my being that are accessible only to God.

Suddenly I looked up to see the train emptying. We had reached the end of the line and were in London's Liverpool Street Station. Still I sat, motionless. Then other passengers began to board the train as it prepared for its return journey. At that I repacked my briefcase hastily and hurried to get off. My heart was pounding, not from exertion but from a strange spiritual excitement. This carried me along the streets to IHQ and to my office where the legal section's work of the day awaited me.

As I write of this I am looking at Chapter Ten of my 1940 *Handbook* and still it resonates as it did on that day long ago. My pencilled annotations from 1989 serve as a reminder of the impact it had upon me then. The language reflects the era in which it was written, but the appeal of its message remains to me undimmed. While the journey to Liverpool Street Station was a profound affirmation to my soul, it served to deepen still further my conviction of the real possibility of 'something better' and also to reinforce my personal desire for the holy life. That desire has never left me. There is always growth, 'something better', in our walk with God.

Holiness is not piety. Holiness is of God and therefore makes us more and more human, conforming us increasingly to his image as we open up to his working within us. Everything becomes sharpened: our awareness of our need; our acknowledgement of those things within us that are inconsistent with the will and mind of God; our clarity of thought; our discernment of people; even our sense of humour! God's refining power is always available and always at work.

Our songs

Of the many songs in our *Song Book* and also of the several helpful songs from other sources which have come into our use since the last *Song Book* was published in 1986, I offer just one for highlighting in this Essay as typical of several that help and challenge. From the pen of Charles Wesley (1707-88), it is Song 714. Verse one expresses the writer's hope of victory over sin:

> 'But can it be that I should prove
> For ever faithful to thy love,
> From sin for ever cease?
> I thank thee for the blessèd hope;
> It lifts my drooping spirit up,
> It gives me back my peace.'

Next he boldly receives God's word of promise and experiences 'at last' what he has longed for:

'In thee, O Lord, I put my trust,
Mighty and merciful and just;
Thy sacred word is passed;
And I, who dare thy word receive,
Without committing sin shall live,
Shall live to God at last.'

Verse three speaks of relaxing into the sure ability of God to make the seeker pure and expresses trust in that divine ability:

'I rest in thine almighty power;
The name of Jesus is a tower
That hides my life above;
Thou canst, thou wilt my helper be;
My confidence is all in thee,
The faithful God of love.'

Finally he expresses a sense of assurance regarding God's care in this life and in eternity:

'Wherefore, in never-ceasing prayer,
My soul to thy continual care
I faithfully commend;
Assured that thou through life shalt save,
And show thyself beyond the grave
My everlasting friend.'

Strangely this song is not to be found in the holiness section of the *Song Book* and in that sense is misplaced. It reflects classical Wesleyan holiness insights and can make a very useful teaching tool when analysed thoughtfully in a group setting. Better still, it offers a helpful framework for private and personal prayer reflection on the inner life, as do many Army songs.

Catherine Bannister

Essay 8 covers my love of books and there I make further brief mention of a slim Army volume entitled *The Practice of Sanctification* by Catherine Bannister. Published in 1936, it was a favourite of Helen's. It consists mostly of extracts from Major Bannister's letters home to her sister, written from Maharashtra in India where she spent 20 years pioneering Army ministry among the Marathi tribespeople. She learned their language and adopted their lifestyle. She took the name 'Yuddha Bai' ('Warrior Sister').

This booklet's power stems from its focus on holy living in action. It appeals to me because it is not remotely theoretical, but offers down-to-earth testimony to living the holy life in a culture not one's own and far from Christian, something both Helen and I have tried by grace to do. Let Catherine Bannister's words speak for themselves:

> *My calling is to be one of those who are free to spend and be spent for the salvation of the outcast and wandering.* [What a wonderful statement!]
>
> *Sacrifice and salvation! Probably essentially and intimately connected – for although there may be plenty of sacrifice without salvation, yet there can never be salvation without sacrifice. So it is with us in all our self-denial and sacrifice. Although the self-denial and sacrifice are essential to soul-saving, yet if the sacrifice is what we aim at we shall miss the soul-saving; our hearts will grow hard and narrow, self-absorbed and self-righteous. The sacrifice is not what we live for, but the soul-saving.*
>
> *Giving my experience in a meeting recently, I said that I did not believe God intended us to walk in darkness, and that since I had reached the point of making no conditions with God I had realised a life of light and joy without a cloud.*
>
> *Truly the profession of a soul-winner is the most exultant one spiritually that it is possible to make, and therefore one which is surrounded by the greatest temptations. The higher the peak we climb, the greater our danger of wounds and bruises if we fall. A soul-winner must be devoted to the salvation of souls, beyond and*

above the mere passive love for and interest in their salvation, which is naturally found in the breast of every Christian man and woman. There must be something more than a mere enthusiasm which can shout through a hearty meeting or work like a slave by fits and starts. There must be a devotion for souls of a kind that will sacrifice time, rest, strength, companionship, human affections, and even life itself, because the Gethsemane passion for souls burns so strong in the bosom – of a kind that has so completely got the mastery over self and pride in every form that it is willing not to hang back by reason of its unfitness; but in the midst of others who excel in natural gifts and powers is willing to go forward and even have the appearance of fools if only they may have a share in giving forth the saving message.

Then let us kneel at Calvary's cross and look into the suffering face of him who hangs there, until the melting, yearning, tenderness of spirit, and the burning unquenchable love of that broken-hearted Man of Sorrows flows into and fills our soul. Then indeed we shall need no spur to urge us forth to the most desperate needs for the world's salvation.

I am not at all afraid that God will forget to keep a crown for me or that he will not make it beautiful enough. I am afraid only that my life will slip away before I have gathered all the jewels that I want to win for his crown. I am sure that when I stand in eternity I shall not think that I have gathered enough nor dug deep enough into the mire of sin and degradation to seek for them. Since I became converted I have cast from me all earthly ambition and have sought neither popularity nor position nor ease but earnestly have prayed to be kept filled with a holy ambition for seeking jewels to place in the Saviour's diadem.

Catherine Bannister was promoted to Glory on 14 July 1910. She had all but completed a new edition of a Mahratta *Song Book*. Published later, it became a lasting memorial of her love for the people and her holy zeal for her Lord. Truly a saint.

Highlighting holiness

Brengle Institutes have become an integral part of the Army's life, focusing especially upon the spiritual condition of Army officers. Named after Commissioner Samuel Logan Brengle, an American officer who became known worldwide for his writings and preaching on the holy life, these 10- to 14-day events are held annually in most parts of the Army world. They are attended by officers as spiritual refresher courses and deeper life gatherings but with a very intentional and explicit focus on our tenth Doctrine. From time to time similar occasions are arranged for non-officers, a trend that deserves to be taken up more widely among us.

We need to recognise and resist any tendency to turn Brengle Institutes into just vague spiritual retreats. The need is for a deeper grasp and a more concentrated focus upon purity of life and all that is on offer from God to help us find victory over temptation and sin daily. There can, of course, be varieties of approach. I have found in my own participation at such events through the years that I have tended to speak less and less of the theoretical aspects of holiness and more and more of the practical outworkings in our daily lives and relationships. Both aspects are important, but when time is limited the need is for the teaching to be grounded in the realities of everyday life.

The 1989 event in Sydney already mentioned was a landmark, transformative experience. A few years later we found ourselves teaching at our second Brengle Institute in an altogether different setting in Aizawl, the capital city of the State of Mizoram, the easternmost part of India. By 1995 we were living in the north-east of England in Middlesbrough and leading the Durham and Tees Division. Thus we flew from Teesside Airport on the evening of 5 January 1995, stayed the night in a hotel near Heathrow Airport and the next day flew on to Delhi, arriving at midnight. Seven hours later it was onward to Calcutta for two days of rest and then the final connecting flight to Silchar, Assam, where we arrived on 10 January to be met by Captain (now Commissioner) Lalzamlova, Education Officer at the India Eastern Training College. There then followed a seven-hour drive south into Mizoram where the plains of Assam gave way to the lofty mountain passes of the Mizo people. Our tiny car seemed to cling like a mountain goat to the narrow, winding roads with sheer drops on one side and vertical cliffs on the other. Darkness fell. We reached our modest hotel late that night. The next two weeks proved unforgettable.

It was the first-ever Brengle Institute in the territory. Except for one woman officer, the delegates were all male. Helen taught on prayer and I presented lectures about the history of holiness doctrine and on the work of the Holy Spirit. Two excellent translators helped us. In charge of it all was the Field Secretary, Lieut-Colonel (now Commissioner) Lalkiamlova who, at my request, taught a series on concepts of holiness in the Old Testament. It all concluded with a beautiful, tender but informal hand-washing ceremony in which gently we bathed one another's hands and dried them to remember Christ washing the feet of his disciples in a spirit of humble servanthood.

With the gathering at an end we packed our cases and hurtled by car back down the mountain into Assam. After a sleepless night in Silchar, where rats shared our room, we flew to Calcutta, visited Lieut-Colonel Joan Williams in the children's home, flew on overnight to Heathrow and then home to Middlesbrough. From the heady days on the Aizawl mountaintop, both physically and spiritually, it was back to the sacred earthiness of regular duty and service at home. My diary for 1995 tells me that after a day of rest we made pastoral contact with several officers, hosted Colonel Ray Holdstock (Field Secretary), launched the annual Red Shield Appeal on Tyne-Tees Television with their Pam Royle and Bob Johnson, and drove to Shildon to address the Annual General Meeting of the Shildon Council of Churches. On 1 February it was announced that the Army was to reappoint us to Boston, USA, and that our beloved Durham and Tees Division would be merged with the Northern Division with headquarters in Newcastle. All of these things held a sanctity of their own for they were part of the business of Almighty God. They required and deserved to be addressed and handled by us in a spirit of sanctification just as much as when we gathered in the sacred conclave of a formal Brengle Institute.

We were to return to Mizoram as the Army's world leaders in February 2007, by which time Aizawl had an airport – no more nightmare car rides on mountainous precipices! Hundreds of Salvationists awaited us as we touched down, our pilot (after some prevarication!) having dared to plunge earthward through the thick cloud cover so typical of that region. Profoundly pleased to be back among the Mizo Salvationists, I had asked that a short reunion be arranged with the Brengle Institute delegates from 1995. All of these officers gathered to meet us. Each was still serving faithfully. It was wonderful. The same faces, the same sense of comradeship, a sense of having shared something sacred. We spoke together, recalled 1995 together, and prayed together. Together in Christ, together in God's Army, together in the sanctified life.

Further teaching opportunity opened up in 2000 when we mounted a Brengle Institute for the officers of the Pakistan Territory. Eagerly the selected delegates convened at the Territorial Headquarters compound in Lahore. Any such event needs to be planned in the context of a specific cultural setting and so we tried to cater for the everyday pressures to which our people were exposed. It was important for the material on offer to be grounded in reality. South Asia is not the easiest part of the world in which to live a holy life.

When we reached New Zealand in 2002 I was able to offer only one or two lectures at the Brengle Institute in Wellington that year, but in 2003 made sure that as the Territorial Commander (TC) I would be present throughout the entire period of the event and would share in carrying a significant portion of the teaching. In this way it was possible to grow closer to the officer delegates. Our experiences taught us that a Brengle Institute succeeds best in achieving its objectives, not only when the material is relevant or when the lectures go well, but also when the members of the teaching faculty and of territorial leadership can interact with all present in relaxed fellowship. The lounge room becomes a place of helpful encounter, as too the meal table. The conversation does not need always to be of spiritual things, but the delegates deserve to sense, when you rise to speak or lecture, that they are hearing a person whose life and relationships are authentically grounded in a shared experience of the Saviour.

It became possible to repeat the Wellington approach when I joined the teaching team at the United Kingdom Brengle Institute at Sunbury-on-Thames in 2005. Residing throughout with the officer delegates, I felt blessed to take my place as a member of the teaching faculty under the leadership of the Institute Principal, Major Melvyn Jones. My abiding memory is of sacred and tender moments, especially at the concluding event of the Institute during which both staff and delegates were given the opportunity to kneel and sign a holiness covenant as a landmark, a milestone, in their walk with the living Christ whose likeness we all seek.

Earlier that same year Helen and I had gone to Moscow at the invitation of Colonel Barry Pobjie to take part in the first ever Brengle Institute held in the Eastern Europe Territory. It was well led and coordinated by Major Anita Caldwell. Helen again delivered her series of lectures on the life of prayer. We gathered in a small woodland hotel, our songs and prayers bursting out through the walls and windows to fall upon Russian ears of staff and other guests. Still I can picture the officers, eager faces straining forward in close attentiveness as the teaching unfolded, and still I can hear the good questions and discussions, the fun and the laughter. It all ended with the signing of sacred covenants, passionate praying, mutual encouragement and the lifting up of happy praises to God. Not one of us left unchanged.

Though not a formal Brengle Institute occasion, I ought to mention the officers' residential retreat held by the Yorkshire Division under Lieut-Colonels Bill and Gillian Heeley near Scarborough in March 2012. They had written to say the Lord had placed it upon their hearts to focus for these three days upon the life of holiness. Would I come to speak on that theme? It would be a lengthy drive and my first residential event since Helen died, but I felt I should go. Lieut-Colonel Heeley kindly allowed my son, Matt, to accompany me in order to carry the lion's share of the driving. In seeking the Lord's help for it all, I came to sense that the teaching needed to be very practical so I asked that the overall theme for the retreat be 'The Life of Holiness: A Down-to-Earth Approach'. We focused our minds and hearts upon the nature of authentic religion as taught in the earthy epistle of James and then moved on to look at practical aspects of how the Holy Spirit works in our lives and what it is like to experience him in a personal way. Grounded in everyday reality, this approach seemed of help to the officers. Day by day they face the challenge of living a pure life in a hectic world and of carrying leadership and pastoral responsibilities that can often drain and debilitate, impacting the soul. That is why events that focus on the life of holiness remain pivotal.

On Boston Common

Living in Boston, USA, for two years (1995-7) had endeared this bustling, vibrant city to us not least because it was Samuel Brengle's city. It was also where General William Booth had preached and had first met the young Brengle.

Sam Brengle underwent a life-changing infusion of Holy Spirit energy after praying all night in his rooms near Boston Common, a park in the city's centre. It happened when he was young, on 9 January 1885 at 9 am. Excited beyond measure, Brengle ran out into the streets and onto the Common, finding a new delight in all the life forms – human, plant, animal – he was seeing now through transformed eyes. To mark in 2010 the 125th anniversary of this moment Commissioner Lawrence Moretz (TC) approved the planning of a commemorative Holiness Convention and asked if Helen and I would travel to Boston for it. We did so readily.

A host of Salvationist teachers and speakers took part, among them Commissioner William Francis and Dr David Rightmire. Helen spoke on the contribution of women to the holiness movement, highlighting Phoebe Palmer and Catherine Booth as well as contemporary Salvationist women like Lieut-Colonel Marlene Chase, Commissioner Lenora Feener, Commissioner Debora Bell and Commissioner Nancy Moretz. Lieut-Colonel Eddie Hobgood led the Territorial Arts Ministry team in presenting his telling musical, *Brengle: My Life's Ambition*.

On the morning of Saturday 9 January we gathered on Boston Common, shivering in sub-zero temperatures. There a host of us knelt in the snow and thanked God for Samuel Logan Brengle and his impact upon our own and countless other lives. Brengle's personal prayer bench was placed among us, having been brought from the territory's Heritage Museum. It was my privilege to kneel upon it and speak in prayer on behalf of all gathered. We sang 'Spirit of the living God, fall afresh on me' and asked that our Maker and Redeemer would render our hearts as pure as the snow beneath our knees. We returned to London greatly encouraged. It was good to have been back in Boston, to most a secular city but to us and our fellow Salvationists sacred ground.

Still I pray for a daily infusion of Holy Spirit power that will energise me for sacred service, but even more earnestly I pray for a daily renewing of Holy Spirit purity that will preserve me in the hour of temptation and let me live above and beyond the limits of self.

ESSAY 3

ℭℬ

SHARING

ESSAY 3
SHARING

THIS Essay is about sharing in relationships, both personal and formal, with leaders in other Christian denominations. I have frequently felt blessed through personal friendships with clergy of other churches, for although our doctrinal stances can sometimes be far apart, our contact as friends and fellow believers can yet prove enriching.

The quality of ecumenical relations from country to country and from culture to culture across The Salvation Army varies greatly. Much can depend on the readiness of the individual officer to devote time and energy to building such friendships. Some are good at it, others are not. Some discern the point of it, others do not. Some feel warmly received by their clergy counterparts, others do not. Many of us, now and then, have known what it is to be condescended to, to be coolly patronised, to be misunderstood by leaders in other denominations. This account of my own experiences will reflect both the good and the bad, the highs and the lows of interdenominational contacts, but I want to make plain at the outset that, when I place my ecumenical experiences on the scales, the balance comes down clearly on the side of things positive, constructive and beneficial.

To add further context, these experiences have taken place in diverse cultures including Western settings where secularism and post-modern influences have intensified the need for the churches to encourage one another. Such encouragement is a precious thing. It can in some places, and at more senior levels of ecumenical contact, be also a rare thing.

As a corps officer

How good it was that in our first appointment, at Burnt Oak in north London, there was a relaxed and cordial relationship between the local churches and their various representatives. From the outset I sensed strongly the importance of this, even though I was not then able to articulate very much more than that. I wanted to get to know the local clergy and I wanted them to think well of the Army. So attending the monthly clergy lunches was no hardship. I was made instantly welcome and it became clear that neither my youth nor my uniform would be a problem.

The Anglican churches were the strongest influences upon the local scene in view of their congregational numbers in those days and also because of the place the Church of England holds in the public and ceremonial life of the nation. My recollections are warm ones, some even amusing due mainly to the fact that the Anglican local lay representative in the Council of Churches was none other than Frank Williams, the actor who portrayed the vicar in the popular television series, *Dad's Army*. His face and voice were known to millions through the nine series of the comedy that ran on BBC Television between 1968 and 1977 and which is often re-screened today. So to sit next to him in ecumenical meetings was nothing but fascinating. I had constantly to tell myself that he was not acting! We invited him to come as a guest to our Christmas Carol Service in December 1972 to read extracts from *A Christmas Carol* by Charles Dickens. Frank, a cordial man, agreed without hesitation and proved a great hit with our people.

The Burnt Oak experience afforded us optimism when a few years later in 1977 we left Mazowe Secondary School in Mashonaland, Rhodesia, to become the corps officers at Bulawayo Citadel in Matabeleland. There we enjoyed friendship with local Methodist leaders but there was no structured or regular clergy gathering in the city. When brutal murders took place in June 1978 at the Army's Usher Institute (see Essay 6) we were grateful for the ready understanding of believers across the denominations and especially of the help of the Dean of St John's Cathedral in responding to our request that the funeral service for Lieutenant Diane Thompson and Sister Sharon Swindells be held in the cathedral church. It was the only place of worship in the city big enough to hold the large congregation. Although it was an Army funeral led by the Territorial Commander, Colonel Richard Atwell, an American, the Dean offered prayers and the cathedral staff were wonderful.

Returning in 1979 to London and to the leadership of Enfield Citadel Corps we encountered for the first time a formal Local Ecumenical Project (LEP). The churches in Enfield in the north of London had drawn up a written covenant and signed it. When first we learned of it, we were excited by the thought of this formal commitment to work and witness together. Disastrously, Salvation Army leaders had instructed our predecessors, Majors Derek and Kath Dolling, not to become signatories because it would involve a financial commitment to help fund a local drop-in and community centre staffed by volunteers from the various denominations. This was embarrassing. We did not feel a lot better about it when we discovered that the local Roman Catholic priest, on the instructions of his bishop, had also declined to commit to the LEP. The non-participation by the Catholics and Salvationists left the project unbalanced and in practice dominated by the Anglicans.

Despite this, the Ministers' Fraternal met regularly month by month over a sandwich luncheon and relationships were largely cordial. A series of ecumenical services was planned, to be hosted in turn by each denomination as a further witness toward unity. Each local leader would plan to include the other clergy in the service in some way, whether or not they were formally involved in the LEP. Sadly, this offer of participation focused far too often on being invited to help administer the sacrament. It was a well-meant but naive approach and in the end served only to emphasise our divisions. I did not feel able to accept any invitation to administer the sacrament. Neither did the Quakers, and when we came to the concluding service in the local Catholic church the priest told us, unsurprisingly, that none of us would be invited to take part in either the giving or receiving of the sacrament. I did not mind, but others from sacramentalist traditions felt marginalised.

Why on earth this initiative was made to focus on the sacrament was beyond me. Why would plans to encourage oneness be structured around a ceremony that has split Christians now for countless generations? A possible explanation was the desire of the local Anglican vicar, a dominant figure in our clergy meetings, to highlight the readiness of the majority to share with others in the administration of the sacrament in sharp contrast to the Catholic refusal to do so. If this was his strategy it certainly worked but the cost was a high one. When the series of ecumenical gatherings ended it was decided not to attempt anything similar again for some considerable time. I could not understand why shared worship should be forfeited in this manner, but realised that for some believers church unity is not remotely about worshipping together, focusing on Jesus together, or serving the needy together. For some it is solely about taking the sacrament of the Lord's Supper together. Everything else is seen as insignificant in comparison. The Enfield experience saddened me. It was, however, a lesson in realism.

Arriving in Bromley, Kent, in 1989 we found there a fellowship among the local clergy that was cordial, open, warm and encouraging. To my relief, there was no LEP. Regular exchanges of pulpits took place when local leaders would preach in other churches on a chosen Sunday morning. The annual Good Friday march of witness was another potently visible example of shared endeavour. Best of all was the instant willingness in 1992 of the St Mark's Anglican Church in Westmoreland Road and of the vicar, Alan Vousdon, to allow the local Salvationists the use of the church during the extensive remodelling of the Army hall in Ethelbert Road. Shared as well as separate services took place. Our Anglican brothers and sisters in Christ showed a wonderful spirit of welcome, acceptance and oneness still remembered to this day.

As a divisional commander

It was Thursday 21 October 1993 at 9 am. I was seated in a room in Durham Castle, in the north-east of England, with two expensively suited gentlemen, one from the Prime Minister's Office in London's 10 Downing Street and the other from the Church of England's ruling synod. They were actively engaged in interdenominational consultations prior to making a recommendation to the Prime Minister as to who should succeed Dr David Jenkins as the new Bishop of Durham. The See of Durham ranks third among Anglicans after those of Canterbury and York. Because I was the Divisional Commander of The Salvation Army in the Durham and Tees Division I had been invited to offer my perspective on the needs of the region and on the life of the churches generally as part of the consultation process. Also I was invited to offer the name of any individual I thought suitable to be the next bishop. I accepted both parts of the invitation.

Driving to the castle I thought of the early patchy history of the Army with the Church of England. They wanted us within their ecclesiastical machinery but did not want our Founder, William Booth, with his strong leadership style which they deemed 'autocratic' (see Bramwell Booth's account of conversations with Anglican leaders during the 1880s in Chapter VII of his 1925 *Echoes and Memories*). When William Booth died in 1912 the *Church Times* for 23 August that year wrote as follows:

> As a religious movement The Salvation Army lacks the sacramental life which the Church alone maintains, and the religion it inculcates is not without elements dangerous to true spiritual growth. It has added one more to the sects which have broken the unity of Christendom.

This was arrogant nonsense. The Army had dropped sacramental ceremonies but not 'the sacramental life' in its deeper, interior meaning. 'True spiritual growth' meant everything to the early Salvationists, with Sunday mornings devoted to 'holiness meetings'. Moreover, to accuse Booth of damaging Christian unity was a bit rich when the Church of England itself was born by splitting from the Bishop of Rome simply because King Henry VIII wanted to grant himself a divorce and remarry a more fertile queen.

Needless to say, these thoughts remained unvoiced that morning and I thought how changed things were now. Most Anglicans (most, not all) hold a warm and affirming view of the Army, something Salvationists usually feel able to reciprocate. Furthermore, I was being taken very seriously by the distinguished visitors to Durham Castle that day. We spoke for about 40 minutes and detailed notes were made of all I said. I was impressed by their intelligence, their background knowledge and by their informal cordiality. It was a small, but good, moment for ecumenical relations.

The retiring bishop had become a controversial figure. His outspoken political views were far to the left of centre and his modernist doctrinal opinions alienated many a believer. He had come to be Bishop of Durham after a career as an academic theologian and seemed not to grasp that matters perhaps suitable for exploring in a university lecture room were not always helpful to the believer in the pew or to the man and woman in the street. It was plainly inept of him to refer publicly to the resurrection of Jesus as 'a conjuring trick with bones'. On the other hand, he spoke out fearlessly for the economic victims of government policy. Indeed, I granted permission for some of our Salvationists, including officers, to march in full uniform beside Bishop Jenkins in protest at the closure of local coal mines. We needed to add our voices to those making plain the human cost of government policy initiated by Prime Minister Margaret Thatcher in relation to the coal industry.

Our second term as divisional leaders took us from Durham and Tees to Boston, Massachusetts. It was a wonderful challenge, but there we discovered an Army somewhat reluctant to engage in wider ecumenical relationships, most of our officers preferring to settle for links exclusively with fellow evangelicals. I was glad we had those links, but was disappointed that so many of my colleagues felt no desire to broaden their ecumenical relationships. I wondered if I could change things quietly by personal example.

We landed in Boston on Wednesday 31 May 1995. A meeting of the Massachusetts Council of Churches was scheduled for the following Monday. Although the Roman Catholics were not members of the Council I discovered that Cardinal Bernard Law, Roman Catholic Archbishop of Boston, attended every meeting and took a forceful, prominent role. He was to host the June meeting at his palatial residence at 2121 Commonwealth Avenue in Brighton, Massachusetts (a property destined to be sold later to raise compensation monies for victims of sexual abuse in the archdiocese). Thus we gathered for a working breakfast at 8 am. I was introduced and given a warm welcome by the full-time Secretary to the Council, the Reverend Diane Kessler, a minister of the United Reformed Church. The main item on our agenda was the matter of abortion. The Cardinal had encouraged Catholics to protest publicly against attempts to liberalise the state abortion laws, but informed us now that he had asked his flock to engage only in non-public opposition because of the shootings of staff at two Boston abortion clinics by John Salvi. Suddenly I was asked if the Army had a stance on abortion. Having drafted our formal positional statement and lectured on the topic for some years, I was pleased to offer a full and nuanced explanation of our position, speaking at some length. I sensed those present were quietly surprised. Certainly the Cardinal was and later said so. In the following two years I prioritised my attendances at these meetings. This further surprised the other participants and to some extent also my own colleagues at divisional headquarters (DHQ).

Soon after the May 1995 meeting I suggested to the Cardinal that he and I should meet in order to further our relationship. His response was a misjudgement. He referred me to his diocesan social programme director, Dr Joseph Doolin, thereby signalling that he saw me less as a denominational leader and more as a social worker. Nevertheless, I took up the invitation to meet Dr Doolin and invited Karen Phillips, our divisional director of social services who also happened to be a Roman Catholic, to come with me. The encounter proved courteous, but I sensed now and again as it progressed that we were being patronised.

The Reverend Diane Kessler proved to be an energetic and kind-hearted colleague. She was seriously committed to the cause of deepening inter-church relations in Massachusetts but tended to overestimate the need to please the Cardinal. She was intent upon persuading him to become a full member of the Council of Churches but it was never going to happen. Yet Diane worked tirelessly and was warm and kind to Helen and to me on a personal level, even inviting us for a lovely meal in her home. Also she had ensured that I was briefed fully, soon after arriving in Boston, about the ecumenical scene in the state and how she saw her role.

Each year in January an Annual Meeting of the Massachusetts Council of Churches was held at which Diane would render a report on her role, a meal would be shared, and an act of worship would ensue. I was startled to learn that Diane was planning a shared communion service for the January 1997 event. At once my mind went back to Enfield and the failure of a similar emphasis there. Duly we gathered. I was accompanied by Helen plus several officer colleagues from DHQ, all of us in uniform. The service began. When the moment for communion arrived and the invitation to come forward was made the large Roman Catholic contingent remained seated, so too did the Greek Orthodox representative, so did the Quakers, and so did the Salvationists. It all fell rather flat. Instead of focusing on what united us, once again the inherently divisive nature of sacramental ceremony was to the fore. I came away deeply disappointed and later wrote to Diane urging her not to repeat this approach and suggesting that we should focus instead on central, unifying aspects of faith: the person of Jesus and his love for all his peoples.

Our stay in Boston was to last only two years. Cardinal Law had by now come to take me a little more seriously and on learning of my impending departure for Pakistan via London invited me to a working breakfast at his official residence. It was Monday 23 June 1997. Major Gil Reynders was with me. I have described this encounter more fully in my 1999 *Who Are These Salvationists?* (pages 3-5). The Cardinal had come to see the Army as, in his words, 'an authentic expression of classical Christianity'. He speculated aloud as to the possibility of union with Rome. His comments were warmly affirming but it was clear that his grasp of Salvationism was superficial. We parted that morning on cordial, comradely terms and with mutual respect. I could not foresee the disaster that would later overtake him and his archdiocese. He resigned as archbishop in December 2002 after allegations that he had covered up sexual abuse by priests under his jurisdiction. He was moved to Rome to take an obscure role there and retired on reaching his 80th birthday. It was a sad ending for a man I had learned to admire for his commitment to Christ and his unashamed devotion to his church and calling. He should be remembered for this, despite being the first high-level Catholic Church official to be accused of actively taking part in covering up cases of child molestation.

As a territorial commander

In our first experience of territorial leadership we gave ourselves wholeheartedly to interdenominational friendships in Pakistan. It was not easy. Many senior church leaders appeared to be in competition with one another, vying for position and the public spotlight. The Anglicans, Lutherans, Presbyterians and Methodists had merged formally in 1970 to create the United Church of Pakistan but old rivalries still lay just beneath the surface. In Lahore we found ourselves relating to two bishops living within a stone's throw of each other. Bishop Samuel Azariah, Bishop of Raiwind, told us with disarming candour that he was really a Methodist. Bishop Alexander Malik, Bishop of Lahore, was a courteous, sophisticated person and a telling advocate for the Christian minority communities. He always received us with graciousness. Dr Malik retired in 2011.

My efforts to form a relationship with the then Roman Catholic Archbishop of Lahore, Armando Trinidade, were unsuccessful. It was arranged that I would meet him at his residence in Laurence Road, Lahore, early in October 1997. I was accompanied by the Chief Secretary, Lieut-Colonel Emmanuel Iqbal. After passing the armed guards we were shown into a waiting room. The archbishop came in and briefly greeted us. He then left. We were served hot tea with a small snack. Thereafter the archbishop appeared again. He offered only monosyllabic responses to my attempts at conversation. Soon we were out on the street. It had been a frustrating, fruitless encounter. Lieut-Colonel Iqbal commented that in Pakistan the Catholics did not usually seek or welcome cooperation with the other churches.

In December 1997 the Archbishop of Canterbury, George Carey, came to Lahore with Mrs Carey. We were invited by Bishop Malik to attend a garden party in honour of the Archbishop and to bring with us colleagues from territorial headquarters (THQ). Gladly we accepted. It was a rare occasion in Pakistan to see Christians gathered together in this way. We occupied seating under the shady trees and after brief formal speeches the archbishop began to move from group to group. Noticing our uniforms he hastened over smilingly to where we were seated. We all rose to meet him. I extended my hand. Not understanding Salvation Army insignia, he brushed me aside and held out his hand to the Chief Secretary, moving on to each of my Pakistani colleagues. 'I always like to see the Army wherever I go,' he declared. Dutifully, we all beamed back. As he moved away I noticed his wife standing forlorn and abandoned in the centre of the vast lawn, so I moved toward her and engaged her in conversation for a moment or two. 'Are you American?' she asked. 'No, I'm British,' I replied. I expect she was jetlagged.

Cardinal Thomas Williams, Roman Catholic Archbishop of Wellington, New Zealand, until his retirement in 2005 was a warm-hearted, approachable man and made me feel welcome when I was appointed leader of The Salvation Army in New Zealand, Fiji and Tonga. Now and then he hosted me for lunch and we would talk of the life of the churches in New Zealand. He was immensely knowledgeable. He could, moreover, slip easily into Army terminology as we conversed. I discovered that he did the same thing with colleagues from other denominations, using their terminology. I have never met any other senior church figure with this gift. Tom and I tended to sit together when we found ourselves present at ecumenical gatherings. He displayed much patience with the Baptist representative who repeatedly sought to goad him. As I look back I am filled again with gratitude for having met Tom Williams. He helped to restore my faith in our relationship with Catholic leaders after the Lahore experience.

Another encouraging colleague was Michael Earle, Secretary to the Conference of Churches of Aotearoa, New Zealand. He made time to seek me out, making regular contact during this period when the formal machinery of the Conference was being called into question. Michael made periodic visits to me at THQ and worked hard to ensure that the personal relationships between Christian leaders did not suffer as a result of changing ecumenical structures. During this time of uncertainty our proactive membership of the New Zealand Council of Christian Social Services also served to further our cross-denominational links.

In mid-2004 we found ourselves once again under farewell orders and returning to London to lead the Army in the United Kingdom and Ireland. I discovered that there were no formal mechanisms of any kind that brought the national heads of denominations together at regular intervals. The Army was part of Churches Together in England (CTE) and also of Churches Together in Great Britain and Ireland but we were represented on these bodies by a free churches representative and our presence lacked real traction. When Helen was asked to accept the role of Moderator of the Free Churches in CTE she accepted gladly, but soon thereafter my election as the General early in 2006 changed our formal relationship to the United Kingdom scene and her role passed by default to her successor as Territorial President of Women's Ministries, Commissioner Betty Matear, who went on to work hard at it.

The annual gathering in London's Whitehall for the Remembrance Day Service in November brought some of the leaders of national churches together in one place but there was little time for more than a cordial handshake and an exchange of pleasantries. My hopes of more meaningful contact had been raised when an invitation reached me from CTE to attend a residential weekend in mid-September 2005 for heads of denominations. The venue was an Anglican retreat centre in Woking. We would be together for three days and two nights. I accepted gladly. However, on arriving I discovered I was the sole head of denomination present! The other church leaders sent only their ecumenical officials. It was a profound disappointment. My despair deepened when the then Bishop of Bradford, representing Archbishop Rowan Williams, made pointedly disparaging remarks about the Salvationist position on sacraments. The Quaker colleague present was similarly patronised. Things did not improve when a representative of the black churches asked me if I was a military chaplain. 'You keep on mentioning the army,' she said. At that point I all but gave up. In the evening Cardinal Cormac Murphy-O'Connor, Roman Catholic Archbishop of Westminster, arrived and stayed just an hour. He had been asked to lead evening prayers in the chapel. Thus we gathered at the close of the day. The cardinal withdrew a slip of paper from his pocket and said he wanted to repeat to us all what he had said earlier that same day to trainee priests in a Catholic seminary. There and then he embarked upon an elaborate eulogy extolling the virtues of the newly elected Pope Benedict. Jesus was not mentioned. Ecumenical evening prayer? I resolved to slip away early the next day and did so with a heavy heart.

As the General

From 2006 to 2011 the matter of our ecumenical relations was high on my agenda. I sensed the need to clarify our global self-understanding and was pleased when eventually in April 2008 we were able to publish a short but formal book about the place of The Salvation Army in relation to the churches. *The Salvation Army in the Body of Christ – An Ecclesiological Statement* was issued by International Headquarters (IHQ) after consultation with the International Doctrine Council (IDC) and the International Management Council. It went out in English, French and Spanish all between the same covers, the first multilingual example of an Army book. High numbers of translations into other languages ensued. A companion *Study Guide* was produced in 2010, also available instantly in English, French and Spanish. The original work on the guide was done most helpfully in the Australia Eastern Territory where Captain Peter McGuigan had written a review of the 2008 publication in *Pipeline*:

When I read the *Ecclesiological Statement* it was like breathing in fresh country air. I don't know about you but I'm tiring of the

Army's so-called identity crisis.... With very clear and concise statements and sub-statements this cuts through the mire of opinion and argument, giving us a picture of ourselves that demands our attention and calls for our recognition and engagement.... The statements have been very carefully crafted. In fact, you get a sense that God is in them.... Not only can this liberate us, but it can help propel us into the future with real confidence and a new zeal in mission.

It was my desire not only to offer clarity by means of these publications but also to enhance our self-confidence and poise in relating to other parts of the Body of Christ.

Soon after being elected by the January 2006 High Council, but before taking office on 2 April, I kept a promise to speak at a gathering of the 'Three Faiths Forum' attended by Jews, Moslems and Christians. Thus on 15 February I went to the Methodist Central Hall, Westminster, as the General-elect. The full text of my short address to the Forum can be found in Chapter 4, *Volume 2* of my *Selected Writings* published by IHQ in 2010. The by now retired Archbishop of Canterbury, George Carey, was present with Mrs Carey. After concluding my address and answering questions I slipped away for I had much to do. On leaving the hall I heard hurrying footsteps behind me. I turned to see the Archbishop hastening down the aisle to catch up. Most warmly he shook my hand, told me he had liked my paper that afternoon, and wished me well for the future. 'I am sure the Army is in good hands,' he beamed. A nice moment.

George Carey had been succeeded by Rowan Williams who inherited an Anglican Communion in turmoil over the issues of women priests and of same-sex relationships. In mid-2006 he published an historic 3,000-word document setting out the challenges to be faced by Anglicans worldwide. Attitudes prevailing, for example, in the Episcopal Church in the USA (ECUSA) differed starkly from those among the leaders of the Council of African Provinces of Africa (CAPA). Unlike the position of the General of The Salvation Army, the Archbishop of Canterbury has no explicit or formal executive powers beyond England and Wales and must rely solely on spiritual persuasion. Williams foresaw the need for mutual respect, restraint and a spirit of 'waiting for each other'. On reading his statement (*The Challenge and Hope of Being an Anglican Today: A Reflection for the Bishops, Clergy and Faithful of the Anglican Communion*) I was moved to send him the following letter:

Dear Archbishop,

I have two reasons for writing to you, both of them very positive. First, let me thank you for the address delivered in St Paul's Cathedral during the service to mark The Queen's eightieth birthday. Indeed the entire service was uplifting, and seldom can I recall being caught up in quite that way on such a formal occasion. The music was sublime. Also your words from the pulpit were so apt and right.

However, the main impetus for writing to you arises upon reading your recently published 'reflection', *The Challenge and Hope of Being an Anglican Today*. I have taken time to read it with considerable care and in doing so sensed much that strikes strong chords in my own Salvationist heart. I hope it does not surprise you that encouragement comes from the office of The General of The Salvation Army. Our respective traditions enjoy a relationship of deep mutual respect, and there are countless personal friendships that give this visible, tangible form.

I have been called to lead a Christian Army that is found in 111 countries and, while our polity and structures (not our doctrine) are closer to Rome than to Canterbury, we are subject to pressures not dissimilar to those addressed in your 'reflection'. I want to thank you most warmly for all you have said for I find in your analysis a number of points that assist me personally as I seek, with the help of God, to hold the global Army intact. I was especially moved on reading the section sub-titled 'The Anglican Identity'.

My prayer is that all within the Anglican Communion will find a way forward together, under God, helped by your guiding hand. Please know that we follow, with prayerful interest and not a little Christian affection, the journey you are all undertaking. May God continue to grant you grace and wisdom in full measure as you lead and serve.

Yours sincerely in Christ

The reply was brief but warm:

> Dear General Clifton,
> A quick word to say a most heartfelt thank you for your kind and supportive letter. These are trying times for all our Christian communities, and it is comforting to know that some of our struggles are felt and understood in other households of the faith.
> Be sure of my prayers and best wishes.
> Yours ever

Soon thereafter in the summer of 2008 the Lambeth Conference took place amid growing tensions among Anglicans everywhere, with truculent threats by some bishops of boycotting the event. This Conference seeks to bring together in London all Anglican bishops worldwide every 10 years. Arrangements were made for a Salvation Army representative to attend throughout. I appointed Colonel Michael Marvell, a British officer residing in Denmark, to this task. He was able actively to participate in the discussions and to address attendees on the subject of Christian mission and ministry among the poor. I was invited to send a formal greeting to be printed in the Conference papers and did so in the following terms:

> To his Grace, the Archbishop of Canterbury and to the Anglican Bishops gathered for the Lambeth Conference 2008:
> Warmest greetings in Christ from all Salvationists scattered throughout 115 countries of the world to our Anglican brothers and sisters in Christ.
> It is a privilege to greet you as you gather on this historic occasion and to pledge our prayers for all of you as you consider, under the presiding hand of God, themes which have high significance not only for the Anglican Communion but for the entire Body of Christ on earth.
> The Salvation Army awaits keenly the outcomes of your prayerful and patient deliberations. May the Holy Spirit be your Chief Guest, inspiring you, directing and guiding you, and gently holding you back from error.

May your fellowship be rich within the bonds of Christ. May your mission for saving the world be enlarged. May your oneness in Christ be deepened. May the unity of the body be preserved.

The Salvationists of the world surround you with Christian love and prayers. The Lord is with you!

I decided to send a further private letter to the Archbishop:

Dear Archbishop,

It was both pleasing and affirming to receive an invitation from The Reverend Canon Flora Winfield to send an official greeting from The Salvation Army to the Lambeth Conference 2008.

However, it has been upon my heart and mind to send to you a rather more personal word of encouragement as the Conference draws nearer. This I now do.

As this letter is compiled I have before me the Conference Schedule. I pledge to uphold you personally in prayer every day throughout this historic event. By the gracious action of the Holy Spirit may you know inner calm, warmth of heart, clarity of mind, and holy courage to meet whatever particular stresses or demands may arise for you day by day during the Conference.

The themes for each day have about them a rightness and timeliness, not only for our Anglican brothers and sisters, but for the whole Body of Christ.

May you emerge from the Conference feeling that the Lord has smiled upon it, has poured out abundant blessings, and has guided all of you safely through. May you also sense from those present much personal affirmation and encouragement for your godly leadership in the sacred task to which you have been appointed.

Yours in Christ

His reply came on 23 June just prior to the Conference delegates coming together:

Dear General Clifton,

Thank you very much indeed for your official greeting for the

47

Lambeth Conference; that the Spirit will be our Chief Guest is a prayer that I shall certainly make my own.

And thank you also for the warmth and brotherly kindness of your message to myself. I am deeply grateful for your prayers in all this: it is a very testing time, but at least we know that God is with us and, as John Wesley said on his deathbed that is 'the best of all'!

Yours in Christ

Toward the concluding days of the Conference Colonel Marvell wrote to me as follows:

I have just returned from a lovely evening at the Archbishop's residence at the Old Palace in Canterbury. I have lost count of the number of bishops who have told me how glad they are that The Salvation Army is here – and they mean it. I believe the Conference is moving in the right direction. I have heard several of the American bishops say that they are changing their minds on some key issues, but whether this will be enough to satisfy the hardliners still seems doubtful.

As I was saying goodbye to the Archbishop and Mrs Jane Williams they expressed their need for our prayers. I assured them that we continue to lift them up to the Throne of Grace, especially during these final and therefore most challenging days of the Conference.

Archbishop Williams relinquished his office in 2012 after serving for 10 turbulent years. My heart went out to him. I understood fully the comment made on that occasion in *The Tablet* for 24 March 2012:

The worth of a churchman is not primarily given in human judgements, but in the example he gives of faith, courage and Christian courtesy and kindness to everyone in good times and in bad.

I hope that one day we might see formal dialogues with our Anglican sisters and brothers in Christ in order to deepen our mutual understanding and respect. Before I took office as the General the Army had embarked on formal conversations with the Seventh-Day Adventists and also with the World Methodist Council. Our links to the Methodists were already strong and this dialogue ensued over a period of eight years. The Council, with its official base at Junaluska, North Carolina, was founded in 1881 and represents 76 denominations with a membership of 75 million people. We visited their offices and museum in August 2008. The talks were aimed at a deeper mutual understanding and a final report can be found in the journal, *Word and Deed*, for November 2012. It records the hope that further talks can take place in the next several years. This is to be encouraged and prayed for.

My experiences of contact with Roman Catholic leaders had convinced me of two things: the willingness of the best among them to approach us with a spirit of Christian warmth; a failure truly to grasp who and what we are. Therefore I asked our representative in Italy, Major (now Colonel) Massimo Paone, to set up a meeting for me with high-ranking Vatican officials in Rome. I had long followed with interest the developing trends within Catholicism: numbers at confession were in rapid decline (only two per cent of Catholics now confessing regularly – *The Tablet*, 18 August 2012); Catholic teaching on abortion, artificial contraception, divorce, and premarital sex was being largely disregarded; clerical sexual abuse was being revealed on an ever-increasing scale; vocations to the priesthood were in serious decline; agitation was mounting as to the role and place of women within Catholicism. I sensed that here was a moment to reach out to our Catholic fellow-believers to offer encouragement. In this I was strongly and wisely supported by the Chief of the Staff, Commissioner Robin Dunster, and by Commissioner Hasse Kjellgren, International Secretary for Europe. Majors Massimo and Jane Paone, wonderfully effective in their leadership of the Army in Italy, were also positive about the initiative I had in mind.

We flew to Rome and met Cardinal Walter Kasper on 28 March 2007 at The Pontifical Council for Promoting Christian Unity. Helen was with me, as were Majors Massimo Paone and Richard Gaudion. The Cardinal was accompanied by Monsignor John Radano, an American priest who had experience of engaging with Salvationists in ecumenical settings and who had been extremely helpful to us in Italy through the positive relationship formed between himself and Majors Paone.

The meeting went exceedingly well. It lasted for about an hour and the Cardinal seemed relaxed, approaching us with dignified cordiality. He spoke in gracious terms of our work around the world but readily confessed his lack of in-depth knowledge of us as a body, so I explained the enriching impact on my life of friendships with Catholic leaders around the world, not least with Cardinal Law in Boston, USA, and with Cardinal Williams in Wellington, New Zealand. I had been reading Cardinal Kasper's recent book on church unity from a Catholic perspective and I expressed appreciation for his erudition and scholarship. He seemed pleased. Then I spoke of the areas in which I saw some commonality between Salvationism and Catholicism: in structures, systems and polity; in the approach to social ethics (not least with regard to abortion, euthanasia, human sexuality and social justice); a shared concern for suffering humanity and a resulting ministry of compassionate social service.

I spoke next of the life of the Army as it is expressed typically through activism rather than philosophical or theological reflection. I mentioned our readiness in recent years to engage in formal interdenominational dialogue and spoke of our talks with the Seventh-Day Adventists and the Methodists. I explained to the Cardinal our Methodist/Wesleyan roots. These preliminaries allowed us then to talk about the potential for mutual gain if only our two traditions could deepen their knowledge of each other. The Cardinal most enthusiastically endorsed that goal. Earlier I had quoted from his book and his statement: 'We must first break down the spiral of mistrust.' Both he and Monsignor Radano nodded and murmured their recognition of these words.

Our conversation had now reached the point where I felt able to ask the Cardinal what he thought might be a sensible and Christ-honouring way of building upon my visit to him and our good conversation. He said that he would indeed like matters to be carried forward somehow but he could not think of anything concrete. I then suggested attempting very low-key, informal conversations to take place between a small number of representatives selected by my office and his, perhaps just three or four from each tradition. Instantly he agreed. At that point I introduced the name of Commissioner Linda Bond and explained her role as our international ecumenical representative. Monsignor Radano recognised her name and recalled having met her. The Cardinal quietly instructed Monsignor Radano to organise a small team from the Pontifical Council to meet with chosen representatives of the General. He asked for Bishop Brian Farrell, Secretary to the Pontifical Council, to be included in the team. The bishop was due to speak the next day at our Europe Zonal Conference on the subject of Christian unity.

Next I introduced our hosts to the name of Commissioner William Francis and explained his recent appointment as Chair of the IDC and said that I would probably ask him to lead our team in any future talks. As the meeting ended I presented to the Cardinal a copy of Colonel Henry Gariepy's *A Salvationist Treasury* (2000) suitably inscribed to mark the meeting between us. I presented also a copy of our 2007 *Year Book*. He gifted me with his recently published handbook on ecumenical relations at a local level. We concluded with photographs.

The next day we received Bishop Brian Farrell among us as planned. The bishop, accompanied by Monsignor Radano, was the Cardinal's senior official. I spoke words of welcome and the bishop rose to speak. How we had prayed over this moment. Suddenly the bishop was folding his notes and replacing them in his jacket pocket. 'I will speak from my heart,' he said. He told us of his boyhood in Dublin, Eire, and of seeing the Salvationists in their blue uniforms going about their good works. 'God has given you a very beautiful charisma, a gift of loving service,' he told us. As he finished I rose to thank him and said I wanted to offer prayer. I prayed for him and for the Monsignor and then for the Pope by name, as well as for all our Catholic co-believers in Christ. As we left the meeting room the bishop took my arm and said with much feeling, 'That was a God-blessed moment in there.' Yes, it was.

Before we left Rome Monsignor Radano gave us a guided tour of St Peter's Basilica. We returned to London sensing that God had been honoured, both by our meetings with Catholic leaders and by the positive spirit among the officers attending the zonal conference.

The first formal dialogue began at Sunbury Court, west London, on 13 December 2011. As planned, Commissioner William Francis led our team and Commissioner Linda Bond was also present. This was important as I wanted to signal our trust in women leaders. The talks were relaxed and mutually respectful. On Sunday morning the Vatican representatives were taken as our guests to the holiness meeting at Staines Corps where the lovely music, sound preaching and welcoming spirit of the local Salvationists touched them deeply. It was an encouraging start.

The dialogue continued annually, the venue alternating between London and Rome and with collegial greetings reaching me from Rome from time to time. I felt proud of our team and valued the warmth and clarity of the papers they presented. We were pleased to note the inclusion, for the later rounds of the dialogue, of a female member of the Catholic team in the person of Sister Patricia Murray. By then Commissioner Bond was unable to attend and I was glad that I could call on Lieut-Colonel Karen Shakespeare to take her place.

After five annual gatherings the dialogue with Vatican representatives reached a conclusion. It is my hope that before too long these talks and contacts will be resumed for a further round. They bring all kinds of benefits, some obvious, others more subtle. Our aim was simply to honour Christ by deepening our mutual knowledge and respect. There was never the slightest thought of seeking to impact each other's structures or freedoms. For Catholics and Salvationists to sit together in this way was of itself a significant step forward.

As my retirement drew near I received the following letter from Cardinal Kasper's successor, Cardinal Kurt Koch:

> Dear General Clifton,
>
> I am greatly pleased to join many in giving thanks to God as you end your service as the eighteenth General of The Salvation Army. As you prepare to retire, please be assured of my prayers for you, Commissioner Helen Clifton, and The Salvation Army as a whole.
>
> The Pontifical Council for Promoting Christian Unity has enjoyed a fruitful collaboration with The Salvation Army which has grown under your accomplished leadership. At your direction a series of theological conversations began which have led to deeper mutual understanding, respect and appreciation. Your prayerful support of these conversations has done much to build trust and fellowship between our communities.
>
> As you retire from active service in the Lord's vineyard I extend my good wishes to you, to your wife, and to the faithful of The

Salvation Army. It is my hope and prayer that our journey together in the work for Christian unity will continue in the years to come. God bless you in your retirement. With gratitude for your ecumenical commitment, I am,

Sincerely yours in Christ

I responded:

Dear Cardinal Koch,

Your gracious letter of 2 February 2011 has reached me here in London and I hasten to record my profound thanks for your good wishes on the occasion of my retirement as the world leader of The Salvation Army, and also for your assurance of prayers. Commissioner Helen Clifton joins me in this response.

I will always be grateful to God for the positive response shown by your distinguished predecessor, Cardinal Walter Kasper, when I ventured to propose deeper contact between The Salvation Army and the Vatican. I give thanks to God for the ensuing conversations that have taken place and which will continue still further. It is my firm belief that this visible and tangible sign of our unity in Christ is honouring to the cause of the Gospel and sends a very positive signal to believers in other traditions.

This comes to you with Christian affection and good wishes for your own endeavours in continuing to lower barriers between Christ's faithful followers around the globe.

Yours in Christ

Still it is my prayer that the Army will go on reaching out in love at all levels, both local and global, to all who acknowledge Christ as Saviour, to offer much-needed encouragement and acceptance at a time in the history of the churches when our faith is less and less embraced and when believers are more and more openly persecuted.

ESSAY 4

☙

SICKNESS

ESSAY 4
SICKNESS

BEING a follower of Jesus Christ brings no immunity from earthly peril. Any believer may have to endure weakness, pain and loss. The only certainty is the divine promise of being accompanied by Heaven through the valley. Even then, there is no promise of being granted an active awareness of God's presence so it becomes needful to cling on, believing he is there with you when all your emotions, instincts and feelings tell you he is not. Sometimes the darkness closes in and you are bereft of all solace.

I want this memoir to record frankly what has happened with regard to my health and also that of Helen. I intend an orderly account, free of self-pity or sentimentality, leaving little out and attempting openness and candour. I want also to pay tribute to the Christlikeness of Salvation Army people. They uphold you in countless ways when you are beset by difficulties.

I ought to mention also what might be deemed a selfish motive, for I hope that in compiling this record, especially concerning Helen, it will act in some way as a catharsis for my soul and my emotions. I confess readily to having been damaged by her death and therefore in need of healing beyond the physical. I seek perspective, but even as I write I sense some of the events are still too recent for that fully to come about.

Where is the plan of God in these events from 1969 to the present day? What was our all-powerful Creator doing? What has it all meant, or does it all mean, for Helen, for our children and family members, for the Army? The whole created order seems in constant hurt and pain. I have no adequate answers, simply questions and then still more questions, as do all who have walked this path and of whom many have suffered infinitely more than me.

1969

I was 24 and happily teaching law at the Inns of Court School of Law in London (see Essay 13). We lived in a tiny flat in Muswell Hill. I began to experience intensive night sweating. Then the itching began. Finally, I was aware of my neck enlarging and my shirt collars tightening more and more. I tried to dismiss it. My energies were still good. Helen urged me to see our family doctor but I resisted. In the end, she made an appointment to see him herself and told him about my symptoms. He summoned me to his surgery, examined me and gave me a stern telling-off for being stubborn and stupid. 'You should have listened to your wife,' he said. He was right.

There followed swiftly a series of X-rays and these revealed shadows on my chest and neck. I was referred at once to the Royal Marsden Hospital in Fulham Road, London, to be under the care of Professor Sir David Smithers. We came to learn that Smithers was a pioneer of what was then a relatively new speciality of radiotherapy and the main driving force behind the founding of the Royal Marsden Hospital in Sutton, Surrey, opened by Queen Elizabeth II in 1963.

At Fulham Road a sample was taken from the growth in my neck. Analysis showed I had Hodgkin's Lymphoma, later to be described to me, for reasons not made clear, as 'a young man's disease'. Rapidly I was transferred by ambulance to the Royal Marsden in Sutton and made ready to receive radiation therapy. I recall the days of preparation and the meticulous care of the radiology department staff in determining which areas of my body should be targeted.

I had never heard of Hodgkin's disease and neither had Helen. Later, after being discharged, I discovered she had looked it up in medical dictionaries which told her that the prognosis was fatal. She said nothing of this to me at the time but this information later explained the initial rejection of our subsequent applications to be trained as Salvation Army cadets (see Essay 5).

Among my more vivid memories is that of being prepared for a lymphogram procedure. The technicians said it was relatively new, but that one of its pioneers was in the room next door. I felt reassured, but was still unprepared for the simply awful pain of having the anaesthetic injected into the top of my feet. My mind went at once, in a reflex, to Calvary where my Saviour's feet were pierced more brutally. I held that image in my mind until the dreadful pain subsided. Then with a scalpel they cut into the top of each foot and raised up minute lymphatic vessels into which was injected, at a very slow rate, a blue dye designed to make my entire lymph system clearly visible for X-ray. By this method any abnormalities can be seen, identified and planned for. Subsequent radiotherapy could thus be more accurately targeted. The lymphogram procedure was to be repeated at the conclusion of the therapy to determine the impact on the tumours. The pain of the needles in the top of my feet was just as intense, but this time I knew it would be so and was prepared, though with gritted teeth.

After two weeks as an in-patient at Sutton I was discharged and told to attend daily for radiation therapy for a further four weeks as an outpatient. Helen came with me in our tiny maroon Mini car every day around London's infamous North and South Circular roads from Muswell Hill in the north to Sutton in the south. She was later to recall that on most of those occasions I drove much faster than was legally permitted. She put it down to the mild tranquillisers prescribed routinely in those days for radiology patients!

Eventually the therapy ended and with it the constant nausea and loss of weight. Professor Smithers saw us to say that both tumours had virtually disappeared. He would see me at short intervals for a few more months and then less frequently over the years.

It was at one such consultation a few years later when we were officers that we spoke to him of the Army's desire to send us to Rhodesia. I can see him now, tall and straight in his white coat. I can hear also his nursing assistant gasping out loud when we spoke of Africa. The Professor looked at us, his face avuncular and benign. 'This means a lot to you, doesn't it?' he said. 'It is our commitment to go anywhere at any time to do anything,' we replied. 'Then you must go!' came the response. 'Normally I would want you under my care for a few more years, but this is more important.' He then gave us details of a cancer consultant in Johannesburg and said, 'If your symptoms return, contact him right away and tell him I sent you.'

The symptoms never did return, thank God. However, nearly 40 years later a tumour was discovered in my oesophagus immediately beneath the tiny blue tattoo spot placed on my chest in 1969 to indicate the centre point of the target area for the radiotherapy. In a small minority of patients treated in this way, the radiation may not only erase an existing tumour but may also cause further malignancy.

We set sail for Rhodesia in January 1975 and served there for four years (see Essays 6 and 13). My health fully restored, I was able regularly to join the students in football matches on the dusty sports field and enjoy games of squash using the court at the Army's nearby Pearson Farm. There Allister and Myra Lewis, the lieutenants managing the farm, always made us warmly welcome, as did Stuart Harding, a loyal Salvationist from Weymouth, England, who served as the farm's assistant manager. Helen and I were still in our twenties and glad to be alive, fit, and busy in the Lord's Army.

2008

It is usual for High Council candidates who accept a nomination for the office of General of The Salvation Army to be asked questions about their health. On three occasions I found myself nominated and answering the long list of probing questions (see Essay 11) and on each occasion was able to report that I was well and fit. After being elected in January 2006 neither Helen nor I had any inkling of the torrid time that lay ahead as far as illness was concerned. We entered upon our trusted roles as the Army's world leaders feeling physically well and ready for our new tasks, including the rigours of further global travel (see Essay 6 and Appendix C).

It was in the autumn of 2007 that I began to experience difficulty in swallowing. Remembering the lessons from 1969, I lost no time in seeing our family general practitioner, Dr Michael Choong, who advised me to undergo a total body scan. This took place soon thereafter at the Sloane Hospital in Beckenham, Kent, only a mile or so from our home in Bromley. There the consultant gastroenterologist, Dr M.A. Asante, told us that the scan had revealed two abnormal masses: one in my lower gullet and another on my right kidney. The latter was about 2.5 centimetres in size but Dr Asante could not be sure of its nature. Therefore he referred me to Mr Guy Dawkins, a consultant at the Chelsfield Park Hospital in Kent, to attend to the matter of the kidney and to Mr Rajab Kerwat, a gastrointestinal surgeon based at the Blackheath Hospital in south-east London, to deal with the problem in my oesophagus.

As soon as the scan results were known I was advised by all the doctors to have the oesophageal tumour dealt with at once, while the kidney problem would be monitored for later decisions. Helen and I met Mr Kerwat, an Egyptian by nationality, early in November 2007. He advised immediate chemotherapy followed by surgery. I consented to this plan and at once informed the Chief of the Staff and my private support colleagues at International Headquarters (IHQ). All the senior officers were similarly informed and an appropriate formal bulletin was released to advise the whole Army of the situation. Commissioner Robin Dunster was the ideal colleague to have as the Chief of the Staff in these circumstances, for she had a calm spirit, a medical background, and needed little by way of explanations. She was also a wise and natural leader in her own right and thus more than able to shoulder the added responsibilities that would be hers while I was unavoidably detained in the operating theatre and the intensive care unit.

In the weeks that lay ahead the Chief liaised with me to very good effect, meeting me at home at regular intervals to seek guidance and decisions and to keep me fully briefed on the life and needs of the global Army. Major Richard Gaudion, my splendid Private Secretary, came almost daily to bring correspondence, to seek directives, but also – and this was vital – to pray with me and Helen.

These practical contingency arrangements worked well. Our overseas travel had of necessity to be curtailed for about six months which meant, ironically, that the day-to-day business of the General's office was more up-to-date than was usually the case!

I cannot speak highly enough of the way our fellow Salvationists rose up in loving concern and support during these months. We were carried along on wings of prayer. The daily messages of encouragement from every corner of the world kept our spirits lifted.

Only one strange reaction arose to surprise us. It came by way of a letter to Commissioner Dunster from a commissioner on homeland furlough in London. He had encountered briefly our younger son, John, at a Sunday meeting and in a fleeting conversation had learned that I was not tolerating the chemotherapy well. John's innocent few words about his Dad were then exploited for other purposes. The commissioner's letter expected swift action by the Chief to invoke the Army's legal constitution. He seemed to want a re-enactment of the febrile 1929 crisis which deposed General Bramwell Booth on grounds of ill health. The Chief rightly brought the letter to me in my office without delay. We agreed that she would send a brief reassuring reply and I would respond more fully. Later I did so, asking why the commissioner had not first contacted me or my wife or the Chief before putting pen to paper. Like him, we were all in London and only a telephone call away. He had relied on a brief, casual chat with a young unsuspecting teenager. I assured him that, due to the temporary cessation of overseas travel, the work of the General's office was more up-to-date than usual and ventured to suggest he would do well, on returning overseas, to focus his energies on turning around his struggling territory.

I tolerated the first cycle of chemotherapy reasonably well, but the second beginning in mid-December 2007 proved very difficult indeed. All the worst side effects seemed to hit me at once, the chief of which were constant nausea and loss of appetite. My weight dropped alarmingly and my hair fell out. The side effects were so debilitating that I was admitted to the London Bridge Hospital on Christmas Day and again early in the New Year. However, I got through it in the end and went on to tolerate the third and fourth cycles somewhat better. I still have the meticulous notes written up by Helen on how each day went insofar as diet and energy levels were concerned. She recorded also the dates on which I was able to be in my office at IHQ.

The doctors had told me to travel no further than south-east England during these months of treatment. Both Helen and I were touched and impressed by the mature understanding shown by the leaders in those territories where official visits had been planned but now had to be cancelled. Their gentleness and patience were a real blessing.

By the end of February 2008 the rigours of the chemotherapy came to an end and there followed another scan to check the impact upon the tumour. It had dramatically diminished in size, resulting in my swallowing being normal. We had endured a few rough months, including the discovery of a blood clot on my lung which necessitated six months of blood-thinning self-injections daily. I was granted six weeks of recovery time before surgery and began rapidly to regain energy and some of the lost bodyweight. By now I was directly under the care of Mr Kerwat who made arrangements for a laparoscopic two-stage oesophagectomy to be carried out at The London Clinic, in Devonshire Place, on 5 April 2008. The surgery duly took place, was done entirely by small incisions for keyhole procedures and lasted nine hours. Mr Kerwat was joined by Mr

Abrie Botha in the operating theatre, and to this skilled duo with Egyptian and South African backgrounds I owe the success of it all.

During the operation Helen walked London's streets with Matt and John for company. Mr Kerwat telephoned her mobile number to tell her when I was out of theatre and able to be seen in the intensive care unit. Here I was nursed meticulously for three days and nights before spending a further 10 days or so in a private room and then being discharged.

Mr Kerwat's subsequent letter to his fellow consultants and to my family doctor reported that 'the tumour was completely excised with clear margins all around' and that there was 'no lymph node metastasis' and 'no vascular invasion by tumour cells'. The disease had been detected at an early stage.

The possibility of post-operative additional chemotherapy was discussed by my doctors but decided against. Dr Paul Ross, my brilliant consultant oncologist, telephoned me at home in mid-May to confirm this and echoed the words of Professor Sir David Smithers to me in 1969 when he said, 'Get on with your life now!' This was music to my ears. As I write, I have just been advised by Dr Ross that after five years he feels free to discharge me and relieve me of the need for any further meetings with him.

Journal, 1 January 2009: The year 2008 is over and I am alive and doing OK! What a year it was! I thank God that I am seeing this new year.

2009

However, there was yet the outstanding matter of the growth on my right kidney. In early June 2008 Mr Dawkins met us and suggested that a period of six months be allowed to elapse to afford full recovery from the recent surgery. The diseased kidney would then be removed. He said the tests had revealed that no nearby lymph nodes were diseased and there was likely to be 'a good long-term outcome'. Mr Dawkins referred me to a consultant urological surgeon, Mr Tim O'Brien at London Bridge Hospital, who in turn passed me on to Mr Declan Cahill. He would perform the operation which he described as 'a routine procedure'.

In order to minimise any impact on our official schedule the operation was eventually performed on 11 May 2009. Mr Cahill predicted a recovery period of four weeks before undertaking international travel. However, he was over-optimistic. The pain levels in those following weeks were far worse than anything I experienced as a result of the oesophagectomy which had involved no incisions into muscle tissue. As a result we cancelled a long-planned visit to the USA Western Territory but Commissioners Israel and Eva Gaither, the USA National leaders, stepped in to replace us and, under the guiding hands also of Commissioners Philip and Patricia Swyers, a wonderful series of meetings took place in which blessings flowed in abundance. Later, during 2012, I was honoured to visit the territory and to take part in several events, including the public welcome meeting for 65 new cadets as members of the Disciples of the Cross Session. In a small way this allowed me to repay the territory for its patience and tolerance regarding the earlier cancelled visit. I remain grateful to the present leaders, Commissioners James and Carolyn Knaggs, for making this possible.

One month after the kidney removal Mr Cahill wrote to me to say, 'Your latest blood tests were great!'

> *Journal, 28 June 2009: This is the first journal entry since the kidney operation. I was in hospital for three nights. The pain was severe for five weeks, much worse that I was led to expect. I was well enough to chair the International Management Council meeting on 2 June. Since then I have followed a pretty regular attendance routine at the office. I need more stamina, more endurance. I am walking in the evenings and have mowed the lawns.*

2010

We went to Newfoundland, Canada, for the Territorial Congress in June 2010, pleased to be back in this unique province which held such a significant proportion of Canada's Salvationists. It was not our first visit for we had been guests of Majors Kevin and Mary Rideout and St John's Temple Corps for Holy Week and Easter in April 1985. That visit ensured a special place in our hearts for Newfoundland and its Salvationists, one of whom was the effective and warm-hearted Major Fran Duffett who worked with us in Pakistan. Also I had toured Canada in 1986 with Enfield Citadel Band, travelling for two weeks coast to coast (from east to west), including two venues in Newfoundland. Helen and I had understood the significant place of Newfoundlanders in the Army's history ever since reading General Clarence Wiseman's 1979 autobiography, *A Burning in My Bones*, and sensed not only the early-day passion and courage of the pioneers but also the vibrant spirit that characterises today's Salvationists there.

> *Journal, 4 July 2010: We were really pleased to be in St John's again. We had a couple of rest days. Lieut-Colonel Alf Richardson, a warm-hearted host, drove us around the Bays and we enjoyed cod and chips in Portugal Cove. Full days followed. Renewing links with Major Fran Duffett in her home on our final free morning was great. Also to meet again Majors Kevin and Mary Rideout who first invited us to St John's Temple Corps for Holy Week and Easter. To meet so many good folk was a lovely blessing. Lord, thank you. Thank you for the fervent seekers and for the frequent outbursts of applause as I preached. I love you, Lord, for letting us go to St John's again.*

It was during this 2010 overseas visit that I experienced an uncomfortable shortage of breath when mounting stairs or walking uphill.

> *Journal, 8 August 2010: I will enter London Bridge Hospital tomorrow for an angiogram and probable angioplasty (stent). Tomorrow is day one of three weeks of furlough. Lord God, who made me, raised me, called me and deployed me, grant healing. Hold me. Hold Helen. Restore my energies.*

As soon as we returned to London from a brief official visit to Korea I contacted Mr Graham Jackson, a consultant cardiologist at the London Bridge Hospital, who had earlier checked my heart in readiness for the surgery to remove my right kidney. His tests now revealed furred-up arteries. He arranged for my rapid admission so that stents could be inserted to widen the blocked passages.

The stent procedure is carried out in theatre with the patient wide awake. So I could hear and see everything, including the images of my heart on screen. Despite his best efforts Mr Jackson could not get the stents into place and told me there and then that the arteries were more furred-up than he had thought. Bypass surgery would therefore be needed. He said I should stay in the hospital for the operation two days later.

On returning me to the ward he came to see me again. I told him I was writing a two-volume work (*Selected Writings*) for publication by the Army and needed only a few hours more to finalise Volume 1. Thus I asked to be sent home for one night to complete the manuscript lest anything untoward should befall me during the bypass procedure. Mr Jackson spoke of his affection and admiration for the Army and of his family's habit of attending the carol service each year in the Royal Albert Hall. He would release me readily, but added smilingly that he had never before heard such an excuse for not staying in hospital. I was grateful for his response, and indeed for all the many good and often spiritual conversations that arose with the medical staff at all levels, from porters to senior consultants, who saw us attending appointments in uniform en route to and from IHQ.

> *Journal, 10 August 2010: The angiogram on the 9th showed my arteries too clogged up to take a stent. So tomorrow I undergo heart bypass surgery. No time for self-pity. Came home from London Bridge Hospital for a night to complete draft one of Volume 1 of 'Selected Writings'. Dear Father in Heaven, take care of all of this please. Guard Helen and my children and grandchildren. Protect the Army.*

After Mr Jackson temporarily discharged me Major Gaudion came and whisked me home to Bromley, the first draft of the manuscript was completed, and I returned to the hospital as planned. Once more I found myself parting from Helen at the doors of an operating theatre, but we both knew that there was nothing left unsaid between us and that, as Paul testifies in 2 Timothy 4:17, 'the Lord stood at my side and gave me strength'. How brave, how calm and reassuring Helen was. It was 11 August 2010.

Once again we experienced the warmth of the Army world as messages of prayer and support flooded in. Commissioner Barry Swanson, appointed by me in May that year to succeed Commissioner Robin Dunster as the Chief of the Staff, sent out an official bulletin to let the Army know the situation.

The surgery was conducted by Mr Graeme Venn, who carried out three bypasses and inserted a new aortic valve made of animal tissue. I woke from the anaesthetic to find my ribcage reset and wired together, a long scar running north to south on my upper torso. But I was alive and had yet again come through a serious operation. There were to follow long weeks of recovery of body strength and the introduction of a regime of regular walking.

I had been at home only a week or so when it became apparent that Helen was not at all well.

2010 – Helen

Helen's energy levels had been low but we put that down to the drain of international travel and then the strain of holding on calmly for family and friends throughout my heart surgery. We were soon to know differently.

For completeness I need to refer back to our years in Pakistan. We were granted homeland furlough every year and while on leave in the summer of 2000 underwent routine medical examinations at the InterHealth centre not far from IHQ. A patch of discoloured skin was noticed on one of Helen's ankles and was in due course identified as a melanoma. She was rapidly admitted to the Lister Hospital in Chelsea, London, and on 5 August the melanoma was removed. After recuperating at her parents' home in Edmonton she returned to Lahore and to full activity. She was checked periodically for several more months and again during our next homeland furlough. All seemed well. The years passed.

Helen woke later than usual one morning in September 2010 and on joining me downstairs tried to speak but the words came out all in the wrong order. I noticed that one eye was very heavily bloodshot. I held her close as we sat on the settee. Soon she was able to express herself normally again and the rest of the day passed without incident. However, the next morning we hurried by taxi to Chislehurst to see our family doctor. My strength was low but Major Gaudion came at once and ferried us home. Helen was referred to the Sloane Hospital in Beckenham for a full scan. The consultant radiologist, Dr Preminda Kessar, saw us and said Helen had a melanoma tumour in her brain. It was located in that part of the brain which governs speech and the ability to form sentences.

> *Journal, 19 September 2010: After weeks of scans the diagnosis is of melanoma in her lovely brain. The specialist says she cannot be cured. Helen is calm. I am less calm in my mind and spirit. Constantly turning to God to plead for her. Lord, you see all things. Have mercy I plead. Hold and cradle Helen, Lord Jesus. Touch and heal her. Boldly I ask at your throne for a miracle.*

By mid-September Helen was in the hands of Mr Martin Leslie of The Harley Street Cancer Centre. He planned several cycles of radiation treatment to her whole brain and she was placed on steroids medication. A further scan on completion of the treatment revealed that the tumour was still the same size. Mr Leslie, who in earlier conversations when we attended in uniform had told us he was an unbeliever, quietly told us that life expectancy would be between nine and eighteen months. Helen received this word with a dignified calm. We spoke further to Mr Leslie of our faith in Jesus and the sure hope of Heaven. He listened politely, engaged in further quiet converse, and referred Helen as a last resort to Europe's leading melanoma specialist, Professor Martin Gore at the Royal Marsden Hospital in the Fulham Road, London. This was where I had first been admitted in 1969.

It was just before Christmas in December 2010 that Professor Gore saw us to say he would simply meet and monitor Helen month by month to ensure that any pain was properly addressed. He linked us to St Christopher's Hospice in Sydenham, south London, and arrangements were made for their Harris Nurses to visit us at home from time to time.

How wonderful it was that my sister, Sylvia, had been able to join us in September to care for Helen and to manage household matters during the final six months of my term as General. She and Helen were able now and then to go out and about for shopping, lunch or coffee. Major Lynn Gibbs, Helen's personal assistant, was a frequent visitor. Her professionalism and caring nature were rich blessings, as were the visits by Commissioner Sue Swanson, the World Secretary for Women's Ministries.

On one occasion when Lynn came and when Helen was unable to say very much, the two were seated side by side on the sofa when Helen decided to pray aloud. Her sentences came out perfectly formed. What a blessing that although her capacity to articulate was failing more and more, her ability to comprehend, to reason, and to recognise people never faded. All her faculties were intact with the exception of the ability to use words. The weeks of the 2011 High Council in late January engaged her full attention. She followed developments day by day and read the official bulletins.

Every two months Sylvia returned briefly to her home in Somerset to attend to her affairs there, something first made possible through a visit in October 2010 by our daughter, Jenny, who flew from Auckland, New Zealand. Matt and Lynne's Army leaders ensured they were free to help us and within reasonable reach. In addition our son, John, by now a cadet in London, was granted leave to come home overnight whenever he thought it best to do so. He came for several days over the Christmas and New Year periods. We were grateful for the patience and gentle understanding of our children's Army leaders.

Journal, 22 October 2010: Helen has had a second round of radiation. Now her hair is all gone. Jen flew in from New Zealand on 7 October for two weeks. Syl has been a superb support. Loving Father God, keep us calm and steady under fire. Thank you for each other, for our children, our colleagues, and for the many prayers offered for us and especially for Helen. 'Let our ordered lives confess the beauty of thy peace.' Help us to role-model trust and poise. I cannot do this in my own power.

Journal, 4 December 2010: Still I ask God for a miracle for my lovely Helen. Keeping poised is hard. Oh, for grace, more grace.

Journal, 19 December 2010: At noon today Bromley Band turned up and stood in the snow outside our house and played carols for 20 minutes. Many neighbours came out or watched from windows. We donned our overcoats and stood together. Helen was excited and radiant, insisting by gestures that I prayed with the band before they left us. Wonderful! Thank you, Lord.

Journal, 31 December 2010: Still I wait in faith. I ask for a calm mind and spirit and a deeper trust. I place Helen once again into your wounded hands. Bless her and guard her every moment. I yield, I submit, I bow, I surrender my all again. Break me afresh for you in the next three months and let me stay poised and wise for you as I near retirement.

Helen's two final appearances in public and in uniform are described briefly in my 2012 collation of her sermons, talks and lectures, *From Her Heart.* On these occasions her quiet determination, with her graciousness, shone through.

We entered retirement and I left office early in April 2011. I replaced Sylvia as Helen's full-time carer. We were to have a mere seven or eight weeks together before it became clear that admission to St Christopher's was close at hand. We talked of it together and Helen indicated her readiness in a rare moment of vocal clarity.

Journal, 13 April 2011: I battle for perspective. I feel robbed of a happy and shared retirement. I cannot tell if Helen also feels like that. She cannot articulate any longer. The hospice nurse will come tomorrow. I have been trying to snatch quiet moments to read my Bible and also my Song Book. Philippians 1:29, 2:27 and 3:10 strike me but in my inner confusion I am unsure how or why. Song 475 helped me this morning.

Journal, 20 April 2011: On Palm Sunday we drove to Westerham, Kent, for hot chocolate in the evening and drove home past the lambs in the fields nearby. Lovely.

Journal, 25 April 2011: A quiet Easter weekend for us. Found it hard to feel afresh the power of Calvary and of Resurrection. I am jaded. I took Helen to Knole Park on Good Friday afternoon, a gloriously hot day. Now as I write this Helen is asleep on the sofa in the lounge. Hold and protect her, Lord. We need you very much.

Journal, 7 May 2011: Desperate prayer, groaning prayer. My waking thoughts are inarticulate, primitive, instinctive, even resentful. I have come to the conclusion my Maker prefers me to approach him like this – all facade, all sophistication stripped away by circumstance and pain. Why? I have no idea and never expect to understand. So I cling on, and cling on…because there is nothing else. And all of it hurts – a lot.

Journal, 13 May 2011: Lord, I come to you yet again for Helen, to place her at your broken feet. Come and help her now. Come and help me now. The death of my closest companion, friend, ally and loved one is before me.

Our daughter-in-law, Lynne, was with us on the morning of admission, Thursday 19 May 2011, and gathered up whatever items Helen might need in the hospice. We drove the short distance from Bromley to Sydenham, tears stinging our eyes, though Helen remained quietly focused. Jenny returned from New Zealand for the final two weeks of her Mum's life. How good it was to have her in the house and at my side each day. Matt and John also came daily to the hospice to help in practical ways and to keep vigil. Our constantly faithful corps officers, Majors Brian and Liv Slinn, supported us. Other family members did so too.

Journal, 20 May 2011: Yesterday Helen was admitted to the hospice in Sydenham. Lynne was with us. God above, come and help us now. The empty bed, the vacant sofa, her things about the house. Hold her, Lord.

Journal, 21 May 2011: I hurt in every part of my soul. God, keep me sane and stable. Cradle Helen.

Journal, 9 June 2011: I am low, very low this morning. I am glad Jen has stayed an extra week. John visits his Mum daily. Matt and Lynne come often. Helen smiles now and then. Last evening in the hospice ward gently she and I held hands for two hours and she caressed my fingers. Often her hand has been limp. I hurt, a lot. I can only guess how each of our children feels. They are good to me beyond measure.

On the morning of 14 June 2011 I arrived at the hospice just after 9 am only to be taken aside at once by the staff nurse. 'There has been a change overnight,' she said. 'Helen's hands and feet are cold. Her heart is shutting down. There are only a few hours left. We will move her to a room where you can be alone with her.'

So this was it. Matt and John came quickly. So too did Naomi, John's fiancée. Helen's brother, Kevin, came with Andrea, his wife. Majors Slinn were present too.

I held Helen's hand, stroked her head, and talked to her. We also talked about her. Now and then we quietly sang 'I know the Lord will make a way for me' or 'Jesus is the sweetest name I know'. At about 9.15 in the evening she opened her eyes for the first time that day and gazed at me. A few moments later she looked again. Then she was gone, her last breath so gentle and relaxed.

Journal, 15 June 2011: It is over. Helen no longer hurts and once again she can speak in the presence of her Saviour. She slipped away so quietly and tenderly, breathing oh so gently at the last, having opened her eyes to look at me only minutes before. What a blessing, but also what pain! It was 9.20 pm on 14 June 2011, a Tuesday. I was pleased for her that the long wait is over, but today I am in turmoil again as we registered the death and spoke to the undertakers. Lovely messages flooding in from all over the world. Fifty-eight emails in the first few hours. She was loved. Dear Lord, caress my Helen for me. Make her wonderfully whole. Grant her peace and joy and may her dazzling smile make Heaven even brighter.

In the moments after Helen died Major Brian Slinn spoke a lovely, comforting prayer and then he and Major Liv Slinn left us to be simply family together in a private way. Never had I felt so lost and forlorn. Even when expected, the end is full of pain for loved ones. Helen had shared my life for close to 50 years. Suddenly everything was changed. Why? Why? There are no answers.

An official bulletin went out from IHQ to announce Helen's promotion to Glory. Countless written items reached our home address, sometimes as many as 40 a day. We requested donations to St Christopher's instead of flowers, and with a significant gift also from the family a very useful sum went to the hospice.

Funeral arrangements had to take into account the time needed for Jenny and Marcus, with Hudson (aged nine) and Lincoln (aged four), to travel to London from Auckland. Meanwhile Helen's body, clad in her Army uniform, lay in the chapel of rest at the premises of the undertaker in Selsdon. We could visit at any time. When Hudson arrived, he insisted on seeing his Grandma. 'I am the eldest grandchild,' he said calmly but firmly. I was proud of him.

On Tuesday 5 July 2011 we gathered at Beckenham Crematorium as a family, but also surrounded by a host of Army comrades. Some had come even from overseas. The coffin was draped in the Army flag on which we placed a simple spray of red roses. The General being overseas, the Chief of the Staff, Commissioner Barry Swanson, presided and I will always be grateful to him and to Commissioner Sue Swanson for their help that day. There followed a Service of Thanksgiving in the William Booth College at Denmark Hill where the famous Assembly Hall was packed to capacity. Bromley Temple Songsters (under Major Ray Irving) and the Enfield Citadel Band (under Bandmaster Jonathan Corry) enriched the meeting. Our three children found grace and courage to speak from their hearts in tribute to their mother. Seldom have I been prouder of them.

With the consent of the National Trust we scattered Helen's ashes at the foot of a beautiful birch tree in the grounds of Knole Park, Sevenoaks, Kent. It was important to do this as a complete family before Jenny and Marcus returned to their ministry on Auckland's North Shore. Marcus carried the urn for us. I spoke the briefest of prayers and then we moved toward the restaurant near Knole House. Helen and I had often been there, walking the estate and marvelling at the tameness of the deer herd.

Sylvia and Helen had been there too in the final months when brief outings were still possible.

> *Journal, 13 July 2011: Today we will scatter Helen's ashes. It seems unreal, a bad dream. I gaze at her photographs. I love to look at her, but it also triggers pain. But look I will. I still feel robbed, cheated.*

> *Journal, 18 July 2011: Duly we scattered Helen's ashes. The sun shone upon us. The children were loving and a great support, evincing a simple and pragmatic spirit. All agreed we had done the right and proper thing, choosing a place of natural beauty, one associated with life, pleasure, openness, and free space.*

Sensing the need for a more permanent memorial to add to the natural setting of Knole Park, I contacted General Linda Bond and sought her agreement for a Mercy Seat to be made that would grace the IHQ meeting room where all the staff gather regularly for united prayers. This was readily and graciously agreed. I met the costs involved. My mind went back to a Thursday morning early in October 1982. I had been asked to lead morning prayers in the Bramwell Booth Memorial Hall at IHQ. I had never seen any person kneeling at the lovely Mercy Seat and I had never done so. It seemed to be the least used facility on the building. I mentioned this and invited those present to come and kneel out of love for, and adoration of, Jesus. There was an instant response, led by the most senior officers present. I suppose nearly two thirds of the staff knelt that morning.

The present headquarters for some reason had been designed and built with no Mercy Seat in the space where the staff gathered weekly for prayers. Now this could be put right. A simple service of dedication was arranged. It took place on Thursday 17 May 2012 and General Bond presided. The dedication plate bears Helen's name and cites Hebrews 13:8, one of her favourite Bible verses: 'Jesus Christ is the same yesterday and today and for ever.' These words import a sense of timelessness, of eternity, and now Helen understands them more fully than any of us who are yet to be called Home to Heaven.

Designed and crafted by Ray and Christine Headley of South Shields Corps, in a style to blend in with the modern feel of IHQ, Helen's Mercy Seat is a sacred symbol of all the Army Mercy Seats in countless lands at which Helen and I have knelt side by side, our hands clasped together. In those many hallowed moments we have thanked God for calling us and using us, and have sought and received added grace, guidance and strength for the often burdensome demands of sacred service.

ESSAY 5

&

SINGING

ESSAY 5
SINGING

THIS Essay touches on selected events from childhood to my retiring from office as the General of The Salvation Army and then the death of Helen shortly thereafter. Its common thread is that of singing and songs.

It began in Scotland

The Army has sung its way around the globe and into 126 countries. It is not possible to grow up in the Army and not sing! Salvationists sing heartily. My sister, Sylvia, a Salvationist by nurture and instinct but who lives in Ilminster, a small Somerset town where there is no Army corps, is very active at St Mary's Minster of the Church of England. She confesses to loving the opportunity to get back into an Army meeting where she can sing without inhibition.

My first experience of choral singing was after being enrolled as an Army junior soldier. I became a member of the singing company at Parkhead Corps in Glasgow. It was 1954 and I was nine. The leader was John McDonald who worked under my Dad as an insurance agent for The Salvation Army Assurance Society Limited. I recall clearly his craggy, characterful features and his brushed-back, wavy, greying hair. There were about 40 of us in the singing company, including my sisters, Sylvia and Mary. We never sang in public with music in front of us. It all had to be memorised. Often I struggled to keep up, bluffing my way through, especially as a new member, but I sensed early the joy of making music as part of a trained and disciplined group.

Our family moved from Parkhead to Edmonton, a north London suburb, in 1957 when I was 12. Helen and her family were there already, and I recall vividly my first sight of her when she was only nine. She was petite, with brown eyes too lovely for words. I did not continue as a singing company member but later, after becoming a senior soldier, joined the songster brigade of 40 or so members. Later Helen was their organist/pianist. I sang in the bass section but knew I had neither a natural bass nor tenor voice. I drifted around between the two sets of notes on the lower stave and nobody seemed to mind. Our songster leader was Ernest

Chapman, an intelligent but socially reserved gentleman. Ernie and his wife, Doris, took me into their home for several months when my parents were moved by the Army from Edmonton to Leicester just in the middle of my final-year examinations at school. Their son, Derek, played solo cornet in the band, rode a powerful motor-cycle and played amateur football on Saturdays. He shared his bedroom with me. I have never forgotten this and still feel grateful. My chief memory of Derek is that he spent much of the time laughing. The Chapmans were a kind and generous Army family, typical of others also in Edmonton Corps (see Essay 10).

Singing cadets

Helen and I became members of the Blood and Fire Session of cadets at the International Training College, Denmark Hill, London, in the late summer of 1971 when we had been married for four years. All cadets were required to sing as an entire sessional group. Major Idwal Evans, a kindly and cordial person, conducted us and Captain Clifford Ashworth was our able pianist. His musicality more than made up for Idwal's occasional failing to bring us in at the appropriate moment! Our sessional song was composed by Bandmaster Donald Osgood of Southall Corps in west London. He was concerned to make the singing of the song a deep experience for the cadets. Colonel Mrs Ivy Mawby wrote the words.

After our Commissioning meeting in the Royal Albert Hall in 1973 Donald asked me if singing the sessional song had been an uplifting experience. 'Redeemed with the precious blood of Christ' was the opening proclamation. 'Blood of his sacrifice, fire of his Spirit' ran the chorus. Yes, I said, we felt inspired. By the words certainly, but the plain and evident truth was that as a full session we were no great singers and the high register taxed our meagre talents. Thank God then for the selected female voices of our Women's Singing Brigade under Captain Jill Buchanan (now Mrs Lieut-Colonel Girling) with Cadet Lorna Farley (now Major Doust) at the piano. Helen was a member of the alto section. This ensemble blended their voices wonderfully and always enriched the Thursday night holiness meetings at Camberwell. When they sang, Heaven spoke.

After being commissioned as an officer I took no further part in choral singing of any kind. It was a pleasure forfeited.

Sacred songs

I want to share something of the impact of the Army *Song Book* upon my life. Many varieties of sung music can penetrate my soul. I think of the Anglican choral tradition of all-age male voices. Attending Evensong in Rochester, Winchester, Salisbury or Canterbury Cathedrals is a wonderfully uplifting experience, enhanced by the ancient majesty of these sacred spaces which lend a powerful resonance to both voices and organ. However, the greatest impact upon me has come from Army songs and singing. That is why my *Song Book* (1986 edition) is heavily annotated. My mother also marked her *Song Book*. After she died I found her earlier edition and looked at the markings. Mum knew she was dying of widespread cancer. She loved the songs of Fanny Crosby, not least 'I must have the Saviour with me' (Song 731). The chorus says:

> 'Then my soul shall fear no ill;
> Let him lead me where he will,
> I will go without a murmur,
> And his footsteps follow still.'

In the margin Mum had written 'no fear at all – 1984'. Years later in 2003, when at the hospice bedside of Major David Griffiths in New Zealand (see also Essay 11), I read aloud to him all of the verses and the chorus of this song as he faced his final hours. Present also were his devoted wife, Colleen, and the divisional leaders, Majors Ross and Annette Gower.

I cannot see or sing Song 741, 'Lord Jesus, thou dost keep thy child', without being back at the bedside of our three children. As part of their bedtime prayers we would say: 'Lord Jesus, thou dost keep thy child through sunshine or through tempest wild; Jesus, I trust in thee.' Later, when the children had left home, Helen and I would use these lines as part of our close-of-day devotions, adding the adoration expressed in the concluding lines of the verse: 'Thine is such wondrous power to save; thine is the mighty love that gave its all on Calvary.'

Turning the pages of my *Song Book* I see many a single sentence or phrase underlined because of its impact upon me:

'Inward knowledge no learning can bestow' (Song 6)

'We shall find ourselves at last presented faultless at his Father's throne'
(Song 70)

'Fill, thou, our lives with charity divine' (Song 181)

'Purge the dark halls of thought' (Song 416)

'Write thy new name upon my heart' (Song 444)

'Into thy hands, Lord, take me and mould me' (Song 501)

'Saviour, breathe forgiveness o'er us' (Song 607)

'O thou knowest all the yearning of my heart' (Song 614)

'Thou hast the guarding of my soul, and I am not afraid' (Song 717)

If only I had space to cite them all! Let me add selected lines from the
pen of the incomparable Catherine Baird, taken from Song 631:

'Thou art…come for my need'

'Thou art…my secret fortress and my soul's release'

'Whate'er I am I bring into thy care'

I admire also her passionate, pacifist anthem found in Song 705: 'We
lay all carnal weapons down', in favour of the Cross.

The songs of Herbert Booth, son of the Founders, remain powerful
and eloquent to me. Herbert's personal history and his strained relations
with his father and his brother, Bramwell, seem to render his verses all the
more poignant:

'Before thy face, dear Lord,
Myself I want to see....
Am I what I ought to be?
O Saviour, let me know.'
(Song 409)

Then there is his penetrating, self-searching Song 420, in which he writes of his 'fears', 'hopes', 'feelings', 'tears'. He brings his 'heart', his 'life', his 'sins', his 'all' to the Saviour who 'hath seen how my soul desireth to be clean'.

Add to this Song 713, 'Blessed Lord, in thee is refuge'. My *Song Book* tells me how the singing of these verses brought us into an awareness of the Holy Spirit among us on a Sunday in March 1995 at Guisborough Corps. Commissioners Dinsdale and Win Pender, then our territorial leaders in the United Kingdom (UK), led this meeting. It was rich in blessing.

Herbert's words have claimed an even deeper personal meaning for me in his song, 'I bring to thee my heart to fill' (Song 489). Verse two is one of those we sing all too easily, with its staggering promise to be willing to die for the cause of Christ: 'But with thee, though I mount the cross, I count it gain to suffer loss....' When our Army leaders assigned us to Pakistan in June 1997 we knew we were being sent into harm's way. The Army's township at Shantinagar (see Essay 6) had just been torched by a rampaging Moslem mob and later, on visiting there, we found our Army comrades routinely carrying automatic weapons for self-defence. After being asked by General Paul Rader (via a telephone call from Commissioner Earle Maxwell, the Chief of the Staff) to lead the Army in this Islamic Republic, Helen and I found ourselves attending an Executive Officers' Conference at the USA Eastern Territory's headquarters and staying at the Holidome Hotel in Suffern, New Jersey. Pakistan seemed another world away! Quietly we spoke to one another about Shantinagar as illustrative of the risks of living as Christian leaders in Lahore and of those to which our son, John, then aged 10, would inevitably be exposed. Our matter-of-fact conversation turned naturally to the possibility of losing our lives there, of mounting the cross, for the sake of our sacred callings as officers. Herbert Booth's words suddenly became starkly relevant, but so too did his concluding stanza:

> 'No tempest can my courage shake,
> My love from thee no pain can take,
> No fear my heart appal;
> And where I cannot see I'll trust,
> For then I know thou surely must
> Be still my all in all.'
> (Song 489)

Our five years in Pakistan took us again and again to our knees. Death threats and security issues became commonplace. It was the air we breathed. The dangers were shared by some fine expatriate officer colleagues who served with us at Territorial Headquarters and at the training college. They were shared also by our Pakistani fellow-Salvationists. The reality of the dangers and the endemic violence of the culture were most tragically demonstrated in the murder of Colonel Bo Brekke there in September 2007 (see Essays 6 and 10).

Albert Orsborn was an inspired songwriter. For generations his lines have proved powerful under God. Of them all, it is his song about Calvary, 'Many thoughts stir my heart' (Song 119), that calls to me and speaks for me:

> 'O the charm of the cross! How I love to be there!'

Then that final line of verse two, saying for me of the Cross what I cannot say for myself:

> 'Surpassing my reason but winning my heart.'

Orsborn was born in Maidstone, Kent. Long before Helen became ill, and before retirement, we accepted an invitation to lead meetings there for an Albert Orsborn Memorial Weekend. Despite Helen's death I wanted to honour this engagement. By the time it fell due, I had not been on an Army platform for five months and this after being constantly in the spotlight as the General. It felt very strange indeed to be leading meetings and Helen not there at my side, but Majors Grayson and Janice Williams and the divisional leaders, Lieut-Colonels Anthony and Gillian Cotterill, were insightfully supportive and kind throughout the weekend. The Sunday evening meeting was a farewell to four candidates to the officer training college. The day ended wonderfully with a lined Mercy Seat and several new commitments to the service of God.

Toward a new 'Song Book'

Throughout the Army's history some of our Generals have been adventurous in publishing new editions of the English language *Song Book*. In recent years, the all-pervading use of large screens in our halls, and the onset of clever computerised technology, has relegated our printed song books to a minor role. In the English-speaking territories, few any longer carry them to the meetings, anticipating the use of a screen, which has changed our posture in times of prayer and devotion from bowed-head humility to screen-gazing scrutiny. The age of the screen has also seen fewer and fewer Salvationists taking their Bibles to the worship meetings.

Was there any point in seeking to produce a further, more-modern edition of the English *Song Book*? I decided, as the General, to consult widely across the globe. The feedback was clear: we should never abandon the idea of an up-to-date published *Song Book*. It is a crucial component of our self-expression as a distinctive people of God and a generation-by-generation restatement of our central theological positions.

Thus I felt my duty was plain and a year before I retired I convened a new Song Book Council to pilot things through. To ensure speed of progress I decided to chair this Council in person. The members took to the task with a will. I asked that the words content of the new book should be settled before I retired and that the rewriting of music for bands, keyboards, guitars, and for those countries using the tonic sol-fa system, should be well under way before I handed over to my successor. All this was accomplished. I approved the removal of about one third of the contents of the 1986 edition and felt comfortable in so doing since other Generals had been similarly radical as each new edition came along.

It was decided to abandon a separate 'Chorus Section' since many of the modern entries could not easily be classified as either 'song' or 'chorus'. To help meeting planners we would introduce a series of much more user-friendly indices, including especially an index of Bible references since each song would have a key Bible reference at the top alongside the tunes to be used. The new book would be available online and all our previous song books would be made similarly available so that in effect nothing of the past would be irretrievably lost.

When I retired I was able to inform General-elect Linda Bond that the work was well under way, with the words contents settled. I owe a huge debt of gratitude in all of this to the Council members and to Commissioner John Matear and the United Kingdom Territory for readiness to commit people and money resources to producing the new music. Lieut-Colonel Rob Garrad and in particular Major Christine Clement gave great support, dealing with countless details.

A footnote

The years have brought me untold blessings in listening to Army singing, whether choral or congregation. Here I want to mention right away the choir at the Army's Mazowe Secondary School in Mashonaland, Zimbabwe, where we served as newly commissioned lieutenants from early in 1975 to mid-1977 before being reappointed to Bulawayo Citadel Corps in Matabeleland. Zimbabwe was then Rhodesia.

The school choir consisted of 30 or so male pupils aged up to 17. Their voices were resonant with all that is central southern Africa: deep, melodious, harmonising spontaneously, feeling naturally for the rhythms. Few of these young men could read music, but they could all feel it. When Colonel Bernard Adams, Bandmaster of the International Staff Band and leader of the then renowned Upper Norwood Songsters, retired he came to Rhodesia and heard our Mazowe choir sing. His response was one of profound delight. I can see his beaming, surprised face even as I write of him. Gladly he accepted my offer to send him a taped recording of the choir.

The same spirit of Africa is to be found in the sounds of the Zimbabwe Territory Songsters. They came to us on the evening of Thursday 5 July 1990 in Bromley as part of their tour in England for the 1990

International Congress. Our hall was packed to overflowing on a hot and humid night. The sounds of the songsters filled the building and could be heard out in the streets beyond. African voices singing in a polished choral style blessed us again when we heard the Soweto Songsters from Johannesburg during a visit to Zimbabwe, where they were the invited guest section.

Let me digress for a moment or two. Soweto is an abbreviated name concocted by apartheid-driven white political leadership years ago to denote the **South Western Township** of Johannesburg. It was our privilege eventually to see Soweto for ourselves in August 2006. I was able to visit the Apartheid Museum and receive a guided tour as an honoured guest. Major Richard Gaudion was with me. I have never forgotten the poignancy of this experience and its impact upon me as the full awfulness of the apartheid years was brought home afresh to my soul and mind. It was during our early years in Rhodesia that I first saw Johannesburg, having been asked to go from Mazowe to South Africa to be the guest leader of an Army youth event. Major Stan Anthony, a fine Canadian colleague, was my host. On arrival it became clear that only white young people were to attend, a sign of those bewildering, highly-charged times. However, two memories stand out. The first is the privilege of meeting Major Carl Sithole, the first black officer in the territory to be made the Territorial Youth Secretary. The second is of walking through the city streets of Johannesburg and seeing apartheid signs everywhere: 'whites only', 'non-whites only'. Returning home I told Helen of the black pedestrians who, on seeing me nearing them on the sidewalk, lowered their eyes and instinctively stepped aside into the road and the hurtling traffic to let me pass by without breaking my stride. I felt ashamed and embarrassed.

The ebullience of the Pasadena Tabernacle Songsters from California has always brought blessing. Our International Staff Songsters are also wonderfully skilled. These days I am a regular recipient of blessing when the songsters sing at Bromley Temple Corps, reviving memories of similar experiences of the songsters when we were stationed at Enfield Citadel Corps (1979-82). There Brian Cuthbert took things in hand and produced a blended sound that blessed the listener. In contrasting style, but equally effective, was the Danish folk choir, the 'Gospel Factor', that came from Copenhagen to set alight our divisional gatherings in the Durham and Tees Division in April 1995. What a sound! What uninhibited, skilled performances! Led by Anne Jakshoi, daughter of Lieut-Colonel Miriam Frederiksen, they were an 'open' Army group, making space for unsaved persons to join in and perform. It worked well and God used it all.

I ought to conclude these reminiscences with a frank footnote. When Helen died I found myself simply unable to sing in any setting. I had to let the singing of others touch me instead. This went on for many months, easing gradually, but still returning at intervals. Sometimes we sing sacred songs glibly. The words come to our lips too readily, perhaps until we are badly wounded and then the soul may cease to sing even if the lips try to do so.

Dietrich Bonhoeffer, in his 1949 *Life Together* (*Gemeinsames Leben*), ventured the opinion that too often congregations sing thoughtlessly. He even went so far as to suggest that congregations should sing always in unison so that no undue distraction would arise from hearing our neighbour's individual voice: 'The singing of the congregation, especially of the family congregation, is essentially singing in unison…. The purity of unison singing, unaffected by alien motives of musical techniques…is the essence of all congregational singing…. It becomes a question of a congregation's power of spiritual discernment whether it adopts proper unison singing.'

I have some sympathy with this view, but try telling it to an Army congregation. They would think you very strange and, understandably, take little or no notice.

A further footnote

When Helen and I found ourselves at an unexpected crossroads on the path to officership, and when I was most earnestly tempted to settle for a life teaching university law students and writing academic legal textbooks, it was a song from our *Song Book* which brought me to my senses. Due to my health history as a young man (see Essay 4) our application for officer training was rejected. They believed I was going to die as a result of Hodgkin's Lymphoma.

On receiving the rejection letter my first reaction was one of relief, for I felt I had done my duty by offering and it was others who had slammed the door. However, in the end this would not do and I came under clear conviction that we should heed the loving counsel of our corps officers (Major and Mrs William Simkin) and our divisional youth leaders (Captain and Mrs Ian and Beth Cooper) and reapply. The newly appointed and highly persuasive National Candidates Secretary, Major Hubert Boardman, was also urging us to ask again and was actively lobbying our territorial leaders, asking them to take a calculated risk (a 'sanctified risk' as I called such cases in later years) in our case.

It was in a powerful Sunday evening meeting at Edmonton that God spoke. I was seated in the cornet section of the band (my tenor horn playing days were by then behind me) and we were playing 'Men of Harlech' as the congregation sang Song 693. After the opening bars I ceased playing and followed the words of verse one:

'Dare ye still lie fondly dreaming,
Wrapped in ease and worldly scheming,
While the multitudes are streaming
Downwards into Hell?'

My heart was moved, my spirit deeply stirred, and I knew we had to ask again. Still we had a God-given vocation to be Army officers. Would God let man-made procedures continue to frustrate his will? Helen most readily agreed that we should reapply. After considerable further correspondence back and forth, including an unfeeling letter to us saying the Army would wash its hands of financial responsibility for us if I were to fall ill again, we entered the college in the summer of 1971. The rejection had humbled and tested me. Through it all Helen stayed calm and steady, a rock at my side.

In my *Song Book* I have written beside verse one of Song 693: 'Words that changed my life'. Thank God that George Scott Railton ever penned them. Perhaps the new *Song Book* should have a warning on its cover: 'Open only if you are ready to be changed for the cause of Christ.' Such is the potential impact of sacred songs.

ESSAY 6

☙

SOCIETY

ESSAY 6
SOCIETY

NO TWO societies are the same. Social and cultural forces are endlessly varied. Our experiences living and serving on five continents taught us deep respect for local culture, its complexity and elusiveness. This Essay, by far the longest in the book, describes something of what happened to us when serving and living in social settings far from home.

Culture shock

On reaching Africa in 1975 we experienced classic culture shock. Nothing was familiar. At first it was all a novelty and we felt like tourists. We had not asked to be posted overseas but had unexpectedly been approached by International Headquarters (IHQ) who wanted to use us both, but especially Helen, in Rhodesia in teaching roles. We were willing to go anywhere and do anything. Such has always been our calling.

Once the novelty wore off a few weeks after arriving, we went into the well-defined syndrome of culture shock. We tried not to let it show, but we began to wonder just what we had agreed to and what we had come to. Everything looked different, sounded different, tasted different, smelt different. Landscape, vegetation, food options, modes of attire, accents, even the way the Army saw and expressed itself – it was all different!

Some colleagues intuited our need and were kind. Others did not and were not. As the months passed and familiarity grew we found the strangeness easing. The 'shock' of culture shock had hit me harder than it did Helen. Gradually it all began to pass, but it took nine months or more. As we approached the start of our second year things improved. Suddenly we felt at home, at ease, comfortable, useful: classic culture shock. I have never forgotten the experience and in later years, when in senior leadership, intentionally spoke of it to others who were about to face an unknown environment.

Culture shock is normal and it passes, but it is good to anticipate it and to recognise what is going on when it happens. Reverse culture shock can be equally traumatic. It may hit you upon your returning home after being immersed in, and committed to, the culture of others among whom you have been called to serve. So it was that as young lieutenants we were exposed to social forces, factors, influences and sensitivities that were to mould us for ever. We could not know that God and the Army would ask still more of us in the ensuing years.

Mazowe and Bulawayo, Rhodesia

It took two weeks at sea, in a hot, cramped cabin well below decks near the ship's rumbling engines, to get from Southampton to Cape Town and our first sight of Table Mountain. Next it was three days and nights by train northward through South Africa's Great Karoo then on and on, stopping for lengthy periods in Kimberley and Mafeking, before entering Botswana and traversing the eastern edge of the Kalahari Desert. Crossing into Rhodesia at Plumtree, we used the prolonged halt at Bulawayo to make contact with Salvationists there, little knowing that one day we would live and serve among them in that city. Finally the train took us north-eastward and to our destination, Salisbury (now Harare).

The rail journey was much less stressful than the boat because Matt, then aged only 22 months, could play in total safety in our reserved compartment, in contrast to the ship, the *Pendennis Castle*, which surprisingly had no safety provision for children on the deck railings. On reaching Salisbury we were met by a smiling and friendly Major Neil Young, Principal of Mazowe Secondary School, and driven north to the school campus located among farmlands several miles outside the city limits. Our modest bungalow was clean and welcoming. It was 20 January 1975.

That same evening I was in my new office. I was to assist in the administration of the school as well as teaching English and religious knowledge. I occupied the office and did the work of the vice-principal, with that designation on the door, but it was not until November 1975 that I was given the title to go with my role. Helen started her teaching of English to the senior classes three days after we arrived.

We soon became aware of tensions among the indigenous teaching staff. Some of them saw us as yet more imported foreigners blocking their chances of promotion and openly said so. Several very able African colleagues were heads of departments (science, English, history, etc) but the Principal was an Australian and I was British. Our best efforts to socialise with local colleagues did not always meet with success. There was much political turmoil in Rhodesia coupled with dreadful outbreaks of violence and our African colleagues were determined not to be seen as socially close to overseas staff. We had to learn fast and sought constantly to allow for these sensitivities.

Over and above my main duties I was asked to take charge of the school brass band and of the debating society. I was happy to do both and took my first band practice on the Saturday morning five days after our arrival. I had three first cornet players, six on second cornet, two baritone players and three percussionists! Quite a sound! No basses, horns or euphonium. Nevertheless, eagerness was in ample supply and made up for many a deficiency. The debating society had already had its first meeting of the new school year, arguing the pros and cons of school uniform. I convened a planning meeting four days after arriving and agreed a second debate for mid-February on the proposition: 'That war is immoral.' We ran both a junior and a senior society, visiting other schools for competitive debates. In June the following year, 1976, we reached the National Finals held in Salisbury in the Harry Margolis Hall. I was proud of our students. They did not win the Finals but gained much credit and upheld the reputation of the school.

Soon after we arrived at the start of 1975 we learned that the Principal had arranged for a blood donation unit to visit the school. Senior students were invited to give blood but they all refused. They thought their blood would be used to benefit government military forces, thereby postponing the day when Prime Minster Ian Smith and his administration would fall. Here was another telling lesson in cultural factors determining behaviour.

The students of Mazowe were highly politicised and followed closely the ebb and flow of political events, openly and naturally supporting their nationalist political leaders. Many of the indigenous teaching staff encouraged this. Some of our expatriate officer staff disapproved. I could not for I felt a large degree of understanding toward the outlook and hopes of our African students and staff colleagues and tried to imagine my own reactions had I been in their shoes. They wanted majority rule, no more and no less. When asked if this would bring about less efficiency in Rhodesia's then vibrant economy and in law and order, they would reply simply, 'It is our country and, if need be, we have the right to make a mess of it.'

Our first year in Africa moved on and gradually we found our feet. An old second-hand car, a Morris Traveller, bought for 475 Rhodesian dollars gave us a measure of independence. In March 1975 I preached at the request of the Territorial Commander, Colonel Richard Atwell, in Salisbury's Anglican cathedral in a series of lunchtime services based on the theme: 'We Believe in God.' In May we travelled south to Gwelo (now Gweru) to lead youth gatherings and were glad to get to know Captain and Mrs Fred and Hilary Jackson, the Canadian District Officers there. We liked them both. I organised visits to Parliament for our students and they saw for themselves the dominant white minority government at work.

We were delighted when, in late August and early September, General and Mrs Clarence Wiseman came to Rhodesia as our world leaders. I was in the Salisbury Citadel Band which met them on arrival at the airport. They looked wonderful as they emerged from the terminal to be greeted by us all. On Thursday 28 August 1975 we gathered in the Courtauld Concert Hall with government, civic, business and community guests filling the prestigious front rows. How proud, how encouraged, I was to hear the General say candidly that his sermon had been planned with the invited guests especially in mind: 'You help us and respect us, you give us your money and we are deeply grateful, but do you truly understand us? My friends, if you want to get your finger on the Army's pulse you have to understand about the Mercy Seat for it symbolises everything we are called to do for God.' He then expounded with passion the theological place of the Mercy Seat and its biblical foundation in the book of Exodus. He referred to the row of reversed chairs at the front of the concert hall constituting a temporary Mercy Seat. I felt so pleased and proud. A chord was struck in many a heart that night in 1975.

On the following Wednesday the General and his wife came to Mazowe. He found a moment for private conversation to thank me for my little volume, *What Does the Salvationist Say?* He was graciousness personified. This Newfoundlander Canadian won my admiration all over again.

It was a wonderful day when our second child, Jenny, was born on 31 October 1975. Now Matt had a baby sister, born in the Lady

Chancellor Maternity Hospital in Salisbury. How pleased we were to send a cable to our loved ones in England to share the news. The dedication ceremony took place at Salisbury Citadel on the Sunday before Christmas and was conducted by Captain Colin Fairclough. Colin and Sonia Fairclough had arrived in Salisbury only a few weeks after us and we became firm friends, a lovely blessing and a help to us during this first time of serving out of culture.

Our appointments and roles brought us into social or professional contact with diverse groups of people, each with its own cultural nuances. Moving into our second year we found we had adapted quite well, grasping more and more the cultural subtleties that surrounded us. Understanding the students was foremost in our minds. Some were the sons of Salvationist families and many had officer parents. They represented the Shona and minority Ndebele (Matabele) tribes. The latter showed greater academic aptitude on the whole. Relating well to the African teaching staff – something we saw as right at the heart of our being present in their country – required us to get past the social reserve they each automatically conveyed to any white person in a position of authority. The politics of the time dictated this. Few of the local teachers were Salvationists and this was a further cultural factor to be considered.

Building relaxed friendships with the expatriate officer staff was ultimately rewarding but took time. We worked with Australian, American, Dutch, British, Canadian and New Zealand colleagues. Each had their own nuanced take, not only on Rhodesia and its politics, not only on the school and our life together as a community, but also on the Army as a whole throughout the Rhodesia Territory, on their own place in it, and their expressed or unexpressed hopes for personal advancement. Some of our overseas colleagues were skilled, humble missionaries deeply committed to their work. They felt a strong vocation to be there. One or two others saw 'a spell overseas' as a stepping-stone to advancement and promotion on returning home, even saying so openly. As a young, novice officer I found this troubling.

Mid-1976 saw tensions rise at the school when the students decided to 'go on strike'. They had a history of doing so, refusing to come to classes and remaining in their dormitories. Disorderly, even threatening behaviour sometimes erupted. The ostensible reason for these strikes would be, for example, complaints about school meals but in fact the protests often coincided with a heightening of political tensions in nearby Salisbury. The protests needed to be addressed calmly. They usually subsided after a day or two.

By the end of our second year the security situation throughout the country had deteriorated considerably. A key security briefing session was convened by the police commander at nearby Concession but for some reason the Principal decided not to inform us. Anxiety levels thus rose further. Two months later in early February 1977 terrorists stuck late at night at St Paul's School at Musami. Seven Roman Catholic missionaries, including four nuns, were brutally slain.

During the night of 18 February gunmen entered the Mazowe School campus and enquired as to the whereabouts of the overseas staff. George Chatambarara, our neighbour and a gifted teacher of mathematics, told them we were all away at a conference. He saved our lives. In fact we were only a few metres away next door. It happened that our lights were out early that evening and it was the only night for many weeks when Jenny did not wake up and cry, so our house appeared empty. This incident led to arrangements for the overseas staff to work at the school by day but to spend the next several nights in the safety of Salisbury or at nearby Pearson Farm. Lieut-Colonel (General Secretary) and Mrs Ron and Hilda Cox came from territorial headquarters (THQ) and gave tremendous support. It was stressful for everyone – African and overseas staff alike.

These events served at last to focus the minds of our territorial leaders upon matters of intercultural relations and personal safety. In late February the territorial commander interviewed us to ask if we would take an appointment in Bulawayo. In view of the political situation he wanted to promote an indigenous teacher to be the vice-principal. Naturally, we agreed without demur. Soon thereafter Commissioner Stanley Cottrill, then International Secretary for Africa, visited Rhodesia and interviewed us, as well as others, at Mazowe. We spoke frankly about safety issues and the seeming lack of provision for the security of all the personnel – indigenous and expatriate – working at the school. The commissioner's response was to share reminiscences with us of his Second World War experiences and of Singapore when the Japanese invaded. It was interesting and he meant well. Our reality was different. We all lived with the daily, hourly possibility of attack by men of violence who could emerge without warning from the bush. I proffered the commissioner my views in writing, saying I thought it was only a matter of time before an Army centre would be the object of a violent assault. I could not know then that our Usher Institute, an Army boarding school for African girls and located south of Bulawayo, would be the first to be attacked. A week after the commissioner's visit the Army's Bradley Institute was forcibly closed down by the government for security reasons.

Soon afterwards, in early March 1977, two white female missionaries were shot dead at St Paul's Mission, Lupane. In October a Dutch Reformed Church minister and his wife were ambushed and shot near Que Que. In early June 1978 two Roman Catholic monks, one from Germany and one from Switzerland, were shot at the Embakwe Mission School on the Botswana border. Then a Southern Baptist evangelist was murdered at Sanyati. Next, eight British missionaries and four of their young children, including a three-week-old baby, were bayoneted to death at the Elim Emmanuel Mission School in the Eastern Highlands. Two more male Catholic missionaries were murdered a few days later at St Rupert's Mission, north of Hartley. Despite these atrocities no additional steps of any kind were taken to tighten security at exposed Salvation Army mission stations like Mazowe School or the Usher Institute.

We left Mazowe for Bulawayo Citadel on 4 May 1977. The following 18 months were to prove in many ways the best, but most traumatic, appointment we ever had. We did not know we were to face both triumph and tragedy.

In Bulawayo our congregation grew rapidly. Often the worshippers had to spill up onto seats on the platform. On many Sunday mornings we simply ran out of chairs. The Mercy Seat was used week after week so we kept the Seekers' Register permanently to hand on our office desk at home, making the entries each Sunday evening with glad and grateful hearts. George and Mirjam Claydon, Jock and Gwen Cook, and Major and Mrs Chris and Ellen Ramild Jørgensen were wonderful encouragers and became our lifelong friends (see also Essay 10). Many came to faith, and new Army soldiers and adherents were made, the oldest being Mr Charles King who became a soldier at the age of 90.

Opportunities to engage with the wider community arose through the Rotary Club and by means of frequent radio and television broadcasts for the Rhodesian Broadcasting Corporation. They involved me in religious broadcasts and also in panel debates. A new toy library for the city was begun and I was able to draft its first legal constitution. We embarked on corps rehearsals of the musical *Jesus Folk* (Gowans/Larsson) and performed it – with Helen at the piano – for the corps and later for the staff and students at the Usher Institute located about an hour's drive from the city along the road to Figtree.

We started midweek Bible studies in our home. On the night of Wednesday 7 June 1978 we were immersed in Acts chapter 9 when the telephone rang at 7.25 pm. It was Major Jean Caldwell, Principal at Usher. 'Shaw, it has happened,' she said, going on to describe a violent attack on the school by armed men. Lieutenant Diane Thompson and Sister Sharon Swindells had been shot dead. Captain David Cotton and Major Gunvor Paulsson had been badly wounded. A full account of this atrocity can be found on pages 16-19 of *Mobilized for God – The History of The Salvation Army, 1977-1984 (Volume 8)* written by Colonel Henry Gariepy. The part thrust upon me that night and afterwards is recorded there. Although the Territorial Commander, Colonel Richard Atwell, was present in Bulawayo, he was too overcome to function well and, reacting instinctively, asked me to handle the entire situation for him.

Thus I spent the night liaising with Major Caldwell at the school, with the police, with the military authorities, with the local hospital where I was asked to formally identify the bodies of Diane and Sharon, and also with the local bus companies as I had to evacuate the hundreds of girl students as early as possible the next morning. Soon after dawn I reached the school, accompanied by Major Andrew Kirby, to find a small detachment of the fearsome Selous Scouts there already. They were about to embark on tracking the gunmen (in the end this proved unsuccessful). My focus was on evacuating the students, gathering key files for Major Caldwell, taking into safe-keeping the Army flag in the Assembly Hall, and getting the major back into Bulawayo as fast as I could. Also I wanted to visit Captain Cotton and Major Paulsson in the hospital as soon as was practical.

All caught up in these events were marked indelibly. The dignity of Sharon's and Diane's parents throughout the aftermath was and still is a wonderful testimony to the grace of God and to the reality of Christian forgiveness even when the worst happens to you. We met them at Bulawayo Airport. Accompanied by Major Svend Bjørndal representing IHQ, they handled the press interviews with grace. Diane's parents, Doris and Bob Thompson, became Christians because of it all. They knelt at the Bulawayo Citadel Mercy Seat on the morning of Sunday 11 June and gave themselves away to the Saviour. It was my privilege to kneel with them and to counsel and pray with them.

Still I have the outline notes of the sermon preached that morning. The paperclip on them is rusty with age and the edges of the yellow paper are fading to white, but as I read them now I am transported back to 1978 and to our packed out hall in Bulawayo, back to the power, poignancy and pain of that meeting. I read Matthew 6:7-15 and began: 'This is not the sermon I had first intended to preach this morning. The events of last Wednesday night have, very naturally, conditioned my remarks. Evil is a fact of life. We feel it, we sense it, we struggle against it, sometimes we are defeated by it, but at other times we are gloriously victorious over it. Let there be no doubt: evil is alive and well! Jesus knew about evil: he faced up to its power and might; he lived to fight it; he died to defeat it; he rose to end its power.' Then came part of a prayer by Michel Quoist: 'I should give everything, until there is not a single pain, a single misery, a single sin left in the world. I should then give all, Lord, all the time. I should give my life.' The sermon neared its close: 'Sharon and Diane were two born-again, dedicated, Christian women who faced up to evil and overcame it as did their Saviour with the most eloquent gift of all, the gift of their lives. Who will stand in the gap they have left? Who will take their place in the ranks of Army officership and service? The voice of God is calling: "Go and make disciples of all nations…Lo, I am with you always, even unto the end."' How glad we were to have a Mercy Seat that morning.

The Usher Institute was closed down. I supervised the bricking-up of the classrooms, laboratories, library and dormitories. The expatriate teaching staff flew out of Bulawayo on 24 July, having been hosted readily and lovingly by several of our corps comrades. Later in October the stock, farming implements and machinery from Woodleigh Farm adjoining the school were auctioned off and the farm shut down. Captain Allister Lewis and Major Andrew Kirby were present with me that day. Following the attack on the school, each time we needed to visit the Usher campus or the farm we took practical and visible measures for self-protection.

Our term in Rhodesia expired at the end of 1978 after four years. By then I was 34 years of age and Helen was 31, but we felt older in terms of having experienced all that overtook us in Africa. We would leave behind us the blue skies, the wonderful jacaranda trees in full bloom, the orange groves of the Mazowe valley, but above all, the people we had learned to know, respect and love. Had it not been for the physical dangers and the exposure to high risk of our two infant children we might well have accepted Colonel Atwell's warm invitation to return for a further term. Africa and Africans, as well as many missionary colleagues and white Salvationists, had won our lasting esteem but we knew we needed time and space now to absorb and evaluate it all, to reconnect with our deeply anxious families in the United Kingdom (UK), and above all to let the constant tension about personal safety drain from our bodies, minds and spirits.

We flew from a hot and sunny Bulawayo to an overnight hotel in Johannesburg on Saturday 25 November 1978, from there to Brussels for a night, and then onward to a frosty, freezing London. A large family gathering was at the airport to meet us. Now they could see for themselves that we were safe. Their relief was audible, almost tangible. Matt (by now six) and Jen (now three) were hugged and kissed over and over again. Jen was seeing her four grandparents for the first time. Family is sacred.

Soon thereafter we were asked to attend IHQ for debriefing interviews. Expecting penetrating questions about the security of Army personnel in Rhodesia, we encountered instead only cursory, token conversations. The sole exception was our meeting with Commissioner George Nelting, then the International Secretary for Africa and the Far East. Although he had not served in Africa, he evinced deep concern for our safety and put to us a series of directly relevant and perceptive questions to which we responded with candour and some relief. Months later I was able to speak to him in private conversation of our appreciation for his insightful handling of what for us was a very sensitive encounter. 'You were the only one that day who asked us the right questions,' I told him. His face lit up into a wide smile. As this is being written Commissioner Nelting's promotion to Glory in mid-October 2013 has been announced. Sight of the bulletin brought back deeply appreciative memories of this godly, intelligent officer.

Boston, USA

After spending three busy, happy years (1992-95) leading the Durham and Tees Division in the north-east of England, we learned that we were to be assigned out of culture once again. This time it was to be the United States of America. I will describe something of our time in Boston, Massachusetts, using only extracts from my Journal:

2 February 1995: Three days into the inaugural Brengle Institute in Aizawl, Mizoram, the Chief of the Staff (Commissioner Maxwell) contacted us by telephone at our hotel there. Would we go to the USA? Yes, we would. Yesterday IHQ released our new appointments: leading the Massachusetts Division, USA Eastern Territory, with lieut-colonel rank as of 1 June 1995. We feel comfortable about it. The Chief stressed that this move was for 'orientation' but did not elaborate further. I resisted the urge to ask what he meant. John is very excited, I am glad to say. Matt and Jen seem pleased too. We shall live in Boston. Thinking of Joshua 1. Yesterday in our family prayers with John we read Jeremiah 1:6-8.

19 May 1995: In a few days we shall leave the UK for Boston. All contacts with the USA have been full of kindness. This helps us feel comfortable. At the same time we are seeing signs of real warmth toward us among the comrades of Durham and Tees. We in turn feel the tug, for we have developed strong affection and spiritual ambitions for our people and the centres. Our work is never done. The division is to shut down and be merged with the Northern Division. We cannot close Durham and Tees feeling easy. I never want to close anything, let alone a whole division, ever again!

To the USA Embassy (Visa Branch) on 17th. Secured three visas. Waited four and a half hours in the waiting room. Then British Rail went into one of its periodic meltdowns, so getting home took eight hours from King's Cross to Middlesbrough via St Pancras, Birmingham, Derby, Leeds, York, Darlington, and then by taxi to Middlesbrough. We changed trains at each of these stops! Had we asked for our bags to go via that route they would probably have told us it could not be done!

All our main belongings are now packed for sea freight. The final Durham and Tees Youth Councils was on 8 and 9 April with Colonel Douglas Davis, Chief Secretary, and the 'Gospel Factor' Youth Chorus from Copenhagen. It all went wonderfully well. The chorus were remarkably good. Colonel Davis was direct and helpfully simple in his speaking. He asked me to do the final appeal: over 60 seekers taking 90 minutes, about 25 per cent of all present. Some really good decisions with two offers for officership. Praise God!

Took Matt and John to White Hart Lane to see Spurs beat Norwich 1-0. A lovely treat. Saw the gifted Jürgen Klinsmann in action for Spurs. To Denmark for the weekend of 21-24 April. Many seekers in the meetings in Århus. This was my fifth visit to Denmark and I preached five times making 50 in all in that lovely land. I was pleased Helen could come. She is much more at ease now with being translated since the experience in India Eastern Territory. Jenny came home from university in Kingston upon Thames to look after John while we were away.

Final lectures at the International College for Officers on 4 and 5 May. I am sad that after lecturing to 62 sessions it will now end. My visits to the ICO have influenced me positively and kept me internationally aware. I record my thanks to God for these opportunities. Helen's final Home League Conference in Saltburn went well and was full of blessing. She relates so naturally to her people. She performed her first-ever Army ceremony when she led the dedication of Georgia Constance, baby daughter of Jill and David Mackey, on the Sunday evening of the same weekend.

Took the whole DHQ team for a lovely farewell lunch as a special treat.

Final meeting of the Durham and Tees Division held on 17 May. A truly wonderful meeting used by God. Many seekers, even at 10 pm. Preached from Isaiah 35 and the Way of Holiness. The 'Founder's Song' to end it and flags waving high. They can merge us, but never ignore us. This meeting, I told them, was no funeral, but a launching pad. Dear Father God, you took this meeting and touched everyone there. I praise you from my heart. Next time I rise to speak for you I will be in Boston, USA, according to your will.

I will go to live in the USA out of obedience to Christ. I feel and know we are loved and held by God. Dear Lord, please make us wise and fruitful in that land.

25 August 1995: Met in Boston on 31 May by Major Gil Reynders, General Secretary. A good, cooperative man, very sincere and a good support. They took us that first evening to Maximillians, a local restaurant in Needham where we will live. John fell soundly asleep from jetlag with his head on the restaurant table. The next night we met all the DHQ officers at a barbecue at the Reynders' house. Everyone was friendly.

On 2 June we went to DHQ and were officially welcomed. Each department gave us a gift, including many tickets and free passes for local museums, tours, etc. On 3 June all our effects were delivered, both the sea and air consignments. Everything turned up. We were very pleased and impressed.

I am seated in the public library in Needham where we live. We are on furlough. Matt and Jen are with us from England for a few weeks. I feel useful here. I have also felt stretched but that is beginning to wear off now. My role as a divisional commander is both similar and dissimilar compared with the UK. Here I have a huge staff at DHQ: 12 officers, 65 employees plus a further 200 employees around the division and about 90 officers throughout Massachusetts. We raise and spend nearly US$24 million annually in Massachusetts alone. We are only a medium-sized division by American standards, but this is another planet compared with Durham and Tees. The Sunday meetings are very sparsely attended and there is no soldiers' roll above 90. The division has been steadily shrinking in memberships for 30 years. But now, on a 12-months comparison, we are up in senior soldiers, junior soldiers, adherents and in Sunday meeting attendances. This is the first time since I came that all of these categories have been up at the same month end. I thank God for it and pray we can maintain it.

Our quarters in Needham, 30 minutes west of Boston, is very adequate. Helen and I have a car each. My metallic-green Buick is superb! We like Needham, a quiet town but with enough going on to be of interest. It has 20 churches for its 20,000 population. Best of all, there are football programmes (soccer) for children. How good God is to have sent us where John can play all the football he wants. We have all developed an interest in the Boston Red Sox baseball team [see Essay 14] and have enjoyed several visits to watch them at Fenway Park.

John has settled really well and has shown much character in all he has faced since leaving England. He is bright, cooperative, sociable, sporting and athletic, with a pleasing personality. He comes with me to the gym at the YMCA. I am trying to keep toned up. I need to lose some weight but I am fit and can work hard on the treadmill and weights for an hour at a time. My back has not impeded me of late although it is stiff each morning.

We are missing Matt and Jen a lot and I know Helen is especially anxious for them. Her ministry in the division is pastorally very telling. She is universally liked and respected. I love her. She has made a major contribution to our being well-received here.

We are learning how to cope with American nationalism (different from patriotism), with the lack of awareness of other cultures, with ignorance of other histories and events beyond American shores. We have met some genuinely friendly folk. The trees of New England in the Fall are breathtakingly lovely. Much kindness has been shown to John.

22 August 1995: Today with all our three children we explored Harvard Square and Harvard University Campus in Cambridge. We have a fine corps there and Captains Steve and Betzann Carroll are perhaps the best corps officers in the division. Harvard Square is full of second-hand bookshops to my delight! I note how Matt and John love to browse. We lunched in the refectory in the Science Building, used the free computers there, and showed Jen the Law Faculty Building. We visited the Harvard Memorial Church. By American standards this university is quite old. It also possesses vast wealth and has a generously enlightened view of the need to assist clever students whose families cannot pay the fees of US$26,000 per year.

We have excellent colleagues at DHQ but the administrative structures are outmoded and clumsy. Commissioner Irwin, Territorial Commander, has given me a free hand in changing these structures and I respect him for that. We now mirror the cabinet system at THQ resulting in a reduction of mundane work for the General Secretary, more meaningful roles for the women officers, the creation of new councils where good ideas can be fostered and outdated ones gently set aside, and wider consultation among officers and employees to help shape the future. Commissioner Irwin wants to appoint Helen as the Associate DC but IHQ will not permit this. Nevertheless, he has issued to her and to all the married women in divisional leadership a Brief of Appointment as though she and they held that designation.

I find Commissioner Irwin highly intelligent, single-minded and determined. Capable of great charm, he is also decisive and I have found that helpful.

I am exercised constantly since coming here by the almost universal ignorance among the American public of the Army's soul-saving and evangelical purposes. Social work agency, yes! A church, impossible! This is the response I get at all levels, even from people who have been on our advisory boards for years and years. Many of them know nothing of our congregations, discipling, worship, Bible study, prayer life, membership rolls, ecclesiology, doctrines, Protestantism or ecumenical stance. I have been told by one officer never to use the word 'church' when seeking money donations or else all flow of dollars will dry up. My response has been very simple – to state explicitly, vigorously, unambiguously at every turn and on every occasion and to any and every audience that the Army is a worldwide evangelical Christian church. We are also a human service agency, and a non-profit (charitable) organisation. I've had it printed on our letterhead and on our envelopes, have clarified it with advisory board members, and have repeated it endlessly on TV and radio. I have told also the local Roman Catholic cardinal, Bernard Law, and he was too polite to deny it, though he cannot possibly (according to his own doctrines) accept us as a church. Happily, it is not his view that counts [see Essay 3]. I have urged the officers not to appoint non-Christians to our advisory boards. Some have waited years to hear this. Others pay it lip service and await my farewell orders! But I must record that my DHQ officers are strongly with me. Furthermore, the income is up and nobody at all has left our advisory boards. Honour God and he will honour you. It is that simple.

23 August 1995: High humidity today. Temperatures in the 90s Fahrenheit. We have excellent air-conditioning everywhere. We have been emphasising to the officers that we should put people first. When we arrived we wanted to make pastoral visits to all the officers in their homes but, to our puzzlement, were told we should instead visit them in their offices at the corps buildings. However we pressed on and made pastoral visits to everyone, including our DHQ officers, in their homes. This was well received and many said it was the first time a leader had come to see them at home. The concept of routine and regular pastoral visitation in the homes of corps folk has been abandoned in this division. I do not know if this is true of the rest of America.

The result is we have been losing people hand over fist for many decades. Most of my officers think that 'working' means being in their offices looking at a computer, or outside driving a minibus. So we are trying to role model a different approach.

25 August 1995: There now appears weekly in the 'Boston Globe' an advertisement showing the addresses and times of worship services on Sunday at Salvation Army centres across Massachusetts. Our box appears alongside those of many famous Boston places of worship, just one small further step in repositioning the Army as a church. I am still glad to be in ministry as an officer, despite frustrations at times. To know I am daily in God's will for me outweighs all else.

We find the USA Eastern Territory a little less informal than things in the UK. One has a clearer and firmer sense of hierarchy here. I do not think this is altogether bad, but sometimes it stifles honest discussion. We are trying to ensure that in Massachusetts we strike the proper balance. Some of our officers do not believe us when we say we are truly interested in what they think. However, we see signs of progress in this. Some are beginning to open up to us.

17 September 1995: A wonderful 'Soul Saving Rally' in Boston Central hall led by Commissioner Earle Maxwell, Chief of the Staff, with the Territorial Commander, Chief Secretary and all THQ Cabinet members in attendance. THQ had asked us to put on a musical festival but I disregarded this and sent word to IHQ (via THQ) that we would pack the place with unsaved people who would attend with their corps officers for a 'Soul Saving Rally'. Commissioner Irwin expressed approval. The Massachusetts officers cooperated well and Boston Central hall was packed to overflowing. Commissioner Maxwell preached powerfully on Paul before King Agrippa in the book of Acts and made it very plain what a true Christian experience should be. Prior to the meeting he said I should lead the appeal and prayer meeting. We wrestled for souls for more than an hour and the Mercy Seat was lined over and over with both the unsaved and the saints. It was one of those hours when you know why you were born. God is so good. Great singing to end it all.

18 September 1995: Hosted the Irwins and Maxwells for a morning tour of Boston. We took them to Copley Square, Trinity Church, Boston Public

Library, and to the Hancock Tower, with lunch in the Copley Plaza Hotel. It was a relaxed, happy morning.

20 September 1995: Lunched with Dr Gordon MacDonald of Grace Chapel, Lexington, the largest evangelical church in New England. He is a keen Samuel Logan Brengle fan, a prolific writer, and a warm supporter of Army ministry. He invited me to preach at Grace Chapel.

I should record that in late July I met Marion Heard, head of Massachusetts Bay United Way. I found her very assertive and without the faintest idea of the Army's true identity. When I told her we are an evangelical church she could only gasp with surprise and warned me that in pursuing that line the Army would lose income. Same old story. I could reply only that the Army is not for sale, even to the United Way. Monies from that source had in any event been declining in Massachusetts for many years. My conversation with Mrs Heard meant that at least we were level-funded compared with reductions in previous years, covering about 11 per cent of our social expenditure in Massachusetts Bay. I refuse to be deflected from presenting with absolute clarity the Army's spiritual motives, whatever the consequences to our income. I repeat, we are not for sale.

My second attendance at a meeting of Massachusetts church leaders. I found myself in the company of bishops, a cardinal, and several moderators. The dialogue struck me as guarded. I tried to inject some courteous directness, but nobody seemed to notice.

4 November 1995: Hosted Captains Bill and Susan Dunigan in Boston. I found myself liking them and offered them Dorchester, a new opening. There is no building, no programme, no staff. I said come to Boston and just go for it and let God shape it. They will move into a large rambling house and will both live and work in it. It has 19 rooms and almost one acre of ground. It is a very socially deprived district. God will guard and use them.

22 December 1995: Massachusetts State Governor William Weld came and rang a handbell at our Christmas Kettle stand at Downtown Crossing and I stood with him. Much armed security with him, which made me very nervous!

26 December 1995: There is no such thing in the USA as Boxing Day. Everyone returns to work. So we took the day and the rest of the week as furlough.

6 January 1996: Went to the cinema to see a film about Richard Nixon. Long, but intriguing. He was depicted in the movie as highly politicised and highly skilled but also as foul-mouthed and foul-minded. Blizzard and snow. Jen caught the last flight out of Boston to London. Winter brought a record snowfall in Boston of 120 inches. We went sledding with John but even he got fed up with all the snow, ice and slush in the end.

12 January 1996: Recorded a religious panel-discussion radio show lasting two hours for Radio WRKO. I did all I could to monopolise the airtime and managed to get about two thirds of it. A kindly Catholic priest and a cordial Jewish rabbi got the rest.

21 February 1996: Lent has started. Have maintained the discipline of not using certain favourite drinks and foods until Resurrection day. It does me good, both in body and spirit.

29 February 1996: Went with Helen to a Mozart concert in the Symphony Hall. Found the choice of music anaemic. Longed for the meat and passion of Sibelius or Beethoven or Liszt.

1 April 1996: Start of Holy Week. Meetings at noon all week in the ground floor chapel at DHQ. Another needful innovation. All the meetings were full of help to my soul. Later discovered my officers do not know the meaning of Maundy Thursday, but now they do.

5 April 1996: Good Friday. Preached on Nicodemus to a packed Boston Central congregation with some advisory board members there. God is good. Many at the Mercy Seat. Ended in joyous singing and we could sense the glow of Easter morning beginning to beckon us from the sorrow and loss of the Cross. Christ's suffering and rising still grip my heart and mind. If ever anything will hold me to my faith it is these. I am with Albert Orsborn: 'Surpassing my reason but winning my heart.' Still I long to be in Christ's service. I am serving feebly, but I am serving.

7 November 1996: In Winnipeg, Canada, for an Ethics Conference at the Army's Ethics Center where the able Dr James Read is in charge. I led two sessions and experimented with new material based on my adventures as the IHQ legal adviser. I met Colonel John Bushy, Chief Secretary for Canada, who was warm, friendly and intelligent. Preached at Heritage Park Temple on the Sunday morning. Spent time with Major Herb Rader and enjoyed getting to know him better. One senior THQ officer poured out his heart to me about the decline in the territory. He spoke of falling revenues, declining candidate numbers, and generally low morale. I listened most carefully but was unsure how rightly to respond to him as an outsider and guest in the territory.

4 January 1997: Yesterday we held the annual Divisional Farewell Conference at Hillcrest Lodge in Sharon. Over and over again I am trying to instil the following principles when it comes to reassigning officers:

1. *Minimum moves;*
2. *Longer, and yet longer stays for corps officers;*
3. *Length of stay alone is no reason to move an officer;*
4. *Move officers only for absolutely compelling reasons;*
5. *Commit it all to God in prayer and then see it through with sanctified common sense and a spirit of humility;*
6. *Have multiple reasons to present to THQ for each proposal for change. They may knock back a couple of reasons but will tire after that;*
7. *Pay close attention to the children of the officers and their needs;*
8. *Think of each officer as though he or she were your son or your sister or your parent and act accordingly;*
9. *Never dislodge an officer merely to make way for another you need to place – there must be another solution;*
10. *Pray about all this. Then pray some more!*

26 February 1997: The Territorial Executive Council met last week at West Nyack. It was a very good event, upbeat and visionary. A surprise was in store for us. Commissioner Irwin took us to his office and returned a telephone call to the Chief of the Staff in London. Commissioner Maxwell told us that as of 1 September we would become the territorial leaders in Pakistan with promotion to the rank of colonel. I felt numb. This was totally unexpected. Our first thought was for John's education. The Chief gave us the option to decline. The following day we returned his call and said that of course we would go because we are called to serve at any time in any place and in any capacity. It has always been thus for us and will not change.

John will attend the International School in Lahore and remain in the American system. The Chief said that General Rader was making the move because he wanted me to be at the next High Council along with some other younger leaders. Commissioner Irwin was the soul of kindness to us in his office and offered every practical help for John should it be needed. How do I feel? Calm, a settled peace. Helen too. Very pleased by the trust shown in us. Ready to learn again and this time to adapt to a Moslem culture.

18 March 1997: The visit of the Irwins to our division went very well. They were at ease among us. They liked the direction the division is taking. In private conversation I urged him to make the General Secretary my successor. We are to be in Lahore for 1 August and the public announcement will be made on 1 April. We have still not told our children about this move but we are at peace with it. Peace is the gift of God. Joshua 1 and Isaiah 43. We must remain humble. We feel ready. Helen feels very ready for this change. What a great adventure it is to serve God! This will be our fourth continent on which to serve.

1 April 1997: Snow! Thirty inches of it! DHQ closed! Our farewell to Pakistan has been officially announced. When we told John, aged 10, we were to leave Boston he turned his face into the settee and sobbed for a long time. These are the moments our leaders do not witness, but perhaps have known in their own family. John did not even ask where we were to go. We told him it was Pakistan. All these weeks later as I write he is ready and has made the adjustment. He knows about the Lahore American School. He is a fine youngster. The USA Eastern Territory has made tremendous provision for us financially, treating us as one of their own. God is good.

24 July 1997: Now in London awaiting visas for Pakistan. Yesterday we had morning tea with Commissioner and Mrs Don and Solveig Smith. They were warm, lovingly welcoming, and prayed with us before we left them. Went on to Chris and Val Walford's home in Bromley for a lovely lunch. Two very worthwhile visits.

12 August 1997: At last we have three visas! These will need to be renewed annually in Pakistan but they allow for six exits and re-entries per year. It took many long hours in London at the Pakistan High Commission in Lowndes Square on a sticky and humid day. We had expected some contact from either the General or the Chief of the Staff during the six weeks we waited in London, but no contact arose. They have much to do. My next Journal entry will be made in Pakistan. Lord, give us a love for that land and its peoples, use us by your grace and keep us in your will and guardian care.

Lahore, Pakistan

From Boston to Lahore! Could there be a more contrasting transition? We were helped by a short spell of pre-embarkation leave in London, where we saw our loved ones and where in mid-July I was able to attend a crucial meeting (it focused on upholding our teaching on sacramental ceremonies) of the Spiritual Life Commission chaired ably by Lieut-Colonel Robert Street at the training college, Denmark Hill.

As described above in my Journal, a visit to our friends, Commissioner and Mrs Smith, enthused John for his new environment through hearing Don's vivid descriptions of having slept on the rooftop of his house in Lahore in the heat with nothing but a wet towel draped across him. As things turned out, we found we did not have to do that! Our due date of promotion, 29 July 1997, came and went. Because we had no visas we were told in clear terms by our leaders at IHQ not to use our new ranks of colonel until the visas were to hand. As recorded above, we secured these on 11 August on a scorching, stifling day. We understood the muttered protestations of the elderly Pakistani gentleman in the High Commission's waiting area as repeatedly he mopped his brow and gasped, 'Garam, garam!' ('Hot, hot!'). We had been learning lists of Urdu vocabulary and enjoyed testing one another daily. We left Gatwick airport on 12 August, arriving in Lahore the next day via Islamabad.

Journal, 17 August 1997: We cleared customs in Islamabad easily. A porter approached us and seeing our uniforms told us he was a Christian. He ushered us right through without our bags being X-rayed. The Chief Secretary, Lieut-Colonel Emmanuel Iqbal, met us. He was very useful and got us onto an earlier flight to Lahore where we arrived at about 11.00 am.

As we loaded our suitcases into the car the sky darkened, winds swept across the airport, and lashing rain began to fall. In minutes the concourse was under a foot of water. We drove to THQ with the streets in places three feet deep in water. All the staff were lined up to meet us but had gathered at the rear entrance because of the storm and because there we could alight from the car under cover. We shook hands with and greeted everyone and then climbed the concrete stairs to Flat 4, stairs used by many faithful folk through the years. Ghulam, the cook, was there. Lunch was already all set out. His reputation as the finest cook in Lahore seems entirely deserved. His son, Saleem, is our driver. Outside it is 41°C (103°F). John has just updated me on the temperature which is now up to 116! The gauge ends at 120!

Our Welcome Meeting was held on 14 August and coincided with the 50th Jubilee of the creation of the state of Pakistan and the 1947 partition from India. We made mention of this in the meeting and everyone cheered loudly as I produced John's huge Pakistan flag. He and I spread it and held it aloft for all to see. I told them three things:

1. We would love them unceasingly;
2. We would always be truthful with them;
3. We would wait on God for making decisions.

Memories of their smiling faces and endless handshakes live on in us. Even the malis (the gardeners) and cleaners came forward to greet us. We have heard them all say many times that they receive us as a mother and a father to them. Lord, help us in this.

Journal, 19 August 1997: Tomorrow we complete one week since our arrival. It has gone quickly. Vivid images! Today John and I walked in the busy, noisy streets of Lahore outside the compound for the first time. It was 5.00 pm: dust, traffic, hooters, potholes, donkeys and carts, endless streams of bicycles and motorcycles, dark brown eyes staring upon us, hopeful shopkeepers, banana trees, the Shezan Bakery and the manager's gracious welcome, the salute of our guards at the compound gate, humid air, the cool relief of our apartment 30 minutes later, and shepherd's pie made by Ghulam!

School has gone well for John. His first Urdu class took place today. He alone in Grade 6 has opted for Urdu and thus is taught one-on-one twice a week.

The next five years were to be full of challenge, but God's grace, provision and protection were to become more and more real. He blessed us with fine colleagues: Rudy Moore was my gifted, intelligent and loyal Anglo-Asian private secretary; Jean Albert (whose husband, Wilburn, was a constant help as our travel agent) became Helen's excellent personal assistant; Major Ethne Flintoff from New Zealand worked tirelessly on the social programme and community projects; Major Fran Duffett from Canada gave great support in so many ways; Ashley Dawson, a young Salvationist from London, was an able property administrator; Major John Dyall, experienced in diverse cultures, was a tremendous asset and later became the Chief Secretary; Lieut-Colonels Yousaf Ghulam and Rebecca Yousaf offered us friendship and loyal support, as did Lieut-Colonels Gulzar Patras and Sheila Gulzar; Lieut-Colonels Emmanuel Iqbal and Rashida Emmanuel gave solid help when first we arrived and throughout our early years; so too did many others like Majors John and Valerie Townsend, Lieut-Colonel Emmanuel Paul, and Majors Morris John and Salma Morris. Every one of these comrades, with others too numerous to mention, was a cause for gratitude.

Thrust again into an entirely new culture, we needed to learn fast. We had immersed ourselves in Pakistani literature as soon as we knew Lahore was to become our home. We experienced no real culture shock for this was the third time we had been assigned to serve outside the UK and felt ready for the impact of living in yet another new social setting. I pay tribute to the resilience of Helen and John amid this upheaval. As Salvationists in the Islamic Republic of Pakistan we were part of the Christian minority (three million among 150 million Moslems) and also a minority church among the other Christian denominations. That said, we were numerically significant compared with other parts of the Army world and, by the time we left, Pakistan was the fourth largest Army territory in terms of soldier strength. We were able also to begin work in the remote North West Frontier Province, opening corps in Kohat and Peshawar.

The term 'Christian' was used to denote the non-Moslem minority. It was an ethnic label and did not signify a saved person or any commitment to Christ. Our evangelical efforts therefore sought to introduce ethnic Christians to the Saviour, making them faith-Christians. The Moslem majority habitually looked down on the Christians, holding them back from employment and educational opportunities. Because the minority citizens took lowly jobs they were despisingly known as 'sweepers'. Only the lowest of the low took work that involved hand contact with the ground. Despite all this, the Pakistan legal system made provision for the granting of 'missionary visas' and we entered the country having that status. We were barred from evangelical work among Moslems, though many of them sought to benefit from our social programmes.

Islam holds the person of Jesus in high respect as a prophet but denies Christian teaching on our Lord's divinity and resurrection. We discovered that Moslems believe in the efficacy of Christian prayers. We were expected to know our faith and not to hide it. The more 'Christian' we were, the more respect was shown to us. Thus we presented the Army openly as a Christian church and found our Moslem contacts very much at ease with this. It therefore alarmed us that representatives from IHQ, despite our repeated pleas to the contrary, persisted in referring in official paperwork to the Army in Pakistan as a non-governmental organisation (NGO) and continually sought entry visas on that basis. This put us all at risk because foreign NGOs were often perceived as a destabilising influence upon the population, as acting contrary to the wishes of the government, and thus subject to the constant threat of instant closure and the deportation of staff. In contrast, our constitutional status as a Christian church made us indigenous from a legal point of view and therefore safe from arbitrary action by the authorities. We needed colleagues in London to grasp this.

It took time to grow accustomed to the heat! Average temperatures in summer could reach well over 41°C. We kept our skin covered from the sun. Our flat above THQ had air-conditioning but power and water supplies were constantly interrupted. We learned to manage, adapting readily to local conditions: Helen walked half a pace behind me in the bazaars; we never touched each other in public; we ate our food with our right hand; we ignored the burping of our Pakistani colleagues at the close of a meal; we became glad to have armed guards at our gates day and night; we filtered and boiled all our drinking water; we accepted gratefully the help of our cook, Ghulam, and of his son, Saleem, our official driver; we never ventured beyond the city limits without an Urdu or Punjabi speaker with us; we learned when and when not to shake hands with members of our own or the opposite gender; we entered fully into local cultural festivities like the Basant kite-flying festival at New Year; we enjoyed visits to Lahore Fort and the ancient Badshahi Mosque, its porticos so cool and tranquil; we took our visitors (Peter Cooke, Captain Martin Hill, Cyril Bradwell and others) to Wagha for the dramatic border-closing ceremony at dusk (described by W.F. Deedes in *The Weekly Telegraph* for 20 January 1999 as 'an extravaganza', 'a soldier's ballet', 'more than a pantomime'); we developed lasting respect for our local Advisory Board made up mostly of retired Christian military officers and led by the gentlemanly Brigadier Jivanandham; we learned to run the entire territory on an annual budget of US$1.5 million (in Boston our divisional budget alone exceeded US$25 million); eventually, slowly and somehow we dealt with local expectations, ingrained for centuries, as to 'facilitation fees' – bribes! – and introduced official procedures accordingly.

No sooner had we arrived than we were thrown into a whirlwind of activity:

Journal, 23 August 1997: Heavy monsoon rain yesterday and flooded streets just like the day we arrived. I went to Standard Chartered Bank in The Mall to exchange travellers' cheques and took our chief accountant with me. Rana appears urbane and friendly. We enjoyed the ride in the rain but would have been obliged to wade through six inches of water to enter the bank had not Saleem, after some minutes of tortuous manoeuvring, got us right up to the front steps. We dashed inside. I was greeted warmly, given tea, and shown other courtesies, something no other bank in any country has offered me before or since. When we came out the waters had risen a lot further! So I simply took off my shoes and socks, rolled up my trousers and waded to the car. Rana took his cue from me. On reaching our HQ I entered barefoot. I am not sure everyone appreciated my dishevelled state!

Journal, 2 September 1997: We drove to Jaranwala in pouring rain for officers' councils and two days later for a similar gathering in Sahiwal. Potholed roads, the rigid minibus shaking our bones for three hours there and three hours back, water buffalo and donkey carts everywhere, green fields, lots of mud, several large factories belching dark smoke along the route, faces staring at our whiteness, the driver a little reckless, tiny shops in the towns and villages looking squalid and uninviting, mosques everywhere with loudspeakers on their roofs. Then the arriving! Smiles, shouts of joy, flags, motorcycle escorts, bunting, officers lined up, flowers, garlands galore, rose petals thrown over us, speeches, hearty singing, warm handshakes and (for Helen) hugs from the lady officers. I tell them again that we shall love them in the name of Christ and always be open with them.

En route to Sahiwal our vehicle becomes stuck in deeply muddied potholes right in the middle of the main street in Okara. I jump out and get stared at by the passers-by. I ask all the men to get out and the ladies to remain inside. Our driver spins his rear wheels, all in vain. From nowhere a tractor materialises and pulls us free, then just as quickly vanishes again into the morass of hooting, grinding buses and lorries all negotiating the road that is now a swampy pond. Coming home we stopped to buy Pepsi and bags of peanuts from a street vendor!

Journal, 4 September 1997: We are beginning to feel at home in our flat. All our effects are now here. I flew to Islamabad to clear it all through customs. It became a bit of a pantomime. Arriving in Islamabad at 9.00 am, I was taken to the airport customs house by the local agent of Crown Pacific USA. After two solid hours of meeting endless officials in ascending order of importance I had made no progress at all in obtaining our boxes. Everyone refused to help me because my visa was for one year only and they said that in order to get my things it needed to be for two years. I cajoled, reasoned, almost begged but all I got was smiles and a brush off. They said only one very senior official could make an exception for me and he was 15 miles away in central Islamabad in a secluded government office to which I could write! My flight back to Lahore was due at 2.30 pm and time was ticking away!

So I get into a taxi, a bit of a rust bucket: wires all hanging out; battery on the floor and wired into the engine; steering column stripped for all to see; no glass in the window frames. Anything for Jesus! Anything for my luggage! A rickety ride at breakneck speed gobbles up the 15 miles. I find the Central Bureau of Revenue building, a lovely building as it happens. I go in. I cannot get past the receptionists in the main entrance who tell me they have never heard of the man I need. I have been praying like fury for the last three hours! 'Lord, if you are Lord of the mundane and practical as well as Lord of my eternal destiny let this thing break open and overrule these people who will not help me.' Even as I prayed I was wondering if this was equivalent to asking God for a parking space!

Somehow I find myself simply walking past the receptionists and ignoring their polite but firm refusals of entry. At long last I am up on the second floor and I locate an office marked 'Secretary – Customs Law and Procedure'. I enter the side office to see if there is a receptionist. Yes, more than one. They are all male of course. I am stared at. I present my card which shows my rank of colonel. Please will the Secretary for Law and Procedure see me? More silent prayers.

Within minutes I am in his office and he is suave, cultured, educated and stylishly attired in Western clothing. I tell him my problem. With a smile he says, 'But this is no problem. They should have helped you. I will phone them for you.' He picks up the phone and speaks to the last customs official I had seen at the airport. It is now 11.10 am. He tells the customs official, 'Why are you making a problem over this Salvation Army matter? You can help him. It is all damn simple (voice rising)! Give the fellow his things! It is just a few books and toys. Give him his things!' He rings off and smiles at me: 'It is solved. But now I must detain you here (slight emphasis on 'detain'!). My heart goes cold but I try not to show it. 'Detain you for a cup of tea I mean,' he says and grins broadly at me, knowing full well the effect his use of 'detain' has had on this stranger from afar. Tea is brought and we engage in 15 minutes of easy conversation about his visits to the USA and London. He calls for his personal car and gives me his official driver to take me back to customs at the airport where suddenly everyone is falling over themselves to help me.

It is now nearly noon. Time is passing fast. Paperwork galore. My agent runs all over the building while I sit in the office of the Customs Superintendent, a self-important fellow who nevertheless smiles at me every 10 minutes or so, and tells me everything is going well. To redeem the idle moments I get out my 'Expository Times' and read an article about clergy marriage! Suddenly my agent comes in to tell me it is now time for the lunch break and no officials will be available until after 2.00 pm. I summon up my most serious scowl and say, 'No! Mr Abassi, the Customs Secretary in Islamabad, wants me on my 2.30 pm flight.' So everyone stops eating. They ask me what is in my baggage. I tell them in broad outline and they ask me for 60,000 rupees, about £1,000. I shell out the cash and get a handwritten receipt on Salvation Army letterhead. Suddenly our boxes emerge from the locked cage area. By 2.00 pm I am in the departure lounge and at home in our flat by 4.00 pm having been met at Lahore airport by our driver, Saleem, whom I greet in Urdu! I get a big grin in return!

Our boxes had to come by road across the 300 kilometres between Islamabad and Lahore. The vehicle is so big it can travel only at night by local law. At 3 am there are loud shoutings outside our window down below. We get up. John is already awake and peering down into the gloom of the compound where we see all our things on the back of a truck. The phone rings and the armed guard at the gate tells us our boxes have arrived. John is especially pleased. His bike is here and so too is his cornet.

We celebrated my 52nd birthday by attending a piano recital organised by the British Council and held at our favourite hotel, the Avari. The prizewinning pianist, Anthony Peebles, gave a polished recital of classical music by Liszt, John Ireland and Beethoven. Reviews in the next day's papers praised the pianist's skill but bemoaned his playing of exclusively 'pre-composed music'! Pakistanis prefer improvisation!

In early October Helen and I went to Shantinagar, the site of anti-Christian riots during the weeks prior to our departure from Boston. There had been no loss of life but many homes and Salvation Army buildings had been burned out with widespread loss of personal possessions. The government did well and stepped in with a large compensation fund. It was to be administered by THQ because this community had a Salvationist identity strongly linked to our earlier strategy of settling converts on land colonies. Shantinagar was our largest corps with over 1,000 senior soldiers. Let my Journal describe our visit:

Journal, 11 October 1997: I am alone in the apartment. Helen is travelling back from Karachi and will land at 8.40 pm. John is playing cricket on the far side of the THQ compound in William Booth Street (renamed by me soon after our arrival and an improvement on 'Staff Housing'!). The Sibelius Second Symphony is playing. It still calls, somewhere deep within me. I do not know where or why.

Shantinagar was a very strange, yet moving and exhilarating experience. Our journey times went like clockwork. We saw both of the Army schools, the three Army halls and our three clinics as well. In each of these I prayed and rededicated the land, the renovated buildings and the people to God, and asked for divine protection. I unveiled several new foundation stones. We were welcomed on the outskirts of Shantinagar by a convoy of motorcycles each with an Army flag and a pillion rider. Nearly all the pillion riders had guns – new, shiny, automatic weapons. They fired into the air repeatedly as we entered the town. (Suddenly I was back in Mazowe with my old .303 beside my bed, glad to wake up each new morning and to know the night had been free of incident and of intruders.) I rededicated the repaired and refurbished Army hall, our largest in Pakistan. It was packed with people, over 1,000, all seated on the floor. I spoke to them of faithfulness, suffering, the example of Jesus who did not strike back, of health and other basic blessings, and of Salvationists around the globe who were thinking of them. 'You are not alone!'

I felt it was all a bit feeble and futile to be honest. Just words? When I think of what happened, with me and mine safely in Boston at the time, my words that day seemed weak and of little effect. My desire was (and is) for them to sense we wanted to identify with them and that we cared. As we left I spoke with a group of young men and asked about the guns. 'For our protection,' they said. 'They will not attack us again.' Quietly I responded, 'I understand. I do understand. But be careful. I do not like to see our people armed.' As I spoke, the whole Mazowe and Usher Institute experiences came surging vividly before me again and I did not know whether I was asking of these people what I did not do myself as a young lieutenant all those years ago. Would I arm myself again in the same circumstances? I think perhaps I would. God forgive me. Lord, do not put our Pakistani comrades to the test. Let no gun be fired in anger either at or by your people here.

October 1997 was an eventful month. After the Shantinagar visit our telephone rang in the middle of the night with the news that the divisional commander in Karachi had been arrested and charged with the manslaughter of an elderly Moslem lady by running her down on the highway. The truth was that he had merely witnessed the accident and had stopped his vehicle to get out and help. He was in uniform. His arrest took place at the hospital to which he had taken her for medical attention. The message was plain: the officer would remain behind bars, the only Christian among Moslem prisoners and Moslem police officers, unless I would authorise a payment of a fine of 20,000 rupees to the local police superintendent. If I did so, the divisional commander would be released. Within the hour the major was restored to the safety of his family.

A few weeks later I discovered that my predecessor had insisted on a policy of sending home from the training college any married woman cadet found to be pregnant. The result: clandestine abortions. So, in consultation with senior colleagues at THQ, I announced a new policy: yes, cadet pregnancies were to be discouraged, but if one did occur the couple concerned would be evaluated on their past record as cadets and allowed to remain in the session if the evaluation proved positive. Careful guidance was also given to each married cadet couple concerning contraception. We had no further problems and no longer felt complicit in rushed, secret abortions.

General Rader convened an International Conference of Leaders to gather in Melbourne, Australia, in March 1998. It was our first experience of such a gathering. We were pleased when IHQ approved our request to take John, aged only 11, with us to Melbourne. We were not prepared to leave him alone in Lahore for any lengthy period of time. In Melbourne Majors Craig and Laurel Campbell took him into their home and gave him a wonderful time. We remain indebted to Craig and Laurel for this gift of help and hospitality. Craig taught John to throw a boomerang.

At the conference I was asked to respond formally to the presentation on 13 March of the new *Handbook of Doctrine* called *Salvation Story*. I was not able to endorse the new publication without reserve for I felt it relegated the Scriptures to a minor role and thus ran contrary to our first doctrine. It could not therefore represent our best work. Unsurprisingly, this produced lively debate! That day there became fixed in my heart a quiet determination to remedy the matter if the opportunity ever arose (for more detail on this see Essay 12).

It was April 1998 when we bought land for the construction of a new training college for our cadets.

> *Journal, 25 April 1998: We have purchased 10 kanals (about the size of a football field) east of Lahore for a site on which to build a new training college. We have paid 5.6 million rupees, US$127,000 or £77,000. I took the entire Finance Council to view the land and to finalise the deal. Then we went back to the site and prayed there, gave thanks to God, and planted a small Army flag in the mud, claiming the land for God and the Army. I hope to open the new college there in 18-24 months from now. Lord, over to you!*

Commissioner Ronald Irwin responded gladly and positively to my request that the USA Eastern Territory should be our partner in this venture, a huge undertaking for the Pakistan Territory. I could fund 50 per cent of the costs by the sale of the old college if he could match me dollar-for-dollar. Readily and most generously he did so, sending a gift of

US$345,000. We sold our Model Town site to Kikar Associates, telling them we needed 60 per cent of the sale price upfront and that we would need to continue in occupation of the site for another year. They would pay the balance of 40 per cent on taking possession. It came together well. Our architects, Zor Engineers, represented by Dan Bavington and Dennis Norris, both from England and committed Christians, worked tirelessly for us. The ground-breaking ceremony at Ali Alam Gardens east of the city was held on 21 January 1999, the foundation stone ceremony following on 25 May.

Earlier we held what proved to be a moving ceremony at the old college site as we walked from room to room giving thanks to God through the use of Scripture, song and prayer, for his help and presence there over many years to the blessing of multiple cadets and staff. Carefully we had removed the wood of the Mercy Seat from the chapel and kept it safe until our carpenter could reshape it (into a cross and 'S' intertwined) to stand in the chapel of the new college.

All seemed well. Prayers had been answered for this large building project. However, our architects, usually so proficient, had failed to inform us that our new site was in a military zone and subject to additional planning approval by the local military commander.

> *Journal, 2 January 2000: A shock concerning the new training college! Having been assured by the developer and also our architects concerning planning permission, we have been notified by the Lahore District Council that we are obliged to demolish the entire structure in the next seven days. I have managed to pacify the LDC and have submitted a formal application 11 months late. I have also formed a good relationship with Major Mehmood Nawaz, the military liaison in charge, following the military coup. He is gracious and even sent us a Christmas cake. We await approval. I will send Major Nawaz a courtesy gift of a cake for Eid on 10 January.*

Thanks to splendid work by my private secretary, Rudy Moore, we at last received a 'No Objection Certificate' from the military commander at 22 Brigade Headquarters and took up occupation of the site on 20 July 2000. Staff and cadets moved in under the wise and caring supervision of

Majors John and Valerie Townsend. The inaugural Spiritual Day meetings took place on 5 September and the full and formal opening ceremony was held nine days later.

Let me return to late 1998. On 20 August that year, with the overt support of the UK government, the USA launched attacks on Afghanistan and the Sudan in retaliation for assaults upon embassies in Kenya and Tanzania. Suddenly all Westerners in Pakistan were somehow assumed to be Americans and hence targets for retaliation, especially for the action against neighbouring Afghanistan. All the expatriate staff were suddenly at risk. Echoes of Rhodesia! All Americans in Pakistan were advised by their government to leave the country forthwith. The UK High Commission was more measured and issued a calm but clear word advising UK citizens merely to avoid border areas to the north and west. I circulated detailed information to all the overseas staff and offered practical security guidance, placing a ban on travel beyond the city limits of Lahore and advising all our missionary colleagues to remain in their homes between 5.00 pm and 10.00 am. I provided full briefings on a regular basis also to IHQ. We reached the new year of 1999 without mishap.

Journal, 2 January 1999: Here are my main prayer concerns as we enter 1999: for Matt and Jen so far away from us; for our parents who are growing older; for John's safety and development; for our territory – its growth, reinforcement personnel, the new college, the several new corps openings; for the forthcoming High Council; for my relationship with the new Chief Secretary here in Lahore and with the new International Secretary in London.

I need also to pray for Helen, that she will put up with me when I feel despair and frustration. Her love to me is everything. I must also pray for myself because I am still going through a numbness of spirit. It is now that I have to go on without feelings toward my faith and its truths, just holding on and somehow trusting until the night passes.

Suddenly, Helen has put on a tape of Bristol Easton Road Songsters and I hear 'Of all in earth and heaven' (Annie Laurie) and I am defenceless before the words and the melody. They penetrate the numbness. 'My blood-bought life I give him, the Christ of Calvary.'

Oh, how I miss in this place music and words that feed my soul! I must refill my inner being from our tapes and CDs more often. Dear God, hold on to me.

Journal, 20 January 1999: I have made my first ever proposal to promote an officer to the rank of lieut-colonel. He is Major Yousaf Ghulam. Will IHQ agree? God must hold on to Yousaf. I have also sent to London my proposals for several executive officer moves. The Territorial Appointments Board has been meeting frequently and I think we have the general farewell in place for April. We have settled the first appointments for the cadets. Also we have chosen 33 candidates from the 75 applications for the 1999 college intake of cadets.

Then in April came the Commissioning, the first at which I had officiated.

Journal, 19 April 1999: I have tried to analyse my feelings and thoughts both during and since the commissioning. I felt very deeply and keenly the sacredness of what I was doing. Because of mistaken past practices in the territory, I told the congregation that in the Army we do not place our hands on any cadet when they are commissioned because their commissioning is that of the nail-pierced hands of Jesus and no merely human hands can ever replace our Lord's wounded hands. The cadets did well all weekend and now we have 27 new lieutenants. As each one came forward to be commissioned I was able to look into his or her eyes and speak clearly the words of commissioning and ordination. I feel both pleased and unworthy to have been able to do this sacred and solemn task for God. I felt truly alive in the midst of it all. By the end I was utterly drained. Lord, keep and guard and use these 27 people whom we have sent out in your holy name.

In May, soon after this first commissioning, I attended my first High Council (see Essay 11). We were tasked with finding a successor to General Paul Rader. Commissioner John Gowans was elected after five tense ballots.

July took us back to London for homeland furlough and the wedding of Jenny and Marcus at Denmark Hill (see Essay 8):

Journal, 7 September 1999: The music for the entry sounded out, loud and rising, dramatic. The bridesmaids went in. Marcus and his best man lined up. The guests all stood and turned to the door. The Assembly Hall was a wonderfully subtle blend of pink and gold in the sunlight. The seating arced in gentle curves inward, the wide aisle accommodating each entrant. Then it was our turn. My heart pounded. Jen hesitated and I said, 'We'll be icy cold and professional now.' I was not so sure. I said it more for me than for her. Taking a firm grip on her left hand under my right arm, we set off. Katie Baddams held Jen's train as we came to the top of the aisle, adjusted it as we paused, and then we all went forward. It seemed to take ages. I placed her next to Marcus and then stepped forward to the podium.

Matt's musical group was truly fine. The singing, in modern vein, was tremendous. Even the Assistant Registrar sang and said 'God bless you' to them. I was very hot. My tunic was heavy on me. I wore my new specs for fear of not seeing the small print in the Ceremonies Book but they kept sliding down my nose [see Essay 8]. I spoke to Jen and Marcus about their choice of Psalm 139 with verses from Ephesians 5 for the readings. Suddenly we were all outside in the sunshine (30°C!) and under the shade of the huge tree in the quadrangle. Laughter, banter, smiles, photographs. In the reception when Marcus spoke he gave his testimony, open and direct. By 9 pm he and Jen were in casual outfits and off in a limo to the hotel at Gatwick as husband and wife. We are parents-in-law!

How glad we were to be in England. I know why some people kiss the ground on returning to their home country. No intense humidity or scorching heat, no unremitting dryness, no billowing dust, no underlying air of menace, no subtle uncertainty about cultural dynamics. Instead, green fields, cool sky, protective clouds, our mother tongue, easy accents, rational traffic, and nobody pushing me for directives or decisions.

Ilfracombe and our much-longed-for two weeks at the seaside. A lovely view over the Severn Estuary. A gorgeous, gentle meander in the

127

car over Exmoor once Taunton is behind us. Cream teas available everywhere! We discover Exmoor and the north Devon coastline. We find Woolacombe Beach where John buys a surfboard and then swims with it almost every day. We walk for miles in sun and rain. We hit golf balls on the driving range and watch the sunset. We eat out a lot. We have a wonderful time, just wonderful. This includes attending a 'Songs of Praise' in Lynton Church. I want to record here that this was a turning point for me. I had been very numb within. The experience of just singing, among strangers, brought new life and feeling. On 15 July we marked 32 years of marriage and celebrated by eating fish and chips out of doors. Helen is as lovely to me as ever she was.

If you live in Pakistan you have to understand that everything is precarious, especially its politics. It was mid-October 1999 and I had travelled to Karachi to meet Major Ethne Flintoff and visit a number of our social services centres. We were on board the plane to return home to Lahore and taxiing to the runway when suddenly the pilot addressed us: 'Ladies and gentlemen, we have been ordered to return to the terminal building where you will all disembark without delay.' His voice was anything but relaxed. As we left the terminal building armed soldiers swarmed past us toward the runway and the control tower. Returning to the hotel, we learned that a military coup had taken place and Prime Minister Nawaz Sharif had been placed under house arrest. Every airport in the country had been shut down. General Pervez Musharraf, the four-star general in charge of Pakistan's military forces, had landed in Karachi just as we neared the runway and had ordered the coup from his aeroplane. It was claimed the Prime Minister had given orders that he be refused permission to land. He was returning from Sri Lanka, had little fuel left, and on board with him was a party of schoolchildren returning from a sporting event in Colombo. General Musharraf was to remain in power for the next seven years. His perspective on these years can be read in his 2006 memoir, *In the Line of Fire*.

The coup changed everything. Suddenly, each government office was under the supervision of a military officer. Suddenly, nobody in public office was asking for a bribe. Suddenly, the electrical supply was more consistent. Suddenly, even the street lights came on after dark. Suddenly, we felt a lot safer. Leaders in the West quickly and predictably condemned the coup, but we did not. Our experience was first hand, theirs was not. As I write this, the news bulletins are announcing General Musharraf's arrest on accusations of responsibility for the death of Benazir Bhutto in 2007. Mr Sharif is now back in power.

We entered 2000 feeling truly integrated into Pakistani life, but missing England and our loved ones, especially Matt and Jen, very deeply.

Journal, 2 January 2000: New Year! Much irritating media hype across the world about a new century and a new millennium – all 12 months too soon!

What are my outstanding memories of 1999? Jen's wedding; Matt entering the training college in London; the High Council and my being nominated; John becoming a teenager; our longest ever (eight weeks) break from duty; being more worn and tired out than ever before. Then there are the underlying and on-going things: Helen's love to me; the love and prayers of our parents; learning week by week how to be a better territorial commander; the prayers of our many friends around the world; a constant sense that I am simply not good enough to justify my calling; trying to be a wise parent; trying to stay well in Pakistan; wondering if we will have the stamina to continue here much longer. God has held and helped us.

Early in March 2000 General Gowans telephoned and informed us of our promotion to the rank of commissioner to take effect at the end of that month. He was very kind in his conversation and said that he and Commissioner Gisèle were looking forward to visiting Pakistan later that month.

Journal, 17 March 2000: The Lord is telling me that this promotion has very little immediate significance and, although it relates to his Body, it is really only a worldly bauble. Of itself it does not result in even one more soul saved, nor does it mean that I am more like Jesus or that my skills are enhanced. It does, however, increase my responsibility to be a role-model as a soldier, officer, and leader. I need divine help for these things.

129

Journal, 2 April 2000: Well, the great visit is over. It went well. All our prayers, work and planning were rewarded. God is good. The General seemed relaxed. Huge crowds came to the meetings, with over 2,000 on Sunday morning at our compound in Lahore. Ran out of rice for the communal lunch. The Officers' Councils brought all the actives and retireds together for the first time in years. Lahore Central Hall was packed to capacity!

On the final evening we took a private meal with our guests. Conversation turned naturally to our personal and family situation. We spoke of John's education and said he needed to be in the USA or in London soon. The General said, 'That is not impossible.'

Two more years were to pass before the General took action. Meanwhile we focused on securing visas for our delegates to attend the International Congress in Atlanta, USA. It had been tough to get the visas but personal conversations between my office and senior staff at the USA Embassy in Islamabad eventually led to success. We had created a 'Territorial Folk Dance Group' specifically to perform at the congress. They were wonderfully received and danced gracefully to Christian music.

Journal, 23 September 2000: The congress was good. Our delegates were tremendous, the dancers blessing and winning many hearts and friends. Everyone came home and I emailed the USA Embassy to say so. In Atlanta we were accommodated on floor 42 of the hotel! A dizzy height! Met many old friends and felt very relaxed throughout. I found I could give myself to it more easily than I imagined I would. The plenary worship meeting which I was invited to lead made little demand upon me. The remarkable Joni Eareckson Tada overran her time and I had to cut the appeal and closing song so we could all march through Atlanta on time that afternoon. The Reverend Dr Bernice King (Martin Luther King's daughter) was the speaker who seemed to touch the delegates most deeply. She spoke on Lazarus.

God's hand seemed to rest upon the Brengle Holiness Institute planned for late November 2000.

Journal, 2 December 2000: Colonel Linda Bond and Lieut-Colonel Marlene Chase arrived in the small hours of 9 November. The Brengle Institute started on the evening of Sunday 12 November. It has proved to be a very helpful, meaningful experience to the 17 delegates and the eight members of the teaching staff. The visitors lectured well and identified with our emphases and goals. Their respective styles were contrasting and this helped. The Love Feast went well. The final Covenant Meeting at the new chapel in the training college was very special indeed, proving to be a spiritual high point. I have been doing very badly in my spirit since then. Like Elijah after the victory over the prophets of Ba'al. I will be alright again given time. But truly I wish these experiences were otherwise.

General Gowans unexpectedly appointed me to chair a small group to review and revise the Undertakings entered into by Salvation Army officers, together with those signed by his newly-created non-officer 'lieutenants'. I travelled to London and we convened at the Roman Catholic Emmaus Centre in West Wickham (see Appendix A). It was a good group and our work was received warmly by the General. Our recommended changes to the documents and to the related regulations were accepted and implemented as submitted.

Journal, 21 January 2001: I was in London from 6-12 January and saw much of Matt and Lynne. Lynne volunteered to show me around the Bromley shops on my final morning and this pleased me. It spoke of her courtesy and poise. The Undertakings group went well. The members adapted readily to my style. To make progress I needed to produce a draft on the second morning and this, with some changes, became the revised Undertakings. We also produced Undertakings for the new so-called 'lieutenants'. I do feel God helped us as a group in this sacred work. It was a good feeling to come away pleased with what we managed to do.

A lovely aspect of being in London was being able to call my Dad on my mobile at 7.00 am each day as I walked out in the cold darkness before breakfast. Each time he seemed pleased and very willing to chat. I do love him. I called Helen's parents twice, especially on their wedding anniversary. I took a gift for them, plus gifts from Matt and Lynne. Matt gave me Christmas gifts for us all. I was able to hear him preach again at Forestdale. He can win and hold his congregation well.

The work of the territory was progressing well, with seven new corps all opened on 19 April 2001 to coincide with the commissioning of new officers. Helen and I received personal blessing and uplift to our spirits through a visit to Bangladesh at the invitation of Lieut-Colonels Bo and Birgitte Brekke.

Journal, 13 May 2001: Our Dhaka visit enriched us and taught us a lot: that the Army and the poor are still interlocked; that God is blessing the Army in Bangladesh; that the Brekkes are fine officers and in a very impressive mould of their own.

A further step forward was the welcome arrival of Major John Dyall to succeed Major Cedric Sharp as the Property Secretary, the Sharps having moved to take charge of the training college in succession to Majors John and Valerie Townsend. Major Dyall was to become a most valued colleague, calm and unruffled, intelligent in his handling of people and of business matters, and undaunted when tensions arose in the community.

No sooner had he arrived than our lives were significantly changed by the 11 September 2001 attacks on the World Trade Center in New York, upon the Pentagon in Virginia, and by the hijacking of a third aeroplane that eventually crashed in Pennsylvania. I have written briefly about this dreadful event in my 2004 book, *New Love: Thinking Aloud About Practical Holiness*. Chapter 5 is entitled '"Angels in the Rafters" – Holiness and Terrorism'. There I refer to the impact upon our personal safety as a result of Western forces invading Afghanistan in October 2001 and later invading also Iraq on what was later to prove the false premise that weapons of mass destruction were being made ready there.

Journal, 22 September 2001: On 11 September four hijacked planes crashed in the USA. Over 3,000 killed, due mainly to the collapse of the World Trade Center towers in New York. Horrendous.

I have no words. President Bush at once launched into war/crusade rhetoric. The target is Osama Bin Laden from Saudi Arabia and in exile in Afghanistan. A self-confessed terrorist, he was Bill Clinton's target three years ago. The USA and others will attack Afghanistan again. Pakistan has come out in support of this but is only one of three states recognising the Taliban government in Kabul. We expect a long period of tension here and a possible backlash against foreigners, automatically assumed to be supporters of Western political initiatives. It could turn into a Moslem/Christian confrontation.

The UK High Commission has advised overseas residents to leave Pakistan. Three years ago this was not the case since there was no advance warning save for the sudden and unexplained evacuation of the Lahore American School. I have made provisional flight bookings for all overseas staff. This will continue indefinitely. I am meeting all the overseas staff weekly. IHQ has agreed that I can send them all to London if need be. I cannot leave. Helen and John may have to go without me. The Pakistani staff need me now as much as the overseas staff.

I have added extra guards at the training college. London will ensure that Avalon in Chislehurst, near Bromley, is ready at short notice to receive nine missionary officers. I am ensuring a ready supply of cash at THQ in US dollars and British pounds. We may need this in a hurry. We have built up domestic food supplies in case we cannot get out to the shops. Yesterday saw a public call for street demonstrations and a strike in response to the actions of the West. Karachi saw much violence to property and four persons were killed but there seemed to be no specifically anti-Christian or anti-foreigner element in it. Lahore was quiet and orderly. The bazaars were open as usual, a good sign. However, we had the main THQ gates padlocked just in case. Many messages of prayer support are coming in from family, friends and other territories. I have banned travel outside Lahore for all overseas staff but I hope that the plans for the visit of Commissioners Paul and Margaret du Plessis, starting a week from today, can go through. Lord, keep us all safe in your love and hold us in your will. Guard the Christians of this land and guide the leaders of the nations so that no more innocent lives are lost.

Our travel agent, Wilburn Albert, secured rolling flight reservations for our overseas staff over many, many weeks. I told Helen that she and John would be evacuated with the others if need be, but that I would stay whatever happened. How could I run and then return knowing our Pakistani colleagues had nowhere to run to? Major Dyall begged me to let him stay as well. I agreed. Major Flintoff said she too would stay, but I felt it would be too risky. I admired her spirit.

Journal, 8 October 2001: Western forces attacked Afghanistan last night. Violent reactions in the cities of Pakistan. I have confined all overseas staff to their offices and quarters. Floods of prayer support messages are helping us. Just now John is still at school. I will collect him myself at 3.00 pm today, just in case. The International Secretary, Commissioner du Plessis, has cancelled his visit. We have decided to carry on with all the public events nevertheless in order to keep up morale. So I flew to Karachi with the Chief Secretary and Helen headed by road to Islamabad for a Home League Rally there. The array of welcome banners still carried the names of our missing IHQ guests!

John will be 15 tomorrow.

Bombs in response to bombs solve nothing. Lord, heal the nations. Let no more innocent lives be lost. I hate this aggression. There must be other ways. Not all the peaceful options have yet been exhausted. My soul is much troubled.

Journal, 12 October 2001: Western bombing of Afghanistan goes on night and day. I doubt its morality. Civilian victims, non-combatants, mount in number daily. Tensions rise on our streets but Lahore is still a reasonably viable place in which to live. Quetta and Peshawar are suffering more. All overseas staff seem calmer now.

John's American School has 25 armed Pakistani soldiers in it every day in addition to police and the regular security guards. He is attending normally and is now the only Western, non-Pakistani student there. We cannot see the American staff returning to the school in the near future. Our feeling is that they could have, should have, stayed.

I feel more and more deeply that military action in Afghanistan by the West is wrong. The non-combatant casualties grow daily. Western leaders have no right to harm a single hair on the head of a single innocent Afghani person. Osama Bin Laden remains untouched, but hundreds are dead or wounded by so-called collateral damage.

Late 2001 brought a telephone call from General Gowans to tell us our service in Pakistan would conclude by March 2002.

Journal, 19 November 2001: Farewell orders! In the late afternoon of Friday 16 November the General telephoned to inform us he was sending us to take up the leadership of the New Zealand, Fiji and Tonga Territory. The Chief Secretary, Lieut-Colonel Gulzar Patras, will succeed me. He and his wife, Sheila, shed quiet tears of humility in my office when I informed them of this. The public announcements will be made on 29 November. So much to plan and do. Lord, you have acted again to move us to new pastures, a new flock, and a new field of service. Please go before us. Please smooth the way. Thank you for using us during these five years in Pakistan. I thank you for the new soldiers, the new officers, the new cadets, the new college, the 15 new corps. Grant us holy insight and sensitivity for New Zealand, Fiji and Tonga. Dear Lord, guard and hold us all, especially John. Thank you because you keep us in your holy will.

We were thrust into the throes of packing and the complexities of securing visas for New Zealand. We said farewell to our Pakistani comrades amid many tears and embraces. Some of the tears, of course, were our own. We flew from Lahore to Singapore where our visas were, in the end, readily issued to allow us to live and work in Wellington.

A Pakistan postscript

After three years in Pakistan, on the evening of 1 June 2000, Ascension Day, I found myself compiling a detailed note on how the whole day had gone:

A Day in the Life of a Salvation Army
Territorial Commander in Pakistan

Up at 5.45 am. A hot, sticky night. Today temperatures will rise to 45°C and humidity will be 80 per cent. Hoping the air-conditioning keeps going. We need rain.

John's last day of Middle School before the summer vacation. Briefly we pray with him as he goes out at 7 am. Saleem is already waiting with the car downstairs.

Into the office at 7.45 am. Daily, early prayer and consultation with the Chief Secretary. We start with him praying aloud for me and my family (we alternate each morning in praying for one another before we talk business).

The social secretary and financial secretary ask to see me urgently at 9 am. Suspected loss of funds at a social centre. Obvious culprit is very ill, recovering from major cancer surgery. I speak to the regional commander in Karachi by telephone and ask him to report back to the social secretary within 24 hours.

We are waiting tensely for word on the USA visas for our congress delegates. Still no word after three weeks.

Morning prayers at 10 am. I speak to the officers and staff about Ascension Day. Jesus went home to Heaven. He is preparing a place for us there with himself. I speak about the Plan of Salvation: Incarnation, Crucifixion, Resurrection, Ascension and Session (being seated at the right hand of God the Father). Many have never before given a thought to Ascension. I feel glad we can speak of it.

Monthly Literature Board at 10.30 am. Goes smoothly. Good articles and photographs for 'The War Cry'.

Christian Lawyers Association of Pakistan officials ask to see me. I greet them warmly for I have agreed to be, as they call me, their Patron. Three have come. They want to make contacts with lawyers overseas. Somehow the conversation turns to preaching. With the Pakistani lawyers I discuss 1 Corinthians 1:18 and the meaning of 'the message of the Cross'. It becomes a hallowed moment as their eyes glow at the thought of grace, love, forgiveness and adoption into God's family. They are three good men, but they are marked and they live in danger from Moslem opponents for they are involved in human rights cases and in upholding the Christian

136

marriage laws of Pakistan. I know that at least one of them goes armed, so I pray with them before they leave me and I ask for divine protection over them. They are so gracious.

I talk to the CS about a local carpenter making a cross from the wood of the old Mercy Seat from the training college site now sold.

I meet our computer graphics designer about the territorial campaign poster for 2001. I approve the draft design and authorise an initial payment.

I examine and sign five variation orders for the work of our new training college. We will save 600,000 rupees on the air-conditioning units.

The cashier comes in with numerous cheques and bank drafts to be signed. He presents me with our monthly allowance in hard cash. It has gone up slightly since our promotion to commissioner rank.

Noon and a light lunch with Helen upstairs in the flat. Fifty minutes to unwind. We tell cook, Ghulam Masih, not to return that evening for we shall eat out. He goes off with a cheery wave of the hand as usual.

Suddenly the phone rings and it is my private secretary to say the training principal is asking to see me urgently. It is serious. Major Valerie Townsend has been diagnosed with a detached retina and must be repatriated urgently to New Zealand. The timing is wretchedly inconvenient, but now nothing matters except to get her home. The next hour is spent contacting IHQ, THQ in Wellington and the travel agent. We get Val and John business class seats so that Val can recline fully during the long flight. Her New Zealand specialist has been alerted. Banner Medical Insurance in the UK will cover all the costs but this arrangement takes five telephone calls to finalise. I instruct the financial secretary to go to the training college next day to take into safe keeping all cash and books including the cheque book. John and Val need to be de-registered as Atlanta Congress delegates.

Finally I offer fervent prayer with them both, committing them to the hands of God. I tell them just to walk away and not worry. We can handle things here and they must focus only on getting Val well and homeland leave thereafter.

Throughout all this a land agent is waiting in my outer office for my signature and thumbprints on legal papers in connection with the sale of the old college. He comes in and we go through all the papers. I sign. I give my thumbprint (left hand for men, right for women!). The blue ink stain on my thumb will last for days.

The Chief Secretary calls to say he is sick and needs rest. I urge him to leave the office and go home. He has blood pressure problems.

The field secretary speaks with me about a corps officer who has suffered a stroke. Can this colleague sustain his appointment or not? He wants to do so but we need a full medical report.

Problems continue in our THQ compound with water supplies to the residences of indigenous officers in William Booth Street. I need to go out to inspect the work. It is hot. The sun burns me through my shirt. The work is not complete and I decline to authorise payment to the contractor. I tell him to come the next day when the work is finished. Readily he agrees and smiles for he knows he has asked too soon for the money. I walk back to the office through the rose garden and across the lawns. Despite the lack of rain our grounds look fresh and green. Our malis (gardeners) do a good job. We must get them out to the new college to seed the lawns there.

I need to prepare for our specialling in Melbourne in August. We are trying to compile a photographic display of the work here. I turn to it on and off throughout the day but simply cannot get a run at it without interruption. Finally give up.

THQ closes at 4 pm. Things go quiet. Helen goes to her Urdu class. Eventually I get upstairs to the flat to find that the second England v Zimbabwe Test Match (cricket) has been delayed by rain. I wish I could have some rain! So I change out of uniform into shorts and a T-shirt and watch a bit of 'Songs of Praise' from England's Cotswolds. My sister, Syl, has sent this to us. I like the hymns and the countryside scenes. A longing to be there fills me. But my work is here. I feel very tired.

Then more telephone calls from Banner Insurance and from Major John Townsend who graciously expresses thanks for what has been done. Not all colleagues remember to do this, so I am grateful.

I need to check the email. Several messages from various parts of the Army world. Most need replies. I compile and send them out.

About 6.30 pm we manage to get out to the Avari hotel for a relaxed supper. We are greeted warmly there by staff and the manager, a British citizen whose son attends the same school as John. Supper, including tip, comes to 600 rupees, about US$12.

Home. Fall asleep in the armchair. To bed about 9.15 pm. Exhausted. My last thought is, 'Lord, send the Congress visas, send the visas…' Suddenly I am reaching to answer the bedside telephone. It is the field secretary waking me up to say the police in Hyderabad have arrested our corps officer there. I give instructions for action by the regional commander in Karachi. He is a good man and will do what is right. I find this thought reassuring.

However, sleep is impossible now. Helen sleeps on. So I go back to live coverage on TV of the Test Match. Ramprakash is out. Atherton, a model of slow play, is there with Hussain. The bowling is feeble so the gung-ho remarks of the English commentators about an English revival mean nothing. We invented the game but now we are the second worst Test team in world cricket! I fall asleep in the chair and wake to find Helen moving about the room in the light of the flickering TV screen. She says she has forgotten to make a note of something. Her mind is racing too. Back to bed. We put on a cassette tape of an American evangelist to see if he will distract our tumbling thoughts. Soon sleep comes again. My final thought: 'Sweet will of God....' The ascended Lord sees us, soothes us, and watches over those we love. Outside, the insects make night noises and the guards at the gate check their guns.

Wellington, New Zealand

New Zealand is a lovely place boasting lakes and mountains, wonderful coastlines, and stunning vegetation. Having the same land mass as the UK which holds 65 million people, New Zealand's population is a mere six million. It is a beautiful, uncrowded, uncluttered land. Its citizens carry those self-sufficient characteristics often found among island dwellers within rugged, rocky coastlines: they are proud, independently minded and outspoken, often choosing candour above courtesy; they can be opinionated, argumentative and cantankerous. So right away I found myself warming to them. These were all traits I understood. Transparency is preferable to dissimulation.

It was 4 March 2002 when we landed in Wellington to be met by Colonels Robert and Gwyneth Redhead, members of the Territorial Cabinet, and other friends.

Journal, 26 April 2002: Arrived in Wellington a few weeks ago. Met at airport by cabinet, plus Cyril Bradwell and Majors John and Val Townsend. All very warm toward us. A nice beginning. Supper at

139

'The Captain's Table' overlooking Wellington harbour. John ordered a T-bone steak, much to Colonel Redhead's amusement. He seemed to like John's unaffected manner.

Before we left Pakistan General Gowans had told me that Colonel Redhead would not be with me for very long as the Chief Secretary. Plans were in hand to move him and Gwyneth to Canada. Robert proved to be a warm-hearted colleague and I valued his friendship in those early months.

Soon John was enrolled as a pupil at Wellington High School, where Corps Sergeant-Major Cyril Bradwell, recipient of the Order of the Founder, had once been headmaster. John opted for this school for two reasons: it had no student uniform; football was preferred to rugby. Moreover, the school's intake was culturally very varied and this appealed as well.

Journal, 26 April 2002: John has now taken his place as the youngest player in the Wellington High School football 1st XI. He is pleased and so are we. Thank you, Lord, for paving the way for John.

IHQ had arranged for Commissioners Earle and Wilma Maxwell to travel from Australia to conduct our public installation meeting at Wellington City Corps on the evening of Sunday 10 March. This pleased us for we held the Maxwells in warm esteem and had appreciated their ministry and fellowship when they came to us in Boston.

Journal, 26 April 2002: Wellington City Corps building was packed for our welcome meeting. It was very well led by the Maxwells and Redheads, but strangely the divisional commanders of the territory did not attend. Helen spoke well and very naturally as she always does, all without notes. I preached on John 1:14, 18 and felt much passion and freedom. I gave a promise to place Christ at the centre of everything, to be open and truthful with the people, and not to offer them leadership based on hollow gestures or short-term gimmicks.

The next day I telephoned each divisional commander to make comradely contact in view of no invitations having been sent to them when our installation meeting was being planned.

Journal, 26 April 2002: Called all the divisional commanders to break the ice. An interesting variety of reactions. Some comradely, some surprised. Lunched with the Maxwells. He wanted to chat candidly about the next High Council, I valued that.

Have met Cardinal Thomas Williams. He was very warm and pleasingly unstuffy. Met also our official legal advisors, Bell, Gully & Co, over a lovely lunch with a great harbour view from their offices. They seemed interested in my former legal role at IHQ and also in my doctoral dissertation. Seems they had been well briefed prior to our arrival.

In mid-March we held a weekend retreat with cabinet members on the Kapiti Coast. I have added two women officers to the cabinet. The retreat was a good experience with much prayer and open discussion. On the Sunday morning we visited a Christian Maori murai (compound) and followed the Stations of the Cross.

The cultural variety of the territory was a wonderful thing. Learning all we could about the history of New Zealand brought much pleasurable reading, and discovering the traditions of the Maori peoples was a source of deep fascination. Helen later attended Maori language evening classes at Wellington High School. Added to all this was the richness of Fiji and Tonga. We were keen to encounter these island races at first hand and welcomed the opportunity to spend Easter 2002 in Tonga. John came with us. We arrived on Good Friday at 1.30 am.

Journal, 26 April 2002: Easter in Tonga! Wonderful. Hot. A small but lively Army. It needs mature leadership. Encountered a fuss on leaving Tonga airport as John had no return or onward ticket out of New Zealand and was on a visitor's visa pending formal registration at his school. They refused to let him board the plane home with us so I telephoned from Tonga to the immigration authorities at Auckland airport. They at once waived the restrictions. Phew!

In early April we learned that Lieut-Colonels Garth and Mel McKenzie would succeed the Redheads and return to their native New Zealand. They came with good reputations. Meanwhile we were settling in rapidly.

Majors John and Anne Read hosted us for a Saturday morning brunch at the famous 'Chocolate Fish' café and spoke of their pleasure at our coming to the territory. Early contacts were established with radio and television outlets and I was pleased to meet in particular Maureen Garing of Radio NZ, a kindly but penetrating interviewer as well as a person of Christian faith. The members of the Territorial Cabinet and the finance council were competent colleagues, ready to discuss, willing to disagree, but loyal to their callings as officers and supportive once policy options had been explored and a future course agreed. Helen and I liked these comrades and enjoyed their fellowship as well as their fidelity to the cause. However, problems soon surfaced concerning the local culture of the Army.

First came the discovery that a handful of corps officers were holding fake, privately invented 'sacramental' ceremonies in the Sunday morning meetings, presiding in priestly fashion over the distribution of red fruit juice. THQ had ignored this, senior officers even taking part on occasion. I had not encountered anything like it before so made it a matter of much prayer, consulting widely in an effort to identify what had led to it. Despite the wishes of some in the territory, I did not feel it was a matter for swift or formal disciplinary action. I strongly preferred to begin patiently with dialogue and persuasion. It was clear that the officers doing it needed guidance so I arranged to meet them face-to-face on an individual basis. No two officers offered the same rationale for their actions. Some said it was 'nice', some told me the newcomers from the Baptists had asked for it, and others for some strange reason seemed to think leaders at IHQ had encouraged it. No officer had acted out of doctrinal or theological conviction and this made it easier to deal with. Those I spoke to responded helpfully and showed interest when I raised the matter of the 'Love Feast' tradition. None of them had heard of it or knew of its place in our history. I offered to visit their corps should they wish to have me preside over such an occasion.

These conversations were mutually beneficial, but of course each officer colleague knew only too well that persistent intransigence in the matter would, in the end, give rise to the question of whether or not they could be allowed any arena for Army ministry. It was, and is, lacking in integrity and inconsistent with our understanding of the holy life to take an arena of Army officer ministry, take Army accommodation, take Army financial allowances, wear Army uniform, and yet openly flout a central Army doctrinal position such as our historic witness to the real possibility of living a sanctified life without sacramental ceremonies.

Next came the matter of some corps officers telling newcomers and young people nearing the age for senior soldiership that they did not have to join 'the international Salvation Army' but could instead sign a covenant invented by the corps officer which would be a temporary commitment only to that local congregation. Some officers were teaching the people that 'the international Salvation Army' was an altogether separate body from local corps branches of the Army in New Zealand. It was scarcely credible. Again, here was something that had simply not been addressed by THQ. So we had to find gentle but firm ways of making it very clear that the Army was one body globally and that every corps and centre was part of that one Army. For the avoidance of doubt, I gave instructions that the word 'international' was not to be used before 'Salvation Army' in our periodicals and other documentation. The officers involved were instructed to abandon the inventing of so-called local membership covenants and instead conform to normal Army polity as expressed in junior soldiership, senior soldiership and the adherent members' system. I embarked upon dialogue with General Larsson about adding a simple faith commitment to our globally-used adherents' certificate and in due course this became official international policy with the term 'adherent' being changed to 'adherent member'. This ended the debate as to whether or not adherents were Salvationists. I had always thought they were, but the General insisted they were not. The matter was helpfully resolved.

A third matter was the very low number of persons responding to the call of God to be officers of The Salvation Army. Negative comments about the training college were made openly and often. This puzzled and distressed me, especially when corps officers stated flatly that they would never seek to send a person to the college as a cadet. Now the fact is that the New Zealand training college comprises a beautiful set of buildings situated on a lovely campus in a scenic valley. Majors John and Anne Read had arrived, giving added credibility to the college which was already staffed by intelligent, gifted and committed officers and employees. After consultation with the cabinet I announced a modest territorial faith goal of 15 cadets for the next sessional intake. We sought to talk up the college. It proved to be slow and hard work.

A fourth concern was the laissez faire attitude as to whether or not every Salvation Army hall should have a Mercy Seat. Each corps, especially those recently built, had been allowed to choose! I felt utterly at a loss to understand how this could come about. Some said glibly, 'We need the space for the drum kit, keyboard and guitars.' Of all of our symbols in the Army it is the Mercy Seat, grounded in the Scriptures, that most powerfully, most eloquently expresses the reason God raised us up, for it represents the encounter of a seeking soul with the Saviour. 'There…I will meet with you,' declares the Lord (Exodus 25:22). An Army hall without a Mercy Seat is like a body without a heartbeat. Earlier in this Essay I have recounted General Wiseman's potent preaching on this truth when in Salisbury, Rhodesia.

My Journal records early events:

Journal, 26 April 2002: Chaired a training college council meeting. The staff members were not used to seeing a territorial commander present. I need to reorganise the college boards and councils and create a new governing council with the territorial commander in the chair, the normal way things are done.

Hosted Major Janice Smithies, Colonel Robert Redhead and Cyril Bradwell for supper at home. A good company. Attended a memorial service at the Anglican Cathedral for the Queen Mother and was asked to read one of the prayers. On 11 April held Spiritual Day meetings at the training college. A tiny group in the chapel. All rather hard work but those present showed much sincerity.

Have attended a concert by the Wellington Sinfonia at the Michael Fowler Centre where we preached during the Congress in late 2000. Wonderful violin playing by a young Australian, Niki Vasilakis. A good night.

John's first football match for his school against Onslow College, Johnsonville. Drew 3-3. The youngest player on the field, he was not out of his depth.

Pleased to host Commissioners Hillmon and Lorraine Buckingham, with their son and his wife, Captains Lyndon and Bronwyn

*Buckingham, and their two children for supper in our home. Hillmon
has been very sick. A lovely evening together.*

Mid-2002 brought an encounter with Gregory Fortuin, Race
Relations Commissioner for New Zealand. He asked for a meeting in
my office and I agreed at once, pleased he had initiated contact. Mr
Fortuin was a cape-coloured South African of mixed African and
European heritage and, as I later discovered, a figure surrounded by
political controversy. Colonel Redhead and I received him most readily
in my office in Cuba Street. We offered him a cup of tea or coffee. 'Coffee
please.' 'Do you take it black or white?' With that Mr Fortuin frowned
and rebuked us for referring to coffee with words like 'black' and 'white'.
For a moment I thought he was joking, but he was not. 'You should ask
if I want it with or without milk,' he insisted. He had been in my office
for only a minute or so. 'Thank you, Mr Fortuin. We respect you as our
guest, but please answer the question. Do you take your coffee black or
white?' I did not then know that his days as Race Relations
Commissioner for New Zealand were numbered. The government had
decided to replace him. He served for only 16 months. As I write this in
November 2013 the New Zealand *War Cry* carries a three-page feature
on Mr Fortuin to mark his having been hired by the Army to head our
Employment Plus programme in New Zealand. The article most
naturally caught my eye.

My Journal records briefly many useful encounters and engagements
in our first New Zealand winter.

*Journal, 25 June 2002: To Hamilton, Midland Division, and
flights to various venues in a five-seater plane chartered by the
divisional commander. Great fun! Our good friend, Nesam Noble,
came from London to stay for a few days starting 1 May. I have held
urgent talks with our investment advisers with a view to increasing our
revenues.*

*Have met the Anglican Bishop, Tom Brown. He seemed ill at ease.
A wonderful weekend in early May in Fiji where we have a great little
Army! I felt very free and at home there. Visited the Army farm, Jeff
Farm near Dunedin. It has 5,000 acres. Was very impressed by it all*

and pleased to meet agricultural students receiving Salvation Army scholarships to assist their studies at Telford College.

On 27 May took morning tea at Government House with Dame Sylvia Cartright, the Governor-General. She spoke of her Salvationist origins and I was pleased to offer prayer with her. The next evening we mingled with officers at the Five Year Review where I emphasised the life of holiness and other Army distinctives. Soon thereafter went with Helen to Dunedin, Christchurch and Nelson. A good series of gatherings in the company of the Divisional Commander, Major Lyn Buttar, a fine colleague. Much freedom in preaching about Jesus, only Jesus.

Early June and the Northern Division Retreat on Waiheke Island. Drew on the Epistle of James. Emphasised the real practicality of holy living. Then to Rotoroa Island by helicopter to see our addictions services at work there. I do not like helicopters.

In mid-June we held the Territorial Executive Conference where some delicate and long-standing issues were aired. Then it was the public farewell to the Redheads on 13 June, an excellent, warm-hearted meeting.

Yesterday we visited the zoo. Great fun! John played football last Saturday for Seatoun Rangers, a local men's team. He did fine. Played the same day also for his school and won 2-0.

Bandmaster James Williams of Enfield Corps has been awarded the MBE (Member of the British Empire) by the Queen. We are very pleased. We hold him in warm regard.

The McKenzies took up their new appointments on 1 July 2002 and were publicly welcomed at Wellington City Corps on the following Sunday evening.

Journal, 26 July 2002: The new Chief Secretary is doing fine. Keen on detail. I find he can be clear and firm. He is also open to direction.

Journal, 14 August 2002: Garth and Mel McKenzie are doing well. Garth has tightened up considerably on all details of administration.

Meanwhile, the next High Council began to come more into focus:

Journal, 26 July 2002: The High Council qualifying date of 12 July has come and gone. We have both been duly summoned to attend. Over 50 of the 87 members will be at their first High Council and a small handful at their fourth. It will be my second and Helen's first as a member in her own right.

We left Wellington for London on 10 August having arranged to take some days of furlough prior to heading to Sunbury Court. General Gowans presided over a plenary session of the General's Consultative Council (GCC) for two days. The public welcome meeting for the High Council members was held at London's Regent Hall on a hot and uncomfortable night. The High Council began on Friday 30 August and as expected Commissioner John Larsson was quickly elected (see Essay 11), taking office on Wednesday 13 November 2002.

The General and Commissioner Gisèle Gowans duly came to our territory in early October as part of their concluding overseas campaign. The Maori welcome held at Wellington airport was wonderfully impressive. The guests gave all they could throughout the six days they were with us.

Journal, 16 October 2002: The General's visit has now passed. I am very pleased with the outcome of all the many preparations. Very smooth. Huge attendances at all events. Much positive feedback, some of it glowing. The organising committee did a great job. I thank God for his powerful presence at these events. I pray that confidence throughout the territory will lift as a result.

Soon afterwards I had the opportunity to meet Prime Minister Helen Clark. Leader of a left-wing political party, she made no secret of her personal rejection of religious belief, but twice each year set aside time to spend several hours with the leaders of the larger churches.

Journal, 20 December 2002: I have met the New Zealand prime minister with other Church leaders. Helen Clark has a good mind and a compassionate heart despite what some say about her rejection of religion.

She actively sought our views on current social issues. I was helped by Major Campbell Roberts who had known the Prime Minister for many years and was on first name terms with her. As a result she held the Army in warm regard and paid attention when we spoke in these gatherings. I was pleased also that she was unwilling to be pressurised by the larger nation states. For many years New Zealand had refused harbour and berthing rights to any sea vessel carrying nuclear materials and especially those with nuclear weapons. This proved frustrating for the USA. Offered highly attractive terms in trade deals with New Zealand if she would relax this embargo, Clark's reply was simple: 'New Zealand is not for sale.'

Homeland furlough at the start of 2003 came as a most welcome interlude in our busy lives.

Journal, 7 February 2003: Our furlough was a delight. We encountered long delays in Los Angeles but arrived in Sidney, Ohio, only two hours late. The jet lag did not prevent us savouring to the full our first sight of baby Hudson Collings. What a lovely moment as Helen, John and I crept into his nursery at 1 am to see him asleep in his cot. Marcus could not resist picking him up and we all had a little hold and cuddled him. Wonderful. I think we all felt very strong impulses of love and protection toward him. So small, so vulnerable, yet so beautiful. He proved to be a smiling and responsive child, with clear, intelligent eyes that home in on you and hold you. He would go very still when sung to, kicking his feet and smiling after each song. Jen and Marcus seem well and tell us they are considering officership in New Zealand. No pressure from us.

Journal, 9 March 2003: Hannah Elizabeth Alice Clifton was born at 6.45 pm on 23 February 2003 at Mayday Hospital, Croydon, London. A great day! Matt rang us at 11 pm New Zealand time on Sunday evening. Hannah weighed in at 11lbs 4ozs. So we are grandparents twice over in just a few months. We feel keenly the distances from the children, but Matt and Lynne and Hannah will come for three weeks in May.

Becoming a grandparent was a watershed. It brought new thoughts and responsibilities, but above all new insights. I gave voice to some of these in my 'Thinking Aloud' column for the New Zealand *War Cry* in late February 2003:

About Being a Successful Grandpa

I have recently become a grandpa twice over. The feelings that go through you when this happens are strong: relief that all is well with the baby and with Mum; pride in one's kids; protective instincts; hopes for the future. Then there are the fears.

I find myself afraid that Hudson and Hannah have been born into a world that is probably at its most dangerous for several decades. War and rumours of war are on every hand. Will they grow up to be peacemakers?

Then there is the fear that they may grow up to reject Christ. This is to think the unthinkable. But it could happen. These tiny people, cousins to each other, have been granted free will. They will make their own choices one day. Will they choose Christ?

Another lingering fear is that they will hear the shrill calls of the world more clearly than the call to self-sacrifice and to live for others. They could turn out to be selfish, ambitious in all the wrong ways, and addicted to materialism. Will they discover the power of servanthood in the image of Christ?

I have to mention too some fears for their parents. Will they be up to all the modern demands of raising children? Have I set them a sound example in my parenting of them? Will they have enough wisdom, patience, good sense, strong love, gentle firmness and all the other attributes it takes?

I am also afraid for me. Can I become a successful grandpa? Now here is a fine ambition. Nobody wants to fail, least of all in these precious human relationships. Will these two small people come to find in me all that they need in a grandpa? I am thinking that success in matters of family are perhaps as elusive as ever they were. Happy the man who can claim to have achieved the fourfold goal of successful son, successful husband, successful father and successful grandparent.

Success here cannot be measured by outcomes. Rather, it has to be gauged by fidelity – fidelity to the inherently covenantal commitment in each role. Unconditional commitment, made over and over again as the years tick by, commitment to one's parents, to a spouse, to a child, to a grandchild.

I want to align myself with all Christian grandpas, those seeking God's face to ask for his help in being faithful to the many Hudsons and Hannahs of the world. Lord, let them see in us something of you: your heart for peace; your readiness to live for others; your wisdom; your grace. Let them intuit, even before they can speak or walk, how infinitely precious they are to us as their grandparents, and let them see in us some gleam of the light of Christlikeness.

My Journal records both Army and global political events in early 2003.

Journal, 9 March 2003: Tonight is the Territorial Welcome to the Bridge Builders Sessions of cadets, 12 in all. We have a further nine in Suva, Fiji. This is the first event of its kind for several years in this territory. Lord, be my Helper when I rise to speak. Quicken my tongue.

It is now 10.50 pm and the welcome meeting is over. Helen and John are asleep in bed and I have come quietly to write here that God, in his love and mercy, heard and answered my prayer. Hearts were softened. The seekers kept coming forward for about 40 minutes. Each time I was about to end it others came. Some officers too, maybe 15 or 20 by the end. Three of the cadets spoke well and easily, showing much poise. The image of cadetship is thereby already enhanced. I feel spent and tense as I always do after a meeting like this. It is hard to wind down. We all needed a meeting like this one. Thank you, Lord. As we sang at the end, 'Thine be the glory.'

Journal, 7 February 2003: I am deeply anxious about Western political belligerence toward Iraq. President Bush seems dangerously sincere in his intention to invade. Prime Minister Tony Blair echoes his every utterance. Lord, save the nations from folly.

Journal, 19 March 2003: Iraq is to be attacked. War is again upon the nations. The USA, the UK and Australia will launch the attacks.

I cannot find it in my heart to think this assault is just. Saddam Hussein is capable of great evil but he poses no real threat to any of the states that will attack his country. Early this morning alone in our lounge, as I watched the news reports and heard the bellicose words of Western leaders and saw images of ordinary Iraqi citizens helpless before the onslaught, again I wept for the state of the world – for folly, greed, vengeance, the spilling of innocent blood, for children, for families, for my own powerlessness and sense of futility. Christ's words of forgiveness from the cross were my prayer. There is a fundamental wrongness about this attack and millions in the democratic world sense it. The Salvationists in my territory sense it too. We have not heard any word of guidance on it all from IHQ. This is an added regret to me. Booth would have spoken to his people.

I have spoken formally to the Salvationists here and have called the territory to prayer over the Iraq crisis. I have also united with other church leaders to pressurise the New Zealand government into a non-aggressive stance. This seems to have worked. Still IHQ remains silent.

Journal, 21 March 2003: I have been making written and public statements this week on the Prostitution Law Reform Bill and the Death with Dignity Bill. I have sent a letter about euthanasia to all members of Parliament. Our fellow Christians in other NZ churches have expressed appreciation. Good responses from around the territory too.

Journal, 8 August 2003: The Death with Dignity Bill has been defeated, 60 votes to 57, on its first reading in Parliament. Hurray! I hope my letter to all MPs helped a few of the waverers.

Journal, 13 April 2003: American and British troops have ended the rule of Saddam Hussein in Iraq. It has cost many lives, most of them innocent. Now there is chaos – looting, vigilantes, the burning of everything. Still no weapons of mass destruction found. I feel a deep, quiet inner anger about this war. I have signed yet a third public statement on behalf of the Army. The New Zealand prime minister has done well in all this. Very moderate, very principled. Now we expect show trials. No victor is ever put on trial. Can I truly be a 'victor' if I crush a beetle under my boot? Western powers are saying much about giving humanitarian aid now the main fighting is over (I am reminded of the man who broke into a house, raped the woman who lived there, and then made her a cup of tea). Still IHQ remains silent.

Despite the silence of IHQ, good statements on the conflict were published from Alexandria by USA National Headquarters, from Melbourne by the Australia Southern Territory, and from London by the UK Territory. There was no collusion. Each statement differed slightly from the others. In order to preserve them for future reference, I reproduced them all in *New Love* when it was released in 2004 (see pages 86-89 of that volume).

Meanwhile Matt and Lynne came to visit us in Wellington. Hannah was just three months old. Helen, John and I delighted in holding her and fussing over her. As I watched Helen with her, there flooded back vivid memories of the births of our own three children. Matt and Lynne revelled in all there was to see and do during their holiday, including a day trip to Picton on the Interislander ferry when we marvelled at how glassy-smooth the sea waters were, and time at the Te Papa Museum in Wellington, where Lynne enjoyed the simulated bungee jump machine! A brave new Mum!

The winter months saw a memorable Brengle Holiness Institute, which I have described in Essay 2. An entry in my Journal in April that year reveals something of my inner need at that time.

Journal, 13 April 2003: I feel the burden of my officership. I think God allows me to be a capable officer but I know myself well and am not what I want to be. Almost invariably I preach beyond my own inner experience. So too did John Wesley and William Booth! On the wall in front of me now, where I am seated writing this in my study at home in Wellington, are pinned up two statements: 'Not for weight of glory….' And then 'Though he slay me, yet will I trust in him' (Job 13:15 Authorised Version). The first cautions me against worldly aims. The second is simply true for today. I know that each day God helps me die to self in small ways, unseen and unnoticed by anyone else.

New Zealand is accustomed to interaction with events in Australia. August 2003 saw two instances of this, one good and one bad. The good came by way of an invitation to visit the Army's Collaroy Campsite to speak at a men's Bible convention there. Helen came too and was enrolled, amid much good humour, as 'an honorary man'. What really impressed me was that the newly appointed Territorial Commander, Commissioner Les Strong, attended in residence for each of the three days and mingled easily and without fanfare as just one of the delegates. Prior to the convention I had delivered the 2003 Coutts Memorial Lecture at the Sydney training college.

> *Journal, 8 August 2003: Our first visit to Collaroy. The conference centre is a fine facility in a pleasant location. About 200 or more men. My theme was 'Heroes of the Faith'. The men were attentive, sensitive, and ready to laugh. They lined the Mercy Seat in the final meeting. Some really solid decisions. Ken Heffernan and Graeme Jones from the conference centre were ideal hosts, and Graeme Press proved to be a fine worship leader. We thank God for this open door for ministry.*

The contrastingly bad experience came in the form of a torrent of legal claims against the Army in New Zealand alleging abuse in our children's homes in the 1950s and 1960s.

> *Journal, 4 September 2003: The Army has hit the media headlines and come into strong public glare over allegations of child abuse several decades ago in Army children's homes. Already we have received 80 complaints following similar exposure in Australia. I have been on TV twice already and on radio three times. Endless press enquiries. God is helping us retain our poise. He will also protect our good name. Dear Lord, where will this end? Help me handle it with holy wisdom, holy dignity, and with calm.*

> *Journal, 8 October 2003: We now have 106 legal claims to handle. Hot media attention. Dear Lord, guide me in this for I cannot handle it without you. We need you very much.*

New Zealand had already witnessed a flood of similar claims against both the Roman Catholic and Anglican churches. Now it was the Army's turn to come under the searchlight. Members of the Territorial Cabinet responded with skill and wisdom. My legal background helped too and we resisted any inclination to panic. Rapidly but calmly we devised a strategy. Working closely with our liability insurers, an essential part of handling any legal claim no matter how large or small or embarrassing to the Army, we offered every single claimant (those alleging sexual abuse, as well as those alleging general abuse due to the legally imposed disciplinary regime years ago) a face-to-face meeting with a senior officer. A support person could also attend. All interviews would be recorded and a copy provided to the claimant. No claim would be disputed and an on-the-spot non-negotiable sum in compensation would be offered. Rapidly many claims were finalised. Media interest was naturally strong. I did all the TV and radio interviews, insisting these went out live and therefore unedited. Major Alistair Herring handled the printed media and did well.

However, the key to resolving the whole episode was the careful and skilled work done by the Secretary for Personnel, Lieut-Colonel Wilfred Arnold, and Mr Murray Houston in meeting each claimant face-to-face. By the time we farewelled from Wellington all but a tiny handful remained to be settled. The media proved understanding toward the Army's position and responded encouragingly to our manner of handling it all. To my immense relief, no officer of the Army was implicated. The allegations were against a small number of non-Army employed staff and also against some older boys who were found to have abused some younger boys systematically. The trauma experienced by the victims cannot be overstated. We hoped and prayed that providing opportunities to tell their stories and to be believed would result in a measure of healing. Some who came forward declined our offer of compensation, saying that being heard and being taken seriously was enough.

Amid the storm good things were happening across the territory, one of which was John deciding to become a senior soldier of the Army.

Journal, 7 September 2003: Today John stepped up to the plate for God by opting to become a senior soldier of the Army. How smart he looked in his blue uniform. Tall, slender, so young. He clearly felt the powerful emotion of it all as he was invited by Captain Buckingham to kneel alone at the Mercy Seat at Wellington City Corps. The captain then invited Helen and me to kneel with John. Thereupon many others also came forward to enfold and support him. John had opted to speak a few words of thanks and witness. He was moved by it all but got through pretty well.

In this meeting, and watching intently, were 25 male pupils from the choir of St Patrick's Roman Catholic School. Seeds were being sown

Seeing John beneath the flag, I could only marvel at God's touch on his life and wonder where this might one day lead him. He has a lot to give and much to develop in Christ and for Christ. All three of our children are, by their own free choice, active Salvationists now. Lord, enfold them in your love and keep them true. They must find their own way, but you will be with them.

Jen was the first to be sworn-in. This was at Bromley Temple Corps where I did the ceremony. Then, when we were far away in Pakistan, Matt at Woodford Corps by Major Fred Thompson. Now John by Captain Lyndon Buckingham, who went on to preach a great, pungent message for Father's Day. Again, the boys of St Patrick's listened keenly. It was an Army meeting that moved and blessed us deeply. Just a wonderful morning in God's house.

I am father to three fine children. If ever they read this Journal they are to know I love them, am immensely proud of them, and want them only to be all that Christ can make them. Key to this is obedience to his holy will for their lives, in matters large and small. I am not an ideal father, but have done and am doing my best. I want Matt and Jen and John to be their own people, independent in thought, loving and considerate in actions, ready to defend the weak and to redress an injustice, open to God in everything, not pushy or proud, but having a due and proper self-regard, giving God credit for their talents, giftedness and achievements. God has given Matt and Jen spouses in whom we take delight and pleasure. Lord, lead John to the girl you would choose to be his wife.

In any Army territory there are causes for both joy and sorrow.

Journal, 10 October 2003: Today I learned of a couple wishing to resign their officership. When the Chief Secretary entered my office and told me of it, I tried to pray with him about it but could only weep quiet tears of sorrow with him. Feelings too deep for words. It falls to me now to meet this couple and gently probe their reasons and their souls. Ah, Lord....

Our time in beautiful New Zealand was soon to end. I did not know this when I flew to London early in November 2003 to attend a meeting of the GCC. The venue was the Army hall in Upper Norwood. I had been invited to present a paper on the effect of cultural influences upon the Army. I gave it a rather longwinded title: 'The Impact of Culture (Post-Modern and Traditional) on Salvation Army Core Values and the Search for Army Non-Negotiables'. Later this was to become the basis for Chapter 1 of my book, *New Love*.

Journal, 22 November 2003: I was in London for the GCC. It went quite well, better than I had dared to hope I do confess. General Larsson chaired in a clear but relaxed manner. The open discussions were better than at my last GCC. My main paper on The Salvation Army and culture was, to my surprise, received with tremendous applause and warmth. The General said it was 'a watershed document'. We will see.

The General took me aside to say we are to move from New Zealand next year. He is appointing us to the leadership of the UK Territory as of 1 June 2004.

This creates real difficulties for John's schooling. We have asked if the move could be in November but the General is asking for June. So June it is. John's attitude is mature and calm. We may have to leave him here alone for six months. Please, Lord, sort this out for our son.

General Larsson had caught me off guard. The timing of leaving New Zealand would be all wrong for John's education. I telephoned Helen with the news. She also expressed concern for the impact on John. Later dialogue with the General made it clear that our move to London could not be postponed. We thought it could but were in no position to resist our leaders. Should John move with us or remain alone in Wellington?

Journal, 16 December 2003: John's preference is to stay behind and complete his pre-university education in Wellington. The General has promised all needful financial support. We value this commitment. Lord, please guide us as a family. Open up the right path for John. Lord, your word in Genesis 18:14 says that nothing is too hard for the Lord. We love and trust you. Hush our clamorous anxiety. Please quieten us with your love according to Zephaniah 3:17.

What can I say about the beautiful readiness of Dawn and Tony Bernstein and their daughter, Jacquie, to take John into their home for six months until his school education was complete? They received him as one of their own. What a gift this was to us as a family. The Bernsteins cared for him, checked up on him, but above all allowed him to feel at home. Add to this the many at Wellington City Corps who took an interest in him. The Lord had provided yet again.

From first arriving in Wellington we felt a strong empathy with the Army's ministry among the Maori, the *tangata whenua*, the indigenous peoples of New Zealand who, according to legend, came 1,000 years ago from a mythical Polynesian homeland. They comprise 14 per cent of New Zealand's population. Early Salvationist pioneers reached out to these indigenous peoples but the culture of the Army was not always an easy fit with Maori ways. Our systems, structure and quasi-military expression needed to be rendered more flexible if Maori converts were to feel at ease.

After careful consultations we were able to relaunch the Maori ministries in late November 2003. A building and ground were set aside at Wanganui where the first Army contact with the Maori had taken place. We invited any and all from across the territory to attend. Captains Wayne and Harriet Moses, and later Auxiliary-Captains Joe and Nan Patea, were appointed to lead the Maori work. They were free to travel the length and breadth of New Zealand to contact and inspire, and hopefully lead to faith and recruit, those who shared their ethnic identity.

The public relaunching of the Maori ministries at Wanganui was a tremendous experience. How wonderful when Helen rose to speak and did so without notes in perfect Maori, telling of her family history, her place of origin, and offering according to Maori custom details of her antecedents and present family. You could have heard a pin drop. When she finished the entire Maori congregation rose to their feet to clap and cheer. What a moment! I felt as though I might burst with pride. Still today Helen's words are remembered by our Maori comrades, for when she died they wrote to tell me so. She had shown them deep cultural respect, sometimes a rare and precious commodity.

The New Year of 2004 saw us on furlough in Ilminster, Somerset, and in London. Our appointments to the UK were made known publicly at the end of January. We returned to Wellington and soon thereafter were pleased to welcome the Chief of the Staff, Commissioner Israel Gaither, and Commissioner Eva Gaither to the territory. I had recommended the award of the Order of the Founder to Lieut-Colonels Lance and Faye Rive jointly. The presentation to them in Auckland by Commissioner Gaither proved to be a highlight of the visit.

After a weekend spent at the two southernmost corps in New Zealand, Invercargill and Clifton (yes, Clifton!), Helen and I travelled in late April to New York for a plenary gathering of the GCC. There I delivered, at General Larsson's request, the same paper on Salvationist core values given at the GCC in London five months earlier, but I need to record honestly that it fell rather flat. Far better were the visits we made to Battery Park and the Railton Memorial there, and also to 'Ground Zero', the site of the World Trade Center atrocity of September 2001. We felt moved and privileged to stand in both places.

It was customary for an outgoing territorial commander in New Zealand to have a photographic portrait prepared and placed alongside pictures of all the previous (exclusively male) territorial commanders. I broke with tradition and placed on view a photograph showing both Helen and me. When it was unveiled at headquarters during morning prayers there was a spontaneous outburst of approving applause. Another innovative moment, even if a small one. I had earlier moved all of the territorial commander photographs out of the seclusion of the boardroom to a place of greater visibility in one of the corridors, allowing me to use the boardroom walls for framed depictions of moments from the life of Christ. These helped to keep us focused on the main thing during board meetings as we poured over our agendas and balance sheets.

Duly we dropped off John at the home of the Bernstein family and left New Zealand on Sunday 23 May 2004. London beckoned.

Journal, 17 April 2004: Before leaving Wellington I asked my private secretary, Major Joyce Langdon, to add up my travel over the last 27 months in connection with formal speaking engagements, etc. I have undertaken: 155 air journeys, both within and beyond New Zealand; 94 car journeys; two helicopter trips; two sea ferry voyages. Quite a few miles! It is the Lord who has placed these open doors of service before me. I leave it all with him.

Journal, 21 May 2004: We have only two nights left in our Wellington house. It has been a wonderful home to us, a real blessing. The view is beyond equal. The territory has gifted us with a framed panorama of this view as a parting present. It stretches out over Lyall Bay, across the airport and to the hills beyond. Lieut-Colonel Wilfred Arnold arranged it on behalf of the Chief Secretary and it was unveiled at our farewell meeting at the office yesterday. Another blessing.

I have presented Major Joyce Langdon with a Certificate in Recognition of Exceptional Service for her splendid help to seven territorial commanders over a period of 20 years. This was presented at our public farewell meeting and most warmly received. Three further similar awards were made to faithful local officers, including Bandmaster Eric Geddes.

This is my final Journal entry in New Zealand. Dear God, thank you for bringing us here and using us here. Forgive my sins of commission and omission in this place. Cleanse me and prepare me for service as your servant in the UK and Ireland.

Enfold our son, John, in your care. I love him. Thank you for Helen. Guard Jen and Marcus who will soon come to Wellington as cadets, and bless little Hudson too. Bless our new proximity to Matt, Lynne and Hannah. I'm glad I'm a salvation soldier.

ESSAY 7A

❧

SPEAKING

ESSAY 7A
SPEAKING

EARLY in my officership I confided to Colonel Catherine Baird, then our neighbour in Balham, south London, that each time I was due to speak in public I grew quietly but increasingly nervous as the moment drew near, with 'butterflies' in my stomach. Her counsel was blunt and wise: 'When you no longer feel like that it is time to stop!' Well, it has gone on now for years and is still the same, so I suppose it is not yet time to stop. Nerves can be mastered and put to creative, positive use. If you are a servant of the Lord they are also a frequent and needful reminder that, when you speak for him, you do so not in your own power, but in his strength. Paul's words in 2 Timothy 4:17 have come to me again and again both before and after speaking: 'The Lord stood at my side and gave me strength.'

This Essay (ending with an Excursus) looks at my experiences in speaking to Salvationists and others when preaching and teaching. After that I want to record also something of those occasions when I have been asked to speak *for* Salvationists and on behalf of the Army in situations calling for advocacy. So Essay 7B which follows next covers my time as the legal and parliamentary adviser to the General at International Headquarters (IHQ). The final segment of the same Essay is about my writing. This is speaking, as it were, through the printed page. I also take the risk of including some mention of my half-hearted attempts at poetry!

Preaching

My calling has always been at root a calling to speak for Christ. Preaching and speaking for God are vocations we can trace back to the Old Testament. Only the certainty of that call can keep God's person sure and true amid strife and slander, and even in the face of temptation to choose another path. Moreover, the place given to preaching in the Protestant – and thus in the Salvationist – tradition has meant that I have never been even remotely drawn to contemplate the exercise of my calling in a setting other than the Army. I was called not only to Christian ministry but to ministry in the Army. They say of Salvationists (and under

God's direction we affirm it of ourselves) that we adopt no outward sacrament. I do assent, however, to the assertion of P.T. Forsyth (*Positive Preaching and Modern Mind*) that 'the great, the fundamental, sacrament is the Sacrament of the Word'.

In saying that preaching is a large part of my sacred calling I do not mean that this makes me a fine preacher. Eloquent or not, articulate or not, impressive or not, if you are called to preach then preach you must. It is not brilliance that matters, but obedience. So God's speaker rises and stands in weakness, though assured of the divine readiness to take and use what has been prepared in the quiet place and which must now be declared before the people.

Furthermore, I have perceived my calling to be not only to preach but to preach for a verdict. The matter is too urgent and the need of the human heart too great for the preacher to indulge in ear-tickling peroration. The people may or may not expect to be entertained, and may or may not sit in judgement upon the preacher of the day. Whatever their expectations, the message must be of God and intentionally aimed at the hearts of the listeners. Preaching is not about entertainment. Humour and anecdote have their place, but as soon as they become the meat rather than the gravy the preacher has failed.

I need now to quote Dietrich Bonhoeffer and do so from his 1960 *Christology* (*Gesammelte Schriften*) and the section entitled 'Christ as Word': 'Preaching is the riches and the poverty of the church. It is the form of the presence of Christ to which we are bound and to which we have to keep. If the whole Christ is not in the preaching then the church breaks in pieces…. Man's word of preaching is the Word of God by virtue of God's voluntary association, by which he has bound himself to the word of man…. So Christ is present in the church as the spoken Word, not as music and not as art. He is present as the spoken Word of judgement and forgiveness. Two things must be said here with equal emphasis: "I could not preach if I did not know that I was speaking the *Word of God*"; and: "I could not preach did I not know that *I* were not speaking the Word of God." Human impossibility and God's promise are one and the same.'

When this was first underlined by me in my copy of the book I hardly understood it, but for some reason it leapt off the pages and spoke to me.

I was then but a cadet in training. Now, many years on and countless preachments later, I am beginning to grasp its depths.

A sacred calling is no excuse for being casual or slapdash and so I have long ago taken an organised and systematic approach to the preparation and cataloguing to my sermons. Like William Booth, I have been prepared to preach broadly the same sermon in different places as long as its message still burned in my heart. My habit is to record on the reverse of my notes the place, the date, the occasion and any additional useful factors.

Many of my notes are outlines only. I have studiously avoided, as best I could, preaching from a full verbatim script and have found moreover that when doing so the result is often stilted. My notes can be very brief, perhaps only a few key words or sentences plus Scripture references. This has meant that translators or editors hoping to see the full script of a sermon in advance have often had to settle, in the case of translators, for an outline briefing before the meeting and, in the case of editors, for note-taking by themselves during delivery.

Unlike some brave preachers I never discard any notes of any kind. Everything is catalogued and filed away. Some sermons get preached once, others more often. I suppose my files house about 800 sermons and this does not include copious material used for conferences, seminars or lectures (see below).

During the five years of my tenure as the General I rose to speak on five continents in public on 650 occasions, an average of 10 or 11 speaking commitments per month. Add in frequent media interviews, plus regular writing commitments, and some idea will emerge of the demands we place upon our Generals, even before taking into account the primary role of the General which is to determine under God not so much his own travel plans but the direction of travel for a global Army, overseeing key boards and being available for face-to-face consultations at IHQ, where policy is discussed and finalised. All this, and jetlag has not even been mentioned yet!

The first sermon I preached in our first appointment (to Burnt Oak Corps in north London) while we were still second-year cadets (they called us 'Cadet-Lieutenants' until Commissioning Day came along) was delivered on Sunday 28 May 1972. It was based on 1 Corinthians 1:23, 27 (*Revised Standard Version*): 'But we preach Christ crucified....God chose what is weak in the world to shame the strong.' Paul was referring to his own weak and nervous preaching so it was an apt choice for a novice preacher newly arrived from the training college at London's Denmark Hill. There were six people present. One of them was me, so five heard the sermon! Five or five thousand, the preacher's sacred obligations are the same. The need for careful, prayerful preparation is constantly present. There is, moreover, a sense in which it takes more to preach to five than to five thousand. The smaller the congregation, the more intimate the interaction between speaker and hearers. It is a subtle thing.

My preacher father would often say that if you are doing things properly when preaching then you expend as much energy as doing an eight hours shift of manual labour. Even if this was not to be taken literally, it holds much truth. More often than not I have concluded a meeting feeling utterly spent, even when at the height of my physical powers. Usually there then follows the handshaking as the congregation leaves. Sometimes this can take quite a time, so the upshot can be fatigue on departing the venue, with only a few hours before the next public appearance, these hours holding the further expectation that you will socialise over a meal and interact energetically throughout. Other than those close to you, few grasp any of this. I mention it here merely to describe it. It is the cost of being called to preach and must be borne with poise and patience.

Certain preaching experiences somehow stand out in my mind. Let me recall some of these. Come first with me to the seaside and to Boscombe Corps on England's south coast. Each year an Easter Convention takes place and folk gather from near and far, enjoying also springtime near the sea. It was long the custom for the invited leaders and preachers to be of the rank of commissioner (or above!) but back in 1984 Major Handel Everett, the corps officer, decided to break with tradition and invited Captain and Mrs Shaw and Helen Clifton to lead the weekend. The guest musical section was the Upper Norwood Band under Major George Whittingham.

In those days the Saturday evening and Sunday meetings were held in Bournemouth Town Hall in order to accommodate the Easter crowds. It was all rather daunting but we felt blessed and honoured to be invited. So I found myself preaching twice on Good Friday and again twice on

Easter Day. What a marvellous calling it is to declare the message of Calvary and of Resurrection! Before we left Boscombe that year we were asked if we would return for the 1986 Convention at which the Enfield Citadel Band under James Williams would also take part. It was not hard to say yes. The invitation was graciously renewed yet again for 1994. Later Majors Peter and Val Mylechreest invited us to lead the Convention in 2007 as the Army's world leaders.

Other visits to Boscombe took place in 1988 and 1989 for Bible Sunday meetings. We were there on furlough in the summer of 1992 when a message reached us at our hotel to say arrangements for the leadership of the following Sunday's meetings had broken down and would we step in at short notice? We did so, but had not taken our uniforms to the seaside. It was the first and last time that I led meetings and preached in civvies. At least I had packed a tie! The corps folk were very understanding!

Although we were never given appointments which held direct responsibility for children or youth, it was a tremendous thing to be asked to lead special events catering for these age groups (14 to 30 years). Between 1982 and 1993, until just before we left England for Boston, USA, we found ourselves as the invited guest speakers at no fewer than 18 divisional youth councils weekends. A Saturday and Sunday would see young people gathering from across the division (there were then 25 divisions in the UK).

Working closely with divisional youth secretaries (DYS) in planning these events we came to admire the skill and dedication of so many young, gifted officers as they sought to cater for the spiritual and social needs of their youthful comrades. Often we would factor into the planning ample time to discuss the pressing moral issues of the day such as abortion, divorce, human sexuality and nuclear weapons. This, combined with excellent music, candid preaching and good audience participation would culminate in many clear-cut decisions at the Mercy Seat (the place set aside for response and prayer). God seemed to use it all.

Typical of the many caring and passionate, indeed excellent, DYSs at that time were Captains Anthony and Gillian Cotterill who received us in the Birmingham Division in 1993. It was so easy to work with them and to feel encouraged by being at their side. I have often wondered why the position of DYS was abolished (soon after we left the UK in 1995). Losing officers in this role and replacing them with sincere but junior employees, some of whom were not committed Salvationists, has not always enhanced our mission to youth and partly explains the now diminished numbers in our UK cadet training sessions. Furthermore, employment law hampers any desire to re-officer our youth work at divisional level.

Statistics show that where much intentionality is found with regard to candidates for officership and where this work is a primary (not secondary or tertiary) focus of an officer, rather than an employee, the flow of candidates continues healthily. The recently productive work of Lieut-Colonel Gillian Cotterill in the London South-East Division is a case in point. God grant that in the land of the Army's birth we shall see again training sessions numbering at least sufficient cadets to take the place of the 60 or so officers who enter retirement each year. When the number of retired officers in a territory exceeds the active officers we need to hear the ring of warning bells and turn to God for guidance. It is no answer to say, as I have heard, 'It is God's business, not ours,' or 'God is pruning us.' This is head-in-the-sand defeatism. Across the globe, including parts of post-modern Europe like Denmark and France, we can point to places where candidates for officership and cadet numbers are again increasing due simply to intentionality about it all on the part of visionary, dedicated officers – at corps, divisional and territorial levels.

In 1989 a marvellous door of opportunity opened up to me. I accepted an invitation from Commissioner Will Pratt, the Territorial Commander in Canada and Bermuda, to be the guest speaker at Youth Council gatherings held on the campus of the University of Guelph in May that year. A total of 1,300 young people aged 14-30, plus youth leaders, came together for three days. It was a hectic time in our lives. We were under farewell orders and packing up, after seven years, to move from my legal role at IHQ to go to Bromley Temple Corps in the south-east of London. We had led the officers' residential retreat at Sunbury Court for the Nottingham Division early in May and I had spent four days teaching at the officers' refresher course in Finland. Small wonder then that I arrived in Guelph jaded and jetlagged, with the opening meeting taking place at 10 pm on the Friday evening! The youthful delegates were, as expected, excitable and noisy. I hardly got through that opening meeting and felt I had not truly connected with the attendees, but by the end of the weekend and with the wonderful help and encouragement of the territorial youth leaders, Majors David and Margaret Hiscock, and the members of their team it all seemed to come together. As well as the Hiscocks I must mention Majors Alf Richardson and John Cameron. How gracious and affirming these godly colleagues were to me. We rejoiced to see about 150 youthful delegates kneeling at the Mercy Seat in the final meeting of the weekend. The whole event was enhanced by the music of the contemporary gospel singer, Connie Scott.

I reached home on the evening of Monday 22 May, went into my office at IHQ the next day, lectured in ethics at the International College for Officers (ICO) two days later, and moved to Bromley with Helen and our three children on 31 May. On 19 May, in the midst of all this, we were promoted from captains to majors so needed to re-trim all our uniforms!

I want to record here my lasting gratitude to leaders at IHQ during this period of our lives when a high number of overseas invitations were coming our way over and above travel for my legal role. The Chief of the Staff, Commissioner Caughey Gauntlett, saw me in his office and said that usually the international commitments of headquarters officers had to be curtailed for practical reasons. Then, smilingly, he went on to say that I should not feel myself bound or hindered by such considerations and he would leave it to me and Helen and our good sense to decide what overseas speaking engagements to accept. Commissioner Gauntlett's successor, Commissioner Ronald Cox, took a similarly helpful view of it all.

We said yes to an invitation to spend a week ministering in Denmark in March 1991 by kind invitation of Colonel Edward Hannevik. It was one of several visits to the Army there. What trust was placed in us and what kindness we experienced. We were allowed to address the officers, to encourage a gathering of the local officers, to lead many Bible studies and to preach in evangelical rallies. We had done nothing to deserve any of it, save to say yes to the call of God.

Our son, Matt, married Lynne on 16 June 2001 in St Augustine's Parish Church in Broxbourne just north of London. Helen and I travelled from Pakistan with John to attend. It fell to me to preach at Matt's and

Lynne's request, a delightful honour. Choosing the words of Jesus from John chapter 17 verse 11 ('that they may be one') and verse 17 ('sanctify them by the truth'), and Paul's words from Colossians 3:3 ('your life is hid with Christ in God' *KJV*), I spoke from the lofty pulpit and began: 'It is an honour to be asked by Lynne and Matt to address you all today. The depth of the honour is matched only by the difficulty of preaching on the occasion of the wedding of one's own child. A certain degree of objectivity in the preacher is a most useful thing. Today that is simply not possible. I am a parent first, and only thereafter a professional. My words will inevitably be of a personal nature.'

On this occasion I preached from a full verbatim script in order to let the happy couple have a lasting record of what was said. Central to my words was this statement: 'Your deepest unity springs from *each* of you being united to Christ. He is the Vine and you are *each* a branch of that Vine.'

I had cause to be grateful to God that I was well enough to engage in public ministry again after oesophageal surgery in 2008 (see Essay 4). So it was that we made our way to the USA Southern Territory for the annual Bible Conference held at Lake Junaluska. Commissioners Max and Lennie Feener, hosting us with gentle understanding, gave us ample time and space to ourselves for rest between the meetings. Commissioners Israel and Eva Gaither, the USA national leaders, were there too, offering as always warm and gracious support. With us at Junaluska and sharing in the leading of the sessions were Lieut-Colonel Clive Adams and Major Mark Tillsley, two articulate colleagues. I spoke at some length in four sessions and Helen did so in three, taking as her theme 'In The Arena', studies on Daniel and Esther from the Old Testament and of Stephen from the Acts of the Apostles. I have published her study on Daniel in Chapter 47 of *From Her Heart* (2012). Her public speaking style was always direct but gracious. Many a time I have seen folk in congregations sit up and pay close attention to her, folk who evinced less interest when I was speaking. Such is the benefit of being called and of ministering as a team together.

Teaching

I turn now to what has been and still seems to be a key facet of my work and calling across many years. Preaching and teaching the things of

God are two closely linked tasks and frequently overlap. For now I want to reflect mainly on the opportunities to teach and to lecture.

Like preaching, it is an onerous thing to be called to a teaching ministry. The writer of the Epistle of James is explicit: 'Not many of you should become teachers. As you know, we teachers will be judged with greater strictness than others' (James 3:1 *Good News Bible*). Daunting words! Teaching the things of God (James is not referring to school teaching) incurs greater accountability. Thus the exercising of a gift of teaching in the Body of Christ is both a blessing and a burden.

Most of my teaching, at least in terms of time spent, has been carried out at the ICO in London's Sydenham. However, other rewarding moments stand out in my memory. I think of two illustrative occasions, both from the late 1980s, in North America and Australia.

In February 1988 I was allowed to spend 10 days delivering lectures, with some preaching assignments also included, in Winnipeg and Chicago. Snow hampered the flight schedules and at one point I slept for only an hour in two days. Given the huge privilege of the assignments these setbacks were minor. I recall the warmth of Captains Ray and Cathy Harris at Heritage Park Temple Corps and that of Major Greg Simmonds as he received me at Winnipeg Citadel Corps. So too the kindly encouragement and hospitality of Majors Earl and Benita Robinson, the major being President of the newly established Catherine Booth Bible College (now Booth University College), where I was able to deliver six academic lectures on ethical issues and preach at the 'Deeper Life' meeting for students and staff. This time of worship saw 20 kneeling at the college Mercy Seat.

From Winnipeg I moved on to Chicago despite long snow delays and separation from my suitcases. The Training Principal, Major Eric Britcher, received me with much cordiality as did the entire staff of the School for Officer Training. Broadly the same six lectures (I say 'broadly' for I was not using verbatim notes) as in Winnipeg were given to the cadets but my main memories are of the spiritual meetings which took place at both Norridge Citadel Corps and at the college. What a blessing to preach amid the schedule of academic lectures. The Thursday evening United Divisional Meeting for the Chicago Metropolitan Division ended with nine seekers at the Mercy Seat and at the conclusion of the Sunday evening holiness meeting at the college the Mercy Seat was lined and lined again and again. Sacred tasks, holy privilege. My files retain my three handwritten letters to Helen while in Winnipeg and Chicago:

'I've just spoken to you by telephone and it is about 4.15 am. So glad to talk to you and to hear your voice. Do pray for me. I have a sense of being out on a limb, but I've looked at Joshua 1 again and feel reassured.... I commit you and the children now, here in the small hours of a Western day, into the care of God, to whom there is no east or west to divide those who love and serve him and who has taught us that in his Son love is unconquerable. That includes our love as husband and wife and as a family all together.... I have a further sense of being sustained and of being prayed for.'

Due to a cordial invitation from Commissioner Roy Lovatt, Helen and I flew to Sydney, Australia, in late 1989 to take part in the tenth National Brengle Institute. The venue was the training college at Bexley North and the Training Principal, Lieut-Colonel Keith Parkinson, welcomed us in his capacity as President of the Institute. Our gifted co-lecturers were Lieut-Colonel Lucille Turfrey and Major Mrs Margaret Goffin. A total of 53 officers attended, most of them from the two territories that make up the Army in Australia, plus Captain and Mrs Boiva Nehaya from Papua New Guinea and Captain and Mrs Terry and Glenys Heese from New Zealand.

My role was to offer 15 lectures on the theology of the Holy Spirit and on the historical development of the Army's holiness teaching. Helen shared in leading and speaking in the worship times and served also as counsellor to the delegates. My memories are of wonderful, comradely fellowship throughout the 10 days. We worked hard and thought deeply together, but we also laughed a lot and could unwind readily, prompted by the relaxed, unstuffy social interaction of the delegates. This was our first taste of a Brengle Holiness Institute, the first of several. It changed us. It certainly changed me. The need to prepare and to think in depth about the holy life had its inevitable personal impact which I have described more fully in Essay 2. We came home to London and to our children feeling tired but content. Again we had gained more than we had given.

For many, many years the main formal outlet for my teaching has been lecturing at the ICO. This began in August 1979, a few months after we returned to the UK after four years in Africa. We found ourselves on furlough with Matt and Jen at the seaside resort of Broadstairs, Kent, when a message reached me from the ICO Principal, Colonel Victor Keanie, saying that General Frederick Coutts (Rtd) was no longer able to deliver his lectures on 'Modern Morality' and asking if I might be free to come at short notice to stand in for him. Pleased to be invited (we had barely reached the rank of captain) I drove back to our home in Enfield to gather papers and notes and also a uniform. This first experience of lecturing at the ICO was on 7 August 1979. Nervously I got through the two hours. Victor Keanie was warm and kind to this very junior colleague. Despite my nerves, I loved it. I felt at home there.

Thus began a formative relationship that was to last for many years. With an interlude of 10 years during which we were serving overseas, I was blessed to lecture to 89 sessions of officers at the ICO between 1979 and 2011. Each session consisted of 26 delegates from every continent. So I met there a total of 2,314 officers through the years. Not once did I visit the ICO without coming away enriched and having learned something new about the Army and the countless cultures in which we work. It proved a constant blessing to meet such a host of people who shared my sacred calling and yet had backgrounds and cultural origins so different from my own. I felt then, and now still remain, intensely grateful. Every visit became a further tangible reminder of the vast length of the beneficent shadows cast by William and Catherine Booth and of the marvel, the miracle of Salvationist expansion around the globe.

I always ensured that my presentations allowed time for interaction and dialogue, for I needed to learn from my fellow-officers. At first these ICO lectures focused on modern ethical issues. From a list of eight or nine subjects provided by me, the delegates would select in advance the three or four issues they would like to be addressed in depth. Later the hours allocated to this were doubled at the prompting of the delegates. From August 1984 I taught also aspects of the Army's international and legal constitutional apparatus, including the legal arrangements governing each High Council and the election of our Generals. Earlier these sessions had been conducted ably by Keith Wright, the senior partner at our external legal advisers, Messrs Slaughter and May, Solicitors.

Gradually further opportunities at the ICO opened up. From time to time specialised sessions were held: for divisional commanders; for youth secretaries; for finance officers, etc. I would find myself included in the teaching faculty. Specialist courses in Army administrative processes were also mounted and, pleased to be invited to partner the now Commissioner Victor Keanie, I shared the lecturing with him. Early in 1986 an invitation came to offer a further two hours lecturing on the theme of global peace and this went on to become for many years a fixed part of the ICO curriculum entitled 'Peace, War, and The Salvation Army' (see the Excursus below). By this time I was offering 10 hours of teaching to every ICO session plus regular lectures in ethics at the cadet training college in Denmark Hill.

Working with several ICO Principals, I found them to be colleagues of grace and intelligence: Colonel Victor Keanie, succeeded by Commissioners Leo Ward, Ingrid Lyster, David Baxendale, Edward Read and Ian Cutmore. Each of these was wonderfully supported by more-than-able assistant principals and other staff.

After we came home to London in 2004 Commissioner Margaret Sutherland invited me to resume teaching at 'The Cedars', as the ICO was known, and I was very pleased to agree. This allowed me to develop an uncomplicated presentation entitled 'Thinking Theologically about Officership'. It sought to encourage gentle reflection and re-evaluation by the delegates on their vocations as Army officers. The peaceful setting of 'The Cedars', away from the pressures and routines of their various appointments, was an ideal setting for this. The big house on Sydenham Hill, filled with sacred memories to carry home, was and remains holy ground for countless officers.

After taking office as the General, and with Helen either accompanying me or offering lectures in her own right, carving out time for visits to the ICO was treated by us as a priority. We would go to lecture, to lead Sunday worship, and to take part in open 'Questions to the General'. Still we felt the benefit and blessing of interaction with the delegates. Never did we make a visit in those five years without coming away blessed and uplifted.

I hope these reflections convey adequately the debt I owe to the Principals already mentioned and their early formative impact upon my ministry. This added to the enrichment granted by meeting the members of each ICO session. The relevance and effectiveness of the ICO is crucial to us as an Army, something that came home to me even more powerfully when serving as a member of a 1992 Working Party appointed by General Eva Burrows to review, and make formal recommendations upon, the ICO curriculum. We met under the chairmanship of Commissioner David Baxendale. I sought to make a contribution based on my personal experience, not only as a member of the teaching faulty, but also as one who had experienced at first-hand what it was like to attend and reside as a delegate, having done so in April-June 1990 (Session 126) when stationed at Bromley Temple Corps only a few miles distant from Sydenham. My chief aim was to influence Army leaders to make the curriculum much less UK-oriented and far more international and multicultural. I wanted also greater curriculum time given to spiritual reflection, for as a delegate I had benefited profoundly from the early morning Bible studies offered by the then Principal, Commissioner Edward Read, a gifted and insightful teacher of sacred things.

Excursus: War and books about war

In Essay 8 I write about books. However, I pause here to reflect on books about war, a topic on which I have often been asked to teach. I feel deep respect and even admiration for those in our ranks who, especially in the two World Wars, adhered at much personal cost to pacifist convictions (among them outstanding people like Carvosso Gauntlett, Catherine Baird, Frederick Coutts and Ben Blackwell). However, when it comes to conventional warfare I am not a pacifist. Some evildoers cannot be restrained without the use of force. This is where the Christian tradition of 'just war' thinking is helpful, though I accept that its historic principles need constant revision as weapons technology and the ruthless inventiveness of terrorists grow ever more sophisticated.

Weapons of mass destruction are altogether different. I find in my heart a deep revulsion toward them. The gap between conventional weapons and nuclear weapons, though sometimes blurred by the advent of 'mini-nukes' for so-called battlefield use, is more than a difference merely of degree. The nuclear nations, despite some reduction treaties, still possess sufficient nuclear weaponry to obliterate the entire human race. Leaving aside the obscene waste of scientific resources and funding, such weapons reveal at one and the same time humanity's cleverness and fallenness. If there can be something called nuclear-pacifism, then I am ready to be labelled a nuclear-pacifist.

In *From Hiroshima To Harrisburg – The Unholy Alliance* (1980) Jim Garrison takes us on a terrifying journey from the development and dropping of the atomic bomb on Hiroshima to the near meltdown of the nuclear reactor at Harrisburg, USA. Garrison is a persuasive author. He writes factual history with pinpoint accuracy in every detail, but his main aim is to influence the outlook of the reader concerning what the human race has done to itself and to the created order in the development of weapons of mass destruction. We were and still are and forever now will be the people who can destroy themselves and their own planet many, many times over.

A volume I could not put down is Craig Collie's *Nagasaki – The Massacre of the Innocent and Unknowing* (2011). The book's power is found in its direct engagement with eyewitnesses to the horrendous bombing of Nagasaki following the destruction of Hiroshima in 1945. The main portion of the study is based on personal interviews with Japanese survivors of the attack, including medical staff, newspaper publishers, students, shipyard workers and a Japanese Franciscan monk. There are also interviews with the American personnel involved, including the crew of the plane which dropped the bomb on Nagasaki. We meet members of the Japanese government. We encounter also their Emperor. There is input from American and Soviet Russian political staff. All this is a powerful mix. The reader is drawn in irresistibly to interact with a diverse cast of living, eyewitness characters. Interestingly, hardly any two witnesses give matching accounts of what happened. One of the most moving passages of the book focuses on the night before the raid when the commander of the bomber aircraft sought out his Roman Catholic priest to quiz him on the morality or otherwise of what was being planned. Where do we find right and wrong in all of this? What are we to think? The profound horror of the nuclear age casts us back again and again to the Creator and his love for the fallen human race. There is the constant offer, held out to us by the One who made us, of finding our true selves, whatever our past, by means of a decisive act of self-giving in response to Heaven's love.

Three novels bring alive the awfulness, the moral complexity, and the human challenge of war. Nevil Shute's *On the Beach* (1957) is set in south-eastern Australia in the aftermath of a nuclear holocaust. The rest of the planet has been laid waste in a spasm of mutual mass destruction and now the earth's weather systems are carrying the radiation-laden winds inexorably toward the last surviving towns and cities. It is a troubling novel. So too is Morris West's 1981 *The Clowns of God*. Here the survivors of nuclear war are in Europe and among them is discovered, in human form again, the returning Christ. West wrestles with politics, morality, religion and much more in a narrative that even if read two or three times still disturbs and yet rewards the reader. The third work is *Birdsong* by Sebastian Faulks, first published in 1993. Set in the trenches of France in the First World War, it conveys the agony and futility of the massive loss of life in the cause of gaining or regaining just a cluster of muddy fields. The horrors of conventional warfare are conveyed all too powerfully. Why 'Birdsong'? Because in the fields of battle there was none.

War poetry, mostly arising from the 1914-18 World War, has long ago found its place in my heart and mind. The poems of Wilfred Owen still retain their power after nearly a century. Owen was killed, aged 25, only a week before the November 1918 armistice. He had said, 'All a poet can do today is warn.'

G.A. Studdert Kennedy was both poet and military chaplain in this same war and carried the nickname of 'Woodbine Willie'. Woodbines were a brand of cigarette which he distributed to the soldiers. Helen never got to know her maternal Uncle Harry (Willis) for he was killed in Singapore in the Second World War. His mother (Helen's grandmother), Eliza Willis, received news of his death by telegram from the War Office, a procedure captured by Kennedy in his stunning short poem, 'A Scrap of Paper':

> 'Just a little scrap of paper
> In a yellow envelope,
> And the whole world is a ruin,
> Even hope.'

As I quote these lines, my soul rises up in agonised prayer for those caught up in the strife of war. I ask also for an ongoing absence of strife in all of my own personal relationships.

ESSAY 7B

❧

SPEAKING

ESSAY 7B
SPEAKING

NOT all speaking for Christ is done from the platform or indeed in a public setting. Neither is it all done with the lips. Sometimes it is the pen that speaks. This Essay is about speaking in advocacy and in offering advice in the seven years spent as the legal adviser at International Headquarters (IHQ). It is also about speaking through the written word.

Back to the law

Eleven years had passed since leaving the lectureship in law at Bristol University. Time as cadets, service in Africa, and just over three happy years at Enfield Citadel Corps meant of course that my close knowledge of things legal had grown stale. You never forget the basics, but the law changes on a daily basis and if you are not involved regularly you grow rapidly out of touch.

Word reached us that we were to farewell from Enfield and become part of IHQ as of mid-1982. No appointment was mentioned for Helen. I was to succeed the very able Major Bramwell Baird (who held a Master of Laws degree) as the Legal Secretary (later the Legal and Parliamentary Secretary) attached to the central Secretary's Department and directly accountable to the Chief of the Staff. It was a privileged role.

Yes, the intervening years had left me rusty on the law, but it was not too long before I felt comfortable. Like riding a bicycle after a long time off, you wobble at first, but soon you are steady. I was expected to handle matters involving an unusually wide range of legal aspects. Normally a legal office will have individual specialists in various fields of the law, but I was expected to know a little about everything! The key was not to attempt quick, on-the-spot answers but to take time to ponder and research. Moreover, for the really specialised issues I had recourse to our official external legal advisers, Messrs Slaughter and May and the senior partner, Keith Wright. In recent years their Richard Clark has been an invaluable resource and support to the Army. For matters in Scotland we used Messrs Norwell and McKay, where Robert Forman was unfailingly helpful. In parliamentary matters I could turn to the admirable Jeremy Francis or to Paul Thompson of Dyson, Bell and Co, specialists in the complex processes of the British legislature. Completing our external advisers was Richard Rosser who provided notarial services and was frequently called upon for the processing of legal documents drafted by me, signed and sealed by the General, and then sent out to senior leaders in legal jurisdictions overseas.

Despite this array of expert outside help, my office handled 90 per cent of matters internally. My secretary, Mrs Jean Wilson, worked tirelessly as did my clerks, Peter Jones and later Grahame Whitehead. They kept things ticking over very well on the many occasions I had to travel overseas. Five principal obligations fell to me.

First in priority was the proffering of advice to the General and the Chief of the Staff concerning the Army's legal status and constitutional machinery in every land where the Army was present (see Chapter 11 of my 2010 *Selected Writings – Volume 1, 1974-99* for an overview of our legal constitutions worldwide, with similar processes and mechanisms still in use by the Army today). This work brought me into frequent contact with the overseas departments at IHQ and I came quickly to appreciate the excellent under-secretaries in the zonal offices at that time. A key to their success was their longer-than-usual duration in these appointments. Their corporate memory and patient procedural skills made them highly effective and impressive colleagues.

Second was the interpretation and application of the Salvation Army Act 1980, our principal constitutional document for IHQ as well as for the Army in the United Kingdom. The Act provides, among other things, the legal framework for the election (or removal) of Generals of The Salvation Army.

My third main duty was to be a resource to territorial leaders globally in any matter touching the fundamental legal status of the Army in the country or countries making up the territory, and to work with local legal advisers on any such problems that arose. This meant that sometimes I would draft legal and constitutional documents to safeguard our legitimacy in lands overseas, ensuring that in every case the primacy of the General was guaranteed by the constitution as well as securing our Christian identity based on the Eleven Doctrines.

The fourth role was to advise the British Territory and the British Commissioner in all things legal. Later there came significant structural reform when the United Kingdom Territory was created. My office served as one of the key resources in the planning for this historic change. The main day-to-day need of the territory was for guidance in employment law, contract law, and regrettably in criminal law as well.

My fifth and final responsibility was to speak for the Army to the UK Government and to Parliament at Westminster whenever we wished to influence the shape of legislation. This could arise in connection with public bills on matters of social policy, for example on prostitution, drugs, the welfare of children, and so on. It arose also whenever our freedom of the streets and of public religious witness came under threat, on which see below. It was my responsibility also to monitor private bills, often sponsored by city councils or other local government bodies, to ensure Army interests would not be adversely impacted.

So I had my hands full! Not once did I wish it otherwise. The role stretched and stimulated me. I kept Day Books throughout these seven years. Still in my possession, they record every conversation and every telephone call or meeting, giving a short record of the matter discussed. These five volumes record a total of 9,932 such encounters!

Getting going

The initial Day Book records that on the morning of my first day at IHQ, 20 May 1982, I met with Major Geoffrey Havercroft from the Reliance Bank Limited, received Commissioner Eva Burrows, then the Territorial Commander (TC) in Scotland, to discuss a key piece of Scottish legislation, spoke by telephone to the Portuguese Consulate in London, and advised Captain Ann Woodall on fiscal matters in Zaire. In the afternoon I met Jeremy Francis of Dyson, Bell and Co before he and I took Commissioner Burrows with us for discussions with the Minister of State at the Scottish Office in Whitehall on the impact upon our open-air witness in Scotland of the Civic Government (Scotland) Bill. It was a good meeting. We won our point and the Bill was in due course amended in the terms we needed.

For my first full week at IHQ my Day Book includes the following:

Monday:
- settle into new office;
- meet General Jarl Wahlström to discuss payment of the General's allowances and the General's Trust Fund, our constitutional structures in the USA, sexual orientation issues in Canada, our regulations on marriage and divorce, and the intended length of my appointment at IHQ.

Tuesday:
- coffee with Commissioner Denis Hunter to discuss my transfer to IHQ, the Nationwide Initiative in Evangelism and my representing the Army therein, and personnel matters in the British Territory;
- meet Colonel Ronald Sketcher, Finance Secretary, on Social Trust assets;
- meet Major Peter Chang, Under-Secretary, on legal matters in Japan.

Wednesday:
- problems with a British hall keeper's contract of employment;
- Colonel Will Layton, Chief Secretary, on a claim for unfair dismissal;
- visit to the Charity Commissioners in Ryder Street for lunch and introductory discussions;
- Major Michael Pressland, Candidates Secretary, regarding officer candidates with criminal records;
- Major Audrey Neal and my participation in the Corps Cadets' Seminar at Sunbury Court.

Thursday:
- see the Chief of the Staff regarding the Army and other churches working in Israel;
- advise on legal aspects of a dry rot problem at Plymouth Goodwill Centre;
- offer advice on the law of divorce to a comrade officer.

Friday:
- contact Scottish solicitors regarding a road accident claim.

My feet had hardly touched the ground! I look at my Day Book entries for several days one year later in mid-1983 to find as follows:

- draft a statement for General Wahlström on nuclear disarmament;
- advice to the international auditors on our work in Spain;
- prepare to lead meetings in Denmark (28 April-9 May);
- advice to the British Territory on officers giving evidence in criminal trials;
- our constitutional arrangements in the Republic of Ireland;
- advice to Colonel Douglas Kiff of Reliance Bank Limited;
- contact the police at New Scotland Yard regarding criminal records;
- draft legal documents for use in Holland and Denmark;
- plan and deliver lectures at the International College for Officers;
- attend meetings as a member of the International Doctrine Council;
- work on our legal constitution for the European School for Officer Training;
- draft wills for retired officers;
- plan social ethics seminar for Norwich Citadel Corps and Major Alan Atherton;
- advise IHQ leadership about the ongoing administration of the Army in the case of a major international emergency, including nuclear attack;
- discussions on proposal to offer a knighthood to the TC in New Zealand, Commissioner Dean Goffin;
- problems regarding the officers' pension fund in Sweden.

From day to day it was simply impossible to predict the issues that would crop up. I liked that.

The General

It was a rare privilege as a young captain to have ready access to the General, whether being sent for or at my request. Not once in those seven years did it ever occur to me to think I might one day occupy the General's chair. However, regular contact with Generals Wahlström and Burrows taught me much. I came to appreciate their breadth of vision and their valuing of people. I liked also their sanctified ordinariness and approachability when meeting them one-to-one.

Routinely the General needs to seal and sign legal documents, so I would often go in to obtain the needed signature on commissions for TCs (a corresponding bond would be signed and returned by the recipient) and on power of attorney documents by which the General delegates legal powers to his or her local representative overseas. Not once did either General demur or even raise a question about the contents of any such document. It seems my work was trusted. I confess that later, when I was the one having to sign, I felt at liberty now and then to press gently for further details on the content of the documents and I always scanned through the powers of attorney before signing them.

There is a particularly sensitive and burdensome duty imposed on our Generals and this is in relation to Commissions of Inquiry. I am glad to say that these were convened only rarely, for such a Commission is held mainly when an officer is accused of serious wrongdoing. If he or she is found culpable, there is an automatic right of appeal to the General, who can reverse or uphold any finding of guilt and can affirm, soften or abandon any sanction recommended by the officers constituting the Commission's membership. When an appeal is launched the bulky files, holding all the papers and a verbatim transcript of the proceedings, are forwarded via the relevant overseas department to the office of the General. My role on such occasions was to read the entire record, make a written synopsis for the General, and recommend possible responses. I admired the calm and intuitive wisdom I saw demonstrated on such occasions and remembered it in later years when similar appeals came to me.

A very serious and potentially damaging crisis arose in Spain early in my service in the legal office. Work to solve the problems extended over many months (from early 1982 to April 1983) and took me on several occasions to Madrid, Valencia and Barcelona. I still have my hardback notebook recording in detail the daily activities and outcomes of these visits. I remember clearly the fine work and good spirit of Majors Siegfried and Lise Clausen, who hosted me on these occasions and handled the sensitive pastoral matters with patient love and more than a little skill.

An untrained and inexperienced local officer of Spanish nationality but living in Switzerland was suddenly commissioned to the substantive rank of captain by General Arnold Brown in a public meeting and therewith sent to Madrid to open the work of the Army in Spain. The new captain was energetic and imaginative but failed to consult or inform his leaders when seeking to register a legal constitution in Madrid. Unknown to IHQ he registered a constitution which stated that the officer in charge of the work in Spain had to be of Spanish nationality as well as having been an Army soldier for a minimum of 15 years. He intended that, of all the officers worldwide, only the captain himself would satisfy these conditions. The legal body created and registered by him inappropriately included his wife, his daughter and his son-in-law as his co-directors. These younger persons were resident not in Spain but in Switzerland. All three then signed over to the captain sole and exclusive delegated powers to control the Army's assets in Spain. Nothing of all this was shared with IHQ. It was entirely irregular, unprecedented and unauthorised.

I uncovered these events almost by accident during one of my visits to Madrid and Barcelona, but the captain refused persistently to regularise matters. A long process was then set in motion to recover control of our assets and place them under the direction of Major Siegfried Clausen (sent in by the General to replace the captain) and others approved by the General. It was my task to sort it all out. General Wahlström said that if need be he would close down the work in Spain until the matter was resolved and then go in again after a due lapse of time. It was my hope that such measures could be avoided.

We engaged the services of a Spanish attorney, Señor Jesús Ortiz, who had met and admired the Army when studying in America. Crucially, he had good contacts with senior staff in the Ministry of Justice and its Department of Religious Affairs where church constitutions were registered. General Wahlström had given me a free hand to do whatever was necessary to recover control of our fledgling work in Spain. The Clausens were positive, patient and wise throughout these trying months. I recall sitting in their apartment in Madrid and out of my head drafting longhand on a yellow legal pad an entirely new constitution for our work in Spain. In due course this became the first constitution to be registered at the Ministry with the approval of the General. Among much else it spelled out the relationship of the Army in Spain to IHQ, affirmed the authority of the General, and stated the centrality of our Articles of Faith which were recited in full.

The errant captain was treated with dignity despite his actions and was allowed by the General to take early retirement. Throughout this long saga I was helped, indeed impressed, by the quietly dignified but very determined intentions of General Wahlström together with the firm support of Commissioner Caughey Gauntlett, Chief of the Staff, and of Commissioner Anna Hannevik, the International Secretary for Europe.

As General Wahlström's term in office drew to a close a High Council was duly and constitutionally convened by Commissioner Gauntlett to meet at Sunbury-on-Thames near London in the early summer of 1986. It fell to me to prepare the preliminary documents and to draft a memorandum of procedural guidance for the officer elected to serve as President of the High Council. This proved to be Commissioner Norman Marshall, with whom I had already had fruitful dealings and whose election as President served to reassure me that matters would be in wise and godly hands. I was present in the Council chamber for the opening session and, when called upon to do so by the Chief of the Staff, confirmed formally that by the grace of God the High Council was properly and lawfully convened. Election of the President and other office-holders ensued.

Commissioner Marshall at once asked me to meet him in the privacy of his room and together we went through my memorandum of guidance, pointing out various ambiguities or complexities in the processes. We focused carefully on the voting majorities needed to bring about a conclusive and lawful election and on how to calculate the minimum votes required, given the number of officers who would vote. The commissioner privately arranged for the minutes of each day's proceedings to be sent to me by express courier. Accordingly, once it was known who had accepted a nomination to stand for election, I was able to prepare the requisite number of Deeds of Acceptance of Office (one for each candidate) for use as soon as a conclusive ballot was confirmed. Seven members agreed to stand, but of course only one Deed of Acceptance would ever be signed. The others would be destroyed.

Decision day was 2 May, a Friday. I drove early to Sunbury Court and waited alone in the main lounge for the voting to be finalised. Eventually the Recorder, Colonel Lyndon Taylor (whom I had always admired and who had been helpful to me when I was a cadet in training – see Essay 13) emerged and in whispered tones invited me to enter the Council chamber. I asked him, also in a whisper, who had been elected but he declined to tell me, feeling instinctively bound by a duty of confidentiality. Quietly I explained that I had all seven Deeds of Acceptance with me and needed to bring into the chamber only the correct one for presentation to the Council. After a further lengthy pause he murmured simply, 'Commissioner Burrows.'

The rest was straightforward. I went in and with the permission of the President proffered the Deed to Commissioner Eva Burrows. Beginning now to relax a little after the tension of the balloting and seated beside the President on the dais, duly she signed, becoming in that moment the General-elect. Notarised copies of the Deed would be sent out from my office to all parts of the Army world. My final task was to move from member to member in strict order of seniority to obtain their signatures on an informal but traditionally important document which declared each member's support and loyalty toward the General-elect. Eva Burrows took office on 9 July 1986. I had a new boss!

This outline account of speaking advice to assist the General ought not to omit the matter of formulating orders and regulations on the tender subject of divorce and separation by Salvationist married couples. Well before joining the staff of IHQ in 1982 I had been made a member of a Study Commission convened by General Arnold Brown. Chaired by Commissioner Norman Marshall, then the International Secretary for the Americas, the members met on 13 February 1979 for an inaugural meeting in the General's Advisory Council Room at Queen Victoria Street. General Brown entered the room and sat at the head of the table. His autobiography, *The Gate and The Light* (1984) contains an entire chapter, Chapter 19, devoted to the vexed question of introducing new regulations on divorce. It had never been done before.

The 1984 account does not explain the dramatic legal and cultural changes which swept across many Western countries in the 1960s and 1970s. Prior to that, most legal systems permitting divorce (some historically Roman Catholic countries had no law at all on divorce) recognised the reality of marital strife and the need sometimes to end a failed marriage, but the processes were often slow, expensive and involved harrowing appearances in court by both spouses. Many countries thus began to enact new laws which made divorce procedurally less humiliating and far less costly. Furthermore, the legal processes were greatly speeded up. For example, the British Parliament passed the Divorce Reform Act 1969 which abolished the old concept of matrimonial offences as grounds for divorce and made the sole criterion whether or not the marriage had irretrievably broken down. The results were revolutionary. The number of divorces rose rapidly, suggesting that many failed marriages had remained tokenly and visibly intact only because the legal processes required to end them had been costly and enervating. Inevitably, The Salvation Army was impacted by these social shifts and the incidence of Salvationist divorces, especially in Western countries, began to rise significantly.

It was against this background that General Brown addressed us in the Advisory Council Room. Earlier he had spoken in public to thousands of officers at Wembley, London, in 1978 at an International Congress event and had expressed heartfelt concerns for the sanctity of marriage and the place in our lives of the making of sacred covenants. Some officers present, who had experienced what it was like to be the victim of an unfaithful spouse and to undergo divorce, found the General's brave remarks that day inevitably a cause for pain. Now wisely he was consulting our group and asking for advice on what regulations might be introduced to be applied when Salvationists turned to the divorce courts or lived apart without ending their marriage.

I recall his remarks with great clarity. I was a young captain recently returned from Africa and had never sat in a boardroom with a General! I paid close attention to every word and made my own informal notes. The General's account in *The Gate and The Light* speaks generously of the work of the Commission, but omits one crucial fact. In addressing us the General made it clear that he wanted us to produce a regulatory tool that would make it all but impossible to be a divorced person and also be active in service as an officer of the Army. This startled me. He went on to say that he needed a regulation that could be applied globally so that similar cases of marital breakdown would be treated in similar manner from country to country, irrespective of the personal views about divorce, liberal or otherwise, held by the leader dealing with the case. I saw at once the need for an international regulatory approach, but felt unsure in my heart about how tough it needed to be.

So it came about that after several meetings of the Commission it fell to me to draft a regulation in keeping with the General's instructions. I did so without conviction in the matter and simply as a junior officer working to the General's brief. Eventually a final draft was placed before the General. It created Matrimonial Review Boards in every division but separated clearly the disciplinary function of leaders from the clear need for high quality pastoral care of the parties and of any children. General Brown liked the overall thrust of the draft and decided to have it debated at the International Conference of Leaders in Toronto in 1979. It received a markedly mixed reception. Further time was granted in the following months for every territory to examine the draft more fully and to proffer further feedback to the General. Some territories simply procrastinated and failed to respond while others welcomed the proposals.

In October 1981 a High Council came together at Sunbury-on-Thames to elect a successor to General Brown, who tabled the latest draft of the regulation for debate during the pre-High Council conference. Helen and I were at Swanwick, Derbyshire, for officers' meetings when I was told that the Chief Secretary, Colonel Will Pratt, wanted to see me. 'They want you at Sunbury Court,' he said. 'You are to leave at once.' I realised of course that this instruction arose from the planned debate on the new draft regulation which I had prepared. Leaving Alfreton Station that same afternoon at 1.30 pm, I reached London St Pancras Station by just after 4 pm and went home to Enfield to collect my car and papers. I arrived at Sunbury Court at 10 pm and slept in a bunk bed in one of the huts far from the main house and used for children's activities.

The next day I appeared at the pre-High Council event, accompanied by Major Bramwell Baird (then still the IHQ legal adviser). We sat with the members from 12 noon to 5 pm, General Brown presiding, to discuss the draft in detail and to explain the thinking behind it. It fell to me to introduce the document and to respond to questions from those present. Some of the members were gracious, but others could not conceal their impatience with the proposals. I felt at ease throughout. My role was to provide objective help to the General, not to proffer my private views. Two days later the members were publicly welcomed as the 1981 High Council. They elected Commissioner Jarl Wahlström from among the 44 members. No sooner was the election ended than General Brown promulgated the new divorce regulation. These were *Orders and Regulations Relating to Divorce, Separation, Reinstatement and Remarriage.* Some territories, not least those in the USA where the incidence of Army divorces was high, declined to circulate and implement the new system, feeling the need to take local legal advice. Others put the regulations into effect forthwith.

Soon after taking office, General Wahlström asked to see me. By now I was in post as the IHQ legal adviser. The General spoke of his sense of disquiet with regard to the new regulations and of his plans to soften some aspects with immediate effect. It was clear that his private views on divorce were different from those of his predecessor. Therefore at once I drafted the required changes and these took effect before the end of 1981. General Wahlström's next step was to convene a new working party to be called the Commission on Marriage, under the chairmanship of Commissioner Albert Scott, who had succeeded Commissioner Marshall as International Secretary for the Americas and Caribbean Zone. Again I was made a member and again it fell to me to draft a different, softer regulatory structure. This was not difficult and eventually *Orders and Regulations for Officers*, with other relevant regulations, were amended to include the new provisions. The Brown regulation was rescinded finally in June 1985.

This second regulatory structure remained in place, occasionally undergoing helpful and softening amendment, for many years until completely abolished by General Gowans. Today we have no overall guiding set of regulatory principles covering marital breakdown and divorce and have returned to a regulatory vacuum, the situation before General Brown, courageously in my view, wrestled with the matter (see also Essay 12).

A pleasing side-product of my involvement in this vexed issue was the publication in 1984 of *Growing Together – A Salvationist Guide to Courtship, Marriage and Family Life*. Helen and I edited this volume jointly and I say more about it below when reflecting on speaking through the printed word.

A new territory

Toward the end of my seven years at IHQ there arose an historic issue affecting the Army in all its aspects and expressions throughout the United Kingdom. Our structures in the land of the Army's birth, for reasons of history, had grown complex and even cumbersome. Across the years there had been sporadic minor reforms toward a more streamlined structure but none of these was sufficiently radical to address the core issue, namely the day-to-day relationship of the General to the work in the UK. For a mixture of historical, geographical and legal reasons the General was much more closely caught up in the detailed life of the UK work than was the case in relation to any other part of the Army world.

In Chapter 8 of his 2007 autobiography, *Saying Yes to Life*, General John Larsson gives us a lucid account of this background. He writes about it with authority for in 1988 he was appointed by General Burrows to devote himself to the whole matter of how IHQ and the office of the General should or could relate in a more modern and less intensely detailed way to the work and witness in the UK. Right at the heart of things were two principal tasks: 1) to identify changes that were desirable, wise and helpful to our sacred mission; 2) to identify changes that were legally possible. My help was frequently sought and I felt I was playing at least a small part in an historic reformation. When my appointment at IHQ ended in mid-1989 arrangements were made for my ongoing participation as a resource to Colonel Larsson and as a support to my successor, Captain Peter Smith.

Countless conversations and innumerable meetings later, including consultations with our external legal advisers and the UK Charity Commission, an overall plan for change was approved by the General and published in May 1990 for all to read. The new 'United Kingdom Territory with the Republic of Ireland' was duly birthed on 1 November

1990 and Colonel Larsson became its first TC with promotion to the rank of commissioner. The Chief Secretary, Colonel Ian Cutmore, was also accorded that rank. This unusual step, in part understandable in view of the size and scope of the new territory, was not treated as a binding precedent and has not been repeated.

The Salvation Army Trustee Company (SATCo) became the main legal mechanism for the day-to-day administering of the assets of the new territory rather than of the Army internationally but with the General still retaining ultimate control in accordance with the Salvation Army Act 1980. A new corporate entity was created to serve a similar purpose at IHQ. This was The Salvation Army International Trustee Company (SAITCo).

Despite these reforms, the office of the General retains a unique constitutional relationship to Army work in the UK. History has made it so. Later, as the General, I appreciated very much the spirit of comradely cooperation shown by Commissioner John Matear, whom I appointed to succeed me as the TC in London. He evinced a surefooted balance of both independence and collegiality, always ready to accept the inevitable interactions of sharing a city with the General but also exhibiting poise in the exercise of his key prerogatives as the TC.

Serving as a resource to senior officers throughout this period of complex change caused me to thank God again for those earlier years in the law when I honed my skills in the field of the English law of trusts, and especially of charitable trusts. It did the Army no harm at all whenever external advisers and government officials realised that the Army's in-house man, the lawyer in the uniform, understood things.

Running parallel to all of these changes in 1988-90 were significant discussions and consultations as to the reform of the administrative structures of IHQ. Serving there as the legal adviser from 1982 to 1989 I had no cause to think there was any pressing need for change. From my perspective things worked pretty well. However, it became clear that those more senior to me did not see it like that. My views were sought as to the possibility of change, even though by that time I had left IHQ. I valued this. I still retain a copy of a letter sent by me to the Chief of the Staff in September 1989 by way of response to an interim report on a revised international administrative structure. I wanted to highlight two matters:

the frequent turnover of senior officers at IHQ; the length of a General's term in office.

For the record this is what I said about turnover: 'During seven years at IHQ I lost count of the number of changes in senior leadership in London. I recall that after five years on the staff I tallied up some 30 or more changes in those holding the rank of commissioner or those appointed to lead the various associated headquarters. The total after seven years probably reached 40 or more such changes if the offices of the General and the Chief are included. I have no solution to the condition described, but appointing people to leadership at younger ages has to come eventually so that they stay in post longer.'

On the matter of tenure by a General I wrote: 'May I record here my ever-deepening conviction that the time is ripe for looking again at the arrangements governing the tenure of office by both the General and the Chief of the Staff. It is my view that the term for the General should be not less than seven years and that there should be no upper age limit at which the General would automatically retire. In other words, a High Council could elect any active officer whatever his or her age at the time of election and that person would serve for seven years thereafter regardless of the age to which that term of office were to take them. Present demands upon the office of General by way of travel and the present needs of the Army for truly deep and perceptive reflection as to policy and our mission and place in the world call us perhaps to reconsider these things. It is the upper age limit which is so restrictive upon us. It deprives us of a truly wide choice as each High Council meets. It means that all kinds of accumulated wisdom and hard-won experience are automatically denied the Army by an arbitrary age limit ruling out those of certain years from any chance of election.' Since this was written no reforms have ensued. When I was active as the General I contemplated initiating such changes, but in the end held off lest any initiative be seen as self-serving. I now regret that choice.

Working closely with Colonel Larsson during this time gave me reason to be grateful for his analytical skills. These, combined with his capacity for detail, afforded the Army just the right person for the task at hand. I cannot think of many then in our ranks who could have carried out the research with the same assiduity. Furthermore, I noted his not infrequent expressions of appreciation, sometimes spoken and sometimes written. How could either he or I know that years later I would succeed him in the Army's highest office for, after all, he was a commissioner and I was but a newly promoted major? Maybe Heaven was looking on back then with something approaching wry humour!

Persuading

Speaking up for the interests of the Army came readily to me. I believe God raised us up and therefore whenever I was needed as a spokesperson I had an inner sense of speaking not only for the Army but also in the strength of the One who brought us into being under the Booths. More than once while serving at IHQ it fell to me to be the voice of the Army.

In 1982 word reached me that the United Kingdom Government was in negotiation with the government of the Czech Republic to claim monetary compensation for foreign assets expropriated under former communist rule in the 1950s. I spoke to the Chief of the Staff. Commissioner Gauntlett had been born in Gablonz, Czechoslovakia, so the whole matter won his close attention. On behalf of the General he approved my plan to take advantage of the situation. Contact with the Foreign and Commonwealth Office (FCO) in London's Whitehall clarified the process. The Army could make a claim upon the Czech government by using the FCO as a go-between. The formal negotiations between the two nations had resulted in the passing of the Czechoslovakia Compensation Order whose terms allowed church organisations, among others, to claim compensation for lost assets.

Working with Major Sandy Morrice, the able Under-Secretary for Europe, we unearthed and collated as much documentary proof as we could to establish the Army's ownership of the confiscated assets. Contemporary editions of *The Salvation Army Year Book* and past audit reports showed the buildings and bank balances we had owned. I duly submitted the claim. The sums in compensation, if any, would be based on values at the time of the expropriation with no adjustment for inflation. The outcome was a cause for delight for we were awarded double the amount we had claimed. I contacted the FCO to record our pleasure and thanks but also to ask why the settlement was so generous. The official replied, 'We had money left over when all the claims were processed so we thought the Army should have it.' The monies were duly received and allocated to a special fund to provide financial assistance to those former Army officers still then living in the Czech Republic and who in troubled and persecuted times had remained faithful, even gathering in secret and whispering their songs lest they be overheard and betrayed.

Later in 1985 a similar deal was struck between the UK and China for the expropriations, also in the 1950s, made by the communist leaders there. We began work to make a further claim with explicit encouragement from the FCO who told us we were the only Christian organisation willing to seek reparation. However, it then emerged that in 1997 China would resume sovereignty over Hong Kong, where we had substantial work and assets. Leaders at IHQ had no wish to risk antagonising the Chinese authorities and so our claim was allowed to lapse. The staff of the FCO expressed some disappointment but the policy decision had been made and reluctantly I closed my file on it all, tendering warm thanks to the skilled civil servants and diplomats who had stood ready to support us.

Speaking for the Army arose again in a most unusual and unexpected way when the name of Mrs Victoria Gillick hit the media headlines. I should explain that we were closely caught up in the National Campaign for the Family (NCF), whose aims were to place marriage, children and family life once again at the centre of government social policy. The NCF was a coalition of Christians, Moslems and Jews all sharing the same societal values. I was the Army's representative to the NCF, having served briefly as its first chairman. I was a member of its executive committee and organised meetings hosted at IHQ. So when the Gillick case arose we paid close attention both as the Army and as a founder member of the NCF.

Victoria Gillick was married, had five daughters as well as several sons, and was a Roman Catholic. I found her to be an engaging, determined and devout person despite some of the more negative images of her presented in the media. In 1983 she initiated legal action seeking a declaratory judgement in the High Court to prevent medical staff who worked for the West Norfolk and Wisbech Area Health Authority from giving contraceptive advice and treatment to her daughters without her knowledge and consent while those daughters were below 16, the age of consent. The case attracted publicity and through my office the Army, instrumental in the 1885 raising of the age of consent to 16, made known its support of her cause. I gave interviews to the press and radio. We regarded the protection of underage children as vital, so we advocated for the full involvement of parents in the medical treatment of those under the age of consent, especially in relation to contraception. Furthermore, we took the view that where such a girl was prescribed the contraceptive pill it was better for a parent to know in order to ensure the (low dose) pill would be taken at the required regular intervals.

Gillick's claim was denied when the High Court judgement of Mr Justice Woolf ruled that medical confidentiality between the underage child and the doctor took precedence over the relationship between parent and child. Thus the child, even if aged only 12 or 13, could bar the doctor from contact with the parents. This seemed to me to be contrary to normal good sense and a judgement that was at root anti-family. Gillick appealed the judgement to the Court of Appeal in November 1984. On the 19th I attended those proceedings, at the Law Courts in the Strand, in uniform, accompanied by Mrs Commissioner Marjorie Gauntlett, World Secretary for the Home League. We wished to make a clear and visible signal of our interest and support. We were very pleased when the three judges in the Court of Appeal overturned the judgement of Mr Justice Woolf. It was now unlawful for doctors to prescribe contraception for children aged below 16 without parental involvement.

However, this was not the end of it. The Health Authority in turn appealed to the House of Lords Appellate Committee, then the ultimate judicial authority in the land (recently renamed, for some reason, the Supreme Court). In late 1985 a ruling was given, by the slimmest majority of the Law Lords, which upheld and restored the original judgement of Mr Justice Woolf. Gillick had lost. No stone had been left unturned to help her cause. The Army contributed a significant sum of money to facilitate the engagement of a further specialist senior barrister to plead her cause in the House of Lords. Strangely, her own church declined to speak out in her favour or to help her case in practical ways.

To this day I believe the Gillick cause was just and I feel proud that the Army stood by her. Some said that had she won her case for the involvement of parents then the girls would have stayed away from the doctors and teenage underage pregnancies would have risen sharply. Not so. Statistics for teenage pregnancies in the nine or ten months between the Court of Appeal judgement and the reversing decision in the House of Lords show fewer underage pregnancies than in either of the similar surveys taken before and afterwards. Without closer analysis I cannot explain this but I can speculate. Perhaps it was the case that during these months the doctors involved the parents and this resulted either in ending the sexual activity or, alternatively, in the efficient administration of the pill. So pregnancies went down. Alternatively, it might be that the girls stayed away from the doctors, fearing parental discovery of their relationships and as a result said 'no' more frequently to their older male companions whose sexual contact with girls so young was in any event a serious criminal offence punishable by imprisonment.

Earlier in this Essay I mentioned the Army's 1982 success in obtaining changes to the Civic Government (Scotland) Bill and the securing of our freedom of the streets in Scotland. A few years later we found ourselves having to exercise the same influence upon Prime Minister Margaret Thatcher's government in relation to our open-air activities in the then deeply troubled and violent setting of Northern Ireland. Again it fell to me to speak for the Army. Contact was made with the Northern Ireland Office after I had briefed our parliamentary agent, Jeremy Francis. Jeremy was at once understanding and supportive.

Written representations produced little to encourage us and therefore we sought and were granted a face-to-face meeting with Mr Nicholas Scott, Minister of State for Northern Ireland. This took place in the minister's office on 10 February 1987. Jeremy and I were accompanied by the Divisional Commander from Belfast, Major William Main, and Lieut-Colonel Edwin Grainger representing the British Territory's leadership and the office of the Chief Secretary. The minister was accompanied by his Permanent Secretary and his Private Secretary. It was 4.30 pm.

With the formal introductions duly completed, Jeremy outlined the Army's case for change to the draft legislative order. The minister listened courteously but said that the government had its hands very full in Northern Ireland and could ill afford any exemptions of any kind to the new measure. Prime Minister Thatcher would most certainly not be open to such an amendment. So Jeremy turned to me.

We had planned carefully what to say if our requests were not at first accepted and, with the earlier assent of the General, I told Mr Scott in respectful tones that, while we fully grasped the reasons for the new street procession laws, our freedom to engage in Christian witness on the streets of the United Kingdom, including Northern Ireland, was a non-negotiable aspect of our calling under God. I reminded the minister that Salvationists had often endured imprisonment in defence of this freedom and he should be under no illusions as to our determination. I added that I was duly authorised to say to him, and through him to the Prime Minister, that if the draft laws were not modified to exempt us from their restrictions Salvationists would march and witness on the streets of Northern Ireland in any event, in defiance of the new legislation. It would then be for the government to arrest and charge us with any resulting offence. I concluded by saying that victimising The Salvation Army was hardly a vote-winning tactic and that if we were outlawed by the new measure we would also take our case without hesitation to the media to seek their support. We would not limit our media contacts only to those in the United Kingdom but would feel free to alert others across the globe.

We paused for the minister's response. His officials looked taken aback and his body language spoke for itself as he began to shuffle about in his chair and frown. 'I thought you might say something like that,' he began. I spoke again, 'I cannot overemphasise the significance of this matter for it is about fundamental freedoms of religious expression.' He turned to his Permanent Secretary and asked for his views on whether or not our request for change to the measure was procedurally and technically possible. At that point I began to think we might have won. Jeremy Francis chipped in with skilful suggestions as to how any parliamentary or procedural obstacles might be overcome and with that the meeting ended. Courteous handshakes took place all round but we left without any explicit promise from the minister regarding our request.

Outside on the street Jeremy paused and looked at me. 'I do admire the Army, you know,' he said. 'Thank you, Jeremy, for your help and support once again,' was my reply, 'but will we get what we want?' 'Oh yes,' came the answer. 'They will change it for you. You have won.' We parted company and I returned to my office not at all sure we had won. However, a few days later Jeremy telephoned to say that he had received written word from the minister's office to inform him, and through him the Army, that the changes we wanted had now been included in the new legislation. The Salvation Army was the sole organisation to be exempted from the restrictions.

Before the year was out we found ourselves again locking horns with the British Government. This time it was caused by a major legislative initiative of the most controversial kind introduced by the talented, redoubtable, even formidable Margaret Thatcher. I refer to the 1988 Local Government Finance Act which introduced the hotly disputed 'community charge', nicknamed 'the poll tax'. The Act sought to raise local revenues by the primitive means of a headcount of every person living in each residence. The Army and other voluntary bodies were directly impacted because we would be legally obliged to collect the tax from all persons residing in our social centres, including our hostels. In due course this legislation led to street riots.

We decided that, while the measure was still in its parliamentary birthing stages as a Bill and before it was passed into law, we would seek to have it amended to exclude any adverse impact upon our widespread and historic social ministry. I thank God that Colonel Margaret White was at that time leading the social work in Great Britain and Northern Ireland. Clear-headed and determined, she worked with me and others on our strategy for exemption. The newly appointed Chief of the Staff, Commissioner Ronald Cox, agreed to see me on 10 September 1987 and, on being briefed, urged me to press on with all speed. Later in the evening of that same day, with Mrs Commissioner Hilda Cox, he was publicly welcomed and installed as part of a rousing meeting held at Camberwell Corps in south London. Commissioner Caughey Gauntlett had consistently backed me whenever we needed to do battle on legislation and I was delighted that his successor showed the same mettle and a similarly intelligent grasp of what was at stake.

I had made early contact with both the Department of the Environment and the Department of Health and Social Security to initiate dialogue on the Bill and its impact upon us. It became clear that the Prime Minister was taking a typically very tough and determined stand and our early representations, though received with courtesy, produced no real hope of us having our way. Our case was a simple one: the needy and homeless turn to us trustingly for help or refuge for many different reasons and chief among these is the plain fact that we do not represent officialdom in any way. Imposing upon us a legal duty to collect taxes from our clients threatened that relationship of trust. We would resist this happening and would simply refuse to collect the tax, leaving the government to decide on their next step.

We did all we could to spell this out to the civil servants during our early meetings. I recall one such meeting when I was accompanied by Colonel Margaret White and Colonel Gordon Sharp, Finance Secretary at IHQ. Again I put the Army's case as articulately as I could. 'Thank God for Shaw,' Colonel White was heard to murmur as we rode the lift to the street afterward. It was nice to be appreciated.

Eventually I managed to establish contact with the Under-Secretary for Social Security, Mr Michael Portillo. Portillo was then a rising star in the Conservative Party. I found him ready to listen and unfailingly courteous. He understood our position, but indicated that the minister in charge of the Bill was the Minister for Local Government, Mr Michael Howard. Howard went on later to become leader of the Conservative Party. Michael Portillo offered to arrange a meeting where we could speak to Mr Howard face-to-face. He would be fully briefed beforehand.

Things ran on and it was 28 January 1988 when the meeting took place at the House of Commons. We met initially with Mr Portillo and his staff. Mr Howard would join us later at 3.45 pm. I was fully prepared. Suddenly Mr Howard burst into Conference Room 59 pursued by several aides looking harassed and flustered. Passing over a bundle of papers to an aide, he sat down across the table from me. Mr Portillo effected the introductions and reminded the meeting of the matter to be decided. He then invited me to speak but, after only a sentence or two, Mr Howard cut me off with a scowl and a dismissive sweep of his arm. 'Write to me,' he said curtly. Thereupon, without another word, he got up and walked out, as did his cluster of nervous aides. He had been in the room for only two or three minutes. The meeting had taken months to arrange. Utterly speechless, I turned to a crestfallen and embarrassed Mr Portillo. 'Michael is a very busy person,' he muttered. 'I will speak to him again.' With that we took our leave. In all of my many meetings with politicians and government officials across the years, and around the world, I have never encountered anything like the abrupt, discourteous dismissal shown to us by Mr Howard that day.

Happily, Mr Portillo proved as good as his word. Not long after the disappointing meeting just described, a government spokesman announced on the floor of the House of Commons that amendments would be introduced to the Bill at the instance of The Salvation Army whose representations, he said, had been made in a manner which served as a role model for all such approaches to government. I sensed Mr Portillo's courtesy in this remark. Soon, and most unusually, his staff were writing and telephoning me to ask if I might be willing to assist in drafting suggested amendments to the relevant clauses to the Bill. This I did readily and in due course the new wording was agreed and included in the final Act. God's Army had won.

Seventeen years passed before I met Michael Howard again. It was 2005. By this time he was the high profile Leader of the Opposition in the House of Commons and I was leader of the Army in the United Kingdom and the Republic of Ireland. Every year in November a Service of Remembrance is held at the Cenotaph in Whitehall to honour the memory and sacrifice of those killed in war. I was there among the church leaders to represent the Army. Mr Howard was attending as the leader of a major political party. Following the brief outdoor service in the presence of Queen Elizabeth II, members of the royal family and countless diplomatic representatives a reception is customarily held in the buildings of the Foreign and Commonwealth Office. Helen had joined me there.

Noticing Mr Howard across the spacious room, I approached him and offered my hand. He shook it readily, noting my uniform. Smiling I said, 'This is not the first time we have met. You will not remember me from 1988 but we met when you were handling the poll tax legislation and I tried to put to you the Army's request for amendments to the Bill. Michael Portillo was also involved.' 'Ah, yes,' he replied, 'Michael was doing that as I recall. I do hope I was helpful to you.' What was I to say? 'Well, it was a long time ago. You seemed to be exceedingly busy, though Michael Portillo was unfailingly helpful and gracious.' He nodded his head in silence. I do not think for a moment that he remembered me. We shook hands again and I moved away in search of the Bishop of London, Richard Chartres, to thank him for the dignified service he had just led at the Cenotaph.

Soon after that Helen and I retrieved our overcoats and went down to Horse Guards Parade in time to see The Salvation Army contingent march smartly by as part of the huge procession that always follows the televised service and to hear a splendid military band strike up the Bramwell Coles stirring post-war (1919) Salvation Army march dedicated to Salvationist military service personnel who had served 'Under Two Flags', the 'Union Jack' of Great Britain and the 'yellow, red and blue' of God's Salvation Army.

The College of Arms

Situated opposite IHQ on London's Queen Victoria Street is the College of Arms. Behind the ornate, wrought iron gates sits the ancient red brick building with its dingy corridors and creaking wooden staircases. Salvation Army staff members pass it day after day going to and from their work. Many have done so for years without giving it a second thought.

New focus was brought to bear when General Burrows invited one of its senior officials, the Canadian Dr Conrad Swan, to take lunch with her at her office. It was June 1986 and the General's distinguished guest was intrigued to see the insignia of the Army in its various manifestations. Gently he enquired of the General whether or not the Army had ever sought and been given a 'Grant of Arms'. Uncertain as to the answer, the General passed the question inevitably to my office. The answer was a simple 'No'.

Oh dear, now it began. A gracious luncheon invitation became the unintentional precursor to a long, drawn-out, technical process by which the Army's historic use of insignia, not least in its crest, was to be questioned and eventually deemed unlawful. Could it be true? Regrettably, yes. The English laws of heraldry are the most ancient, and perhaps also the most obscure, of all English laws. It was in 1484 that the College of Arms was established to create and maintain official registers of coats of arms and pedigrees. The College officials are members of the Royal Household and act under Crown Authority. Its jurisdiction extends to England, Wales, Northern Ireland and to most countries of the

Commonwealth including Canada, Australia and New Zealand. When designing and implementing Salvation Army insignia, the earliest Salvationists had no inkling of any of this. In 1986 things changed when Dr Swan came to lunch!

It was clear that matters needed to be regularised. Dr Swan, a most distinguished royal official, was gracious throughout. At the same time he was quietly insistent that we put things right. It was my job to make this happen. Fees to the College of Arms would be in excess of £5,000. Though by legal cost standards this was a modest sum, neither the General nor her Chancellor of the Exchequer was pleased to learn of it. My hands were tied. The money would put us at last on the right side of the law and, crucially, would afford us legal protection for the design of our insignia in every country where the Queen was queen. Thus we set about designing a Salvation Army Coat of Arms. The General would have the right to display it on letterhead, business cards and so on. This privilege has never been taken up by any of the Generals to this day. I must confess to having thought about doing it when elected, but decided it could be taken as pretentious.

General Burrows simply left me alone to get on with designing a Coat of Arms. I was no artist, but eventually sat down with pencil and paper to make a very rough sketch. First the scroll underneath would say 'He is risen'. The centrepiece would be an open Bible. The supporting figures on either side would be one man and one woman, each kneeling, one on grass and the other on sand. One would be white, one black. One would wear Western uniform, one tropical uniform. Each would hold an Army flag. I wanted the design to speak of Jesus, of our reliance on Scripture, of our internationalism, of our quest for gender equality in ministry, and of our spirituality. Having sketched things out, I asked Major David Blackwell, Chief Architect, if he could help to make the depiction more presentable, a little more polished. Graciously he did so. I arranged to meet Dr Swan and placed the design before him. He liked it at once and told me it could remain largely unaltered. Later, to our pleasure, we discovered that never before in the long history of heraldry had kneeling human figures been used.

In due course the College completed the design production on vellum. Surrounding it were the time-honoured words recording the decision of

the reigning monarch to grant Letters Patent to General Eva Burrows of
The Salvation Army and to her successors in office. Attached at the foot
of the large document were three huge seals of the Kings of Arms. Dr
Swan, who was later to become in 1992 Garter Principal King of Arms,
came again to meet General Burrows on 6 March 1990 and to present
the Grant to her in person. Thoughtfully, the General arranged for me to
come from Bromley to be present for the occasion and I was allowed also
to be in the photograph as Dr Swan made the presentation.

I am not sure that my leaders ever grasped fully what all this was
about. To this day the legal protection is still in place to be invoked if
anyone in the Queen's realms were to usurp our crest and insignia. All
this applies over and above any local copyright laws that might also be
in our favour. Thus the initial irritation in response to learning of the
fees payable (today these would be doubled or tripled) ought not to be
our enduring reaction.

On becoming General and examining the contents of the cupboards
in the General's office early in April 2006 there I found a dusty, oblong
presentation box. Taking it down and opening it I was transfixed to find
rolled up the Grant of Arms presented in 1990! Clearly its significance
had not been fully appreciated by any of my several predecessors, but at
least it had been kept from harm. Right away my staff had it professionally
mounted, framed and placed upon a display easel in a corner of my office.
Often in the years that followed it became a talking point for visitors and,
because of its design, a natural icebreaker for speaking of our spiritual
purposes and identity. [For a photograph of the Salvation Army Coat of
Arms, turn to page seven of the second section of photographs.] When I
retired I left a detailed briefing note for my successor to highlight and
explain the significance of this unique, irreplaceable artefact.

An unexpected bonus

It was a Tuesday, 15 September 1987. How could I know that a
conversation was to take place that one far-distant day would bring a rare
benefit to both Helen and me?

Commissioner Cox asked me to see him. He was exercised on behalf
of the General. Each time she left the United Kingdom and re-entered on

her Australian passport she had to line up in long queues and this after much demanding ministry and many a tiring flight. Her aide, Lieut-Colonel Jean Issitt, could pass through the immigration controls on her United Kingdom passport far more swiftly than the General. Surely, the Chief said, there was something I could do about it to relieve the General of all the delays. I refrained from saying it was hardly a legal matter and instead indicated I would think it over.

The British Airports Authority (BAA) grasped the situation as soon as I made contact with them. We discovered that certain persons, classified as Very Important Persons (VIPs), could bypass almost all the normal airport waiting processes, going in and out of the United Kingdom with very great ease. I was sent written details of the arrangements and invited to submit a request for the General of The Salvation Army to be accorded VIP status. No sooner was my letter received than the status was granted. Access to the airports would in future be through special security gates leading to private lounges where the VIP and any accompanying staff could relax in comfort, be offered refreshments, clear passport control and customs without leaving the lounge, be checked in, and be offered the choice of boarding the aeroplane either before or after all the other passengers. An official car would then take the General's party from the VIP suite to the airside area where they would board the flight from the tarmac.

All this worked well and afforded General Burrows and all of her successors in office an entirely cost-free facility that allowed rest, privacy, dignity and calm both before and after the demands of international travel. Each General holds this privileged amenity in trust for his or her successor. Helen and I felt honoured to make use of the arrangements, Major Gaudion accompanying us. The airport staff always received us with warm courtesy and much efficiency, remembering our names and saying quietly to the flight crew as they handed us over at the door of the aircraft, 'This is the General of The Salvation Army.' On returning to London the VIP team would meet us as the doors of the aeroplane opened, again greeting us by name and escorting us at once to our private vehicle waiting on the tarmac below the wing of the aircraft at the gate. What a blessing!

Speaking through writing

Writing is an impulse. It is an urge that just seems to overtake you and somehow there is born, in a place between your head and your heart, the concept of the next article or next book.

The Salvation Army has been generous in giving me outlets for writing, something that had not entered my head when we were young candidates and then cadets in training. I have no idea if I would ever have been published had I chosen a secular path. True, as a young law lecturer I daydreamed about producing legal textbooks but that was very much a future hope. Having said that, I did have an academic article accepted and published by the *Solicitors Journal* in the 14 May 1971 edition when I was still only 25. It was a piece about the more technical, idiosyncratic aspects of the English law of defamation. I was paid handsomely for it!

So it seems that speaking through writing somehow came naturally. The first time I saw my name in print in an Army journal was when I was 14. I had been asked to testify at the East London Division's annual Young People's Councils. I still have the notes! I talked about sanctified ambition and Christlikeness: 'My highest ambition is to be like Jesus, to be completely God's man.' Major Muriel Linkins, responsible for the youth of the division, sent my notes to Major Will Burrows, editor of *The War Cry*, who reworked them (as newsprint editors almost always seem to do, unless you are the General!) and published them in the issue of 31 October 1959. I have the cutting.

Years later I found myself immersed for a few passing months in the Literary Department at IHQ. My theological studies completed, Helen and I were awaiting visas to travel to Rhodesia. It was 1974. Our neighbour, Colonel Catherine Baird, contacted her longstanding colleague and friend, Commissioner Kathleen Kendrick, Literary Secretary, to ask if she might be able to give me work in the department for the few months prior to our departure by sea from Southampton. So it was that I became a short-term insider in that department at IHQ for the second half of the year.

My main duty was to assist Major Clifford Kew in the production of *Living and Believing*, the Sunday school teaching manual. Cliff was kindly to me but rightly expected high standards of accuracy in anything I wrote.

(**Top Left**) Annie Fiddis and her daughters. My mother, Alice, is in the middle

(**Top Right**) My mother, Alice Shaw, before becoming a cadet

(**Centre Left**) My dad, when a cadet-sergeant in 1938

(**Above**) My parents, Albert and Alice, on their wedding day, 18 November 1939

(**Left**) My grandfather, CSM Ernest Clifton

(Below) I was a blonde baby!
(Right) Sylvia, Shaw and Mary, 1949
(Below Left) With my grandpa in Goole, 1947
(Below Right) Sylvia, Mary and Shaw, 1954

(Top Left) Sylvia, my sister, on her wedding day, 1967
(Top Right) My dad leaving Ilminster to preach
(Centre Left) At the cricket in Somerset, play delayed by rain (Dad and I swapped hats!)
(Left) Helen and her dad on our wedding day, 15 July 1967
(Above) Shaw and Helen, husband and wife

(Above) Matt (5) and Jen (3) as we left Rhodesia in 1978
(Top Right) Our beloved MG Midget, 1971!
(Right) Bulawayo Citadel hall in Rhodesia, 1978, scene of many blessings
(Below) With Matt and Jen on the River Thames, 1984
(Below Right) Helen with Jen, 1981, saying bedtime prayers

(Top Left) Helen, Jen and Matt, 1985
(Above) Jen, Christmas 1985
(Left) Matt, John, Helen and Jen
(a bridesmaid), 1988
(Below Left) With John in Boston, USA, 1995
(Below) All five of us in Boston, USA, in summer 1996

(Above) Preparing to walk Jen down the aisle, 30 July 1999
(Top Right) Helen and our friend, Nesam Noble
(Right) Helen in Mizoram, India, 1995
(Below) Helen, aged 15, as a new senior soldier, 1963
(Below Right) Helen on the River Thames, 1984

(Left) On the River Seine in Paris
(Above) Helen in her bonnet, aged 37
(Below) Helen conducting a dedication ceremony
at Shantinagar in Pakistan, 1999

HELEN, WORLD PRESIDENT OF WOMEN'S MINISTRIES

(Top Left) Mizoram, India
(Top Right) Old Orchard Beach, USA
(Above) South Africa
(Right) London, UK
(Below) With Commissioners Izzy and Eva Gaither at the 1999 High Council
(Below Right) Junaluska, USA

(Top Left) Preaching beneath the Cross
(Top Right) Commissioner Robin Dunster addresses the congregation
(Left) With Izzy during the prayer meeting, a tender moment
(Above) Helen and Eva spotting family in the gallery

(Right) First day at International Headquarters as the Army's world leaders, arriving with Commissioner Dunster

(Below) Welcoming Commissioner Barry Swanson to International Headquarters

(Below Right) Johannesburg, South Africa

(Below Left) Being interviewed in Oslo, Norway, by Torbjørn Solevåg

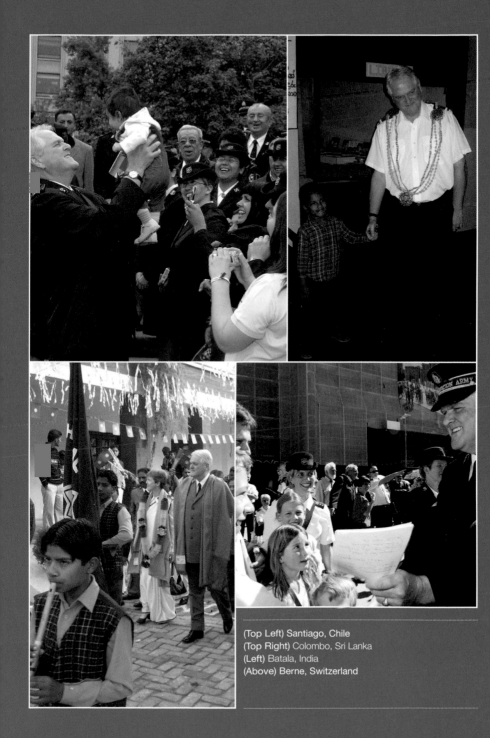

(Top Left) Santiago, Chile
(Top Right) Colombo, Sri Lanka
(Left) Batala, India
(Above) Berne, Switzerland

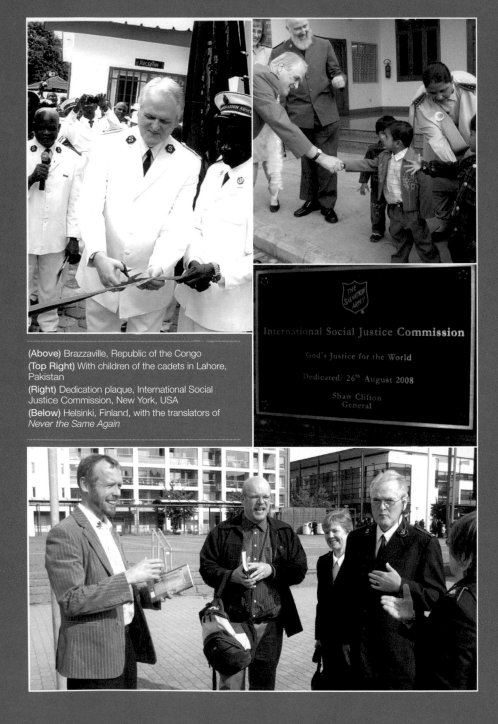

(**Above**) Brazzaville, Republic of the Congo
(**Top Right**) With children of the cadets in Lahore, Pakistan
(**Right**) Dedication plaque, International Social Justice Commission, New York, USA
(**Below**) Helsinki, Finland, with the translators of *Never the Same Again*

International Social Justice Commission

God's Justice for the World

Dedicated: 26ᵗʰ August 2008

Shaw Clifton
General

(Top Left) With Colonel Andrew Kalai in Papua New Guinea

(Top Right) Christmas kettle kick-off in Boston with Senator John Kerry, now USA Secretary of State

(Above) Serious talk with the Senator ...

(Left) At the Vatican in Rome with Cardinal Walter Kasper (to my left)

(Below) With Pu Zoramthanga, Chief Minister of Mizoram, India in 2007

(Above) With President Michelle Bachelet, Santiago, Chile, in 2009

(Top Right) With President Lee, Myung-bak, Seoul, South Korea, in 2008

(Right) With former President George W. Bush and Laura Bush, Dallas, USA, in 2010. Our hosts were Charles and Dee Wyly

(Below) Dr Conrad Swan presents the 'Grant of Arms' to General Eva Burrows in her office in March 1990. I was invited to attend

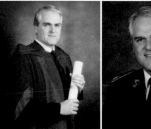

(Above) Grant of Arms to the General of The Salvation Army

(Centre Left) Doctor of Philosophy, 1988

(Centre Right) On promotion to the rank of commissioner, Pakistan, 1999

(Below Left) With Helen in my office as leaders in the United Kingdom, 2004

(Below Right) Speaking for Christ in Hershey, USA, June 2007

SIX PRECIOUS ONES

(Above) With Miriam Helen Clifton in October 2013
(Right) Hudson and Lincoln in October 2013
(Below) Hannah, Amos and Elijah in November 2013

I owe him a lot for this excellent grounding. Much of my time with him was taken up in writing for *The Young Soldier* because that periodical carried a weekly Bible narrative linked to the relevant chapter of *Living and Believing*. I have every one of these early articles in a scrapbook. They ran from 2 November 1974 to 10 July 1976 and were syndicated to Army periodicals in Canada, Australia and South Africa. Producing those pieces was a wonderful discipline because the number of words was strictly rationed and I was writing for children. Deep truths needed to be communicated in straightforward language. Major Kew proofread everything and helped to keep me up to the mark.

Other tasks came my way from the kindly Commissioner Kendrick. I was asked to prepare the index for *No Discharge in this War – A One Volume History of The Salvation Army* by General Frederick Coutts (Rtd). No computers in those days! I spent two weeks poring over the manuscript, going through it 26 times, firstly underlining and listing all the index words starting with 'A' and lastly all those starting with 'Z'. Then I typed up each list and the corresponding page numbers. Inevitably some questions arose for clarification so Commissioner Kendrick arranged for General Coutts to come and see me in my tiny office as though this were a routine thing. I had never been in close proximity to an Army General! In he came, his high-collared uniform bearing the golden insignia, and sat across the desk from me, occasionally commenting, nodding, and assenting to the need for these few clarifications. Gracious and unassuming, he thanked me for my labours and promised to contact me again to finalise things. Published in 1974, this paperback history of the Army is a very fine piece of work. Its index is not so bad either!

Major Will Clark was then editing *The Officer* magazine and invited me to write short reviews of Christian books, a further helpful discipline. With much kindness he accepted from me an article on Martin Luther and used it before we left for Africa. He then kept in touch while we were overseas and encouraged further submissions. A series on ethical issues appeared in 1975 and was later published as a slim book in 1977 with the title *What Does the Salvationist Say?* General Clarence Wiseman came to Rhodesia soon afterwards and took time to speak words of thanks to me about the book. I have never forgotten this (see Essay 6). Many of these articles can be read in my 2010 *Selected Writings – Volume 1*,

Chapter 2. As the years have passed I have had frequent cause to be grateful to other editors of *The Officer* for using my material. Each has been comradely and encouraging. I wonder what might have been had Colonel Baird not spoken generously to Commissioner Kendrick back in the summer of 1974.

Earlier in this Essay I have written about attempts by Army leaders to find an appropriate regulatory approach to marital breakdown. In 1984 General Wahlström approved a proposal from the Commission on Marriage for a book that would be a useful teaching tool and which would reflect the Army's internationalism. Helen and I were invited jointly to edit this volume. It was no small task. We were supported wonderfully by Commissioner Albert Scott, Chair of the Commission, and by the then Lieut-Colonel Will Clark who had become Editor-in-Chief and Literary Secretary. Entitled *Growing Together*, the book took the form of a global symposium with contributors from the five continents of the world.

We received and edited the material with the clear intention of allowing each individual and cultural voice to come through even if that occasionally meant English syntax that was less than highly polished. It was something of a tussle, conducted in comradely fashion, to persuade Major Raymond Caddy, Book Production Officer, about this. He and I seemed to march to different drummers. We needed to dig in our heels also about the cover design after being offered one that made the volume resemble a book of orders and regulations. Commissioner Scott supported us in our request for a more modern and less formal approach. We arranged for a photograph of male and female hands touching at the tips with a wedding ring also visible. We asked for a colour tone that would allow the hands to be perceived variously as black or brown or white. All this was done. The hands used for the photography by Robin Bryant were those of Captain Diane Lillicrap (now Lieut-Colonel Diane O'Brien of the USA Western Territory) and of Kevin Ashman, Helen's brother.

Every territory in the world was told in advance of the publication and asked to submit orders. They had all been sent details of the concept and the titles for the chapters. This led to an initial print run in 1984 of about 15,000 copies, unprecedented for any Army publication. It meant also that the price per book would be very low. Several favourable reviews were published but the one that brought us most satisfaction was that written by the Reverend Dr Kenneth Greet, a former President of the World Methodist Council. It was published in *The Expository Times*. He wrote: 'This is a book that may be commended for many beyond the ranks of The Salvation Army.'

Helen and I had prayed and worked hard on the book. It had its shortcomings: it was limited in length for reasons of cost; some aspects of married life and of human sexuality were treated with less depth and detail than was ideal. However, its uniqueness among a host of similar volumes (then available from authors like Walter Trobisch, James Dobson, Anne Townsend and Joyce Huggett) was its international panel of contributors. Not all of these were experts but they wrote with spontaneity and in a guileless manner from their personal life experience. Rereading the volume today renews a lasting sense of gratitude that the assignment came our way.

The following year *Strong Doctrine, Strong Mercy* was published, also by IHQ. Beneath the title ran the following: 'A Salvationist looks at some major moral questions of the late 20th century.' It was an expanded treatment of the material in *What Does the Salvationist Say?* Though it is now out of print, I am glad to hear from time to time of it still proving helpful. General Wahlström needed to approve its publication and went to the trouble of seeing me face-to-face to discuss its contents and to ask for one or two changes. Today I understand more clearly why he did so and the need for the General to be parent to the totality of his global family. He explained that certain passages in the chapters on nuclear warfare would or could be taken amiss by American readers. He asked that I remove them. Naturally this was done. These passages offered outlines of different scenarios that might lead to nuclear conflagration and I had included, *inter alia*, the possibility of the USA launching a decisive, pre-emptive first-strike attack upon the Soviet Union, something being openly discussed by the media, by scholars and by military theorists at that time in many lands including the USA. As he spoke with me the General reflected freely upon his time serving in the armed forces of Finland, an interruption to his service as an officer in The Salvation Army. Finland was then at war with the Soviet Union. He and I also discussed briefly aspects of pacifism. General Wahlström was a most gracious person. He spoke to me as though I were his equal, which I was not. He was senior to me and a better man than me. Some underestimated him. This was a major mistake.

If I had to forfeit all but one of the books I have written (this present volume is the tenth) I would single out for retention *Never the Same Again – Encouragement for New and Not-so-new Christians*. How it came to be published in 1997 as the inaugural book of the USA National Book Plan (Crest Books) is quite a tale. It all began with our son, Matt. When he was a student he and I would meet in London whenever I needed to travel down from Middlesbrough in the north-east of England. He was full of questions about faith. We would find Chinese food to enjoy while he probed me with countless and often penetrating enquiries. I began to wish there were a useful, short, but searching book published by the Army which I could put into his hands, but for such material we needed to turn to non-Salvationist publications. So in January 1993 I wrote to the TC, Commissioner John Larsson, and put to him a concept: 'I wonder if there is room for a simple book designed to lead new Christians into a sound grounding in the faith in the immediate aftermath of their conversion experience. It would be a tool for discipling and could be used on an individual basis or in a group setting.' The commissioner's reply was typically warm and offered encouragement.

Several months later I found time to begin work. The book needed to be straightforward and unpretentious. It took just two weeks. Never has anything come together for me so readily. I spent a week working at it on the huge oak table then in the dining room of Caldew House, the Army's cottage in the English Lake District at Sebergham. The second week was spent similarly, but in my sister's lovely cottage in Ilminster, Somerset. Each morning of our furlough was spent in writing. It just seemed to come together. I was writing for a verdict in the hearts of future readers.

Major Raymond Caddy, by now the Literary Secretary at Territorial Headquarters in London, wrote on 29 June 1994 to say he was 'anxious to have the proposed manuscript'. He asked that it be ready by mid-September. On 9 September I sent him two copies of the completed work and a reply came in a two-line letter of acknowledgement with a kindly handwritten annotation: 'Have started reading and it looks great!' However, nine months of total silence then followed.

We farewelled to Boston, USA, to start work as the leaders of the Massachusetts Division on 1 June 1995. As soon as we reached the USA Major Caddy wrote to say: 'It has been decided not to proceed with your manuscript.' Could he not have written or called me a little sooner before we left England? No explanations were given. I was now an ocean away from the major. Any face-to-face communication was impossible. The unexplained delay and the curt tone of the letter left me troubled, especially after his initial enthusiasm. I requested that the manuscript be returned to me and the copyright assignment I had made in favour of the Army be rescinded. This was duly done. Further, I asked for some indication of the reasons for the interminable delay and the 'volte-face'. So Major Caddy wrote again to tell me that the work was seen as generally out of step with the needs of the territory. I felt sad because this was to be a book for new converts. Surely our home territory expected converts. When finally we returned to London 10 years later the number of Army soldiers in the United Kingdom had fallen by a staggering 11,900 – in a single decade.

Soon after reaching Boston we learned of the intention to initiate the USA National Book Plan using the label, 'Crest Books'. During a visit to National Headquarters in Alexandria, Virginia, I fell into conversation with Lieut-Colonel Marlene Chase, the Editor-in-Chief and Literary Secretary. I told her of the recently rejected manuscript and at once she expressed an interest. Events from that point onward were in total contrast to what had happened in our home territory. Lieut-Colonel Chase followed through in a timely, professional manner. Feedback was received from external assessors who read the manuscript. I was impressed by the efficiency, candour and warm courtesy of it all. How grateful I remain to Marlene Chase for her help to me at that time. She was skilled yet warmly personable, restoring my faith in our editorial colleagues.

Colonel Israel Gaither, USA Eastern Chief Secretary, announced the launching of the National Book Plan in a circular to executive officers on 27 March 1997 adding, to my lasting delight, this generous comment: 'We are extremely pleased that this "first offering" of the Plan is authored by one of our own! Lieut-Colonel Shaw Clifton has made an invaluable presentation.' Izzy was always gracious to me. Graciousness also marked the Foreword written by General Paul Rader.

So in the end my simple little book was born in America. It has been found to be of use especially for men and women coming to faith in our adult rehabilitation centres across the USA. By the grace of God it has also been translated for use in India (including into Mizo for use in Mizoram), in Korea, and in Finland. It has also been translated into Spanish in Santiago, Chile. We led Congress gatherings in Finland in September 2008 and there had lunch with the translators of the book, Jorma Pollari and Timo Teräsvuori. We were moved to hear these spiritually sensitive men speak of the impact of the book upon them personally and of how wonderful they thought it that someone would write such a volume prompted by love and concern for his son.

The opportunity to work again with Lieut-Colonel Chase, and to contribute further to Crest Books, arose while we were still in Boston. I had been asked to give the 1997 Chandler Memorial Lectures at the School for Officer Training in Suffern, New York. These lectures, open to the public, are intended to address issues in contemporary Christian mission from theological, biblical, historical and social perspectives. I delivered the four lectures in May that year in memory of Colonel Alfred Augustus Chandler, an Englishman who served in the USA and Canada, influencing Army training programmes.

Lieut-Colonel Chase expressed interest in the idea of a book based upon the lectures so I began to reshape the material accordingly. Before the task was completed we were reassigned in 1997 from Boston to Lahore in Pakistan. Thus the manuscript was finalised there but published in America in 1999 as *Who Are These Salvationists?* Because of its origins in an academic setting I added footnotes throughout, something I usually seek to avoid in order not to interrupt the flow of the text. Two of the chapters take the form of special case studies, Chapter 8 examining Salvation Army freedom of the streets and Chapter 12 drawing upon the material in my doctoral thesis concerning the Army and its policies in time of war. Since first published in 1999, this book has been reprinted four times (in 2003, 2004, 2007 and 2012) and has also been translated into German, Spanish and Russian.

While leading the Army in the New Zealand, Fiji and Tonga Territory I was able to establish 'Flag Publications' in the hope of stimulating a continuing flow of helpful literature from the able Salvationists there.

How pleased we all were to attend the launch of the new label and its inaugural publication, Cyril Bradwell's autobiography, *Touched with Splendour*. Cyril was renowned in Army circles in New Zealand and a recipient of the Order of the Founder. He offered encouragement to our publishing initiatives. For some time I had been thinking of attempting a further book. The theme of holiness kept coming into view and eventually there was born the idea of something very practical, not something of an expository or doctrinal nature but a book that would ground our sanctification teaching in the muddy realities of life. I felt that such a book should allow voices other than mine, and from different backgrounds, also to be heard. So I would write seven chapters and invited guests would provide another seven. It would be titled *New Love: Thinking Aloud About Practical Holiness*.

It was pleasing that my seven invitees all agreed to make a contribution: Lieut-Colonel Marlene Chase, General Eva Burrows (Rtd), Colonel Henry Gariepy, Captain Stephen Court, Commissioner Joe Noland, Captain Geoff Ryan, and our son Captain Matt Clifton. I was especially ready to give exposure to the three younger men – Court, Ryan and Clifton. Each of these could think for himself and, even better, could write with persuasion. Whenever I look at this book I still enjoy seeing Emily Fletcher's cover design with its hovering dove, a symbol of the Holy Spirit's sanctifying presence. The same motif is found scattered throughout the book.

Major Harold Hill kindly sent me a copy when the book was reprinted in New Zealand in 2006. I was surprised but pleased when Colonel Birgitte Brekke told me some years later that she and her organising committee for the World Youth Convention in Stockholm in 2010 had decided to take the themes for the various sessions from the opening chapter, 'Salvationism – Holiness and the Non-negotiables of Salvationism'.

Even more pleasing was a quiet conversation held in my office at IHQ late in November 2010. With me were Helen's personal assistant, Major Lynn Gibbs, and her mother, Major Maureen Baxter whose husband, David, had recently been promoted to Glory. Maureen came all the way from Bristol in the west of England to give me a copy of David's handwritten notes prepared by him for a testimony in a forthcoming meeting but never delivered due to his final illness. I am rereading his notes as I write this. He speaks of his calling to serve God, to know God personally, to be under God's direction, to follow the example of Jesus, and to find purity of heart and mind. To conclude his testimony he had planned to read from pages 38 and 39 of *New Love* which mention Salvationist distinctives. His testimony concludes: 'To sum up, I am glad I am in this Army.' These precious, tender notes were found by Maureen with David's Bible and Army *Song Book*.

I dedicated the book to my father: 'The day-by-day prayers and weekly airmail letters of my aged father, Major Albert Clifton, have made an incalculable contribution to my life and it is to him, with love, admiration and gratitude for his unassuming example of holy living, that I dedicate the pages within these covers.'

A very different dedication appears in my Introduction to *Selected Writings*, two volumes of which appeared in 2010: 'I dedicate these pages to my Saviour, Jesus Christ, and to his people known as Salvationists.' The fact is that the first of these two volumes was finalised on the eve of undergoing major heart surgery. I felt it could well be the last I would ever produce (see Essay 4). The dedication is thus to honour all my Army comrades. I had long felt that we needed to be far more open and much less stuffy about things that go on at the highest level of the Army's administration and so these volumes offer not only early articles from *The Officer* magazine but also global policy papers delivered in more recent years and which would normally be confined to a relatively small circle of senior leaders. The book was published jointly by IHQ and Crest Books, USA; the advertisement in the USA National *War Cry* for 8 January 2011 says simply: 'Readers will be informed, inspired and surprised by his words.' I liked that.

It still seems only a short time ago that *From Her Heart* was released, a 2012 compilation of Helen's preaching and teaching. It too was published jointly by IHQ and Crest Books. It consists of 55 of her sermons, talks and lectures given over 34 years dating from 5 June 1977 to just before her death in June 2011. The book's Introduction explains how it came to be compiled in the period after Helen died. Although earlier I have singled out *Never the Same Again* as the book I was most pleased to have authored, *From Her Heart* holds a unique place for obvious reasons. Moreover, I can hardly claim to have written it. It is more accurate to say I compiled, edited and introduced it. Since its release it has been wonderful to hear of the many for whom it has been a source of blessing, some using it as a daily or weekly devotional tool.

Journal, 25 August 2011: I have been sorting Helen's many files and papers which came home with her from her office when we retired. She threw very little away; hence these papers give a vivid picture of where her chief interests lay. These were in people (lists of names), human trafficking (reports and statistics from every corner of the Army world as well as from secular sources), women's roles in ministry (many lectures, talks and seminar notes by her and also graphics on this theme), pastoral communications to Army women everywhere (many individually addressed according to personal need), departmental papers on women's ministries and publications (such as 'Global Exchange' which she renamed 'Revive'), and policy papers on issues current at that time for the General's Consultative Council, the International Appointments Board, or the International Management Council (these papers often annotated incisively). Add to all this copious books on women in Christian service and on cultural factors affecting the lifestyles and well-being of women everywhere and you begin to get a rounded picture of what were Helen's driving motivations, in addition to her natural concerns for me, our children and the wider family.

Journal, 28 November 2011: Today I completed the first draft of Helen's book manuscript and am pleased with this progress. O Lord, bless this book.

Journal, 21 January 2012: My stay in Auckland continues at a leisurely pace.... I am close to finalising a further draft of Helen's writings and have emailed the literary secretary at IHQ a week ago to alert him.

My plan was to have the book published to coincide with the first anniversary of Helen's promotion to Glory on 14 June 2012.

Journal, 17 June 2012: My book of Helen's sermons and talks has been published exactly on time. I have sent out, via IHQ, an initial set of 24 copies to family and friends.

The first review I read was prepared by Lieut-Colonel Jayne Roberts for the June 2012 issue of *Revive* magazine. It was a warm tribute: 'Clear scriptural teaching is interspersed with fascinating glimpses of both family life and the challenge of service as an Army officer. Her love and prayerful concern for her family and the worldwide family of The Salvation Army are evident.'

Turning finally now from prose to poetry I must at once declare that I am no poet! Now and then, but not all that often, an impulse springs up and I find myself scribbling. The mostly light-hearted results (some of them) can be found in Appendix A. So, Dear Reader, I rely on your patient spirit and perhaps your sense of humour should you opt to turn to that Appendix, where I am pleased to include also some of Helen's verse.

ESSAY 8

൭

SPECTACLES

ESSAY 8
SPECTACLES

YES, this Essay carries a strange heading! Wanting to set down some thoughts on the pleasures of reading, I confess to being at a loss in seeking a better title, one that would keep to my self-imposed alliterative pattern for all the Essays herein. So 'Spectacles' is meant to connote the joys of reading (do I hear you sigh…?).

It is only in recent years I have needed to use spectacles, and vivid memories come flooding back of the first occasion I used them in public. It was 30 July 1999 and our daughter's wedding day. Jenny and Marcus had asked me to conduct their wedding ceremony, a wonderful privilege. We were gathered in the imposing Assembly Hall of the Army's cadet training college in London. Marcus's family had come from distant New Zealand, his sisters being two of the three bridesmaids.

The day was hot and sultry. The print on the pages on my maroon *Ceremonies Book* and in the Order of Service was a trifle blurred to my naked eye so I decided to use, for the first time in public, the low power spectacles I had bought from a nearby pharmacy. The heat was all-prevailing. Everyone felt it. Perspiring, I rose to get things going and donned the half-moon spectacles. Oh dear, they simply refused to stay in place! I pressed on, trying to appear casual, but each push of the glasses upward to the bridge of my nose resulted simply in the wretched things sliding downward again within moments. We reached the ceremony itself. Anyone who has officiated at a wedding will know the need to juggle the *Ceremonies Book*, the Order of Service and the rings. Add to this a presiding officer who is a novice wearer of slithering spectacles and you will appreciate the challenge!

Somehow we got through it. Jen and Marcus looked wonderful, spoke their vows with transparently earnest joy, and everyone shared in their delight. The marriage service over and with folk gathering for photographs, I heard my Dad's voice as he squeezed my arm. 'I didn't know you wore glasses,' he murmured. 'I don't usually,' I gasped, and we both burst out laughing. It was a nice moment.

So let us turn to the joys of reading, one of life's major pleasures, and which nowadays involves using spectacles. My tastes and habits are wide-ranging, from novels (not all serious!) to works of theology (all serious!). What follows is an intimation, a sampling, of the writing that has developed me and helped to shape both my mind and being through the years.

I love books. I love the feel of them, the smell of them, the sight of them arrayed on shelves or piled haphazardly. I find it all but impossible to pass a second-hand bookshop. Hardly ever do I discard a book. If I do, it is most often to gift or lend it to someone. As I write here in the study at home, I glance to my left to see what has come to be called the 'book-room' housing nearly 3,000 volumes. On the wall is my small gold-framed print of Carl Spitzweg's 'The Bookworm' ('Der Bücherwurm') bought years ago in 1970 in Marlborough, Wiltshire, for five guineas. Commuting in those days in my red MG Midget between London and Bristol, I would break for coffee in Marlborough. There I saw 'The Bookworm' in the display window of an art dealer and knew instantly that I had to own it. Five guineas, even 43 years ago, was not a prohibitive price.

Ranging now across a variety of subject matter, I will leave mention of prayer books to the next following Essay which covers spirituality. Here let me ponder works of journalism, novels, Army books, theological treatises, social ethics and, finally, biography and politics.

Newspapers and periodicals

Salvation Army officers need to have a daily, weekly reading diet beyond those periodicals emanating from Army sources, helpful as these are.

Choice of a daily newspaper is often said to betray not only your reading capacity but also your politics. I am not so sure. Here in London we can choose from an impressive array of serious daily newspapers, all with a global reputation. When we lived outside our homeland we found the choice more restricted. Our years in Boston, USA, were enriched by *The Boston Globe*, in Lahore by *Dawn* (Pakistan's oldest and most widely-read English newspaper founded in 1942), and in Wellington by *The New Zealand Herald*.

Good as these newspapers were, they could not compete with *The Times* of London, *The Daily Telegraph*, or *The Guardian* in terms of the calibre and reliability of the journalism. Moreover, they somehow lacked the breadth and scope of reporting on the international scene that seems to come naturally to their British counterparts.

So these days my choice is *The Daily Telegraph*, although my private political views are far more centrist than those of the typical *Telegraph* reader. Over and above the quality of the journalism is the penetration of its investigative reporting. Recently it exposed, with startling depth and detail, the shamefully corrupt practices of many of our members of Parliament in relation to the fraudulent claiming of personal reimbursement for expenses. The *Telegraph* 'Letters to the Editor' page is the best and most amusing in the country. The brilliant cartoons each day by 'Matt' never fail to raise a smile and often an audible laugh! The cryptic crossword puzzle provides a daily workout for the brain.

Before leaving the subject of newspapers I should mention *The Sunday Times*. From 1975 to 1979 my sister, Sylvia, sent this by slow surface mail each week to us in Rhodesia. With no television to watch, it provided much spare-time stimulus. We loved its massive supplements and the in-depth reporting. We were, moreover, fascinated to read the coverage of events some four to six weeks after they had happened and to see that often the speculation of commentators went awry. A further plus was the usefulness to Helen of some of the articles as she sought to stimulate and improve the reading outlook of the senior students at the Army's Mazowe Secondary School where we served.

Turning to periodicals I should mention at once the pleasure and help brought to me over countless years by *The Expository Times*. A monthly publication, it offers serious articles and book reviews on matters of biblical studies, theology and Christian ministry. The Revered Dr Cyril Rodd was its gifted editor for 25 years until 2001. He seemed to know the lives, challenges and privileges of people in Christian service and the journal became for me not only a regular source of intellectual stimulus but also, and more importantly, a provider of grounded encouragement for my day-to-day service for Christ. The last decade has seen a decided shift in editorial policy toward content of a more theoretical kind, plus a focus which is decidedly Scottish, as evidenced these days by the very high number of Scotland-based contributors. Nevertheless, *The Expository Times* remains a helpful publication to me and I am able to pass it on to my son, John, each month. My long-standing habit of annotating the cover (where the contents are listed) was eventually frustrated by the shift from a matt to a slippery, glossy finish. My plea to the then editor, Alison Jack, to revert to a matt finish so that once again I could write on it was politely but firmly rejected. The criterion of user-friendliness, so evident until Cyril Rodd, was no longer to the fore.

Weekly and pleasurable sources of news and opinion are found in the *Church Times* (an Anglican periodical) and *The Tablet* (which centres on things Roman Catholic). This latter is an especially good read. The standard of writing is very high. There is much for the non-Catholic reader to enjoy, not least the willingness of its editorial staff to publish candid comment about the Roman Church. As I write, Pope Francis has just been elected in succession to Pope Benedict, the first Pope in many centuries to retire. *The Tablet* has revelled in these events, offering well-informed, candid commentary but always with an underlying tone of deep commitment to the Church of Rome and its mission in the world.

Fiction

Some Christian folk have a quiet suspicion of novels, as though reading them is a worldly, frivolous use of one's time. I suppose this outlook might be a faint shadow still cast by the puritanical element in our spiritual gene pool. It first came home to me many years ago. I would be invited to take part in candidates' assessment conferences. In the United Kingdom (UK) these are weekend residential events designed to test spiritual vocations for officership in the Army. A team of six or seven assessors would meet a group of candidates. Interviews ensued. My role was dubbed 'academic assessor', for I had to evaluate each candidate's learning and intellectual capacity. It was a privileged thing to be involved. I have always tried to see and sense the sacredness that lies at the heart of any procedure connected to the testing of a Christian calling to ministry. It is a spiritual exercise in discernment, not primarily an administrative thing.

During the interviews I would, among many other things, invite the candidates to tell me what they were reading. Hardly any volunteered a response that mentioned novels. So I would ask if they read fiction. This elicited often stumbling responses, for some interviewees clearly thought the question was designed to trap them. Far from it. I was hoping to find folk who knew and enjoyed what good novels could offer and who might grasp the insights into the human lot that the best fiction reveals. Add to this the ready source of sermon illustration material to be found in quality novels and the case for Christian leaders to be readers of good fiction is complete.

My taste in novels is broad. Who can resist Thomas Hardy? His *Tess of the D'Urbervilles* pulls at our emotions and its grim ending is deeply troubling. Tess was 'the plaything of the gods', a woman victimised and exploited. Although Hardy was an architect of church buildings, he had no time for the God and Father of our Lord Jesus Christ. If there were a deity at all, to this great novelist it would be remote and unfeeling. Hardy is a prime example of someone with a brilliant and gifted intellect who, when it came to faith, was simply wrong. Brilliant but wrong.

Even had I never been involved in the law I am sure that John Mortimer's wonderful character of Horace Rumpole, the ageing but wily English barrister, would still have entertained me. On my shelves are six Rumpole volumes, including *The Second Rumpole Omnibus*. The cover blurb aptly quotes a review from *The Sunday Times*: 'Rumpole is worthy to join the great gallery of English oddballs ranging from Pickwick to Sherlock Holmes, Jeeves and Bertie Wooster.' The books became a popular television series with Leo McKern playing Rumpole. McKern is now deceased. Irreplaceable. The talented Patricia Hodge played Rumpole's younger colleague and pupil barrister, Phyllida Trant, who shared his chambers at the Inns of Court. In December 2004 Hodge took part in our Christmas carol concert at the Royal Albert Hall when I was the leader of the Army in the UK. In speaking with Helen and me she asked very bright, penetrating, but empathetic questions about our work and witness. A memorable, pleasurable encounter.

Spy novels can stretch the mind. Len Deighton's triple trilogy (nine novels in all) offers abundant proof of this. Published between 1983 and 1996, these books give us the vulnerable but 'brighter than he looks' British agent, Bernard Samson. The titles are easy to remember: *Game, Set, Match*; *Hook, Line, Sinker*; *Faith, Hope, Charity*. Deighton has afforded me considerable pleasure and diversion from the everyday for many years now. My final purchase of the ninth volume of the triple trilogy (*Charity*) was made in Lahore, Pakistan, and cost 395 rupees, then worth about £3. Deighton stands with John le Carré as a master of the spy genre but I find le Carré just that bit too obscure. Often he develops his plots by means of nothing but a fleeting, passing allusion, leaving me to turn back several pages to confirm I have not misunderstood! Nevertheless, his enigmatic George Smiley (*Tinker, Tailor, Soldier, Spy* and *Smiley's People*) will long remain a favourite of my generation. My younger relations and friends had opportunity to encounter Smiley when recently *TTSS* came to cinema screens. Comments overheard on emerging from the cinema into the night air showed that most who saw the film – I had to smile to myself – were left bemused as to its plot. Such is le Carré's style. He makes demands of us and that is no bad thing.

I have been able to read only one other fictional triple trilogy apart from Deighton and it has come from the inspired pen of the lawyer-novelist and 1932 Nobel Prize in Literature winner, John Galsworthy. This is *The Forsyte Chronicles* (*The Man of Property, In Chancery, To Let, The White Monkey, The Silver Spoon, Swan Song, Maid in Waiting, Flowering Wilderness, Over the River*) published between 1906 and 1934 with the last volume emerging a year after the author's death. Galsworthy's characters show us the depths and complexities of human nature. The reader sees, as though in a mirror, the finest and the basest of human motives. Here is much grist to the preacher's mill.

I cannot omit mention of the debt I owe also to the novels of Dr A.J. Cronin, of Graham Greene and of Morris West. Cronin was a shrewd observer of human foibles. West imbues his works with religious themes, putting into the mouths of his characters dialogue on profound, even abstruse theological matters which, from a writer less gifted, would bemuse and deter many a reader. I should mention here especially his 1981 work, *The Clowns of God*, set in the context of nuclear holocaust (see Essay 7A). Alongside it I want to place *Birdsong* from Sebastian Faulks in 1994. It too is set in wartime and is further evidence that the novel can provide a telling setting for the serious treatment of issues central to the human lot (again see Essay 7A). Nevil Shute's *On the Beach*, written in 1957 and set in post-nuclear holocaust Australia, is another example.

Two novels deserve mention to conclude this section: E.M. Forster's *A Passage to India* (1924) and Alan Paton's *Cry, The Beloved Country – A Story of Comfort in Desolation* (1948). Each carries me back to two of the continents on which I have lived and served, South Asia and Africa. As I read I can see, hear and smell the authentic sights, sounds and aromas of these places. The books are wonderful achievements but in the final analysis no adequate substitute for actually leaving the safety of home and immersing oneself into the culture of others in far-distant lands, and doing so for the sake of Jesus Christ.

Salvation Army books

Where should I begin? My shelves house over 400 Salvationist publications. Feeling strongly that International Headquarters (IHQ) should take a lead in publishing Army books, I revived its long dormant book-publishing role when elected General, helped so well in this by Lieut-Colonel Charles King and later by his successor, Lieut-Colonel Laurie Robertson (see also Essay 12).

I am confined here by space to highlighting but a handful of the Army books that have impacted me. Chief among my prized volumes is Catherine Bramwell Booth's 1933 biography of her father, *Bramwell Booth*. I have long admired the son of the Army's Founders, my heart going out to him whenever I think of his being deposed from office by the Army's first High Council in 1929. Not everyone caught up in those traumatic events acted from the purest of motives. Bramwell, sick in body and agonised in soul, emerges into history's spotlight with his integrity intact.

My copy of his biography belonged originally to General Albert Orsborn no less. His handwritten annotations appear throughout. It became eventually part of the personal library of General Frederick Coutts and Commissioner Olive Gatrall when they married. Helen and I were privileged to visit them in their home in St Albans for a meal together. The General had agreed to talk about his views on issues of war and pacifism as part of my then PhD researches. We left with *Bramwell Booth* as a lasting memento of the day. 'Take it, please,' said Mrs General Coutts, 'we have two copies you see.' It was a Thursday, the first day of August 1985. I was 39 years of age, just a few weeks short of 21 September when I would reach 40 and Frederick Coutts would also celebrate another birthday, his 86th. Let me quote just a few lines from Catherine's account of her father: 'Certain it is the world would not have known The Salvation Army of the first quarter of this century, had not such a father as was William Booth been given such a son as was Bramwell. William Booth was blessed in having at his side a man of the next generation, whose vision was wide as his own, and who was capable of understanding and appreciating him.'

Following naturally from this I must mention *General Booth's Journal 1921-22* published in London by the Army in 1925. It came to me as a Christmas gift in 1998 from Major Ethne Flintoff in Lahore, where by mutual consent and for pragmatic reasons we restricted gifts between expatriate colleagues to the value of a few rupees or the giving of a personal possession. How pleased I was to receive this volume. Ethne inscribed it: 'To Shaw Clifton, Christmas 1998, to keep in your custody and for many hours of enjoyable rereading.' Like Bramwell, I have long kept a personal journal and feel closer to him, knowing he too sensed his need of finger-therapy.

Two books by Frederick Coutts come next. *No Continuing City* (1976) is as close to an autobiography as this self-effacing leader came and indeed is sub-titled *Reflections on the life of a Salvation Army Officer*. Chapter 12 includes an articulate explanation of the Army's position on sacramental ceremonies and candid comment on the Army's deployment of women in ministry. Of this latter he writes: 'If this be yet another of those deplorable deviations from orthodoxy, pray God there may be yet many more.' Amen to that. My second Coutts book is his account of the life of the Army's leading pacifist, Carvosso Gauntlett, entitled *Portrait of a Salvationist* (1955). Coutts shared Gauntlett's views on warfare. Gauntlett was appointed to lead the Army's work in Germany when war ended in 1945. Coutts's *Portrait* grants us a penetrating insight into post-war Germany and The Salvation Army there. Several outstanding young officers who worked under Gauntlett at IHQ during the war espoused his pacifist views, among them Catherine Baird and Ben Blackwell. I have never been a pacifist but I understand and respect those who were or still are.

Samuel Logan Brengle's books on the holy life rightfully claim a place in the writings I need to highlight. Hugely influential upon many generations of Salvationists, they are less read in the UK now. When I became leader of the Army there I discovered that our trade department had ceased to stock them, that they were no longer required reading for cadets in training, and that they were not featured even in our holiness Brengle Institutes despite these events bearing his name. I did what I could about all that. Here I will but testify to the impulse after personal purity engendered by reading Brengle, an impulse deepened through the holiness songs in our *Song Book* and the writings of others like Frederick Coutts and Edward Read. All of our holiness writers and teachers owe a huge debt to Brengle, and before him to the Booths and John Wesley. Sallie Chesham's *The Brengle Treasury: A Patchwork Polygon* (1988) is a mine of information and useful platform material. It was a gift to us from Sallie's daughter, Julie Kennedy (later married by me to Ro Whittingham), when we lived in Boston, USA. Then also from the States, where Brengle is still widely read both within and beyond our ranks, we have David Rightmire's admirable *Sanctified Sanity – The Life and Teaching of Samuel Logan Brengle* (2003). It is an outstanding work.

Finally I turn to a tiny paperback booklet which Helen would carry constantly in her handbag, often reading it on our many long journeys. It is *The Practice of Sanctification* by Catherine Bannister published by the Army in London in 1936. Eventually I had it rebound for Helen in hardback, lest it disintegrate. These 61 small pages move and challenge me, as they did Helen (see also Essay 2), not least because Catherine was writing from India and practising the holy life as an officer there. Our years in Pakistan (part of Catherine's India) allowed Helen to feel a strong spiritual bond with the author.

Theology and social ethics

Certain writings on moral theology and social ethics have been covered separately in Essay 7B and I touch also on prayer books in Essay 9, so here I will try to offer a sampling of the books that have shaped my theological outlook in a general way. My spiritual and theological formation has been indelibly shaped by my Salvationist heritage. Works from other traditions have sometimes broadened and even deepened all of that, but I learned long ago that all theological literature, without exception, needs to be read with an ever-alert, discerning and critical eye.

The Gospel of John came truly alive for me only when I was able to read and analyse it in the original Greek of the New Testament. I cannot say enough about the enrichment to my soul and mind afforded me by Rudolf Bultmann's *The Gospel of John – A Commentary* (1971). Bultmann, who died aged 92 in 1976, was one of the greatest of modern theologians. I have also the two volumes of his *Theology of the New Testament*, the first of which became my close companion during our 1975 sea voyage from Southampton to Cape Town to take up appointments in Rhodesia (see also Essays 6 and 13). Because it was no longer in print it took me until 1992 to secure a copy of Volume 2, but then to my rescue came Pendlebury's, the renowned dealership in second-hand theological books located, ironically, in the heart of north London's orthodox Jewish community in Stamford Hill.

Other writers on the fourth Gospel to whom I am indebted are John Marsh, C.H. Dodd, and C.K. Barrett. I should mention too Ernst Käsemann's splendid 1968 monograph, *The Testament of Jesus – A Study of the Gospel of John in the Light of Chapter 17*. Add to this the cross-disciplinary collection of essays edited in 2000 by Larry Kreitzer and Deborah Rooke, *Ciphers in the Sand – Interpretations of the Woman Taken in Adultery* which centres on the 12 verses that make up John 7:57-8:11. I find this one of the most riveting and revealing passages in all of Scripture. The woman is at the centre but it is the men accusers and the absent co-adulterer about whom most is revealed. The intriguing 'ciphers in the sand' of our Lord must, along with much else, await the hereafter to become clear.

Hard on the heels of John's Gospel I want to mention the Epistle of James. I feel readily at home in its company because it is so down to earth and not at all, despite my hero Martin Luther's views, 'an epistle of straw'! My shelves house five volumes of commentaries on it: James Moffatt (1928); Herbert Stevenson (1966); Sophie Laws (one of my tutors at King's College, London) (1980) in the Black's New Testament Commentaries series; Alec Motyer (1985) in a preacher-friendly volume from 'The Bible Speaks Today' (BST) series; John Blanchard's *Truth for Life* (1986) written from an unapologetic evangelical perspective. Also deeply instructive for background is the Australian John Painter's work, *Just James – The Brother of Jesus in*

History and Tradition (1999) in the series of 'Studies on Personalities of the New Testament'.

Three trilogies have long proven helpful. Published in 1990 in a single paperback volume are the writings of Francis Schaeffer: *The God Who Is There; Escape From Reason; He Is There and He Is Not Silent.* All three were designed to reach out to both Christians and non-Christians. This they have done to much effect. John McIntyre taught theology in the University of Edinburgh. The first book I bought from his trilogy was *The Shape of Soteriology – Studies in the Doctrine of the Death of Christ* (1992). I got into its pages during a long train journey. An elderly gentleman entered the carriage with his wife and sat opposite me. Noticing the title of my book he leaned forward and asked, 'What is soteriology?' Very un-British, I thought, to broach a conversation with a stranger thus. However, I was pleased because it offered a golden chance to speak quietly of Jesus and to explain that soteriology is simply the study of how we can be saved, the word being derived from the Greek for 'saviour'. My questioner nodded courteously, smiled and lapsed into the more accustomed silence expected of co-passengers! McIntyre's companion volumes are *The Shape of Pneumatology* (1997) on the person and work of the Holy Spirit, and *The Shape of Christology* (the 1998 second edition but first published in 1966). The third of the trilogies comes from the pen of the recently retired Bishop of Durham, N.T. Wright. I have space only to mention them: *The New Testament and the People of God* (1992); *Jesus and the Victory of God* (1996) (a Christmas 2004 gift to me from Helen in which she wrote beneath the title: 'The greatest subject, happy reading!'); and *The Resurrection of the Son of God* (2003). Wright represents a current and refreshing challenge to those scholars who have given up on the quest for the historical Jesus.

I enjoy certain Roman Catholic writings, though many would say that Salvationists and Catholics are at opposite ends of the theological spectrum. Even if that is so, we can by grace remain open and teachable toward one another. The writings of Hans Küng appeal strongly because of his readiness to be intellectually honest and his refusal to be overawed by hierarchical pressures brought to bear by the Vatican. *On Being a Christian* (1976) was gifted to me by Colonel Catherine Baird in 1978. *Does God Exist?* (1980) more recently came to my shelves from a bookshop in Sydenham in November 2012. It makes demands upon its readers, but why not? Küng's *Women in Christianity* (2001) is a much shorter paperback arising from his role as director of a research project on women and Christianity. His starting point is the place given to women in Catholicism. He wants to see this changed. I wonder if Küng knows about the women of The Salvation Army?

I feel indebted to Catholic writings on social ethics, an area where Catholics and Salvationists have more in common. In Essay 3 I recount my dealings with the Vatican but here let me mention the *Compendium of the Social Doctrine of the Church* (2004) published by the Pontifical Council for Justice and Peace. My copy, rich in ethical analysis of a most scholarly nature, was a gift from Cardinal Walter Kasper sent on to me after I met him in Rome in 2007. Add to this and other Vatican publications the writings of Jack Dominion. I have six of his books, typical of which is his *Passionate and Compassionate Love – A Vision for Christian Marriage* (1991). He writes as a Catholic layman grounded in the realities of his work as a psychiatrist. Impressive stuff.

I own eight books by the great, courageous, German theologian Dietrich Bonhoeffer. Of them all my favourite is his *Life Together* first published in English in 1954. Bonhoeffer is entirely unafraid of stretching his readers but the challenge is not confined to matters of theological depth or complexity. He writes for a verdict. In this I find an affinity with the best of Salvationist literature. We need to rediscover what it is to publish for a life-impacting verdict. Jesus told parables with precisely this aim.

Reading the sermons of others brings both pleasure and stimulus. Of all such volumes on my shelves it is Enoch Powell's little-known collection of sermons and articles, *Wrestling with the Angels* (1977), which I prize best. My copy is an autographed first edition. The author was a gifted academic turned politician. Often controversial and much vilified during his later political career, Powell was a scholar of classical Greek and an Anglican lay reader. His sermons are well worth reading and rereading.

Finally I have to record the help received from the writings of Helmut Thielicke, who believed no person could claim to be a preacher who had not preached through the creation narratives of Genesis, the Sermon on the Mount, and the Lord's Prayer. Thus his works: *How the World Began – Sermons on the Creation Story; Life Can Begin Again – Sermons on the*

Sermon on the Mount; *The Prayer That Spans the World – Sermons on the Lord's Prayer*. Some of these preachments were delivered in war-torn Stuttgart. They have a grounded feel to them. Thielicke preached for a verdict. I also have his autobiography, *Notes from a Wayfarer* published in 1995. Movingly he dedicates this volume to his wife 'who even through dark valleys kept me from becoming lost in the hospitality of this beautiful world'. A godly spouse is a very great gift.

Biography and politics

Living in Boston, USA, aroused a closer than otherwise interest in American politics. So it is unsurprising that my bookshelves house several volumes on recent USA presidents. Arthur M. Schlesinger's *A Thousand Days – John F. Kennedy in the White House* (1965) did not come to my notice until I spotted it on sale for $1 in Needham, Massachusetts, where we lived. The author worked with JFK in the White House. Written much later, and with access to additional records, is *President Kennedy – Profile of Power* (1993) by Richard Reeves who writes: 'I was interested in what he knew and when he knew it and what he actually did – sometimes day by day, sometimes hour by hour, sometimes minute by minute.' Then there is *Kissinger* (1992) by Walter Isaacson, another vast tome of almost 900 pages which covers some turbulent years with Kissinger as Secretary of State under President Richard Nixon. As I write, Kissinger, aged 90, is in London for the state funeral of former Prime Minister Margaret Thatcher.

Controversy dogs the steps of George W. Bush. Helen and I had dinner with George and Laura Bush in Dallas. The former President was relaxed and cordial. Mrs Bush was the essence of feminine graciousness and intelligence. Others present that evening represented some of the wealthiest citizens of the state of Texas, all willing to be identified in some way with The Salvation Army. Two volumes on my shelves evoke the memories. One is Bush's own narrative of his presidency, *Decision Points* (2010), noteworthy for the candid account of his alcoholism and of the Christian conversion that rescued him from addiction. The other is Laura Bush's account of her life, entitled *Spoken from the Heart* (2010). Mrs Bush is now a member of The Salvation Army's USA National Advisory Board.

In closing this Essay I must mention two books that impacted me some years ago, leaving me with deep respect for their distinguished authors.

An Humbler Heaven (1977) is a short account in paperback by the former editor of *The Times* newspaper and later chairman of the Arts Council in London, William Rees-Mogg, of the factors which led him to Christian faith. Rees-Mogg died in December 2012, aged 84, after a distinguished career as a journalist. He describes his faith at the age of 30 as that 'of a child', adding: 'I would have thought it shameful to know as little about economics or politics or literature as I knew about religion.' He then testifies: 'I can now say that [my life] has become the life of an unquestioning believer. The love of God is the only thing that matters ultimately in life, that and the love of humans which flows from it and flows back into it. This is the reason of life.'

A Sparrow's Flight (1990) is from a Christian lawyer and politician who held the post of Lord Chancellor in the UK government for a record eight years (1979-87). Quintin Hogg, later Lord Hailsham of Marylebone, was head of the entire judicial system in England and Wales with a staff of 22,000 housed in over 1,000 buildings. He offers a tender narrative, perhaps surprising from one known for pugnacity and tenacity in both the courtroom and in Parliament during his earlier political career. I once watched and heard him in London in full flow at the Law Courts in the Strand when I was a student lawyer.

Hailsham was an openly committed Christian. Especially moving is his account of the suicide of his brother, Edward. He tells of the guilt felt irrevocably by all the family because they would never know if they could have done anything to avoid the tragedy. We learn also of their hurt caused by the refusal of George Bell, then the Bishop of Chichester, to allow Edward to be buried in consecrated ground. He 'condemned us unheard in our hour of need', writes Hogg, before adding an ever-relevant, cautionary word about religious leaders 'who try to exert their authority without either charity or natural justice'. Here is a harsh reminder of ecclesiastical insensitivity, of rules taking precedence over pastoral need. All in spiritual leadership, including those of us in the Army, must by prayer and by taking wise counsel avoid such pitfalls.

So many books read and so many still to be read. Reading is an inexhaustible joy. I must take good care of my spectacles!

ESSAY 9

❧

SPIRITUALITY

ESSAY 9
SPIRITUALITY

IN MANY ways this Essay has been the hardest to compile for it must reveal things that would otherwise remain private. It has been written with some reluctance because essentially I am a private person. I do not mean to say that I am shy, far from it, but I am by nature inclined to reveal intimacies to but a chosen few. So this Essay is offered in the hope that some reader, here or there, might be helped. I add now to what has been said in Essay 2 in order to indicate how prayer, music and poetry help to nourish my soul. A concluding, short reflection will focus on the formative impact Helen made upon my spiritual life.

My prayers

They say there is both good and bad prayer but perhaps there is no such thing as bad prayer. There is both good and maybe not so good prayer. If one key aspect of the life of faith needs to mature with the passage of time it is the understanding and practice of prayer. I have never seen prayer as magical, as though if we somehow find the right words God will produce the right answer like a magician pulling a rabbit from a hat. Neither is God a divine vending machine mechanically responding to the right coin in the slot.

Over time my private prayers seem to involve less and less the sound of my own voice. Long ago I started to write down my intercessions for others, noting the date, name and subject matter and then, to an extent, ceasing to fret. It became possible to go back, at varied intervals, to my intercessions book to check what had become of each person's situation and then simply hand them back to God.

Praying for the needs of others is natural and right. So is praying for one's own needs, but prayer is so much more than 'needs'. It is not all asking. William Barclay tells us: 'Prayer is not making use of God but offering ourselves to God in order that he can make use of us.' The key is the initial entering into the presence of God. This requires stillness, so I need a physical place of tranquillity. Living in retirement has made that part of it easier than before. In earlier years Helen and I would try to find time together in our home, something that became more manageable once our children were grown up. My place of stillness would also often be my office desk, settling there early in the day with the door closed and putting aside the files and papers. Now and then those very documents would become the focus of prayerful thoughts. I could place before God the people and issues they represented.

Invoking the name of Jesus is central too. It was he who prayed the perfect prayer in Gethsemane, putting aside self and centring on the will of the Father. This leads effortlessly to a sense of awe in the divine presence and thus a sense of personal unworthiness. Longings to conform to God's plan in all things can arise spontaneously by putting self aside and relaxing in prayer in a spirit of readiness to co-operate with Heaven. Prayer allows us to place ourselves at God's disposal. The act of prayer thus becomes the fact of availability to God.

I have found that my own words, especially when spoken aloud, can sometimes render my praying more shallow. So I seek a sense of God's nearness by tending to say as little as possible. If words are used, they have to be mostly words of adoration, thanksgiving or self-offering. Intercessions, praying for the needs of others, can often flow naturally from this. Then there are the moments when words just fail. The apostle Paul knew of prayers too deep for words.

When Helen died my prayers were virtually all like this. I became inarticulate in prayer. Hardly could I engage my mind at all. My reaching for God became instinctive, visceral, tearful, desperate. Looking back now I see that these prayers were perhaps the deepest, most honest I have ever prayed. I was left helpless, bereft: my mind could not render assistance; my education was worthless; my rank was an irrelevance; my capacity to articulate was rendered dumb. It was as though I had suffered a spiritual stroke. So I turned to my Maker virtually speechless, with nothing to offer but deep pain, anger and tears. It seemed it would never cease, but a beacon of hope came from knowing that others were frequently speaking my name to God.

There really is no such thing as being stuck for words in prayer. We can relax, forget the words, and know God is all around us. We can sigh or weep, smile or laugh. How liberating this is. How comforting to know that Heaven is neither measuring the time we spend in prayer nor giving us a grade for the words we use. In the end prayer is simply being with God in an intentional way and enjoying his life-changing, soul-formative company.

The prayers of others

Much help has come to my private prayer life through using the prayers of others. Their words have freed me from the quest to find my own, letting me go deeper, more intuitively, into God's presence without 'Shaw' getting in the way.

The Psalms help in this. So too does our *Song Book* (see Essay 5) or reading the Army's daily devotional guide, *Words of Life*. Most used by me is a little volume bound hardback in maroon and called simply, *A Book of Prayers*. Compiled by Ruth Connell and published by Lion Books in 1988, it has been in my hands at three High Councils (see Essay 11) and is now heavily annotated with dates and places to remind me when and where a particular prayer brought comfort. Additional prayers have been copied and pasted in, adding still more to this special collection. Here are two prayers. The first is printed in the book and the second has been inserted by me:

> *Come, Lord! Come with me: see with my eyes; hear with my ears; think with my mind; love with my heart – in all the situations of my life. Work with my hands, my strength. Take, cleanse, possess, inhabit my will, my understanding, my love. Take me where you will, to do what you want, in your way.* (Evelyn Underhill)

My annotations to this say: 'Farewell Orders, January 2002 to New Zealand'; 'Voting Day, High Council, 6 September 2002'; 'November 2007 in hospital with a very different setting for this plea.'

The second prayer is by J.S. Horland. It is called 'A Prayer for Loved Ones':

> *Teach me stillness and confident peace in thy perfect will, deep calm of soul, and contentment in what thou wilt do with these lives thou hast given. Teach me to wait and be still, to rest in thyself, to hush this clamorous anxiety, to lay in thine arms all this wealth thou hast given.*

Thou lovest these souls that we love with a love as far surpassing our own as the glory of noon surpasses the gleam of a candle. Therefore we will be still, and trust in thee.

'All this wealth' means 'these souls that we love': my spouse, children, grandchildren, siblings and wider family. This can also be used to pray for one's spiritual family.

Two more books have helped to shape my soul. *The Soldier's Guide*, first published by the Army in 1907 and republished in 1917, was intended 'for the use of men who would wish to carry it with them to their work'. Its size allows it to be kept in a breast pocket or in the pocket of a military battledress (note the publication date during the First World War). The title page says: 'A Bible reading for the morning and evening of every day in the year together with leaves for mid-day plucking.' I have found it so practical. My well-worn copy was once the property of Sergeant George Tansley, Number 46359 of the 23rd Northumberland Fusiliers, 4th Tyneside Scottish. It is inscribed: 'To Cousin George, with kind thoughts, from Auntie.'

My second prayer companion is nearly a century old. It is *The Priest's Prayer Book*, an Anglican publication from Longmans, Green and Co in 1921. Handsomely bound in leather and embossed with gold, it was bought by me second-hand in Bromley, Kent, in March 1992. A plate inside the front cover shows it was presented in the Lent Term of 1921 by the Principal, L.A. Phillips, to one Conrad Howard Rogers at Lichfield Theological College. Published as an Appendix to the *Book of Common Prayer* and meant for use by parochial clergy, it has been especially helpful to me. I have valued its 'Notes on the Practice of Holiness' and the section entitled 'Private Prayers for Bishops' containing short prayers on 16 matters ranging from 'Wisdom in Ruling' to 'Moral Courage', from 'True Faith and Holiness' to 'Grace to Rule Well'. Often I have made these pleas my own and have used also the section immediately following entitled 'Questions for Self-Examination'. Echoes of John Wesley.

The enriching prayers of others in my life include also those of the wonderfully articulate Michel Quoist. His *Prayers of Life* from Logos Books in 1963 include two that have especially moved me. One is 'The Priest: a Prayer on Sunday Night':

It's hard always to give without trying to receive. It's hard to seek out others and be unsought oneself. It's hard to carry others and never, even for a moment, be carried.

The other is 'Lord, you have seized me':

Lord, you seized me and I could not resist you. I ran for a long time, but you followed me. I took bypaths, but you knew them. I struggled. You won. Why me, why did you choose me? Joy, joy, tears of joy.

Lately I have used also a Canadian volume, *Quiet Moments*, a 1989 collection of prayers and meditations by Lyn Whittall and Judy Hager. They include George Appleton's plea:

Help us to leave no duty undone, no sin unrepented, no relationship unsanctified.

Then a prayer of defencelessness from Avery Brooke:

O Lord, when I am bewildered and the world is all noise and confusion around me and I don't know which way to go and am frightened, then be with me. Put your hand on my shoulder and let your strength invade my weakness and your light burn the mist from my mind. Help me to step forward with faith in the way I should go.

Finally, a salutary thought from an unknown source:

We may desire to bring to God a perfect work. We would like to point, when our work is done, to the beautiful ripened grain and bound up sheaves, and yet the Lord frustrates our plans, shatters our purposes, lets us see the wreck of all our hopes, breaks the beautiful structure we thought we were building and captures us up in his arms and whispers to us, 'It's not your work I wanted, but you.'

My soul and music

I cannot overstate the part music plays in helping to mould and stir my spiritual life. With tastes in music wide and varied, I am readily moved by what I hear. I am also a warm admirer of those whose musical skills provide for the rest of us. Their dedication is a wonderful thing, whether as a skilled amateur like most of our Salvationist musicians or as a gifted professional. Those of us who listen reap the benefit of their commitment. It was the wonderful Russian cellist, Mstislav Rostropovich, who said: 'You play for yourself. The audience are merely eavesdropping.' There is good and bad eavesdropping. This is the good sort.

All kinds of music can touch me, from John Rutter to Elvis Presley. I am among the many in the United Kingdom (UK) who were delighted to discover the Classic FM radio station when it first came on stream. I have been uplifted countless times by the playing or singing of Salvation Army musicians in worship meetings. Sometimes the level of performance is high, sometimes it is not, but there is always a blessing to be gained. Let me give one or two illustrations.

At Enfield in north London the corps would observe Mother's Day in the traditional manner. Wanting to make special those moments when each child presented a flower to his or her mother, I asked Bandmaster James Williams to have the band play, as the distribution took place, the brass arrangement of Edvard Grieg's Elegiac Melody, 'The Last Spring'. Then each year on Mother's Day it would be played again, creating a small but beautiful tradition. Knowing that the Norwegian Grieg came to reject his Christian faith saddened me, but could not detract from the exquisite simplicity of this music. Still it imparts blessing, and will be played at my funeral. Grieg had a modest view of himself. He said, 'Bach and Beethoven erected churches and temples on the heights. I wanted only to build dwellings for people in which they might feel happy and at home.' I think he succeeded.

Dudley Bright, a Salvationist and professional trombone player, wrote in *Salvationist* (10 September 2011) about his fellow Army musician, the composer Major Leslie Condon: 'His was an extraordinarily original, natural, creative talent.' Who could disagree? Les was an approachable person. I recall a holiday long ago at Gwydyr House in Margate, Kent, where the Condon family were also taking a break. One day I found Les sitting in the sun with a musical score manuscript on his knee. He looked up and afforded me, then still a fledgling officer, time for a short, cheery exchange. I wished him an inspired morning. On 19 March 1979 soon after our return from Africa Les came to preside at a musical evening presented by Enfield Band at Wood Green in London's northern suburbs. It was there that I heard his 'Song of the Eternal' first performed in public. I had heard it rehearsed by the band but now here it was complete in a polished performance: 'From that sacred hill, hope is gleaming still. Thy shame and grief he bore, go in peace, sin no more.' I had been moved by Army music before, but not like this. It called to me, drew me in, and demanded gently but firmly some sort of response. I was not the only one with moist eyes that night. When the performance ended Les stood up and self-effacingly complimented Jim and the band: 'It is only when your music is brought alive in this way that it takes on meaning.' Since then I have heard this composition countless times and been blessed. Enfield Band came to play it at Denmark Hill for Helen's funeral and thanksgiving service. 'Hope is gleaming still.'

Helen and I long ago found ourselves captivated by Beethoven's Piano Concerto No 5 (Opus 73) 'The Emperor'. In February 1988 we attended a concert at the Barbican by the London Symphony Orchestra under Sir Colin Davis to celebrate the 85th birthday of the great Claudio Arrau who that night played 'The Emperor' and enchanted us all. It was televised live. Beethoven's Symphony No 5 (Opus 67) was also performed. What power, what majesty! During the interval I heard in the lobby the polished tones of a familiar voice opining, 'It's a rather corny programme, don't you think?' I turned to discover that the speaker was the debonair actor, Peter Bowles, who played Richard DeVere opposite Penelope Keith in the popular sitcom, *To the Manor Born*. I wanted to go over to tell him I disagreed completely, but Helen's restraining tug on my sleeve (a tug which all through the years I came to know well!) meant I did not.

Two other great classical works have come to be my main spiritual companions. The first is Max Bruch's Violin Concerto No 1 (Opus 26) completed in 1867. It is immensely popular. It won me when first I heard it on BBC Radio 3. Back then in the early 1970s we managed to get hold of a cassette recording of it which travelled with us to Rhodesia in 1975.

During the early months there we had no television set, so our hi-fi equipment came into its own. Our bungalow at Mazowe School had a small veranda at the rear where we could sit, usually at dusk, in almost complete privacy. Bruch was frequently playing. My vivid memories are of evening tropical rain hammering down all around me as I sat, sheltered on the veranda, with the sound of Bruch's violin concerto at maximum volume reaching me from the open doors of the lounge within. Those occasions brought balm, help and a soothing to my soul which, because of the lack of safety faced almost daily, was often tense and troubled.

If the music of Max Bruch carried me through Africa it was that of the great Finnish composer, Jean Sibelius, that sustained me through our years in the USA, Pakistan and New Zealand. Among the vast riches he has to offer is his Symphony No 2 in D major (Opus 43), composed in 1901-02, which has captured my soul. While compiling this Essay I heard the Sibelius Symphony No 7 (Opus 105) on BBC television. The charming presenter referred to the Mahler Chamber Orchestra and their conductor, David Harding. She went on to offer remarks about the symphony, concluding her introduction by smiling whimsically at the camera and telling us that Sibelius 'lived long enough to hear Elvis Presley'. Well, I thought, two of my favourite musicians mentioned in one breath!

Born in 1865 Sibelius lived to be 92 but produced nothing of real musical value during the last 30 years of his life. In the five preceding decades he composed prolifically. I suppose many think of Sibelius and hear at once the stirring tones of 'Finlandia', composed in 1899 when Finnish longings to break free from Russian imperial domination were strongest. That work has remained Finland's unofficial national anthem. The composer tried to resist an active part in the political unrest of his day but 'Finlandia' identified him indelibly as part of the anti-Russification movement. He was proud to have received his education in Finnish, although his parents (his father was a military doctor) were natural Swedish speakers like most of the educated classes of Finland at that time.

Despite Sibelius's reluctance toward politics, the Second Symphony in four movements was at once perceived through the political lenses of its Finnish admirers. It proved to be an immediate success. One critic,

Karl Flodin, in 1903 described it as 'an absolute masterpiece'. Not everyone was impressed. Virgil Thomson, American composer and critic, later called the music 'vulgar, self-indulgent and provincial beyond any description'. I am with Flodin, but let my Journal speak for me:

Journal, 23 August 1996: When we served in Rhodesia (1975-79) I was sustained on countless occasions by the Max Bruch Violin Concerto. Now here in America I have discovered the symphonies of Sibelius and the Second has won me entirely. It moves and comforts me. I take it as a gift from the Lord to help me through.

Journal, 11 October 1997: I am alone in the apartment. Helen is on her way back from Karachi and gets in at about 8.40 pm. John is playing cricket in William Booth Street. Sibelius Second Symphony is playing. It still calls to somewhere deep in me. I do not know where or why.

Journal, 20 January 1999: As I write, the Sibelius Second is on the CD player. Loud brass, much timpani, prominent basses and cellos. I like its lower pitch, its intensity, its power and yet it is also strangely delicate. A gentle, perceptive strength. I should have this in my life and personality.

Journal, 8 March 1999: Sibelius is on the CD player. The Second Symphony still speaks to me. Somewhere too deep within for me to identify just where. It is strong and purposeful, yet unorthodox and often gentle. I think Jesus was like that, in perfect balance and inner harmony.

Sibelius: a mounting crescendo, driving on and on, surging forward, pulsating, now reaching the finale with a gorgeous rubato. Lord, thank you for these sounds and the resonances within me. The music is your gift to me. It sustained me in Boston and now in Lahore. Lord, get me through.

Journal, 16 December 2000: It is Saturday afternoon and I have the Sibelius Second Symphony on loud in the flat. It is some time since

I heard it all the way through. It still touches and moves me. It speaks, but without words. It tells me there are realities beyond the expressible in words, beyond the tangible. It tells me there are aspects of my being untapped and unexplored. What are these?

Journal, 13 April 2003: Opposite this entry in my Journal I have placed a photographic portrait in black and white of the great Sibelius, photographed by the renowned Yousuf Karsh in 1949 when the composer was 84 years old. His Second Symphony has long been part of me now. Sibelius had a good face. He was a little portly. Generous cut of suit, but I do not like the foppish breast pocket stuffed with a fancy handkerchief. In the end, the strong face, firm jaw line, and the penetrating, engaging eyes win out. I would like to have known him.

Journal, 18 April 2012: Am in Ilminster with Syl, spending five nights here. Weather wet and windy but we need the rain. The evening of Friday 13 April was one of real pleasure. I went with Matt and John to the Barbican Hall to hear the BBC Symphony Orchestra play Sibelius. It was magical. I sat between the boys just seven rows from the stage. We could see and hear every note, every nuance, every gesture of both conductor and musicians. A last-minute change meant that a young Danish conductor, Thomas Søndergård, presided. What expression, what grace, what eloquence, what power! The major work of the evening was the Second Symphony. I know it so well, note for note. Now here it was live and pulsating, enfolding me in sounds beyond imagining, albeit from a composer whose personal life and habits were not always the best. Dear Sibelius was a flawed man but his music is exquisite. Beauty from ashes. The evening brought me comfort and balm. I could lose myself in the sounds. It was one of the few occasions since Helen died that I have experienced something I might call joy.

A bonus to the Sibelius was the playing of the Ukrainian-born Israeli violinist, Vadim Gluzman. He was using a 1690 Stradivarius, on loan to him from the Stradivari Society of Chicago. We were just a few rows from him as he played, brilliant and effortless. It was the first performance in the UK of the Violin Concerto in B minor by Balys

Dvarionas (1904-72), a Lithuanian composer and the first from that land to produce a violin concerto. For half an hour the music on that rare Stradivarius enfolded us. When it ended Gluzman was applauded for many minutes. We brought him back on stage again and again until at last he settled us all down with an unaccompanied encore. Wonderful! I feel so pleased and grateful to God that all of this was mine. Matt and John loved it too.

Music and movement

If today you find yourself in London and in the northern suburbs, your chosen route might well take you via The Angel, Edmonton. This is where the notorious, traffic-laden North Circular Road intersects with Fore Street and where Edmonton Corps hall is only a few hundred yards to the north. 'The Angel' public house, famed for its links with the highwayman, Dick Turpin, was still standing when we were children. Across the intersection back then was the Regal Theatre. Now it is the site of an unprepossessing supermarket, but when Helen and I were young the Regal was a beautiful cinema behind whose screen was a huge revolving stage. It was there we saw our first ballet, Pyotr Ilyich Tchaikovsky's *Swan Lake*. Curious at first, perhaps even dubious, I was captivated within moments of it beginning. The marriage of sound and movement won me completely. The live orchestra, the grace and power of the dancers, the scenery, the drama – I felt transported.

Since then we have enjoyed ballets in Bristol, Boston, Wellington and various venues in London. These experiences brought escape from daily pressures and uplift to my spirit. Just before our intention to marry was made known, Birgitte and I found ourselves in the Royal Albert Hall for a performance (not on stage but in the arena in-the-round) of *Swan Lake* by the English National Ballet. There was not an empty seat to be seen in that vast venue. We were only a few rows above the dancers. This version of the popular ballet ended with the evil Rothbart (who had first emerged from a trapdoor centred in the floor of the mist-laden arena) defeated and all the swans (60 of them!) set free from his malevolent control. It was all great fun, but also wonderful drama, exquisite movement, and overwhelmingly poignant music.

Poetry

I must not pretend to be knowledgeable about poetry. The many volumes still in my possession were for the most part used by Helen. However, I can recognise a good poem (one that works) when I come across it and I know when I feel engaged, caught up by the language and by what it conveys. I will offer here just two examples of poems that speak to me, both expressions of human love. One is from a Nobel Prize-winning Irish poet and the other from a famous Russian:

> *Had I the heavens' embroidered cloths,*
> *Enwrought with gold and silver light,*
> *The blue and the dim and the dark cloths,*
> *Of night and light and the half-light,*
> *I would spread the cloths under your feet:*
> *But I, being poor, have only my dreams;*
> *I have spread my dreams under your feet;*
> *Tread softly because you tread on my dreams.*
> (W.B. Yeats)

> *When your face*
> *appeared over my crumpled life*
> *at first I understood*
> *only the poverty of what I have.*
> *Then its particular light*
> *on woods, on rivers, on the sea,*
> *became my beginning in the*
> *coloured world*
> *in which I had not yet had*
> *my beginning.*
> *I am so frightened,*
> *I am so frightened,*
> *of the unexpected sunrise finishing,*
> *of revelations and tears*
> *and the excitement finishing.*
> *I don't fight it,*

248

my love is this fear,
I nourish it who can nourish nothing,
love's slipshod watchman.
Fear hems me in.
I am conscious that
these minutes are short
and that the colours in my eyes
will vanish
when your face sets.
(Yevgeny Yevtushenko)

Helen's influence

No Essay about my spirituality – and I cannot claim this one is an adequate account – would make sense were Helen's influence upon me not mentioned. We fell in love wholeheartedly in our early teens but knew even earlier as children that we would be together. So her part in shaping me has been virtually lifelong. I wanted to be good and godly because Helen was good and godly, and I wanted to be good and godly because Helen wanted me to be good and godly.

She was easy to love. She looked so attractive, and I could not resist the powerful draw of her able, clear mind, of her readiness to laugh, of her iron strength of will when something really mattered, and of her deep commitment to Christ.

She had a profound capacity to be committed. She gave herself: to the Saviour; to me; to our children; to our children-in-law; to our grandchildren; to the Army and its sacred cause. Here was femininity quietly enfolding a will of steel.

As she rose in rank in the Army she sought always to remain unfettered from departmental chores. Content to process papers when needful, she never quite understood what drove some women officers around her – and often accountable to her – to yearn for an office, a desk and a department to run. To Helen these things were at best a necessary evil, a ball and chain, taking away precious time that needed to be spent with and for the real needs of real people. At the same time she held a clear and ever-present intention to influence policy matters, but opted to do this in the boardroom in person rather than through a flurry of email correspondence or form filling. All of this impressed and pleased me.

So too did her love of reading, her extensive general knowledge, her love of physical exercise (I think of those long, romantic walks in the Lake District) and her capacity suddenly to be still, alone with her Lord. She used *The Soldier's Armoury* and *Words of Life* and kept prayer journals (quoted in part by me in *From Her Heart*, 2012). Her reading included classical novels, contemporary fiction by African and Pakistani authors, and much biography. Books about people and their lives were her constant focus.

What had I done to deserve the gift of this person? It is as though our Maker sees and knows our needs and, if we are willing, provides for them and goes on shaping us through the gift of those who become closest and most precious to us. Marriage, as God intended it, and for those of us called to that estate, is sacred. When allowed to be the setting for the formation of one's soul, then it is at its most sacred, most intimate.

ESSAY 10

☙

STALWARTS

ESSAY 10
STALWARTS

THIS Essay involves risk. I want to mention people who have been role models or a help and inspiration to me and there is every possibility that some names will be left out. I ask forgiveness for any serious omission. I am thinking of those who have helped me in my Christian walk because they have been easy to admire, been kindly and considerate, or have possessed other qualities more of which I need in my own person.

Most folk mentioned are Salvationists because this Essay is largely about people I have met and known well. It need hardly be said there are others beyond our ranks whose examples or whose writings have been a blessing, but here it is mainly my Army comrades I want to salute. As far as practical, I will proceed in chronological sequence.

Family

My loved ones must come first, not because of what they have done and still do for me, but because of who they are to me.

Helen's unique part in shaping me is recorded in other Essays (see especially Essay 9) and so is the loving impact of my parents (see Essay 1). So first I will focus briefly on my three children. Not only do I love them, I admire them.

Our firstborn, Matt, is of a gentle, amenable spirit but has a mind like a vice. Always ready to point out a flaw in one's reasoning and to sustain his point of view in strenuous but amicable debate, his overriding concern is for others and their dignity. When he commits, it is with a whole heart. God has bestowed on him a gift of articulation through writing. He is a lovely father to his three children and is blessed to be married to Lynne, who is passionate about her calling and greatly gifted in working energetically with people.

Born in Rhodesia and living now in New Zealand, Jen has inherited her Mum's easy, natural ways with those to whom she ministers. Yet, like her brothers she is tough-minded and highly principled when it comes to the issues of the day. Seeing her lead a Sunday meeting or hearing her preach is a blessing. She combines directness with femininity, like so many gifted women throughout the history of the Army. Marcus is an ideal match for her. He is clear about his faith, is an articulate preacher, is committed to his calling and family, and offers firmly intelligent leadership in all he does. Best of all, he does not take his father-in-law too seriously.

John lived on four continents before reaching the age of 18. As a result he relates easily to persons of all backgrounds and connects quickly with those he meets. Said to resemble me in appearance, he is much brighter intellectually than I ever was and shows evidence of real academic giftedness. With Naomi, he has entered upon his sacred calling with intelligent enthusiasm, not settling for the routine. He is ready to push the boundaries outward if it will further the gospel. Naomi complements him wonderfully, being also academically gifted and having a poise when speaking in public that many far more experienced would wish for.

These six people are a blessing to me. It is not hard to admire them. They are generous with their affection, hospitality and support. They have gifted us with six grandchildren, each one so precious: Hannah, Elijah and Amos; Hudson and Lincoln; and even as this was being written, Miriam Helen.

Having two sisters has shaped who I am and also my view of the world. Mary, the younger, died just a few weeks before Helen and showed quiet Christian courage as she coped with many years of illness. Her example as a devoted wife, mother and grandmother lives on to inspire us all. Sylvia, the firstborn of the three of us, is one of the finest Christians I know. She will not thank me for saying so, but her life of availability to others is an inspiration. The value of her presence in our home for the final months of Helen's life can never be repaid. She took care of me when I was small, and still does so today in a wonderfully subtle, supportive and yet non-interfering way. She is loving, wise and selfless. The world could benefit from having more like her.

Student days

The Army relocated my parents from Edmonton in London to Leicester in the Midlands right in the middle of my final year at school. Their plea to leaders for reconsideration went unheard and I found myself lodging in the home of Bert and Rose Jipps, Salvationists in Edmonton

Corps. Essay 6 describes a similar pattern of events years later affecting our son, John. The Jipps were wonderfully kind and allowed me to feel at home. Bert was an ardent Tottenham Hotspur fan. On getting home from work (he was a skilled brush maker) he would toss the newspaper to me and comment cheerily on the latest sports headlines. Rose had a kind heart and was a wonderful cook.

When I started out as a law student at King's College, London (see Essay 13) I needed accommodation. Betty, daughter of Bert and Rose, offered me lodgings. Married to Les Dean, Betty inherited her Mum's skills in the kitchen and fed me well. I owe much to the Deans for their acceptance of me and their kindness all those years ago. Living now in Wellingborough, these loyal Army folk have opened their home readily to us on several occasions in recent years when we have made official visits to the corps.

Also generous with accommodation for a spell were Doris and Ernie Chapman. Ernie was the songster leader and the skilled compiler of the crossword puzzle for the Army's *Assurance Magazine*. Their son, Derek, made me welcome in their home. He played solo cornet in Edmonton Band, was a keen amateur footballer, and rode a hugely powerful motorcycle. He was fun to be around (see Essay 5).

Nesam Williamson was adopted in south India by Lieut-Colonel Vera Williamson. When we were still young local officers at Edmonton she attended the corps and became our friend due to Helen's persistence in making her feel welcome. She married Moses Noble, also an adopted child of missionary officers. Colonel William McAllister conducted the wedding at Edmonton. We enjoyed the company of Nesam and Moses. He had been a ship's cook and introduced us to curry, delighting in my efforts to cool down after eating his hot (oh so hot!) dishes. When Moses died at an early age in the autumn of 1982 Nesam had to raise their two children, Isobel and Rajan, alone. She lived only a few doors away from Helen's parents. Working as a skilled theatre nurse in the North Middlesex Hospital, Nesam provided well for her family, now and then also making the long journey to New Zealand to visit her adopted mother. Nesam is one of our oldest, most loyal friends. After Helen died she telephoned me every week to ensure all was well. How good it is to have friends who never change through all the passing years.

When teaching in the law faculty at Bristol University, I met David Slingsby. We became good companions but lost touch across the years. Recently we have re-established contact. Dr Slingsby is a biologist and for some years has edited the *Journal of Biological Education*. He is also a member of the British Council's Disability Advisory Panel. Although now mainly confined to a wheelchair, David remains active in his church. It was good to have a fellow Christian to befriend and encourage me in Bristol. When we met recently for a meal near London's Russell Square it was as though all the intervening years just fell away. 'We are still brothers in Christ,' said David.

Denmark Hill, Mazowe, Enfield

We met Major and Mrs John and Lydie Ord when we became cadets in 1971. John was refreshingly approachable and often played football (with quite some skill!) with us in Ruskin Park. He and I tussled for the ball and kicked each other's shins in friendly rivalry! Lydie was warm and kind, always ready to ask how we were getting on. How good to have staff who were unpretentious and treated us normally. Later they became our divisional leaders in the East London Division when we were at Enfield. Now commissioners and retired, they still take an interest in me and mine. They have not changed through all the years.

Lieut-Colonel Alistair Cairns, an Australian officer, was the Chief Side Officer for Men. He and his wife arrived as our training days began. We were blessed to have this godly, humane, intelligent man to guide us. Whenever I was with him I sensed an aura of manly sanctity. In later years he would write to us on blue airmail paper to assure us of prayers and interest. Alistair was a very special person.

It was at Denmark Hill that we also met and got to know Chick and Margaret Yuill, two gifted cadets. Each was multi-talented and could readily draw a crowd with Chick's trumpet and Margaret's guitar whenever we engaged in street ministry in central London. Chick, also a fine pianist, went on to benefit many around the world through his writing and public speaking.

Moving to Balham in early 1974, prior to sailing for Rhodesia in 1975, we met Colonel Catherine Baird, the Army's foremost poet, then well into retirement. Here again was a gifted but down-to-earth Christian person who offered us friendship. She doted on Matt, then only a few months old. She had a way of making you feel special. This was her gift to us. Being with her made me want to be a better, more godly officer. Small, even frail in appearance, she had a formidable intellect but never engaged in outward display on that account. She knew words, could use them exquisitely, but more than that she knew people and what was in them. Here was a rare kind of wisdom. Her impact upon both Helen and me was profound. In September 1974, just before my 29th birthday, she presented me with a new copy of the 37th edition of *Hart's Rules for Compositors and Readers at the University Press, Oxford*. It remains a treasured possession. C.B. signed it and added this inscription: 'To Shaw, who likes to have things right.'

Essay 6 describes some of our African experiences. The all-too-short 18 months at Bulawayo Citadel marked us indelibly. My outstanding memories are of good and godly people. John McNabb (now a major and living in retirement in South Africa) was the corps treasurer. It was he who opened the self-denial altar service envelopes with me in our home one evening. Realising how much the giving exceeded that of previous years, John paused and pushed aside the papers and books. 'We need to stop and give thanks to God in prayer,' he said. So then and there in our dining room we prayed. I have relived that moment many times on similar occasions and have thought of John. Still today he writes with news and assurances of prayers. He is another who has stayed the same despite the passing years.

Majors Christian and Ellen Ramild-Jørgensen became our lifelong friends in Bulawayo. Their fidelity to their sacred callings in trying times, and their openness to others, was inspiring. Chris and I laughed at the same things. Bulawayo was where we met also George and Mirjam Claydon. Later returning to England and reassuming the rank of major under Commissioner Denis Hunter, these gifted, intelligent Salvationists became the corps officers at Salisbury City Corps in England. George died of cancer and I led the funeral on 2 December 1985. Mirjam pressed on in valiant service, a true stalwart. Dr and Mrs Jock and Gwen Cook were stalwarts too. Mervyn and Jackie Sadler became our friends. Mervyn and I would meet to play squash and to talk about matters of faith over post-game refreshments. Serving part-time in the military forces of Rhodesia, he was shot dead in an ambush on the road between Beit Bridge and Bulawayo just a few weeks after we left Rhodesia for London. Feelings of despair and helplessness swept over us on hearing this news. We felt we were a million miles away from Jackie and her two children, Heather and Sean. Coming so soon after the deaths of Lieutenant Diane Thompson and Sharon Swindells at Usher Institute (see Essay 6), it seemed that darkness was all around.

Going to our appointments at Enfield brought us into close contact with many good and loyal people. Bandmaster James Williams and his wife, Elsie, were sources of constant encouragement. How I admired Jim's gifted way with the band and his deep inner commitment as a Salvationist. As I write I still picture his conducting, articulate hands and arms drawing out the best from each player to impart inspiration and blessing. Jim was always respectful and gave me my place. Peter Moore was the corps treasurer. A skilled accountant, he brought the same dedication to his Army service as he did to his work for Price Waterhouse Cooper. Alan Cooper, energetic and practical, was the corps secretary. John and Glenys Hill typified the consistency of service and warmth of fellowship that marked out the corps. So too did Stuart and Muriel Garnham, Malcolm and Margaret Hynd, and a host of others. We formed lifelong friendships at Enfield and it is always rewarding to return there.

The legal years at International Headquarters

Seven years at International Headquarters (IHQ) brought me into contact with a host of able employees and officers. General Jarl Wahlström readily won my affection, as had General Clarence Wiseman in earlier years. They seemed to stand in that tradition of confident but unassuming leadership that has marked out many of our generals. General George Carpenter, from all I have read and heard of him, was another in this mould. I learned much by serving under two very able Chiefs of the Staff, Commissioners Caughey Gauntlett and Ronald Cox. Both treated me with humanity and, despite my lack of years and of rank, with much respect. They trusted my judgement, acted on my advice, and backed me whenever I ran into obstacles with others. Not once did either of these gifted men seek to curtail my international travel. They encouraged me to accept invitations to teach and preach, over and above the journeys necessitated by legal things.

Several international secretaries impressed and encouraged me at that time: Commissioners Norman Marshall, Albert Scott and Bill Roberts (Americas and Caribbean); David Durman (South Asia and before that Chancellor of the Exchequer); Anna Hannevik and Egon Østergaard (Europe). Here were competent people, each one normal, unstuffy and real.

The seven years at IHQ saw us involved in the life of Romford Corps in Essex. We lived not far away in Hornchurch. The corps offered much for children and teenagers. At the heart of the youth scene was Joyce Shepherd, a stalwart of the faith and a lasting influence for good and the gospel on countless young people. We had known Joyce since our days at Edmonton prior to becoming cadets and now our own children, Matt and Jen, were the beneficiaries of her loving ministry. Today facing health challenges, but with her spirit and mind as vibrant as ever, Joyce still keeps in touch with assurances of prayer and interest in our life as a family.

To Bromley

Leaving IHQ behind and taking up the leadership of Bromley Temple Corps was a challenging transition for me: no longer easy access to people at the top; no more handling of large, complex issues; no global arena for mission and service; no secretarial back-up. The warm reception from the people at Bromley helped me handle this transition though never did I speak to them about my initial struggle with the change. The corps brimmed with committed, capable comrades typified by Chris and Val Walford, Christine and Arthur Webb, and Paul and Maureen Gettens. Here too were the beginnings of lasting friendships.

When Helen died the folk at Bromley Temple showed instant and practical support. Added to expressions of love and sympathy from the global Army family, this was a huge help. Majors Brian and Liv Slinn, our corps officers, were wonderfully faithful with sensitive care and generous hospitality. Helen and Howard Elliott opened their home to me, as did the Walfords and Gettens already mentioned. Christine Webb made sure I was coping, as did Mrs Colonel Jean Clark. Each hosted me more than once for tea and chat, for they knew what it was to be bereaved of a loving spouse. Lieut-Colonel Colin Fairclough got me out walking each week in the fields of Kent. How I miss Colin. He was promoted to Glory at the end of 2012. Lieut-Colonel Royston Bartlett gifted me with his company and comradeship over many a cup of coffee and a Belgian bun. Peter Cooke made sure I was doing alright. We have known each other for many years and still meet up for coffee. General John Larsson and Commissioner Freda Larsson provided hospitality to me on more than one occasion, as did Railton and Olwyn Holdstock, and Major Hannelise Tvedt. Jim and Val Baddams hosted me and showed loving concern. Major Dean Pallant sought me out in those early months and gave me time and companionship.

The list could go on. I place on record my deep indebtedness to those I have named and to the many more besides, including those beyond Bromley, who have shown me loving kindness. Typical of these is Major Peter Mylechreest who, after retiring and settling in London, proved a cordial and understanding companion on several occasions, even tolerating my hopeless efforts to match him at chess!

In the divisions

Our years in the lovely Durham and Tees Division in north-east England allowed us contact with many impressive Salvationists. Among these were John and Lynda Garrett who have kept in touch through all the years and who, despite now living in the USA, see me in London from time to time. With typical, godly largesse they have set up and financed a trust fund in memory of Helen which reinforces Army ministry in many parts of the world.

As a family we soldiered then at Middlesbrough Citadel and were regularly blessed and helped by the pastoral care and platform ministry of Major Kenneth Morey, a more than able exponent of God's Word. The skill, warmth and energy of Majors John and Sheila Hunt, Major Maisie Bellshaw and Captain Martin Hill ensured that the team at divisional headquarters was not only a happy one but a productive one too.

It was at this time that Commissioners Arthur and Karen Thompson came to lead a divisional congress. I recall good, frank conversation with Arthur during that visit. The outcomes demonstrated that he was a man of his word. I have always warmed to his directness and have been a beneficiary too of his readiness to offer encouragement and affirmation.

In Boston, USA, we met Majors Gil and Warna Reynders, two people who instantly helped us feel at home and who, with their daughters, opened not only their hearts but also their home to us. Gil was the general secretary in the division and a meticulous, competent administrator. I owe him much. A similar debt of gratitude is owed to Commissioners Ronald and Polly Irwin, our territorial leaders in the USA Eastern Territory. We were touched by their readiness to receive and accept us, as well as by their holding us to account for our stewardship of the Massachusetts Division. Here were leaders who led, but who cared as well. Working under them was a formative experience. So too was working alongside deeply committed and godly colleagues like Bandmaster Bill Rollins, our Divisional Director of Music, and at territorial headquarters (THQ) Colonels Israel and Eva Gaither, Lieut-Colonels Larry and Nancy Moretz, and Lieut-Colonels Bill and Marilyn Francis. These six officer friends all went on to become commissioners and to serve both within and outside the USA. I believe our getting to know them during our time in Boston was no mere accident of circumstance. God was in it. He blessed also our friendship with our predecessors, Lieut-Colonels Ralph and Alice Joyce, who hosted us overnight whenever we were in West Nyack. Ralph is now in Heaven, but Alice keeps in touch with news and words of encouragement.

In the territories

Those who blessed and helped us in the three territories entrusted to our leadership are far too numerous all to be listed by name. As I look back to Lahore I see the face of the then Lieut-Colonel Gulzar Patras, helpful, self-effacing and honest. He was of a gentle disposition and never once did I sense in him a spirit of self or of misplaced ambition. He was faithful in leading the extensive Lahore Division and later, after becoming the Field Secretary, demonstrated a rare level of pastoral giftedness. He knew his people, he understood his culture, and he related well to the Moslem majority. All of these things came helpfully to the fore when he was appointed as the Chief Secretary. Never once did he let me down.

I want to record the same of Majors John and Val Townsend, Ethne Flintoff, John Dyall and Fran Duffett. These were all gifted colleagues blessed with a spirit of friendliness and self-giving servanthood. Our lives were made better through knowing them and without them at our side much less would have been achieved.

Where else could one look to see typified the spirit of Salvationism in New Zealand but to retired Corps Sergeant-Major Cyril Bradwell? A deserved recipient of the Order of the Founder, his name and reputation in the territory were legendary. He was admired and loved on every hand. An enthusiast for sports, he connected easily with others, never letting his academic sophistication get in the way. He and Nola were lovely people. Readily they offered us friendship and acceptance. I liked Cyril for all that he was, but not least for his deep pride in his native land, in its culture and in the place and role of the Army there. Another who won my admiration was Major Lyn Buttar, an unfailingly courteous and encouraging colleague who, when Helen died, showed me understanding for he too had walked that same path of sorrow and loss.

Leading the Army in the United Kingdom Territory with the Republic of Ireland drew heavily upon our spiritual resources. It helped to know that scattered throughout the territory were officers and soldiers who still believed the Army was raised up by God and had a distinctive role to play in building the Kingdom. Many were still focused on soul winning. Everyone's work rate across the divisions was impressive. The staff at THQ also worked hard, giving long hours in attending to administrative matters and to travel throughout the territory. Lieut-Colonel Keith Burridge, steeped in its culture and history, was a constant source of knowledgeable counsel. Lieut-Colonel Bill Cochrane stood out as a discerning and independently minded colleague, not unwilling to take a solitary stance on certain matters. I liked and valued his input for he too knew intimately the people and dynamics of the territory.

As the General

It was not a difficult decision to appoint Commissioner Robin Dunster as the Chief of the Staff to follow Commissioner Israel Gaither after he expressed a desire to return home to the USA. Engaging in consultations with significantly more people than was customary when appointing a Chief of the Staff, it rapidly became clear to me that the outstanding candidate was Robin Dunster. She brought an independent mind, long and varied experience in senior leadership, and knowledge of the Army's diverse cultures. Added to our own backgrounds in all five zones of the Army world, her appointment meant that at the highest level of the Army there would be ample personal knowledge and experience of the global scene. Doing full justice to her role and being the first woman to become the Chief of the Staff, Robin gave loyal and unfailing support. It was not difficult to delegate matters to her. She knew what to do and – crucially – how to do it, yet consistently held herself accountable to the General. She had a capacity for people, for the 'big picture' issues as well as the details of her role, and she expended much energy when ministering effectively in the territories and commands.

Her successor, Commissioner Barry Swanson, though having considerably less experience in top leadership and less exposure out of culture, brought a calm and unruffled mind to his task. Of a teachable spirit, he learned rapidly and was of much help to me. Both he and Commissioner Sue Swanson were a blessing throughout the trying months toward the end of my term in office when Helen was so ill.

Commissioners Donald and Berit Ødegaard, overseeing the Army in Europe, were a source of ready encouragement and brought wide and wise experience to their roles. My admiration for Commissioners Amos and Rosemary Makina and for Commissioners Lalkiamlova and Lalhlimpuii compels me to mention them too as outstanding representatives of our IHQ colleagues. These gifted officers held their appointments at IHQ for a record number of years giving oversight respectively to the Africa and South Asia zones. They knew their people and they knew the Army. When they spoke I listened. Unfailingly courteous toward the General, they nevertheless knew how to proffer frank advice within the context of their own cultural norms. I relied on them a lot and was never let down. They represent the many fine officers and employees with whom we worked at IHQ.

Across the wider Army world we were honoured to know and work with outstanding colleagues. I refer not only to those in top leadership but also to the many selfless and devoted officers of lower rank, and to non-officers too, doing equally significant work for God. Let me mention one couple as representative of the many. Colonels Bo and Birgitte Brekke typified all that is best in Army service. Willing to be available in or out of culture, they knew how to get results and brought a consistently inspirational vision to the mission wherever they were appointed. They had a hunger for souls, but also hearts of deep compassion for the downtrodden and the poor. When Bo was killed in Lahore (see my 2010 *Selected Writings – Volume 2*, Chapter 11), Birgitte made it clear amid her unimaginable pain that she still had a sacred and compelling calling and wanted to go on being useful. Since that time she has proven this in countless ways, handling the World Youth Convention with vision and skill, and being a transformational leader of the Denmark Territory. Serving now as the International Secretary for Europe, she became Vice-President of both the 2011 and 2013 High Councils, the only officer to serve at two High Councils in this role.

Pakistan needed help and leadership in the aftermath of Bo Brekke's untimely death. The talented Lieut-Colonel Yousaf Ghulam was very new to his role as the Chief Secretary and wisely asked me to send help. How grateful I was when Lieut-Colonels Roland and Dawn Sewell agreed to step in to support the Chief Secretary until a new territorial commander (TC) could be appointed. If ever colleagues could rightly be termed 'stalwarts' it was the Sewells. They went without demur, they read the situation with wisdom and intelligence, they knew of but were not inhibited by the risks, and they loved and encouraged their Army comrades there. We could do with a few more like them.

Not just private secretaries

Not just private secretaries, but also colleagues and friends, are those who have helped me by working most closely with me in roles of personal support. Joyce McKittrick was a gifted colleague and my private secretary in the Durham and Tees Division. Rudy Moore proved to be a multi-talented private secretary in Lahore, providing not only office skills but also insightful help to me in negotiating the complexities of life as a Christian leader in a Moslem democracy. Major Joyce Langdon was my seasoned, unflappable private secretary in Wellington, New Zealand. How glad I was that she was available to proffer wise help and efficient assistance.

I have left until last any mention here of Major Richard Gaudion for it is he who has worked longest and closest with me, a total of seven years. I discovered his considerable support skills when I became the TC in London and later did not hesitate to promote him in rank and make him Private Secretary to the General when that opportunity arose. Richard is gifted, not only at his desk where he displays an astounding ability to handle endless detail, but also in his ease with people. He travelled very widely with us, readily making friends in every place. Our burdens were eased because of his presence. He placed his gifts at the Lord's disposal long ago and Helen and I became beneficiaries of that commitment. He remains a deeply valued friend and comrade.

My heart is full of gratitude for the many in my life who have shown me friendship, who have taken the time and trouble to get to know me properly, who have continued across the years to be in relationship, and who still accept me for myself.

ESSAY 11

☙

STANDING

ESSAY 11
STANDING

IT NEED hardly be said that standing for election to the office of General of The Salvation Army is no light matter. Three times I have agreed to do it and this Essay describes, entirely from my personal perspective, those occasions.

May 1999, aged 53

> *Journal, 27 April 1999: I fly from Lahore to London early tomorrow morning. Matt will meet me. I will have five days with Dad and Syl and then go to Sunbury Court for the High Council on 4 May, Helen's birthday. I have prepared several questions for candidates for the office of General and have restudied the procedures of past High Councils. I am thinking about the prevailing issues of the day for the Army.*
>
> *Helen will be 51 on 4 May. I have known her since she was 10. I have always loved her.*

The High Council began on Thursday 6 May following two days of discussions under the guiding hand of General Paul Rader, who spoke with his usual intelligence and passion to the 74 members, deepening further my respect for him.

I had left Lahore on 28 April and, somewhat jetlagged, made for Ilminster in Somerset to visit my sister and father. Those days with loved ones proved reviving and I set out on the convoluted journey for Sunbury-on-Thames with a free and glad heart. A coach ride took me to London Victoria, and then I went by Underground and taxi to Sunbury Court on the south-western edge of London.

My accommodation was a tiny single room in the block located separately from the main mansion house. It was clean and functional. Over the next several days it was to become a sanctuary of prayer, of waiting on God, and of deep reflection.

The seating of the members in the High Council chamber was, as usual, arranged according to seniority of rank so I found myself on the

269

back row with only two other members ranked below me. It meant I could easily reach the exit doors when the coffee breaks came!

Prior to the public welcome meeting at the Methodist Central Hall, Westminster, we were received by Speaker Betty Boothroyd at Speaker's House in the precincts of Parliament at the Palace of Westminster. Thereafter the preliminary business of the High Council was rapidly completed. Commissioner Robert Watson, USA National Commander, was elected President. He appointed me as the Liaison Officer, assuming reasonably enough that my junior status and age meant I would be free to function in that role throughout. I was pleased to be asked and, in preparing the daily news bulletins, tried to make them as meaningful as I could. I felt they should avoid a sterile tone and instead emphasise the place of prayer in our gathering and, in order to convey the devotional atmosphere, also give details of the songs and Bible readings used. Later Colonel Dennis Phillips took over the role and continued in this vein.

The High Council reached the making of nominations for the office of General on the fifth day of meeting. It was Tuesday 11 May. When the President read out the names of those nominated I heard mine among the eight. It was a strange experience. I sensed the honour of being nominated but could not at once discern exactly why it should have happened. Was God in it? I was but 53 years of age and had held colonel rank and been a territorial commander (TC) for only two years.

The President announced a generous break in the proceedings to allow the nominees time to consider whether to decline or accept. I had much to ponder. Would acceptance appear ambitious? Would refusal appear disrespectful toward those who had placed my name in nomination? I reached Helen by telephone. In keeping with the Orders of Procedure she would fly at once from Lahore if I decided to stand. She told me I was not at liberty to decline because our calling was to be open and available to God whatever he might place before us. I knew this but it was good to hear her articulate it. She would therefore make plans to reach Sunbury-on-Thames as soon as she could. I contacted Matt and Jen. They saw it in the same way.

The counsel given me by Helen matched that of a seasoned senior officer who, many months earlier, had somehow anticipated my being nominated and had advised me in unambiguous terms to accept it: 'You will not be elected in 1999, but you will be nominated and that will give you an unmatched opportunity to speak and be heard by the Army's most senior people. Your voice is needed. You can influence how we think.'

Thus it was that when the High Council reconvened that evening and when the President called for my response to the nomination, I informed the members I had conferred with Helen and that, under God, I would accept nomination. I said also that Helen was making arrangements to arrive from Pakistan as soon as practicable. She reached Sunbury Court in the early evening of 13 May. Her parents had met her and John at Heathrow and then taken John to their north London home. When Helen walked into Sunbury Court in her uniform, all I could think was how unflustered and attractive she looked. It was a wonderful moment.

Colonel Eva Gaither also had to travel. She came from South Africa to Sunbury Court because her husband, Colonel Israel Gaither, had also accepted nomination.

While Helen was in the air I spent the day of 12 May preparing answers to the lengthy question list prepared by the Questions Committee and approved by the Council as a whole. I needed also to write an acceptance speech. So my small room became a place of intense reliance on the leadings of God. Helen too was required to answer questions. The general questionnaire to all candidates consisted of 35 questions plus one additional question directed solely to me. It raised the matter of my relatively young age. Colonel Gaither and Commissioner Larsson also received individual questions. The questionnaire for the spouses held nine questions.

The next day I managed to confine my answers to nine sheets of paper with single line spacing. My nomination speech extended to four pages. The order of responding to questions is drawn by lot. I went fifth out of the five candidates, and spoke second when the speeches were presented. Each candidate is heard in total silence and every answer has to be read verbatim with the assembled members having the script in front of them. This results in a stilted, artificial atmosphere for an Army gathering. Reading verbatim from a pre-prepared script had never been my habit. As a result I found the experience quite stressful but managed to get through it. The formal questions ranged widely: health and family life; spirituality; leadership style; the holy life; international funding of our

271

work; our administrative systems; choosing a Chief of the Staff; legal matters; developing future leaders; the advancement of women leaders; the place of uniform; mission strategy; opening the work in new lands; ecumenical relations; future membership eligibility of a High Council; the age of retirement of the General.

The most important question, as I saw it, was that which asked for my 'vision of the Army as an evangelical force to be reckoned with'. I had planned that my nomination speech would focus on this very matter and therefore offered only a brief response to the questionnaire and a reference to our Lord's 'New Commandment'. Here is part of my answer: 'Lying at the beginning of evangelism and soul winning are the interpersonal relationships we have right here within the Church, within the Army. The New Commandment is a mission-related commandment. If we love one another little, we shall see little fruit for the Kingdom in terms of converts and new soldiers. This drives us right back to the love-focus of 1 Corinthians 13 and to the sanctified life. If we do not love, if we are not pure and holy for Christ's sake, we shall not grow. Who will look at us and say: "Let me be part of that"? God help us. God make us loving. Make us more like Christ.'

Later in my nomination speech I said: 'God sees all things and knows all things. In the best traditions of the Army, we never ask for, or seek out, a specific appointment. But also in the best traditions of the Army, we are ready to be used and to be spent in whatever manner God chooses and in any appointment, any responsibilities of his design. I think it was the late John Wimber who said, "We are coins in God's pocket, and he can spend us as he likes." That is how I feel today. That is the reason – the only reason – why I am willing to participate as a candidate for office.'

I continued: 'Let me say right away that I am under no illusions as to my relatively young age. The age factor is not new. It comes up again and again in the Scriptures when God is choosing and appointing, but it is never God who raises it. He says simply, "I will be with you."'

Voting took place on Saturday 15 May. The number voting for me exceeded the number who had nominated me. I was eligible to move forward into the second ballot but, in order to speed up the proceedings, decided not to do so and informed the President I would withdraw. The voting continued into a tight fifth ballot involving only Commissioners

Earle Maxwell and John Gowans. It was 3.30 pm when the President announced that Commissioner Gowans would succeed General Rader.

I was glad to be present the following morning, with Helen beside me, in the holiness meeting at Staines Corps. Here we could relax and worship, allowing the intensity of the High Council experience to drain away. Then it was back to linking up with John and to the routine of securing tickets to get the three of us home to Lahore. We flew from Heathrow the following Wednesday, reached Lahore on Thursday morning, and by 2 pm I was in my office catching up on business with the Chief Secretary.

General Rader then sent me a most generous email: 'I read through your responses and your speech and must say it was all quite magnificent… I wouldn't throw away my notes if I were you.'

My Journal entries during May 1999 reflected upon the Sunbury Court experience:

Journal, 26 May 1999: I have returned from the High Council and am unsure what, or how much, to write. I found myself nominated. I was not, of course, elected. I had some days in Ilminster by leaving Lahore early. Matt met me and we had good conversation as he drove me to Somerset. He is pure and godly, much more so than I was at his age, or perhaps even now. I was truly refreshed and relaxed in Ilminster through being with my Dad and Syl. I walked and rested and slept pretty well.

At Sunbury Court I was put into the annexe and room 17. It became my cell, my sanctuary, a place to retreat to, a place to walk away from into the sun and breeze of England's springtime.

The pre-High Council conference allowed the Raders to give an account of their five years of stewardship. They were dignified, incisive and clear. Then the High Council began. The President, Commissioner Watson, was kind to me. We spent days and days over the Orders of Procedure. There were occasional procedural muddles, but the sharper minds emerged in it all and the whole company settled down. We then spent two days in discussion as a Committee of the Whole (when the normal rules of procedure are suspended). I felt this part was too hurried. Then the nominations. The next day the President read out eight names. Mine was first because the order was alphabetical. Commissioners Watson, Edwards and Davis all declined after an overnight break. The President informed me privately of the number of persons who had nominated me. Commissioners Gowans, Larsson and Maxwell, with Colonel Gaither, all agreed to stand.

The rules require a candidate's spouse to be sent for if he or she is not a High Council member. So Helen and Eva Gaither flew in. As I finalised my answers and speech I felt comfortable with them. I prayed for detachment in delivery so that I would not be overwhelmed. Helen answered her short questionnaire well. The personal responses to my speech outside the chamber were many and powerful, but I now know that few vote on this basis. Many of the members vote automatically for the most senior person(s) present.

My feelings now? Too soon to tell. Some sense of confusion. Why did God put me through this? I was not expected to be elected. I seem to have emerged with some credit, but I find it very unsettling. I am told that I am the youngest person ever nominated at a High Council. I think perhaps I am not spiritually ready to be the General. Maybe God does not want to put so much power and influence into my hands. If that be so, then I am content.

Journal, 31 May 1999: Inevitably we continue to reflect upon the High Council, trying to get it all into perspective. A useful antidote has been our annual Executive Officers' Councils which seemed to go well and included a lively discussion on the status of women and the issue of violence against them in the home. It is not usual in the culture of Pakistan to speak of such things.

I am trying to focus on what I need to achieve in the territory when we return from two months of homeland furlough. There is much to be done. We have emailed the Larssons on the announcement of John as the new Chief of the Staff. He replied in a warm tone.

On the evening he was elected, John Gowans took Helen and me to one side in the sun lounge at Sunbury Court and placed an arm around each of us. He said, 'I heard all your answers to the questions. I hope they do not keep you waiting as long as they have kept me waiting. God bless you both.'

I have pasted a copy of my nomination speech into the Journal. These speeches do not see the light of day. Why cannot we have a book of these? Incidentally, I was the only candidate who, in the speeches, made any courteous, positive mention of the others who were also standing for election.

August 2002, aged 56

By the time of the next High Council we found ourselves leading the Army in the New Zealand, Fiji and Tonga Territory. Both Helen and I received the legal summonses to attend, dated 12 July 2002, issued by the Chief of the Staff, Commissioner Larsson. This time Helen would again be present but, due to her rank, as a member in her own right. Naturally, anticipation of a second High Council experience prompted some Journal entries:

Journal, 25 June 2002: The High Council looms nearer. I need to record my sure feeling that I will not be elected. I have spoken to Helen about the possibility of declining any nomination – 'All the vain things that charm me most, I sacrifice them to your blood.' Even as I write I feel unsure of what is best.

Journal, 26 July 2002: The High Council qualifying date of 12 July has come and gone. We have been duly summoned to attend. More than 50 of the 87 members will be at their first High Council. A small handful will be at their fourth. My new Chief Secretary, in our very first meeting together, asked me outright if I would be elected and thus be in the territory only briefly. I told him to discount that possibility.

Thoughts of the High Council keep coming up. I need to record that I have decided to stand if nominated. However, I need to be sure of my reactions when not elected, as seems likely. I do not get my personal worth or my standing in the eyes of God from holding a particular appointment or rank, even that of General. There are many fields of service and being a faithful TC is a crucial one.

Journal, 14 August 2002: We leave for the USA and UK on 16 August. Helen and I have spoken together about a possible nomination. If it comes, I will accept it with Helen's blessing. So I have prepared some thoughts on paper. At 56 I am still young for the Army's highest office. I know I am unworthy in myself. I am praying for an easy mind and a quiet poise of soul.

Leaving Wellington on 16 August, we managed three days of furlough with Jen and Marcus in Sidney, Ohio, then in Ilminster, Somerset, with my Dad and my sister. We reached Sunbury Court with the jetlag largely overcome.

The two days prior to the formal opening of the High Council were treated as a plenary session of the General's Consultative Council (GCC), a body introduced by General Gowans to replace the smaller, more intimate Advisory Council to the General which used to meet without the General at the table. The quarterly meetings of the GCC, however, were chaired by the General with territorial leaders attending from overseas on a rotating and thus token basis only every two years or so. Commissioners based at International Headquarters (IHQ) attended every single meeting. GCC business seemed largely to duplicate the business of the International Management Council (IMC) which the General also chaired. The gatherings known previously as pre-High Council conferences thus became technically plenary sessions of the GCC (see Essay 12).

After a swelteringly hot and humid public welcome meeting at Regent Hall Corps, Oxford Street, on Thursday 29 August the High Council embarked upon its formal business the following day. The 87 members were again seated in strict order of seniority. Helen and I were ranked 50th and 51st. It was good to meet up again with many colleagues and friends, a facet of a High Council which is perhaps the most rewarding. We were housed comfortably in the nearby Shepperton Moat House Hotel, Sunbury Court not having room for all the High Council members.

The preliminary stages were completed more rapidly, but less thoroughly, than in 1999 and the nominating of candidates for the office of General took place on Tuesday 3 September. Of the nine persons nominated, six declined to stand. Again I agreed to stand, as did Commissioners John Larsson and Hasse Kjellgren. Later I was able to put together a piece for the New Zealand *War Cry* in which I tried to share aspects of the High Council experience. I began with a brief rationale for accepting a nomination even when you are unlikely to be elected:

> Twice now it has been my lot to attend a High Council. Twice I have found myself nominated to be a candidate for the office of General. Twice I have agreed to stand, at the ages of 53 and 56. This has therefore been in the full knowledge that election was not going to happen. High Councils are notoriously conservative bodies.
>
> Why then agree to stand? For me the answer is easy – to take advantage of that unique forum in order to have the ear of the Army's gathered international leadership. It is an unsurpassed opportunity to influence thinking, capture hearts, and to influence the Army's worldwide agenda. I thank God for these opportunities. We need to be speaking among ourselves and to the wider world of holiness, the sanctity of marriage, the authority of the Scriptures, our doctrinal integrity, our sacred mission to souls, our callings to be the voice of the voiceless, and much more besides.
>
> Each High Council spends much time in prayer. Prayer flows easily in many, many tongues. This time more of the women members were heard in prayer and also in speaking from the floor in open debate. More voices from the developing territories were raised both in prayer and in making representation on the issues of the day. The gender mix and varied ethnicity of the leadership group that gathered at Sunbury Court a few weeks ago might well prove to have been unique in the annals of the Army, and even of the wider Church.

Following the traditional break of at least one whole day to allow the candidates time to formulate their public presentations, my name was drawn first by lot for answering the questions and second for making the nomination speech. Although the questionnaire was considerably shorter than in 1999, my answers extended to 17 pages, with my speech again covering just over four pages. The questions raised matters very similar to those posed in 1999 but now there was added emphasis on matters of social justice.

There was also a question about Army regulations governing divorce (see Essays 7B and 12). The helpfully pragmatic regulatory system ensuring that like cases across the globe were handled in like manner had been repealed by decision of General Gowans. My answer included the following observation: 'We have always managed to uphold the biblical standard and the sanctity of marriage but now the new regulation allows officers to divorce by mutual consent and remain as officers with their rank. *The new regulation allows, for example, all of us here at the High Council to go home and arrange to be divorced by mutual consent and all still remain colonels and commissioners.* There is no longer any provision for loss or reduction of rank, or even a brief suspension of rank or role, if there is no known sexual misconduct. I believe we need to look at this matter again to seek, not only compassion, but also clear principle. We are sending the wrong signal to the Army and to young people in the Army. We seem to be joining those who see marriage as disposable. We need to think again.'

I wanted my speech to be down to earth. Sometimes a High Council can be too inward looking so my emphasis was on the world outside: 'It is only holy courage granted by God that helps me to stand before you today. I could not do this in my own strength alone. Let me be clear. If God does not want me to take office, then neither do I. If he wants it I will try my best, by his grace. We have gathered to follow Army constitutional procedures which the Lord has honoured for many generations. It would be a mistake to focus on these in a way that made us forget the needs of the world outside. We gather with the world in a state of great peril and tension. The 21st century has begun and we are in the third millennium. Violence and hatred are on every hand. Our world faces great risks. The noises of war and terrorism are all around us. Christianity itself is under attack in many lands. We gather to elect a new leader for the worldwide Army against this sombre and most challenging of backgrounds. We need an Army and a General for an era when the most explosive religion of recent years has been "no religion". We need an Army and a General for a violent, godless age.'

The questions put to the spouses of the three candidates included one about public speaking. Helen answered in the following terms: 'Throughout our officership Shaw and I have shared the platform ministry. He has always encouraged me to feel that I had something distinctive to say, which God might use to touch the hearts of people, my style being quite different from his. In corps leadership we shared the platform fairly equally. In senior leadership and when visiting around the world I have recognised that people want to hear him speak, and so do I. He often discusses with me what he will say and makes me feel I have some useful input into his preaching. I have practised the discipline of trying to say something very significant in the space of six or seven minutes early in the meeting. When occasion demands, or when I am travelling alone, I deliver a full Bible message. I love to open the Word of God and expound it. It is a joyous responsibility.'

Friday 6 September was voting day. Only one ballot was needed and Commissioner Larsson became the General-elect. We knew he would make a godly, dignified leader of wide experience. Prior to the vote he and I had managed a brief moment together when I said that the likely outcome of the election was already clear and that Helen and I would be honoured to serve under his leadership.

Outside the High Council chamber and after General Gowans had publicly announced the name of his successor, I was taken aside on the lawn by our own media staff armed with a video camera. The hired interviewer put strangely intrusive questions to me as though the election of a General of The Salvation Army were a personal, even a political contest. He seemed not to have been properly briefed. My only possible response was to explain patiently that the purpose of a High Council is to engage in a spiritual exercise, not in a contest of any kind. It was not a matter of rivalry to be evaluated in worldly terms. There could be no misgivings or complaints about the outcome. At this point my interlocutor appeared a little crestfallen. It seemed he had hoped for a more worldly reaction. A High Council is not a soap-opera.

Our long journey back to Wellington was a relaxing interlude prior to applying ourselves again to the busy life of the territory. Three of our suitcases failed to arrive with us, but turned up a couple of days later!

Journal, 15 September 2002: The High Council was full of interest,
blessing, self-examination for purity of motive, fellowship and much

more. We had anticipated the election of John Larsson. It was all fairly predictable but we felt we should also take part.

Nine persons were nominated. Helen advised me to accept and I am glad I heeded her. The numbers voting for me greatly exceeded the number of nominations. But as predicted it was all over very fast. So now I have the distinction of being the youngest person ever to be nominated and to stand at a High Council and also of being the only person to have been nominated twice in their 50s.

I tried to be very rigorous in examining my motives through it all. I asked God over and over to cleanse me of personal ambition and of vanity. He has granted me a steady peace both during and after the High Council. I do not share the view of many at the High Council that God's one chosen person is there and it is the task of the members to find him or her, like some kind of party game. I think the High Council chooses and then God graces.

My answers to the questions were full and honest. My speech was a plea for the Army to be related to the world's needs. Neither of my fellow candidates mentioned the world outside.

God gave me a beautiful verse in the holiness meeting this morning from Daniel 6:23 – 'When they lifted Daniel from the lions' den, there was no wound on him, for he had trusted in the Lord.' I am taking this for me. I have emerged from the fire of the High Council, with Helen, and we are unharmed for we trusted in the Lord. Dear God, keep us true to you and your gospel. Keep us in your will and in your love. We want only to do what you approve.

We are praying for the Gowanses, Larssons and the Gaithers. The Gowanses will visit us in Wellington in three weeks.

Helen was very loving to me at the High Council, very affirming, very calm. I am a man blessed.

Journal, 16 October 2002: Reflecting in recent weeks on the High Council leaves me feeling very liberated and detached from disappointment of a personal kind regarding the outcome. One growing sense is that I should be slow ever to stand again. I do not rule it out, but I feel just now it holds little attraction for me.

Many months later, the following took place:

Journal, 15 June 2003: I went to the most northern corps in New Zealand at Kaitaia, led by Majors David and Colleen Griffiths. I found much to encourage me. Two years ago the corps was about to close but the Griffiths have led it back to viability and effectiveness. I visited also Whangerai, one of our largest corps, but I should record an unnerving experience in Kaitaia. Major Griffiths spoke to me on the final day just before I flew back to Auckland. He said he sometimes could not sleep and stayed up all night in deep prayer and that the night before had been such a night. With his wife and the divisional leaders (Majors Ross and Annette Gower) present, he said that the Lord had given him a word, a message for me. He appeared nervous as he spoke and did not look into my eyes until he was done. He said everything twice for clarity. This was his message: 'When you are the General, call the Army back to the old wells. Seek first the Kingdom of God and everything will be added to you.' David emphasised the word 'When'. I made no sign or response as he spoke but felt very moved. His wife, Colleen, wept quietly. I do not know what to make of this or how to evaluate it. It has unsettled me after I had come to terms with it all and put it behind me. When Matt, our son, came to visit us I told him of it. He said I should take it as a warning not to decline if ever again nominated. He says you cannot take your future back into your own hands. I told Helen also. No one else. Helen barely commented. I am putting it all down here in order to preserve it and then forget it.

January 2006, aged 60

The next High Council was convened to begin on 20 January 2006 and for the third time Helen and I found ourselves attending. General Larsson presided over a plenary session of the GCC beginning on 17 January. This time we were not jetlagged. We ranked 19th and 20th in the order of seniority.

Journal, 16 January 2006: We go to Sunbury Court tomorrow for the High Council. I will make my next Journal entry when it is all over. Am receiving lots of assurances of prayers and well-intentioned comments. I feel no real personal ambition about it. Am open to God in it all. I feel loath to stand. I am seeking only dignity for the Army and praying that the Holy Spirit will rule.

Commissioner Todd Bassett, USA National Commander, was elected to serve as President and proved to be an excellent choice. He was impartial, firm, kindly and patient with the Council members, but he was also expeditious in moving us through the preliminary stages. Commissioner Robin Dunster was made Vice-President and did well.

We all gathered at the Methodist Central Hall on Saturday 21 January to honour and bid a fond farewell to the Larssons and to welcome the 100 High Council members to London. General Larsson had kindly asked me to speak words of welcome as the TC of the host territory. I did so early in the meeting and included the following:

'Even though this territory has hosted previous High Councils, our sense of privilege is not diminished on this occasion. You have travelled from far and near, from every corner of the Army world, to carry out profoundly sacred and solemn duties. You have come in the name of Jesus. We greet you therefore in that same holy name, recognising that the task is large and that the eyes of the global Salvation Army are upon us.

'What a wonderful thing it is that Army leaders can gather from every part of the Army world with the main purpose of being in prayer together, seeking the guidance of God. What a marvellous thing that the Army's most senior leaders gather together specifically to wait upon God, to sense his divine prompting, and to obey his voice.

'Also how wonderful it is that we come from every race and every background. We are a visible sign that the gospel of Jesus is for everyone regardless of race or colour. We are a powerful example of the internationalism that is one of the key hallmarks of the Army. And how good that the membership of the High Council shows plainly the place that both women and men are now given in choosing a General. So again I welcome you all in the name of Jesus!'

The process of making nominations began at 12 noon on Wednesday 25 January. The elected Chaplain, Commissioner Alex Hughes, led us in the singing of Edward Boaden's 'Here, Lord, assembled in thy name' (Song 581) and a period of passionate prayer ensued. At 1.20 pm the President told us that seven persons had received the legally required number of nominations. The full figures are never publicly announced, but a nominee is free to speak privately to the President to learn the measure of initial support. After a late lunch the Council adjourned for four hours to give those nominated time for solemn reflection.

Helen and I returned to the seclusion of our room at the hotel. We both knew that this third High Council experience was unlike those earlier. Given my age and added experience there now seemed to be a serious prospect of my being elected. Our room again became a place of prayer. We knelt down together at the bedside and asked God to lead us. What was his will? My feelings fluctuated, my thoughts went back and forth. Still we prayed. Still we discussed it from every perspective. Eventually, we came back yet again to the same solid foundational principle of our sacred callings, that of constant availability to God. How could I decline and still honour that? A settled peace came upon us and we agreed that I would, somewhat resignedly and for the third time, indicate willingness to stand.

The Council reconvened at 5.30 pm. Commissioners Bond and Needham declined the nomination with words of wisdom and dignity. In my turn I indicated readiness to stand, as did Commissioners Gaither, Kjellgren, Lydholm and MacMillan. At 6 pm formal photographs of the five candidates were taken. The following day saw no formal activities of the Council as again time was afforded for the candidates to prepare answers to questions and to compile their nomination speeches.

Drawn second by lot in the ballot for the order of answering the questions, I rose to speak at 11.10 am on Friday 27 January followed by Helen. The nomination speeches were heard again in total, unnatural and unresponsive silence on the following morning when by lot I was required to speak first. It was 9.35 am.

The formal questionnaire held 32 questions and my responses amounted to 17 pages. As before, the areas covered were those to be expected, but one of the more penetrating questions asked for our views on the internal forces that gave rise to concern for the whole Army. Could we identify those factors within our own ranks?

I answered by referring to:

- Financial pressures
- The fact that many Salvationists were still not fully mobilised for God
- The risk of losing our sense of urgency for souls
- Potential loss of nerve about our identity under God
- The impact of changes imposed too rapidly and sometimes destructively
- The apparent diminution in understanding of our sanctification doctrine
- The rising stridency of some voices calling us to abandon our God-given mission in the face of Western cultural changes.

On this last point I included the following response:

'We need to hear and manage the debate that some, especially in the Western cultures, are seeking. Countless ideas are being put forward. Some say get back to our roots. Others say adapt to post-modern culture. Then some want us to drop the military image. And so it goes on. Everyone has their own idea of how we can grow again in the places experiencing a hard time. Dear comrade leaders of the global Army, there is a voice that is hardly ever heard among us. It is the voice of the Old Testament prophets. When things went wrong for God's people, the prophets took the leaders and the people back to basics. They returned to the Covenant of old and asked the hard, awkward, uncomfortable questions. These were questions about *sin in the camp*. They did not debate strategy, or ceremonies, but instead spoke the language that called the people back to obedience, to repentance, to fasting, to their knees. They asked if there was sin in their midst. Thus we come to that same difficult, awkward question: Is there sin in the Army? Is it sin that is causing the blessing to be withheld? Lord, show us if this be true. Have we strayed from your chosen path for us as an Army? Can we allow the next General, lovingly and gently, but ever so clearly, to help us face up to these questions and to seek the answers before the face of God? Can we return to the old wells? These will not be the old methods of a bygone Army, but the old wells that still hold the old and eternal qualities of obedience, humility, self-sacrifice, purity and righteousness before God.'

My nomination speech was considerably shorter than on previous occasions and only two pages in length. Here are some key extracts (the full text was published in *The Officer* magazine for May/June 2006 and made available in full to non-officer readers in *Volume 2* of my 2010 *Selected Writings*):

'I have accepted this nomination with some reluctance. Ever since accepting nomination in 1999 at the age of 53 and then again in 2002, aged 56, I seem to have been living with the loving, kindly-meant and generous expectations of others, including some in this room. I want to say that it is not these expectations that have prompted me to accept nomination again. I desire only to obey God.

'No person ought to accept a nomination for General if they cannot accept the outcome with genuine joy. Here today there can be no winners or losers. That is not the language we speak for it is not the way we think about this sacred matter. We are not competitors. We are children of God together, lending ourselves to the Body to help a sacred process. I salute my fellow candidates and offer them my deep esteem.

'You all know that if you elect this speaker, you will not be getting a perfect General. I can offer you only my weakness, the same that I offer to God every day. He comes to tell me that he loves me anyway, and wants my weakness so that he can transform and use it to his glory. So I am standing here in much weakness, but relying in real faith upon God who says that when we are weak, then he is strong.

'Here is a picture of the Army I believe God wants to see. Already we are an Army loved and used by God. He wants us, however, to be closer yet to his side. It is a wounded side. He wants us to be broken again. He wants to break, melt, mould and fill the Army. He wants us to be purer. He wants all sin cast out from among us. He loves us deeply. He wants to use us more and more and longs for us to put aside the things that hold us back. Some of these things are personal, some corporate, touching the whole Army. He stands ready to reveal, if we are ready to see.

'He calls us back to the old wells. He is not calling us back to old, worn-out methodologies, but to things that made us what once we were: humility; simplicity; nothingness; brokenness; a readiness to risk all for the sake of Christ; obedience come what may; a fearlessness that the world could not comprehend; a total and ruthless rejection of worldly enticements; a refusal to be seduced by anything unpleasing to God; a heart for the lost and lonely, daring to go for souls and go for the worst souls; a spirit that seeks after personal holiness and after our perfect Saviour, Jesus, who alone can give us this gift, growing himself within us to change us, and change us, and change us again, from glory into glory until in Heaven we take our place.'

The solemn process of voting began after the speeches. The first ballot started at 12.17 pm. Three further ballots took place and by late afternoon the result was known: the High Council had elected me. Commissioner Israel Gaither, dignified and gracious, had gathered a significant number of votes in each of the ballots but insufficient to reach the required majority. My heart went out to him. To render the Council chamber private, the President called for the window shutters to be lowered and then asked me to rise in my place. Solemnly he asked if I was willing to accept the office of General of The Salvation Army. 'Under God, I am willing,' was my reply.

There followed the traditional closing formalities and the offering of garlands, handshakes, some hugs, and pledges of loyal support. General and Commissioner Larsson came into the chamber to announce by webcast the result of the election to the Army world. I needed to speak briefly, somehow managing a few words, and then concluded by asking the High Council members to sing a chorus that expressed what I was feeling at that moment:

> 'I have not much to give thee, Lord,
> For that great love which made thee mine:
> I have not much to give thee, Lord,
> But all I have is thine.'

Thereupon the High Council ended and, in legal terms, ceased to exist until formally reconvened at some future date. We snatched a few moments to telephone our loved ones and to speak to my Private Secretary, Captain Richard Gaudion. By late evening we were at home in Bromley trying to wind down and take it all in.

General Larsson invited me to meet him at IHQ on the following Monday morning. He was very helpful to me in the weeks that followed prior to his leaving office. Because Commissioner Gaither felt strongly he should return to serve in the USA I needed to consult widely about choosing his successor. This led to Commissioner Robin Dunster becoming the first woman to hold the appointment of the Chief of the Staff. She and I met to talk it through on Tuesday 31 January and I sensed right away that she would acquit herself with skill and poise. Next came a flying visit to my Dad in Somerset. We did not know that he would be promoted to Glory shortly afterwards. That visit proved precious. His loving, ready, wise affirmation was beyond price.

> *Journal, 31 January 2006: I am to take office as the Army's 18th General on 2 April 2006. I will do so only because God is in this. I will do so incomplete and with a contrite heart, asking God to keep me broken on his potter's wheel.*
>
> *After three days of the GCC the High Council lasted eight days. Helen's love throughout saw me manage to remain calm. She was truly wonderful, a genuine confidante and partner in prayer. So too our three children and our children-in-law.*

Hundreds of messages are pouring in, all loving and affirming, with many assurances of prayers. Commissioner Todd Bassett was a splendid President. Matt and Lynne were with my Dad and Syl in Ilminster when the news broke at about 5 pm on 28 January.

John Larsson is being helpful. Spent over three hours in his office yesterday with Helen and Freda there as well. The General's office is made of glass! No pictures or books! All very clinical.

Lord, what have you done? I know you will help me. 'I have not much to give thee, Lord, but all I have is thine.'

Journal, 1 February 2006: God seems to stay near me. Through the years I have not always felt that. On reading what people say in their lovely greetings I experience strong emotion, a sense of unworthiness, but also a deep inner calm.

Journal, 6 February 2006: We made a quick overnight visit to Ilminster. Dad is very slow and frail now, yet he is still responsive when there is some company and stimulus.

I have worked on a long list of top moves with John Larsson. I am startled to discover a total absence of written protocol for transition in the office of General. Once I take office I can remedy that easily enough.

We now have good plans in place for the Welcome Meeting on 8 April at Kensington Town Hall, a red-brick construction from the 1970s. We visited and found it not unpleasant. Jen, Marcus and Hudson will fly in from New Zealand.

Journal, 18 March 2006: My days have been very full. Even now the messages of greeting and prayers continue to come in. With my staff I have ensured every single one has been answered. All plans for the move to IHQ are coming together well. Very busy days, week after week. Richard Gaudion has risen to it and, despite his protestations, will be promoted by me to major on 2 April. The Chief Secretary has been on homeland leave for five weeks so I have been TC and Chief Secretary and General-elect all at the same time. Several press and radio interviews too. Very glad we opted not to move house as well! Am suffering from a heavy head cold. Better now than in two weeks.

I find myself calm at the prospect of taking office. God will go before me and carry me into it. He knows my needs: wisdom, more and more; holy courage for each day; a deeper prayer life; patience; poise and dignity; vision to penetrate the present and the future. I am thinking five years is very short, with all I see to be done. At once there will be key decisions on senior appointments. There are many impending international retirements. This may create opportunities that might otherwise be unexpected. In making such appointments I will consult widely, openly and then act decisively. My powers are very wide. God will guide.

Our specialling in the UK since the High Council has exposed us to countless smiling faces and warm greetings. Paris last weekend, as General-elect, was fascinating. Only 70 or so active officers. A triple-lined Mercy Seat in the public rally was the work of God. France has huge legal issues, but these are being addressed. I tried out my French on the officers and they took me by surprise by bursting into applause!

Journal, 2 April 2006: It is 7 am, 2 April 2006, a Sunday. Seven hours ago, as I slept, the sacred responsibility of being the 18th General of The Salvation Army became mine. I woke early. Helen made tea and brought mugs to bed. 'You are the General,' she said. 'It has been several hours now. What have you done so far?' Then we just laughed. We read from 'Words of Life', also from Jeremiah 1, Joshua 1 and 1 Corinthians 13, as well as 1 Peter 1.

I feel very calm and unafraid. God is with me. Lord, hold me and do not let me fail you. 'Lord Jesus, thou dost keep thy child through sunshine or through tempest wild; Jesus, I trust in thee.' The issues and decisions awaiting me are numerous and far-reaching. Lord, be my Guide and my Divine Prompter.

Helen seems very ready for it all, just pragmatic and sensible. Her Mum is very ill and this is on her mind and heart. My Dad is also deeply unwell and weakening by the day.

My farewell article as TC in London appeared in *Salvationist* for 4 March. I entitled it 'A fond farewell' and included the following:

'The High Council, under God, has caused a unique trust to be bestowed upon me. They knew because I told them, that I felt reluctant. Our commitment to our home territory was part of that reluctance. We leave with hugely mixed feelings, but we shall still be soldiers here and will try to make a contribution in that way and in our new capacities. At the High Council every member came strongly under the hand of God. Prayers flowed easily and readily. We offered up our adoration and poured out our hearts, using many languages at the throne of grace. We remembered all of you who were not there. We were many, but one. We were different, but united. I commend to you all, in the warmest possible terms, Commissioners John and Betty Matear who will come to give wise leadership to the territory. God will use them wonderfully.'

With Commissioner Robin Dunster we arrived at IHQ on Monday 3 April to be greeted in the entrance by Commissioner Ray Houghton and other officers and staff. Our welcome meeting followed at 10 am. Helen spoke warmly and naturally, as she always did, and then it was my turn: 'I thank General Larsson for his help to me since the High Council ended. He has been thoughtful and courteous. We have been in daily contact, often several times each day. I have a request of you all. Please be patient with me. I have much to learn in my new role and I ask for your forbearance. I am so pleased Helen is at my side today. We said yes to our callings together many years ago. We have sat together now in three High Councils. Without Helen I would not be standing before you today. Please know that we will not change as people. We are still Helen and Shaw. We are very much sinners saved by grace and needing to rely on God every moment of the day.'

Then came the late-afternoon public welcome event on Saturday 8 April at Kensington Town Hall. Two things were important about that meeting: that the Gaithers returned readily at our request from the USA to preside (soon afterwards we in turn conducted their installations as the new national leaders in the USA in a memorable meeting held in the Centennial Memorial Hall, New York City); that the tone of the meeting should be, especially at the start, more like a Sunday morning holiness meeting (less loud, less triumphalist, less militaristic). I asked that, as we and Commissioner Dunster entered and walked quietly through the congregation to the platform, devotional music should be played to set the tone. All three of us would enter quietly, carrying our Bibles to reflect our first doctrine. The opening song would be one of seeking more of God in our lives and thus we began by singing 'I would by thy holy temple' with the chorus, 'Take thou my life, Lord...accept my offering today' (Song 786).

Kindly greetings sent from Australia, Canada, the USA and the UK from the five retired Generals were read. Helen spoke words of personal testimony and next we sang the song by Richard Slater quoted by me on the webcast from Sunbury Court a few weeks earlier as the High Council ended: 'I have not much to give thee, Lord.' Commissioner Gaither offered a moving prayer of dedication over us before calling on me to speak. The following extracts are from my (this time verbatim) notes:

'We are very human and we feel things deeply. I am still experiencing something of those very powerful feelings that swept through me at Sunbury Court, feelings of unworthiness and reluctance, all mingled with a certainty that God was in control. The Council chamber was a highly charged place to be. We had all been there together for nearly two weeks. The sense of the divine presence was unmistakeable.

'Since then there has come a deeper peace to my soul to replace the earlier turbulence. God's people around the globe have reached out to us, holding us secure in Christ. God's goodness is revealed in the Christlike love of his people.

'It was at about 5 pm on Saturday 28 January that I saw the President of the High Council, Commissioner Todd Bassett, look down at me from his podium to put to me the legal question required by the Salvation Army Act 1980: "Are you willing to accept office as the 18th General of The Salvation Army?" I recall rising to my feet to reply: "Under God, I am willing." I felt again that strange but familiar heartache and burden for the world, and for the Army's distinctive mission to the world.

'We are raised up by God. God sustains us in being. God owns us. The General is under God. Your new General is under God. There is no other place to be. I repeat tonight what was said in the High Council chamber. Only under God am I willing to accept this sacred responsibility. Only under God can it be done. Only under God can the burden be carried. Only under God can the General please the One who called him into sacred service long ago.

'I want every person listening, especially every Salvationist, to know that the new General knows his place. That place is under God. I am a servant of God. I am also your servant. I am subservient, under God. I am surrendered, yielded, fully given up to God for the salvation of the world.

'I have a vision. It is a vision of the whole Army kneeling together at the feet of Christ. We are there at the throne of grace from countless countries and countless cultures, using hundreds of languages. But we are all asking for the same thing. We are asking God for forgiveness. We are pleading for more faith, more wisdom, more holy courage, a closer walk with him, more of the Holy Spirit, more of his power among us and within us. You are there. I am there. We are all there together: the General, the commissioners, the senior soldiers, the junior soldiers. We are all kneeling in prayer and the tears are flowing, tears of sorrow and tears of joy. But every tear is a cleansing tear. As we kneel we see those wounded feet. We hear his voice. He speaks and tells us that he loves us.'

Journal, 2 May 2006: The Kensington Town Hall proved a good venue for the Welcome Meeting. God blessed it all. Our loved ones were there. The Mercy Seat was lined over and over. Israel Gaither presided with grace. I put my arm around him during the long prayer time and he said the response to the Mercy Seat was the seal of God upon the High Council election. It was a good moment. After the meeting I felt pleased because God had been present. I did not preach with any sense of freedom or eloquence and so it was all of God. The message preached was of God and has drawn comment from a number of perceptive sources. Thank you, Lord, for this meeting. Please take it and use it. Use the webcast and the DVD.

So it began. Essay 12 seeks to convey a sense of the five hectic years that followed. During the final months of that term I was approached and asked if I would consider continuing in office for a further three years or so until reaching the age of 68. We did not know then that Helen was soon to become very ill. On 29 June 2010, in a formal meeting of the IMC at IHQ, I made the following statement:

'This is a statement of a personal nature. I make it on behalf of both Helen and me. It will be recorded in full in the Minutes of today's meeting.

'During the last several months some senior officers have approached me to raise the possibility of a formal proposal to extend my term in office as the General. This is possible under Army regulations, subject to a vote (by postal or electronic ballot) by those who would be eligible to attend a High Council.

'These conversations have been initiated both in London and in the USA. They have been both face-to-face and by email. I am warmly grateful to all who have approached me. Helen and I have been encouraged and affirmed most deeply. We have given the matter long, detailed, prayerful thought. We have sought for the right thing under God.

'Although my health is normal and we are following a busy schedule both at home and abroad, we have decided that we will retire on 2 April 2011 on completion of my five years term in office. Accordingly, planning for the High Council will move ahead as normal.

'I do not look forward with great keenness to retiring, and this at the age at which my two immediate predecessors assumed office. However, let me say that I need more time to feed my soul. The exceedingly heavy and persistently draining duties of my office leave little time for personal and truly deep attention to one's spiritual health. I do not think I can postpone this even for only one more year.

'In recent months my mind has often turned to the Old Testament narrative of Elijah on Mount Carmel. Elijah did well, but he fell into the trap of thinking that he alone could take the lead. God had to tell him to step back. God had it all in hand. So I thank you all again. We anticipate a very full and positive year ahead. I invite Commissioner Swanson now to lead us all in prayer.'

Our public retirement meeting was held on Saturday 22 January 2011 at the Lancaster Gate Hotel in London. This event was also the public welcome to the 2011 High Council members. By now Helen was exceedingly frail but she donned her uniform and addressed the meeting, surrounded on the platform by our children, children-in-law and grandchildren (see *From Her Heart*, 2012, pages 228-9). I read and spoke from Luke 12:22-34 because there it is recorded that Jesus said, 'Do not be afraid, little flock.' It was as though these words were spoken to and for the Army. Even before I had concluded, folk started to come to the Mercy Seat, moved not by me but by the Holy Spirit.

Some reflections

There is a sacredness which, if you are open to it, will swiftly impact and enfold you when you serve as a member of a Salvation Army High Council. There is also a warm camaraderie, a sense of being bound together for a sacred purpose.

On all three occasions described in this Essay I found almost all of my fellow members ready to be humble before God and willing to be prayerful. Not once did I hear any candidate for office speak in a self-promoting manner. Even though the processes required us to speak about ourselves, I cannot recall any candidate doing so without some sense of awkwardness. The need for openness, candour and transparency about oneself was always matched by the knowledge that none of us was truly ready to take office. The role of the General is one into which any newly elected incumbent must grow. This takes time. Hence the desirability of longer, even much longer, terms in office.

Not everyone holds the same theological view of how a High Council works. Some are certain that God has already chosen the next General. Thus they see it as the job of the High Council to find out who that is. Sometimes the prayers of the members in the opening sessions reflect that belief, with phrases such as 'Your chosen one' being heard.

However, there are others who see it a little differently. They believe that God looks upon and blesses the processes of the Council, always granting wisdom and insight, but allowing the members to exercise sanctified judgement in the nominating and voting processes. It is as though the Lord is saying, 'I have convened you. I will be among you. I trust you. You trust me. Do your work and I will grace the person you elect.' When General Rader addressed us prior to the formal opening of the 1999 High Council he said, 'Make the most informed and responsible choice that you can…. The process is, in a sense, a *mystical* one, but it is not *magical*. God will not elect the next General for you. You must think clearly and choose wisely…. Be open to possibilities that may not have occurred to you.' These were wise words.

God is not confined by time (there is no past, present or future for God, but always an *eternal now*) but he knows the end from the beginning. He foreknows, but does not thereby necessarily cause outcomes. He says, 'Make your choice. I want you to choose. I trust you.' God gives grace, empowering and enabling his servants. The grace afforded to a General is precisely the same grace granted to the corps officer, the cadet, the singing company leader, or the corps sergeant-major. We do not believe in a hierarchy of different levels or intensities of grace, or in some separate, distinctive grace given only, for example, to commissioned officers or to those of higher, or even the highest, rank.

Grace is inseparable. This central tenet is the reason we do not 'lay hands' on a newly elected General or on cadets when they are commissioned and ordained as officers as though some special, distinctive grace is being imparted. We do not lay hands on a bandmaster being commissioned or upon a welcome sergeant. Neither do we put our hands on a person becoming a new senior soldier or junior soldier of the Army. God is bestowing the same grace directly upon all of these believers for the tasks assigned to them. Grace is indivisible.

Thus it is no more and no less for a General. God does not love or grace Generals more than he loves or graces captains or junior soldiers. Jesus died for all and in him there is neither General, nor captain, nor junior soldier. We are all one in Christ and equal in our need of grace.

ESSAY 12

⁊

STRATEGY

ESSAY 12
STRATEGY

SOME leaders settle for allowing things to remain as they are even when not all is well. That has been neither my inclination nor my calling. The need to make choices can never be escaped, and in matters of Army policy is unavoidable if you are thrust into high office. This Essay's main focus is on the more-significant policy choices made by me when in office as the General (on which see also Essays 3 and 5).

Essay 6 records my responses to certain policy issues when stationed outside the United Kingdom (UK). On returning to London as the Territorial Commander (TC) in 2004 I inherited two principal matters demanding strategic decisions: the finances of the territory; the future of the training college at Denmark Hill.

The territory's general reserve had been entirely depleted and yet plans were still being made to go on spending far in excess of income. Cutbacks were thus inevitable and involved some job redundancies. It was not a good time. The Territorial Finance Council was chaired by the Chief Secretary, the UK being the only territory in the world where this was the case. The TC was excluded while the finance council could spend up to £1 million without his consent. It simply did not work. However, the TC chaired a monthly meeting of the Salvation Army Trustee Company board of directors, and so I arranged for every weekly meeting simply to be a meeting of the directors and thus chaired these sessions myself. In this way the territory returned to normal processes in matters of business and spending and we were able gradually to restore financial stability.

When telling me of his plan to appoint me as the TC in London, General Larsson alerted me to his profound anxieties in connection with proposals emerging at territorial headquarters (THQ) to dispose of the iconic training college site in Denmark Hill. I learned that the intention was to sell off this historic set of buildings, devote the sale proceeds to enlarging the Church of England's tiny St John's College in Nottingham, and train Army cadets there in conjunction with Anglican ordinands. By the time I took up my appointment these plans were considerably advanced. St John's, a very modest establishment, made no secret of its dire financial straits or of its delight at the prospect of being bailed out by The Salvation Army. I initiated an independent report on the relative merits of these plans compared with remaining at Denmark Hill. The report's recommendation was unambiguous: we should stay where we were. Thus it fell to me to inform St John's that plans for a merger, made prior to my arrival, would come to an end. Since then the campus at Denmark Hill has been modernised and further upgraded. After my election as General, Commissioner John Matear succeeded me as the TC and handled this often complex property project with patient skill, keeping the office of the General informed at every stage.

Transition, sessional names, and early travel

After the January 2006 High Council it became clear that there existed no formal document of guidance outlining the many matters involved in the handing over of the office of the General. I asked my Private Secretary, Captain (soon to be Major) Richard Gaudion, therefore to keep a record of everything needing action as the date of assuming office drew near. This catalogue was then easily formalised into a Protocol Document containing an exhaustive list of what needed to be done. It continues to be of help to recently elected leaders and refers to 27 separate matters requiring attention during the weeks of transition.

One of the first tasks for a new General is the choosing of names for the cadet training sessions around the world. I sought to make these resonant with key Army beliefs and tried also to incorporate words which had not been used in earlier sessional names, such as 'prayer', 'holiness', 'friends' and 'resurrection'. Thus I chose the following five names:

2008-10 Prayer Warriors
2009-11 Ambassadors of Holiness
2010-12 Friends of Christ
2011-13 Proclaimers of the Resurrection
2012-14 Disciples of the Cross

Helen and I were pleased when our son, John, told us he felt drawn to the name for the 2009 intake.

My first year in office saw the promotions to Glory of two of our parents:

Journal, 31 May 2006: My lovely Dad died last evening. I am deeply, deeply sad and empty. Yet glad and pleased. Dear Lord, receive and soothe my Dad.

Journal, 4 June 2006: I have known all my adult life and increasingly as I have entered middle age that I have loved my father with a love which was unusually strong. In the immediate aftermath of his death I am experiencing very powerful feelings. Two months ago I saw him and spoke to him alone in Ilminster. He told me of his weakness and his anticipation of death. His body was breaking down. Together we spoke of courage and fear. I told him that Sylvia would look after him until the end and do everything possible to let him remain at home with her. We wept together. Kneeling beside his armchair I put my head on his chest. He held me and told me how proud he was of me and that he loved me. I told him he had been a lovely Dad and had been all I needed and wanted from a father.

Syl has been wonderful in taking care of him. I see real grace in her, a self-sacrificing, mature giving and devotion rarely met. Mary and Nick have been with her now for several weeks and have helped a great deal.

Earlier, on our way to Ilfracombe for the bank holiday weekend, we visited Dad. I read all his 90th birthday cards to him. He was alert and knew the names. On our day of returning, the Tuesday, Syl rang us at the hotel to let us know Dad was failing fast. We reached him at 10 am and stayed until mid-afternoon. He was not communicating. Just once he looked into my eyes for a few seconds only. I held his hand. After we reached Bromley that evening Syl telephoned at 9 pm to say he had breathed his last. Dear God, hold my Dad. Thank you for my lovely Dad.

We went with John last Thursday to see Dad's body in the Chapel of Rest. It was hard. Dad was dressed in his Army uniform. We prayed and I was able to kiss his forehead, his noble brow. We finalised the funeral plans with Sylvia. I will lead the funeral in the Minster

301

Church, the vicar will read prayers, and the Methodist minister will pay a tribute. The Army band from Yeovil will play and the corps officer will read the Bible, using Psalm 46 which was read at Mum and Dad's wedding in November 1939. Several folk from International Headquarters (IHQ) will be present. Because Dad is the father of the General, the entire Army world has been told of his promotion to Glory. Truly he deserves that. Emails and cards are pouring in.

Jen in New Zealand feels very distant from the family but the Principal at the training college, Major Robert Donaldson, graciously plans to hold a service for her and the cadets a few hours before we gather in Ilminster next Tuesday.

It is hard to think of Dad not being in the cottage. His voice is stilled but his weakness is now transformed. He is reunited with Mum and face-to-face with Jesus. Fullness of joy. No fear. Lost in wonder, love and praise.

Journal, 2 April 2007: Helen's Mum was found dead by her Dad at 6 am today on the floor of their bedroom. We went at once and Helen will stay on for a couple of nights.

Journal, 24 April 2007: Grandma Ashman's funeral was on Wednesday 18 April and proved to be a dignified, warm and helpful occasion. Granddad handled it all with poise. Kevin paid a fine family tribute. Major Stuart Downham led well and gave a clear gospel address. Many came from IHQ and Edmonton hall was packed. Jenny's written tribute was read by Kevin. Since the funeral Granddad Ashman seems to be coping quite well, though he has much pain in his lower limbs. I thank God for Betty Ashman, a gracious Christian mother-in-law who was kind to me through all the years and prayed for us all consistently.

Journal, 26 June 2007: Today at 10 am we met Helen's Dad with Ruth and Alan, and Kevin and Andrea at Enfield Crematorium to inter Mum's ashes. A fine plaque has been placed next to a beautiful peach rose bush. We read from John 14 and spoke the verses of 'How sweet the name of Jesus sounds'. Helen had chosen a poem to read and then we all placed pink rose petals in the ground to cover the ashes. Next we shared lunch together in a local restaurant. Granddad Ashman seemed pleased with it all and mentioned specifically the words which we had read from the Army 'Ceremonies Book', 1966 edition.

Travelling around the globe as General and making contact in person with Salvationists is important, but I do not want this Essay to become a mere travelogue (see Appendix C). However, my private Journal records details of many such journeys, as illustrated by visits to Johannesburg, South Africa and to St Petersburg, Russia:

Journal, 28 August 2006: On the evening of Monday 7 August we flew to Johannesburg overnight – lots of turbulence and precious little sleep. We were most cordially greeted on arrival and given VIP processing with the entire territorial cabinet in the VIP lounge to welcome us and pray with us. We received excellent personal attention in our accommodation and then moved outside the city to Amazingwe Lodge for the final three nights. There the morning air was full of scents that took my mind straight back to Mazowe, Rhodesia. We were treated well and made very comfortable. They gave us an early morning mini-safari to see kudu, eland, wildebeest and zebra. Amazingwe is across a valley from Pelindaba where the chemical installations remain very visible. This is where South Africa first developed its now abandoned nuclear weapon capacity. The Treaty of Pelindaba 1996 seeks signatories to create an African Nuclear Weapon Free Zone. I was deeply intrigued to see this place, once symbolic of great evil but now associated with the quest for peace.

We had two aims for this visit: to attend the International Theology Symposium; to encourage Commissioners Trevor and Memory Tuck and their staff and the Salvationists of Johannesburg. The Sunday morning holiness meeting was wonderful. Soweto Songsters took part, making delightful contributions under Songster Leader Khumalo, recipient of the Order of the Founder. A lovely response to the Mercy Seat.

We marched with 800 Salvationists through Soweto on the Monday to a venue that had become synonymous with the anti-apartheid movement, the Regina Mundi Church. It was National Women's Day and Helen would be the guest preacher. We mustered at the Carl Sithole Centre, named after Major Sithole who was killed in a traffic incident. He is revered in Soweto for his courage under apartheid. We were honoured to meet his widow at the officers' meeting held at Johannesburg City Corps hall, part of the THQ complex.

A morning with the cabinet members proved fruitful. We conversed for three hours before I was asked to sum up. I did so by speaking, not about programmes or finance, but about the need of each of us for sanctification. Private moments like these come rarely. As I spoke, quiet tears flowed from more than one in the group. I pray that you will bless them, Lord.

While Helen preached at Regina Mundi Church, I spent a precious, unforgettable but deeply disturbing hour in the new Apartheid Museum, accompanied by Major Gaudion. In many ways it was hard to take. Nooses – 121 of them – dangling from the ceiling to commemorate Steve Biko and 120 others who died in police custody. Thank you, Lord, for this unexpected, disturbing experience. Afterwards Helen joined us there and we had our photographs taken outside the museum.

We toured the Carl Sithole Centre and also the home for motherless babies, 'Ethembeni'. It means 'Place of Hope' where many of the infants have AIDS. We felt deeply moved.

Journal, 28 August 2006: In Russia from 30 August to 4 September. Images galore! Happy faces, moving Mercy Seat scenes, meals and table fellowship with so many different groups, the elegant city of St Petersburg, fine hotel accommodation, and good comradeship with Colonels Barry and Raemor Pobjie and Lieut-Colonels Bo and Birgitte Brekke (the latter about to leave for Pakistan to be the territorial leaders there with the rank of colonel). We were celebrating the 15th anniversary of the Army returning to Russia. It is part of a territory comprising eight time zones. The work has begun also in Romania, Ukraine, Georgia and Moldova (which seems to be the strongest at present). We were treated to a guided tour of the famous Hermitage Museum, a rare treat. I asked to be taken at once to

Rembrandt's 'Return of the Prodigal'. Over two and a half metres high, it is overwhelmingly beautiful, a huge painting with such rich colours. I stood and gazed at it for a long time. Now we have a small, framed print of it on canvas at home.

The remainder of this Essay outlines some central policy issues and broad emphases which marked my five years in office as the General. In addition, matters of ecumenical relations are covered in Essay 3 and the initiative on the new English language *Song Book* is described in Essay 5. International travel, a significant but not the most important component of being the General, is catalogued comprehensively in Appendix C. Space does not permit the recording of the countless meetings, interviews, discussions, board meetings and tactical administrative decisions filling each day, week and month.

Communication

I wanted very much to be in direct contact with Salvationists on as wide a scale as possible in order to demythologise still further the person and role of the General. Two main steps were taken.

A new website dedicated to the office of the General was launched by IHQ on 1 February 2007. It offered visitors free information about the General and his ministry, including news reports and photographs of his travels and other official activities. Articles from various sources would also be available.

Next, a month later, I announced my intention to write occasional pastoral letters to all Salvationists. This was in response to a strong, clear urging that had grown in me ever since taking office. In the Army's earliest days William Booth had a luxury no subsequent General has enjoyed: the facility to communicate directly with his soldiers through *The War Cry*, published in London. At that time all the soldiers lived in the UK, but soon came international expansion, first to the USA and then to Ireland, France, Canada, India, Switzerland, Sweden and many other countries. Booth's soldiers were no longer all within easy reach. Now, over 120 years – and 17 Generals – later, advances in technology had made it possible for the General to communicate directly and virtually instantaneously with his soldiers, wherever in the world they might be. Thus I could send out pastoral letters to be distributed electronically. Once received, they could be circulated still further by whatever means was suited to local conditions. I asked that these letters should not be used as articles in Army publications, but that they be placed directly into the hands of as many Salvationists as possible and as widely as possible across the world. The letters would appear also on the new website.

So in the period of Lent in 2007 I wrote the first of these letters. They went out three or four times each year. They would most definitely not be a mere travelogue. I wanted to speak to my brothers and sisters in Christ on spiritual matters, offering understanding, appreciation and encouragement. These letters were translated into many languages and found their way to even the remotest parts of the Army. I tried to write in a straightforward, sometimes even simple style even when the subject matter was quite profound. Also I tried to keep in mind the translators' task. Often feedback would come directly from recipients in distant lands and this warmed my heart. A retired officer, attending a gathering in Brazil, rose uninvited to his feet to express his personal appreciation for the letters. He said they had made him feel that he mattered. I was greatly encouraged.

Consultation

General Gowans replaced the Advisory Council to the General, a compact group, with the General's Consultative Council (GCC) made up of every non-retired commissioner and TC in the world, a total of about 120 people. Members not residing in London attended in what could be only a token manner every two years or so, or roughly one meeting in eight. The agenda tended to duplicate that of the International Management Council (IMC) which the General also chaired. Significant expressions of frustration with the workings of the GCC were beginning to be voiced and were growing steadily louder. Some senior colleagues urged me to abolish the GCC altogether. I resisted these suggestions for such a step would send the wrong signal. Yet reform was clearly needed.

After conferring with senior colleagues I took the following measures: the meetings would be reduced to three each year instead of four, would last three instead of two days, and would be attended by increased numbers of overseas leaders; the agenda would no longer replicate the work of the IMC but would focus on large issues affecting the whole Army. The GCC would become a think tank instead of a management mechanism. Early main themes for the revised meetings included, for example, 'Our Life of Prayer', 'Our Life of Holiness', 'Winning Children for Christ' and 'The Spiritual Formation of Army Officers'. Detailed minutes of every discussion were made and circulated to all GCC members across the world. Thus ideas could be gleaned for adoption and possible adaption locally without any need for the formal involvement of IHQ. In this reformed GCC we avoided the making of formal resolutions or action steps, preferring to let the discussions themselves act as a stimulus for future policy in the event of ideas filtering down and taking root locally. All this was, in a sense, a step toward decentralisation without diminishing the role or powers of the General or of IHQ.

More significant than these modest and overdue reforms of the GCC was my initiating of the International Appointments Board (IAB). It is the absolute prerogative of the General to determine the appointment of any officer. In practice the General makes decisions usually about only the most senior officers, but for many years now all appointments for those of or above the rank of lieut-colonel or of those becoming divisional commanders (DCs) for the first time have required the General's personal approval.

On taking office I found there was no settled procedural mechanism for ensuring regular, effective, consistent consultation in the appointing of territorial or command leaders, or of chief secretaries. The zonal international secretaries were not consistently consulted prior to senior appointments being made in their zones. This surprised me. So, even though Commissioner Robin Dunster (Chief of the Staff) and I had unusually extensive experience of the wider Army, I decided to introduce a new body to guarantee that those with even closer knowledge of the zones would always have a voice and be heard. At the same time I was not prepared to give away any of the General's prerogatives and so the new board would be explicitly a consultative body with the General presiding. It would meet monthly. The formal Terms of Reference stated: 'The Board exists to assist the General in making senior international appointments.

Its function is consultative and advisory, with the General exercising his right and responsibility to make final decisions. The General may also engage in additional, informal consultation outside the board meetings... . The board will not consider promotions. However, the General will consult with senior colleagues as appropriate.'

Thus the IAB was born. It consisted of the General, the Chief of the Staff, the World President of Women's Ministries and the five zonal international secretaries. The International Secretary for Personnel, whose responsibilities for personnel were more procedural than substantive, was not a full member but attended to supply database information as potential appointees were considered. The other functional international secretaries (business, programme resources and administration) were not included for I wanted to keep the group as tight and as streamlined as possible. It also needed to be strictly confidential and therefore I opted for a limited membership. It was the zonal international secretaries who, of all the international secretaries, knew the personnel of the zone with intimacy and accurate insight. I was aware that the non-zonal international secretaries felt they too should be members of the new board, but a smaller, tight-knit, knowledgeable group was to prove not only more effective but also secure in terms of confidentiality. The IAB could not meet without the General being present. Soon we were well into things and able to plan calmly at least a year or more ahead for changes of senior appointments. This gave us ample time for poised reconsideration in the event of some unforeseen factor arising to frustrate an initial plan. I was determined never to rush such decisions. Too much was at stake. The notice given to senior officers of a change of appointment was also modified, from three months to a more humane minimum of four.

Women leaders

It was while perusing the *Year Book* and glancing at the names of the DCs in North America that it dawned upon me that proactive steps were swiftly needed to advance the cause of women officers into more senior leadership roles. At that time, of the 53 DCs or equivalents in the USA and Canada, 52 were men. Further review of the global situation confirmed a similar pattern. If more women, whether single or married, were to rise to senior roles and higher rank then it made sense to start by seeking to appoint more women as DCs. Proposals for such appointments reaching IHQ from the territories consistently offered the names only of male officers. With the support of my senior colleagues at IHQ word went out that I expected to see a significant increase in the number of women being proposed as DCs and also as holders of cabinet positions at THQ. Where a territory continued consistently to offer only male candidates for these positions, the zonal departments were under instruction to return the proposals and ask that women officers also be put forward. It was slow work. Cultural factors were against us everywhere. Male chauvinism seemed to be entrenched in every zone of the Army world and in every cultural group.

Slowly things changed. During our visits to territories I would raise the matter in private with the territorial leaders, in sessions with Territorial Cabinet members, and also in plenary gatherings of the officers as a whole. We sought also to identify women who could, without further delay, take on the role of Chief Secretary. Marital status would be no bar. We would consult carefully and sensitively with both spouses and explain our hopes. Responses were mixed. Some very able married women simply declined advancement despite encouragement from their husbands. We did not give up. Everybody knew that I would not promote a man of merely average ability when there was available a woman, whether married or not, of above-average ability.

Closely akin to this issue, which I saw as one of justice for our women officers, was that of eligibility for membership of a High Council. Many married women officers who had long served in the role of Territorial President of Women's Ministries were not eligible for membership if they held only colonel rank. Other married women officers who had served in the same capacity for shorter terms but whose rank, because of the size of the territory, was that of commissioner were eligible for membership. The excluded women were leaders in the smaller territories and were often African or Asian in ethnicity. This gave the unintended impression of racial discrimination. It was relatively simple to resolve things. After taking legal advice and following extensive consultation I invoked the relevant provisions of the Salvation Army Act 1980 and held a postal ballot to amend the rules of eligibility for membership of a High Council. Now all officers holding the appointment of Territorial President of Women's Ministries would be eligible regardless of rank. This simple change, modest in comparison with past modifications of the rules for eligibility, received overwhelming approval. The last two High Councils (2011 and 2013) have included these long-excluded female leaders. This too was a matter of justice.

New countries

Numerical growth and geographical enlargement are usually signs of good health in any organisation. Due mainly to our numbers in Africa and South Asia the Army is numerically larger now than at any time. In other places, where the tough challenges of post-modern and deeply ingrained cultural shifts have marginalised organised religion, we still see clear signs of hope.

William Booth saw advancement into new lands as a mark of God's favour. The period 2007-11 saw the Army put down roots and become legally established in 12 more countries, making 123 in total:

2007	Burundi	112
2007	Greece	113
2008	Namibia	114
2008	Mali	115
2008	Kuwait	116
2008	Mongolia	117
2009	Nepal	118
2010	Sierra Leone	119
2010	Nicaragua	120
2010	United Arab Emirates	121
2011	Turks and Caicos Islands	122
2011	Solomon Islands	123

Numerous requests had reached IHQ through the years from Greek citizens asking that the Army be established in their land. All were repeatedly denied. Having met and got to know Greek-speaking officers in the UK while TC there, I could sense an opportunity for God and the Army and thus initiated further exploratory visits. So it was that work came to be established in Thessaloniki. We are now also in Athens. We had been in Namibia from 1932-39 but were expelled by the German authorities when war broke out. How good it is that we have returned and how gracious the welcome extended to us. 'We need you for your awareness of the holy life,' said the Namibian Council of Churches. Mali, a mainly Moslem nation, is the most northerly part of Africa in which the Army is found. After prolonged and careful preparations by the Korea Territory, the work in Mongolia was pioneered by Captains Lee, Min-ho and Chang, Mi-hyun. It was my privilege personally to dedicate and send these fine comrades to Mongolia during the celebrations in Seoul to mark the centenary of our work in the Korean peninsula. Then came Nepal at the instance of the visionary and energetic India Eastern Territory. Captains Lalsangliana and Lalnunsangi were sent, with their children, to live and work in Kathmandu. Captains John and Roseline Bundu from Liberia opened the work in Sierra Leone in January 2010. Costa Rican officers, Majors Enwike and Ana Molina, were appointed to lead the new work in the Central American land of Nicaragua. In June 2012 the focus shifted back to the Middle East and the opening of work in the United Arab Emirates. Majors Mike and Theresa Hawley, with Lieutenants Robert and Glenis Viera, supervised this pioneering endeavour. They were the gift of the USA Southern Territory.

Regular monitoring reports from each place showed steady, modest, early growth. This pleased me, for had the growth been sudden and large-scale I would have suspected a lack of depth. I was pleased also by the readiness of several well-established territories to provide initial funding plus support personnel. I knew that if these initiatives were pleasing to God, resources of both people and money would flow. The Army needs always to be open to God in this way. I have never agreed with those who have advocated a moratorium on new openings, for that would be to close the door to the divine impulse.

It is important to understand that little of this expansion was intentionally orchestrated. We did not, for example, plan a specific number of new openings each year. We were continually open to the probability of expansion, but there proved to be a spontaneity about it that marked it out as God's intention and God's initiative. My role was simply to be open to the divine leadings and to offer affirmation and pragmatic support to those engaged in the sacred toil of 'opening fire' in each new land. As I said in my nomination speech at the 2006 High Council: 'It is God's plan that we are a global force. It is not an accident. He wants us to span the world and he will take us into still yet untrod paths and places if we are faithful and obedient.'

Children and youth

The place of children in the Army was constantly on my mind. We believe in the wonderful possibility of childhood conversion. The September 2008 meeting of the GCC focused on winning children for Christ. Out of this came a strong, timely plea that the 2009 International Conference of Leaders (ICL) should give the matter further attention (see on this my 2010 *Selected Writings – Volume 2*, Chapter 16). From that gathering came a unanimous recommendation that, as part of a renewed focus on evangelising children, the Junior Soldier's Promise should once again be made uniform across the globe and restored to its once rightful place in our orders and regulations. In addition every territory and command would revisit and update its junior soldier teaching and training materials. Most importantly, in those lands where evangelising children had been sidelined or virtually abandoned by the Army a change of emphasis was called for and responded to.

The youth of the global Army met with eagerness in representative gatherings during the World Youth Convention held in Stockholm, Sweden, in July 2010. Colonel Birgitte Brekke coordinated this historic event. She and her two committees (in London and Stockholm) proved to be visionary, competent planners. We can be proud of our young people. They are hungry for God and they long for the holy life. They are ready to be deployed in self-sacrificial service. They evince a wonderful spirit and are proud to be seen in uniform and in Army witness-wear. They have a passion for the gospel and copious energy for outreach. Pleased to be associated with the Army, many are experiencing a sacred vocation to serve God as Army officers or in other distinctive ways within our ranks.

For many months after the Stockholm Convention reports continued to reach me of the lasting impact made upon those who attended and in turn their significant influence upon all around them when they returned home.

> *Journal, 21 July 2010: Answered prayers! God has answered the countless prayers over the last two years. He has blessed all the planning and all the complex logistics in crystal clear fashion to make the World Youth Convention in Stockholm a sign that he loves his Army and his Salvationist young people. He rejoices to see them together. He loves their uniforms, their laughter, their chatter, their praying and their praising. He loves them because of their tender hearts and their natural responses to his holy impulses. God has touched us all in Stockholm, stirred us, humbled us, and has told us afresh that he loves us and wants to use us. I pray, Lord, for each young delegate. Hold them in your hands through all the years to come. Let this convention be your rain on parched ground. Flood your Army with Holy Spirit confidence and boldness. Grow lasting fruit from it all. Purify us afresh and bind us into the very centre of your holy will.*

Army books

It troubled me that the book publishing role of IHQ had long since been allowed to fall away. I took the view that it was the natural role of IHQ to take a lead in publishing useful Salvationist materials. Of course, cost was a factor but I have always viewed the subsidising of good Christian literature as part of our overall strategy for Christ. Also I wanted the current generation of Salvationists to rediscover and benefit from some of the good publications of the past. Thus the series of 'Classic Salvationist Texts' was born, reviving works by William and Catherine Booth, Catherine Baird, Gunpei Yamamuro, Clarence Wiseman, Frederick Coutts, Flora Larsson and others. Using a new imprint, 'Salvation Books', to date 44 publications – both 'classic' and new – have been released.

Our 'Handbook of Doctrine'

My personal spiritual life owes not a little to the availability of successive editions of the Army's *Handbook of Doctrine*. So when it was announced that a further edition would be published by 1998 I paid close attention. We were still living in Boston, USA, when a draft was circulated and I was able to offer feedback via Commissioner Ronald Irwin, our TC. My first impression was that the compilers still had much to do to complete the new edition and to render it authentically user-friendly.

Eventually things were finalised and the new *Handbook* was published with the title, *Salvation Story*. It was made the subject of a presentation by Colonel John Amoah, then a member of the International Doctrine Council (IDC), at the ICL in Melbourne in March 1998. An official invitation from General Rader reached me in Lahore asking me to make a formal response to the colonel's presentation. I prepared accordingly, reading the new *Handbook* from cover to cover several times and noting its various characteristics. Each reading left me with an increased sense of anxiety. Thus my formal response in Melbourne became a candid appraisal of the new publication with the following main observations:

1. The useful appendices and the glossary of doctrinal terms were to be welcomed, although the definitions often used overly complex language, sometimes even more sophisticated than the words being defined!

2. The material on the classical creeds was very helpful.

3. The rejection of numbering for the paragraphs in the main text was a mistake. It rendered the book significantly less helpful for teaching purposes, yet it was meant to be a teaching tool for cadets and others.

4. Most significantly, the relegation of the scriptural references to mere lists at the end of each section was a startling, truly disturbing measure. Since our first published doctrine book in 1881 we had consistently been explicit about the scriptural basis

314

for all we believe, liberally lacing our commentaries with biblical quotations in order to allow the inspired Word to speak to the reader. We had always been willing to be clear and plain, spelling out the direct link between Scripture and our beliefs. All this had now been abandoned. The new book gave only a cursory nod to the Scriptures, settling for lists of references after each section which gave no hint of how any of the references related to the main text. No longer would we feel the divine cutting edge of the Scriptures as we moved from page to page. The claim by the compilers that using lists of Bible references instead of Bible quotations throughout the main text of the book would make readers turn to the Scriptures and look up each reference was hopelessly naïve.

5. Of the 121 pages of main text only 24 held a direct quotation from the Bible. Of the 33,000 words used in the book only 275 came from the Bible. Of the 11 chapters, five had no quotations from the Bible at all! These chapters included those on the Trinity, on salvation, on the Church, and on last things. Ironically, the Roman Catholic Church had released a new official *Catechism* in 1994 with over 600 pages of teaching, each page littered with direct quotations from the Bible. Yet it was the Army, not the Catholics, whose first doctrine declared the supremacy of the Scriptures in matters of faith and practice. Now our new *Handbook of Doctrine* signalled that the words of Scripture were no longer to be seen as paramount in transmitting our beliefs.

6. The numbering of the chapters did not align with the numbering of the doctrines, an easily avoided misjudgement.

7. The new book attempted to reword our doctrines, giving the impression of seeking to rewrite them by stealth instead of respecting the prerogatives of the General and the processes for change set down in the Salvation Army Act 1980.

Unsurprisingly, these frank observations triggered considerable reaction from some colleagues present. I felt the matter was far too important to settle for simply going through the usual formality of offering customary polite praise.

It was in March 2008 that I wrote to Commissioner William Francis, Chair of the IDC, to initiate discussion on the publishing of a new *Handbook of Doctrine* to replace *Salvation Story*. I explained my longstanding misgivings about the 1998 publication and referred also to the 1999 *Study Guide* which had been published to be used alongside the 1998 book. I asked if we might merge the two into a more user-friendly single volume. The commissioner received my proposals with immediate enthusiasm, going on to suggest that the title, *Salvation Story*, be dropped in view of the impression given that our doctrines were fictitious, just 'stories'. The 1998 compilers had adopted 'story' to convey a sense of the full historic sweep of God's plan of salvation. However, this was a word connoting to many, especially those using English as a second language, something made up. They were not aware of its use in a scholarly sense. Moreover, it created difficulties for translated editions.

With the helpful backing of the IMC, the detailed work on a new volume began. I was very pleased to appoint Lieut-Colonel Karen Shakespeare to carry out the work of revision, of reorganisation, and of merging the two volumes into one. She was the holder of high theological qualifications and had many years of experience teaching cadets in matters of doctrine. Given an explicit brief as to what was required, she worked with speed, skill and much patience to reshape the book. Her main task was to restore the Scriptures to an explicit and central role in the presentation and explanation of our beliefs. The first draft of the new single volume, ready in mid-2009, was sent to the IDC for close scrutiny. Their helpful feedback led to further modifications and the new volume was released in both hardback and clothback editions in 2010.

From the outset I informed Lieut-Colonel Shakespeare that her name would not appear in the new book. Except for the 1998 *Salvation Story* publication, no personal names of writers had appeared in any *Handbook of Doctrine* since the first in 1881, and there had been no fewer than 26 new editions or reprints through the years, all anonymous. It is customary to retain author anonymity whenever IHQ publishes a formal document representing official Army teaching (for example, our positional statements on moral issues or our publications on ecumenical relations). Karen (now Lieut-Colonel Dr Shakespeare) expressed ready understanding of all this and proved gracious throughout the entire exercise. Through these pages I am now free to salute and thank her more publicly for splendid work on the new 2010 *Handbook of Doctrine*. It has been most positively received and its enhanced user-friendliness widely appreciated. Best of all, we have returned to acknowledging explicitly, and to using openly, the Scriptures in matter of doctrinal exposition.

Impoverished officers

Many parts of the Army world are extremely poor. Not every officer receives the full allowance and many enter retirement on a meagre Army pension and without any state provision.

The better-off territories have an impressive history of giving well to support our work globally and it is often very moving to see such support bear lasting fruit. With this in mind, the Centralised Pension Fund (CPF) was created at IHQ to alleviate hardship for retired officers in the less- affluent countries. We needed to build up a corpus of at least US$100 million in order to generate annual revenues from its investment which would provide for the payment of pensions in countries where the officers were disadvantaged.

I decided to ask the Western territories to give on an unprecedented scale. Speaking personally to each TC in the four USA territories, I secured solid commitments from each that his territory would contribute US$20 million towards the corpus of the CPF. USA National Headquarters also made a significant contribution and so too did many of the other financially independent territories. Thus the fund began to grow under the experienced and guiding hand of the then International Secretary for Business Administration, Commissioner Ann Woodall. It is still growing, providing for hardship, and serves as a lasting reminder that in Christ we are one body, providing for the needs of our brothers and sisters in Christ.

Social justice

Matters of social justice and the making of ethical choices have long been of close interest to me. So too has been my desire to have the Army speak in the public arena when opportunity has arisen. Our people are proud and their spirits are raised when they know that Army leaders are ready to seek to influence public affairs in a non-party and non-partisan manner, articulating the values of our Saviour and drawing upon our long and wide experience of working among the socially deprived.

Essay 7B outlines my personal involvement in such things when serving as the Legal and Parliamentary Secretary at IHQ. Opportunities for further initiatives arose later on my becoming a TC. In New Zealand I was able to set up a new Social Policy and Parliamentary Unit to conduct research and propose social policy initiatives to the government. The unit has published a series of influential 'State of the Nation' reports.

It seemed to me only natural that the Army should establish a kindred unit to carry out research and engage in advocacy on social and moral issues from a wider international perspective. Thus I initiated the International Social Justice Commission (ISJC) to be based in New York near to the United Nations building and to be under the guiding hand of Commissioner Christine MacMillan. Though housed in America, the ISJC functions as part of the Administration Department of IHQ and is accountable to the General in the same way as other IHQ departments.

This initiative drew warm expressions of approval on every hand. I sensed a growing wave of concern and of fresh determination that we should speak out for the cause of right, regardless of the consequences. It is especially encouraging to note that often it is our younger people who show a lead in these matters, something that became abundantly clear during the 2010 World Youth Convention in Stockholm.

The formal opening and dedication of the ISJC at its new centre on East 52nd Street, Manhattan, New York, took place on Tuesday 26 August 2008. Helen and I were delighted to be present, together with the USA National leaders, Commissioners Israel and Eva Gaither, for a moving and inspirational opening ceremony organised by Commissioner MacMillan and her staff. Also present were our United Nations liaison representatives from Vienna (Major Elisabeth Frei) and Geneva (Major Sylvette

Huguenin). I spoke words of warm thanks to Commissioners Larry and Nancy Moretz for making available and upgrading the Manhattan premises and recognised also the helpful support of the leaders of the Greater New York Division, Majors Guy and Henrietta Klemanski. Representing the United Nations was Mr Liberato Bautista, President of the United Nations Conference of Non-Governmental Organisations, who spoke of the need for God's will to be seen to be done on earth. He extended warm congratulations on the creation of the ISJC.

Now directed by Colonel Geanette Seymour since July 2012, the ISJC continues its sacred task of representing God's Army in global issues of social justice and of encouraging Salvationists to be proactive in their own communities. Internships are offered to capable young people who can make a telling contribution while in New York and then go on to influence their communities and governments in matters of social justice after returning home.

Coupled with the creation of the ISJC was the re-establishing of a body at IHQ that would advise the General on ethical issues having a global dimension. Thus the International Moral and Social Issues Council was formed with Commissioner MacMillan appointed as the inaugural holder of the role of chairperson (see also my 2010 *Selected Writings – Volume 2*, Chapters 12 and 17). This step did not restrict the ability of the territories to formulate their own stances on local issues subject to the approval of the Chief of the Staff, a process that had been in place since General Eva Burrows disbanded the original Moral and Social Issues Council which in the years prior to her election had met and worked successfully in London.

Regulations on divorce

In Essay 7B I offer an account of the creation in the 1980s of a regulatory system and the introduction of pastoral measures to cope with marital breakdown. These provisions were repealed a few years prior to my taking office, having been in place and having steadily evolved over a period of almost 20 years.

Toward the latter part of my final year in office I received both verbal and written requests urging me to initiate a fresh look at our international regulations in this field in order to make them once again comprehensive and relevant to the realities faced both by the Salvationists suffering marital trauma and by their leaders called upon to render consequent decisions. These representations came mainly, but not exclusively, from North America and from highly experienced, seasoned leaders there.

The whole matter was carefully aired and analysed in 2010 during one of my scheduled face-to-face consultations with the USA National Commander, Commissioner Israel Gaither. Other senior colleagues, both female and male, were present for these talks. This group felt unanimously that the worldwide Army should no longer be required to handle such sensitive issues in a virtual vacuum, an almost total absence of relevant guidance in the form of written regulations issued on the authority of the General. One senior TC wrote to me with a moving, heartfelt plea for regulatory guidance to be reintroduced. He expressed his feelings of isolation and helplessness when confronted with marital breakdown among officers serving under his leadership.

All of this confirmed my own convictions in the matter. However, I had taken no step to revive the issue since my election and now, with it being raised so clearly, I regretted greatly that so little time was left to me to address it properly. I brought the matter to the attention of the IMC and discussed it carefully with the Chief of the Staff. This led to the conclusion that it would not be wise or helpful to the Army for me to initiate a revision of the regulations when I was due to retire in just a few months. Any major consultation with the Army world and the shaping of a renewed regulatory structure should be initiated by my successor, who would have adequate time to ponder the subtleties and cultural complexities involved without feeling pressurised by deadlines.

Accordingly I took no formal action and left it to the 2011 High Council to raise the matter in their formal questions to those standing for election as my successor. The matter would remain on the ongoing agenda of the IMC.

Serving God as the General

In my address to those gathered for the 2011 High Council I spoke as follows:

'It is my earnest prayer that no person has come to the High Council hoping to be elected. That would be a fatal error. If you hope to be elected, you are likely to go home disappointed.

'Let me remind you of the enormous physical burdens of being the General. Helen and I, with Major Gaudion, have flown almost 300,000 miles since I took office. Add to this the miles travelled by land both in the UK and elsewhere. We have visited 41 countries, undertaking 52 separate overseas campaigns plus 10 official engagements in the UK Territory. I should mention also the 50 visits to the International College for Officers. Since becoming the General I have risen to my feet to speak in public on over 650 occasions.

'All this is a considerable burden and challenge for both the General and the General's spouse. The expectation concerning global travel by the General remains a very high one around the Army world. The Army benefits from these visits, but does everyone understand the draining impact on world leaders due to jetlag and the stress of public engagements? Travel is not the main aspect of the General's job. It is an added extra over and above the General's sacred obligations to set direction and to formulate policy initiatives.

'I turn now to deeper aspects of what it means to serve as the General. You are about to elect the global spiritual head of a worldwide evangelical Christian church. Approximately two million people, in every corner of the world, look to the General as their leader under God. Your task is to elect someone to carry out this sacred function of spiritual and ecclesial leadership. That same person will become responsible also for a vast business empire with holdings and assets which would be the envy of many a business mogul. This alone is a huge responsibility and the Army needs to have at its head a person with sufficient intellectual acumen for it all.

'Salvationists want a leader who has experienced, and who is willing to speak unashamedly, openly and with candour about, the holy life. Salvationists also know that their General should have vision beyond what is normal, being able to see further than others and instinctively anticipating the ultimate outcomes of key decisions. The General must have a heart of compassion, a heart moved by human need and that beats in time to the heart of the compassionate Christ. Salvationists expect their General to uphold everything represented by the word "Salvationism" and to defend it tooth and nail, never watering down our infinitely precious distinctives. The General also needs to be decisive, yet willing to consult and to listen. Our people will not be pleased if they sense the General is yielding to the temptation to be surrounded by "yes" people.

'Nobody in this room is qualified for this role. I was not qualified for it when I sat here five years ago. However, we know that God will grace the person ultimately elected and be their constant companion. All the resources of Heaven will be made available day by day if the one you choose remains faithful and true.'

Letter to an unknown successor

As the date for my retirement drew near I worked assiduously with my personal support staff to prepare a Farewell Brief for my successor. It ran to 80 pages plus 36 separate appendices. It began with a letter to my unknown successor:

Dear General-elect,

I am compiling this letter, and am doing so deliberately before knowing your name or the outcome of the January 2011 High Council. There are things I wish to say to you, things I have intended to share with whoever might emerge as my successor.

First of all, I tremble for you because I know exactly what faces you and, at this time of writing, you do not. However, you are intelligent and gifted. The Holy Spirit will further sensitise you to the vastness of the responsibilities thrust upon you and to the enormous potential now placed in your hands for the accomplishment of good, or for otherwise.

Approximately two million people all over the world are about to look to you as their leader. They will feel connected with you and at the same time feel a responsibility toward you. You will experience a wonderful upsurge of loving loyalty as word of your election spreads. This is a recurring miracle of God that happens following each High Council.

You will most definitely be prayed for by countless persons. I pledge my prayers for the demanding days ahead.

More important than anything else is your personal spiritual walk with the Lord, the Lord who has known you from before your parents met each other, and who has planned for you and called you out from secular paths into sacred service. Guard your spiritual life. Beware flattery. Allow your people to affirm you, but do not believe all the wonderful things many will want to say. Beware also those few who will seek to denigrate you for reasons known only to themselves.

I need hardly urge you to seek persistently and regularly the guidance of Almighty God in all things, but especially in the appointment of senior leaders. This applies particularly to the appointment of commissioners to serve with you in London. Do not yield to the temptation to surround yourself with people who will flatter you.

The Army is blessed to have you. God knows you through and through and is already making provision for your every need. Please know that as the years unfold you will have, in this writer, a most empathetic intercessor at the Throne of Grace.

On the due date of 1 April 2011, at midnight, I ceased to be the General in office. Now I would devote myself round the clock to caring for Helen until the Lord took her home to Heaven. I was called to be Helen's spouse just as powerfully and as clearly as I was called to be God's servant as an officer in The Salvation Army. Caring for her and tending to her needs was a privilege even more sacred, more eternally significant than being the General.

The weeks passed until she died on 14 June with her loved ones at her side. Her death bonded us yet closer together as a family, something that seemed to take visible, tangible form when we gathered for the wedding of our son, John, to Naomi Shakespeare at Denmark Hill on Saturday 23 July. Invited to conduct the ceremony, I wondered how I could possibly get through it for deep within I was fractured and still reeling from Helen's death. The day dawned. I was a confused mixture of excited anticipation for John and Naomi and yet apprehension at having to appear in public feeling broken.

Journal, 21 July 2011: Sympathy cards have diminished in daily number at last. None at all yesterday and only two this morning. I have received well over 600 so far. As I close this entry, I give tonight and especially tomorrow to God as all the family will convene again. This time we meet, not for a funeral, but to celebrate a marriage with John and Naomi. We will feel Helen close among us. Dear Lord, help me to officiate warmly and calmly for John's sake.

Journal, 26 July 2011: John and Naomi are married! It all went well, except that the registrar arrived 20 minutes late and then asked me what time it was all due to start! John was visibly moved at the sight of Naomi walking down the aisle on the arm of her father. I got through it all pretty well. My voice wavered once or twice as the sacred words were recited. John spoke naturally and well at the reception. Matt dressed up as Charles Darwin for his best man speech and made us all laugh. When John spoke he mentioned his Mum. I missed her terribly and felt like a spare wheel at times throughout the day.

I took Jen, Marcus, Hudson and Lincoln to Heathrow Airport on Sunday. Our parting was not too stressful because they are heading for a few days in Los Angeles and I will spend nine weeks with them over Christmas and the New Year. It will be a lonely trip. Never have I flown that far alone before.

Journal, 22 August 2011: Things have been going a little better from day to day. Perhaps I am beginning to find some semblance of balance, some poise. I am not truly sure. Missing Helen is deeply painful. I long for her voice, her touch, her companionship.

ESSAY 13

❧

STUDYING

ESSAY 13
STUDYING

Starting school

SCHOOL was not always a comfortable experience. As a young teenager I chafed under regimentation and authority, and was not an outstanding pupil. This may explain why in later years I opted to pursue studies at tertiary level in subjects, first law and then theology, not taught in British schools.

I was somehow aware of being reasonably intelligent, but applying that to the formalities of the classroom did not come naturally. Contrast Helen who excelled in all things academic from a very young age right through to postgraduate studies at university. She had a highly retentive memory coupled with an aptitude for logical analysis. Opting for the sciences until completing her fifth year at the Latymer School in Edmonton, she then suddenly switched to the arts, languages and literature for her advanced level pre-university courses. Still the annual prizes continued to come her way, culminating in an academic scholarship to read English Language and Literature at the University of London's Westfield College. I loved her for all that she was, and her bright, intelligent mind was powerfully attractive. Put simply, she was brighter than me and I liked that.

My earliest memories of formal study take me to Sholing, Southampton, and starting school aged five in 1950. Our family had moved from Portadown in Northern Ireland under farewell orders from The Salvation Army. My classroom was part of a Second World War Nissen hut. My mother would drop me off and pick me up later. Each afternoon we were all required to put our heads down on our folded arms and sleep for 20 minutes! Was this for our good or for the teacher's? I will never be sure.

The Army moved my parents to Barnsley, Yorkshire, where we lived in Queen's Drive from 1951 to 1954. Our house was opposite a large, empty, grassy area which was sometimes a jungle in which I was the intrepid explorer, or a racing track with me as the fearless bike racer. Each November it became the site of the Guy Fawkes bonfire blaze. Wilthorp Junior School took me in, even tolerating my breaking a staffroom window from outside in the playground! They taught us all to knit, girls and boys alike. It was called 'handicrafts', and I knitted a kettle-holder for my Mum. It was made of thick twine. She received it with appropriate praise heaped upon me, but later dropped it onto the gas hob and all that remained was a pile of charred string. No great loss! I was not an outstanding pupil, but I can remember the giddy heights of coming third in the annual fancy-dress parade and winning a new tennis ball for my pains!

Scottish schools

Our family's odyssey under Army auspices took us next to Parkhead in Scotland's great city of Glasgow. It was here that the Lord first let me hear his calling voice as I recount in Essay 1. The Tollcross School was housed in a stolid 19th century two-storey building. My memories are of pleasant days and of walks through the grassy spaces of Tollcross Park to get to school each day. With Major Richard Gaudion, Helen and I visited the school when we were the territorial leaders in the United Kingdom, arriving in our uniforms and unannounced but being most graciously received by the headmaster. Majors David and Sylvia Hinton, the leaders of the West Scotland Division, accompanied us. Sight of the building and the playground brought floods of memories, mostly good. Near the school lived James and Mary Hamilton. Mary was employed as an agent of The Salvation Army Assurance Society Ltd and worked under my Dad's supervision. As I write, I have just received news of her promotion to Glory. Many a time I delivered business packages to her home on the way to school and was always rewarded with a shining silver sixpenny piece. Ah, what riches! Sixpence could buy a more than adequate supply of aniseed balls and chewing gum!

On reaching my 12th birthday I was transferred to secondary school and the Eastbank Academy. Everything changed. Now there was a uniform to wear, a tram journey to be made each way, and streets to be negotiated that were occupied by Roman Catholic families whose children were off school on certain 'saints days' while we Protestants could be seen in our Eastbank uniforms attending school as normal. It was not unusual to find ourselves pelted with stones by the Roman Catholic youngsters as we came and went. No real harm befell us, but in later years this simple memory would return to me when in contact with Catholic colleagues. We needed to work for, at the very least, mutual respect. Ingrained, negative attitudes did nothing to enhance the cause of the gospel (see Essay 3).

Other vivid memories of Eastbank Academy include my hopeless attempts to learn to play the cello. They include too the regular use of the tawse (a leather strap with split end sections) to discipline the pupils for even minor things. Teachers would slash it across our hands or oblige us to bend over to be whipped on the buttocks, all in full view of the entire class. My parents soon told me to refuse to hold out my hands or to bend over. I recall the first time of refusing, my heart beating rapidly, but the startled teacher backed off and I was never offered this appalling sanction again. Neither were my sisters.

We left Glasgow in 1957 for London. I was not sorry to be leaving the Academy. It was there I found I had some early ability to put words on paper, but it was there also that I was known to be a son of an Englishman, a 'Sassenach', and had to learn to defend myself in the playground. I did not mind the rough and tumble of a playground encounter, for I was well-built, had been taught boxing by my Dad, and soon won respect. It was the structured physical brutality of the school discipline system that appalled me, young as I was. That said, my memories of Glasgow and of Scotland as a whole are largely good ones: holidays on the Isle of Bute; football, cricket and open-air theatre in Tollcross Park; the young people's band and singing company at Parkhead Corps; trips to Edinburgh Castle and Arthur's Seat; the annual band camp at Middleton; hearing my parents preach, especially at Shettleston Goodwill Centre where the Army still has a corps; and being a recipient of Salvationist, Celtic warmth and hospitality on every hand.

To London, Latymer, and Helen

Edmonton, north London, was and is a far cry from Parkhead. As our train pulled out of Glasgow Central Station, and as we waved to Army friends gathered to see us off, my Mum burst into tears, declaring her sense of loss on leaving Scotland. Her Irishness had allowed her to feel a Celtic affinity with the Scots and she had been happy to be in Glasgow. I came to learn that my officer-parents had discovered the precious gift of being content wherever their vocations took them, for their happiness was grounded first and foremost in their love for each other, then in their love for their three children, and all of this undergirded by their shared devotion to Christ.

Leaving our older sister, Sylvia, behind in Glasgow to complete her education at Eastbank, Mary and I became pupils of the Latymer School, Edmonton, whose origins go back to the educational reforms of the early 17th century and stirrings at that time toward more widespread education of the young. The dominant figure was the school's Welsh Headmaster, Dr Trefor Jones, in post from 1957 to 1970. He was to show me patience and understanding as I journeyed through my teenage years. Though I was never a star pupil, he seemed to sense something in me that was worth encouraging.

With 1,400 pupils, the school was organised on a 'House' basis. I became a school prefect, entitled to wear the distinctive striped tie and granted the much-sought-after use of the prefects' common room. I found myself also elected as captain of Dolbé House (named after a former headmaster) and was beginning to feel at ease addressing others in a public setting. I was very pleased when Helen also became a pupil at Latymer, two years my junior. She seemed to excel in every way. The staff liked and encouraged her, though one or two wondered what she saw in the rather pedestrian Shaw Clifton.

I confess to being delighted when invited to return to Latymer in the summer of 2013 as the guest speaker for the annual Foundation Day Service, an honour few of my teachers in the 1960s would have foreseen as ever being accorded to me. The present head teacher, Mark Garbett, with staff members and governors received me most graciously. At the conclusion of the service in the Anglican Church of All Saints, Edmonton, we rose to sing the Latymer School Song. It takes its inspiration from the promises found in Scripture in the Book of Revelation and in the messages to the seven churches. Each message holds a sacred promise for the one who endures to the end and is victorious. Hence the Latymer School motto beneath its coat of arms, *Qui Patitur Vincit* – 'The one who endures will conquer', and the ringing lines from the school song by Alice W. Linford: 'Ye who endure while strife engages, strong in soul shall win at last.'

To university

Leaving Latymer with decent but not remarkable results in my final examinations I applied to study law at university and was given a place at King's College, part of the University of London. King's was well known for its Law Faculty. It was also famous as a place of learning in the field of theology, being a Christian foundation named after Christ, the King, and established in 1829 as a faith-based counterpart to the famous University College, renowned for its humanist and secular emphases. University College, founded in 1826, was known at King's as 'the godless college in Gower Street'.

As part of its Christian heritage King's invited all undergraduate students to take courses in religious studies. These were open to students of every faculty. So in addition to my legal studies I took the courses and the examination, earning a diploma as an Associate of King's College (AKC).

King's has produced 10 Nobel Prize winners. Among its alumni are the poet John Keats, the nurse Florence Nightingale and Archbishop Desmond Tutu. I was partaking of a distinguished heritage. After my election as General the *In Touch* alumni magazine for autumn 2006 carried an interview and profile. My time there was enriched by my friendship with Barry Nathan. He was Jewish and shared my dislike of the claustrophobic, smoky pubs and wine bars frequented by most of the undergraduates. His disposition was always bright and positive. We shared a similar sense of humour. Often our conversation would turn to matters of faith and, as we asked each other searching questions, we would also express respect for one another's heritage. Barry was a keen fan of the famous jazz drummer, Buddy Rich, and spent much time – even at the expense of his studies – in attending concerts. He scraped through his law finals, but went on to make a good career as a barrister.

It was as a law student that suddenly I found my feet academically. A whole new world of learning opened up to me, as never before, in a field rich in academic theory but grounded too in everyday applicability. Law was useful. It had purpose. The long hours of reading judicial precedents in the law library were no hardship to me. I loved it. The tomes, many bound in calf-leather, felt and smelled good. Their musty aroma was a

delight to my young nostrils and the hours spent surrounded by them
sped by all too quickly. Taught the law of trusts by Michael R.
Chesterman, a gifted academic lawyer from Tasmania young enough still
to remember what it was like to be a student, I discovered a special affinity
with the law of charitable trusts, not knowing that one day God would
take and use this in an unexpected way. Vague thoughts were born of
perhaps one day teaching law and of authoring legal textbooks. After three
years at King's I emerged in 1968 with no real idea of what to do next. It
was usual to go on and read for the English Bar or to qualify as a solicitor.
Neither held real appeal for me.

Teaching law

In the late summer of that year my uncertainty was ended by an out-
of-the-blue telephone call from the Sub-Dean of the Law Faculty at
King's, Charles Morrison. He said he was leaving to take up a post as
head of the new law school at London's Inns of Court. It was an entirely
new initiative by the Council for Legal Education. He wanted to gather
around him a team of bright, young law tutors to get it all off the ground.
Would I be interested in joining his team? I could hardly believe my ears!
I leaped at it. Thus I joined the Society of Public Teachers of Law and
set out on a career as a young and very junior academic lawyer, spending
two happy years teaching students studying for the English Bar
Examinations. The law school was housed in pleasant grounds within
Gray's Inn on London's High Holborn. Gray's Inn is one of the four
Inns of Court that serve as the professional bodies for practising
barristers. I became a member of the Inner Temple, famous for its Temple
Church once led by Richard Hooker, a Protestant reformer of the 16th
century (see Essay 8).

My time at Gray's Inn was interrupted by a bout of cancer (see Essay
4), but it was there that I met people from across the globe wanting to
study law in London and it was there I discovered an ability to teach. I
was paid to lead tutorials in the law of torts, of crime and of contract.
Many of my students were second-language speakers of English and I had
to find ways of presenting complex concepts in accessible language. God
was preparing me for another work, but I did not know it.

In Essays 1 and 5 I have outlined the spiritual vocation that propelled me into ministry in The Salvation Army. It was toward the middle of my second year as a tutor at Gray's Inn that matters of a sacred calling crystallised. It became clear under God that any career in the law was to be seen by me as merely preparatory. With this in mind I found myself intrigued on reading of a vacant position on the staff of the popular Law Faculty at the University of Bristol. The post was to be for 12 months only, to cover the teaching of one of the law professors taking sabbatical leave. It was my only chance, before leaving the law, to see if I could handle being a university faculty member. Helen encouraged me to apply. She was by then starting her teaching career in Edmonton, and I would be able to commute by car between Bristol and our little house in Argyle Road, Edmonton, spending four days each week at the university. I was given the job and a substantial rise in salary.

The extra money helped us to buy our beloved MG sports car. It was a two-seater, open-topped, very fast little thing with black leather upholstery and bright-red body paint. How we cherished that car! Here I will digress. Not everyone liked it. Soon after arriving in it at the Army's International Training College (ITC) in London in 1971, a captain on the staff approached me as I was locking it, looked it over, and then and there opined that it was much too flashy, too worldly a car for a cadet. Was I hearing correctly? He seemed to discount the fact that other cadets had arrived in conventional saloon cars that were far costlier. It was the image that seemed to trouble him. Clumsily he asked, 'Are you sure your all is on the altar?' I felt patronised. Clearly he knew nothing about me. I assured him there was no need to fret about the depth of my calling, and held back from saying more even though his gauche remarks invited it. So this was to be college life, I thought! Little did the captain know that the Training Principal's wife, Mrs Lieut-Commissioner Margarethe Warren, had only days before openly admired the MG and even offered to finish washing it down for me to allow me to get to her husband's office on time for an interview! How I liked Mrs Warren! She was so normal! But I must record that I declined her lovely offer. It would have meant giving her the keys and my instincts told me she would probably delight in taking it for a spin through the local suburbs!

It was in the course of driving up and down from home in London to Bristol University that I discovered the joys of the open Wiltshire countryside and of towns like Marlborough. There I bought our precious print of Spitzweg's 'The Bookworm'. It was in Bristol that I met Jim Stevens and John Yelland, both formidably bright. We became good friends as fellow members of the Law Faculty, having all three arrived to take up posts at the same time. It proved to be a full year. I played cricket for the staff against the students, won the staff's annual demonstration moot, occupied rooms at Bristol's Badock Hall located in Clifton, Bristol, and was given responsibility for overseeing the welfare of students living in hall in return for my rooms being rent-free. Among my fellow residents in hall were several students who were good Christians. Their friendship and warm fellowship, especially that of David Slingsby (see Essay 10), enriched me enormously.

The year in Bristol passed rapidly before it was time to pack up and head for the ITC and Denmark Hill. Both Helen and I had felt deeply fulfilled in our teaching roles but there was a persistent inner voice to be obeyed, and obeyed with glad and youthful hearts.

Cadet studies

The college buildings were erected in the 1920s and gave off a heavy art deco architectural presence (but see also Essay 12). I confess candidly that as a cadet I found the surroundings closing in on me. I felt stifled, almost claustrophobic. Helen and I were assigned one tiny room on the top floor of House 6. It had an open-air vent in the wall between us and the corridor, allowing every conversation to be overheard from outside. Bathroom facilities were shared by 10 cadets. We were required to clean these areas under strict supervision. I never understood why we had to use industrial scouring powder on the white enamel surfaces, only to see them steadily eroded.

I came to look forward to time spent in the classroom. There our tutors proved themselves personable and knowledgeable. I benefited especially from the doctrine classes of Captain Clifford Ashworth. He understood our varied academic backgrounds and was gifted in speaking and teaching with clarity. He was relaxed and always approachable, as was his wife, Ann, who supervised the college library and secured for me an entire paperback set of the works of the German theologian and martyr, Dietrich Bonhoeffer. These were to be my leisure-time reading as a cadet. They made me hungry for more.

King's College again

Thus it was that, with Helen's wise counsel, I approached the training college authorities to act upon advice given me, before entering training, by Captain Ian Cooper. He told me how he and Captain John Coutts had taken advantage of the University of London's regulations and had been fast-tracked through the theology department at King's College to gain formal graduate qualifications in divinity. Helen and I decided to seek permission for me to do the same. After speaking to my college leaders about undertaking formal theological studies away from the cadet campus while still following all normal cadet activities outside the classroom, it was agreed I could contact the Dean of Studies at King's, the Reverend Dr Sydney Evans. He assented at once to admitting me to the Faculty of Theology, bypassing the first year and granting me permission to enter for the final examinations after only two years of study. His sole condition was that I should master New Testament Greek beforehand. He would provide a weekly tutorial for me in Greek, free of fees, prior to the start of the following academic year. My Army leaders deliberated on this and, with advocacy on my behalf by two recently appointed training officers, Lieut-Colonel Alistair Cairns (Chief Side Officer for Men) and Major Lyndon Taylor (Education Officer), the plan was approved. It was then decided to free us entirely from the second year of cadet training and we were appointed as Cadet-Lieutenants to Burnt Oak Corps in north London. It was a tiny corps, giving me time to pursue my studies. It also gave us back our freedom and our privacy.

Helen and I explicitly dedicated these years of study to the Lord, not knowing how they might be used but sensing the rightness of it all. The plan gave us a renewed spirit of gratitude and respect for our leaders who had been ready to think outside rigid tramlines. For the second time in my life I experienced the opening up of a new world of ideas, concepts, facts, philosophies, language and learning that I had hardly known to exist. I found my personal faith stimulated and deepened. I saw the Christian faith as having intellectual, rational foundations that were new to me. I felt pleased, excited, responsive. That same hunger of the mind, the love of books, the seclusion of the university library all returned as familiar friends from my days as a student and teacher of the law. This time, though, there was a difference. Now the studying was a sacred trust. God's servants in the Army had allowed it and God's money was paying for it. I was studying as an expression of devotion to Christ: 'Take my intellect....'

The final examinations were only months away (success or failure would depend on the outcome of 27 hours of written examinations at the end of the final year – no continual assessment in those days!) when we were instructed to meet the Training Principal at Denmark Hill. Colonel Arthur Linnett had succeeded Lieut-Commissioner Harry Warren. The colonel, whom we had not previously met, was of a kindly disposition and told us that the Africa Department at International Headquarters (IHQ) had asked for us to be assigned to the Rhodesia Territory when my studies were concluded. The colonel asked if we were willing. Yes, we replied, we were willing to go anywhere and do anything for God in the Army. Very quickly we found ourselves transferred from Burnt Oak Corps to IHQ and to accommodation in Balham, south London, with full freedom to complete my studies on a full-time basis. We lived in a large house split into two self-contained flats. Imagine our delight on discovering that our downstairs neighbour would be Colonel Catherine Baird, arguably the Army's most gifted poet (see Essay 10).

On my setting out each day for King's College, Helen and I would commit it all to God in prayer. My heart held a deep and settled longing for these studies to honour God. So it was that I managed to approach the final examinations with a calm spirit. The results were sent out by mail several weeks later. I found my name at the top of the lists and was awarded the 1974 Relton Prize for my performance in the examinations. God had honoured it all. My efforts had been rewarded, but so too had Helen's constancy, and also the wisdom and generosity of the Army and my leaders. I could not know that 38 years later our son, John, would also be awarded the Relton Prize (2012) for his performance in the MA in

336

Systematic Theology, the only time both father and son have been granted this distinction.

I went to King's in the Strand, sought out Dean Evans and thanked him for taking a risk with me. There in his handsome, book-lined study, he beamed his pleasure and said he had never taken a surer risk and would welcome any others the Army wished to send to him. It was a good moment. Dean Evans held his academic post from 1956 to 1978, to be succeeded by Professor Ulrich Simon, a survivor of Nazism and another whose writings brought me much pleasure and insight. He was born of Jewish parents, grew up in Berlin, came to London when the Nazis took power, and later converted to Christianity, becoming an Anglican parish priest (see Essay 8).

I give thanks to God for these experiences at King's, whose motto is *Sancte et Sapienter*, 'Holy and Wise'. I like that. It is a motto to encourage the seeking of grace to go deeper into Christ whose holiness and sanctity are beyond compare and yet available to be apportioned to the sincere and seeking human heart. As we set sail for Africa in early 1975 I had no thought of ever returning to King's College but events years later, once again through the prompting of Helen, meant I would one day be reunited with this notable centre of learning and research.

Meanwhile Helen had been pursuing theological studies of her own to add to her degree and postgraduate professional teaching qualification. The Army's training college got her started on work for the London University's Certificate in Religious Knowledge (CRK) and during our first year in Rhodesia she completed it and was awarded a distinction. This was in addition to her teaching duties at Mazowe School and her role as wife and mother of two, Jenny being born at the end of our first year in Africa when Matt was three years old.

I was proud of her. I was fully aware also that when IHQ asked us to take appointments in Rhodesia it was primarily Helen they wanted, for she was a fully-qualified professional teacher and I was not. My experience lecturing in law cut little ice when it came to teaching young men in an African secondary school. The same was true of my theological qualifications. So Helen earned a higher government salary than me and thus made a larger contribution to the school's finances since our salaries were paid directly to the school and we received only the much lower allowance for officers. Helen taught the upper forms. I spent much of my time in administration as Vice-Principal and taught English and Bible Knowledge to the lower forms. We loved being in the classroom at Mazowe. The students were responsive and hungry to succeed.

Postgraduate research

It was several years later that the Army decided to make direct use of my legal background. In 1982 we were reassigned from Enfield Corps in the British Territory to join IHQ. I was to succeed the very able Major Bramwell Baird as the in-house legal adviser with the title of Legal and Parliamentary Secretary. My experiences in this role from 1982-89 are outlined in Essay 7B.

In 1985 we celebrated my 40th birthday. 'Life begins at 40,' they say. I recall the onset of strong, irrational feelings that the years were fleeting fast and I seemed to have accomplished little by way of note. Such feelings, I was told, were not unusual in midlife. I could stand outside myself and analyse what was going on in me, but sometimes perspective gets lost and one's feelings do not entirely accord with the objective facts. Helen seemed to understand all this and one day said that although my role at IHQ was absorbing, stimulating, privileged and involved much travel, it was obvious I needed something additional to go at. Thus it came about that I contacted King's College again to enquire about embarking on work for a Doctor of Philosophy degree (PhD). Holders of first-class honours degrees were not required to work initially for a Master's degree but could enrol directly for the Doctorate. The university agreed at once that I could so enrol, to be supervised by Professor Keith Ward, FD Maurice Professor of Moral and Social Theology and author of many books in those fields of study.

My research built upon my long-standing interest in the ethics of warfare and was an ethical analysis of the Army's actions and attitudes in time of war, beginning in 1899 with the Second Boer War and covering both World Wars, 1914-18 and 1939-45. Let me cite here the opening acknowledgement in the finished thesis (which amounted to 135,000 words):

'I wish to acknowledge gratefully the generous, willing help of my secretary, Mrs Jean Wilson, and the guidance received from my supervisor of studies at King's College, London, Professor Keith Ward. I offer warm thanks also to Major Jenty Fairbank of the Army's Heritage Centre, London, and to Mr Thomas Wilsted and Miss Judith Johnson, of the Army's Archives and Research Centre, New York. I am grateful also for the help of my clerk, Mr Grahame Whitehead. Finally, I want to record that, but for the love and encouragement of Helen, my wife, the research would have never been undertaken, still less completed.'

The bound volumes of the thesis record warm thanks also to the King's College Theological Trust, the Gerald Bailey (Quaker) Trust, and the IHQ of The Salvation Army for financial assistance to facilitate the research.

Keith Ward was an approachable, scholarly, Christian academic who gave me every encouragement. He was gracious toward me as a mature student, and warmly respectful concerning the Army. The completed thesis, which had evolved from an exercise in moral theology to become a contribution to the history of religion, was subjected to the usual rigorous scrutiny after four years (you could take up to seven years) of part-time research and writing. The internal examiner for the University of London was Dr Judith Champ, accompanied by Dr Stuart Mews of Lancaster University as the external examiner. They were relaxed and warm toward me during the *viva voce* (oral) examination held on Friday 6 January 1989 and with wide smiles told me the degree of Doctor of Philosophy was mine and I could henceforth call myself 'Dr Clifton'! It was a good day.

Helen had been waiting for me in the imposing entrance hall at King's College in the Strand and could tell at once from my demeanour as I descended the stone staircase to join her that all was well. It was her achievement as much as mine for she was party to much of my researches, aware of many of the sources, and had spent hours in various libraries helping me dig out obscure historical data. Furthermore she had set up our house with space and privacy for me to write, a task that occupied numberless hours. I would write amid mountains of books and documents, always to the muted accompaniment of the music of Enfield Citadel Band on the record player.

Helen was with me also on 13 December 1989 at the graduation ceremony (where fellow-Salvationist, Olwyn Westwood, was also receiving a doctorate that day). I wore my full Army uniform under the scarlet doctoral gown to walk across the platform of the Royal Albert Hall and make the customary bow to Lord Flowers, the Vice-Chancellor of the University. My father was there too. Like every son, I wanted and needed his approval. He provided this naturally, unaffectedly, and in generous measure.

ESSAY 14

❦

SUPPORTING

ESSAY 14
SUPPORTING

WERE I to make no mention of sport this collection of autobiographical essays would be incomplete. I like sport. It is a not insignificant component of my life, taking me away from what can sometimes be the treadmill of work and duty. It is an icebreaker, a bond-creator, a gentle but effective social passport with friend and stranger alike. Ride any London taxi and the chances are that if the driver fails to chat about the weather or politics he will turn quickly to sport. Whether watching or participating, sport is one of life's real pleasures. I have only to think back to games of squash in Rhodesia to relive the exhilaration of exercise, the stimulus of friendly competition, and the camaraderie over post-match refreshments.

My beloved Spurs

Anyone who knows me well knows I am a passionate fan of Tottenham Hotspur Football Club. I was just 12 when my Dad took me to my first game at the famous White Hart Lane stadium in the northern suburbs of London. We lived in nearby Edmonton. Because it was raining I wore my school cap with its distinctive blue circle on top and was able to spot it on the television news later that evening. In those days few spectators sat down. We stood on the terraces to watch and cheer with 65,000 others. My pal, Peter Boreham, and I would meet straight from school if it was a midweek game. We lined up early at the 'Boys Gate', avoiding the hooves of the police horses controlling the crowds in Paxton Road. It cost only nine old pence to get in (there were 240 pence to the British pound back then!).

Peter and I always stood at the front of the crowd behind the goal at the Park Lane end and saw every single home game of the 1960-61 season when Spurs became the first team of the 20th century to achieve the so-called 'impossible dream' of 'The Double', winning both the Football League and the Football Association Cup in the same season. Captained by the elegant, eloquent Northern Irishman, Danny Blanchflower, they were simply unstoppable. Even Bob Wilson, goalkeeper of our arch-rivals,

Arsenal, claimed for many years that this Spurs 'Double Team' was the best he had ever seen.

Bill Brown, a Scot, kept goal. Ron Henry and Peter Baker, both English, were the accomplished, watchful full backs. Blanchflower played in midfield as the right-half back, with the peerless Scot, Dave Mackay, on the left. Maurice Norman, another English international, was the centre-half back. Leading the front-line attack was the Yorkshireman, Bobby Smith, fearless, stocky and strong. Either side of him were Johnny White, one of the most skilful, visionary players in the history of the game, and Les Allen, a prolific goalscorer. Completing the forwards were the Welshman, Cliff Jones, a lightning-quick winger, and the diminutive Terry Dyson who ran and ran for 90 minutes, stretching and startling even the stoutest of defenders. Should a player be injured and unable to start, Tony Marchi stood in, competent in any position. There were no substitutes in those days.

These footballers were my boyhood heroes. So familiar was I with them that I could tell at a glance even 80 or 90 metres away and on a misty evening who was on the ball. They played in rain or shine, on grass or mud, on ice or snow. Masterminding it all was the manager, Bill Nicholson. He had been a formidable player in his own right, scoring against Portugal only 19 seconds from the kick-off when making his debut for the England team. Now he applied his Yorkshire grit and wisdom to mould the best team of British players that until then had ever been created.

Success in 1961 took Spurs into the European Cup (now the UEFA Champions League). I was present at White Hart Lane for the second leg of the 1962 semi-final when we lost narrowly to the eventual winners, Lisbon's Benfica led by the legendary Eusebio, whose death aged 71 has been announced as I write, triggering three days of Portuguese public mourning. We rattled the crossbar in the dying minutes of the game, only to lose by a margin of one goal. My young heart ached that night, but how I glowed with pride when soon afterwards Spurs went on to win the European Cup Winners' Cup, the first English club to lift a European trophy. They trounced Atletico Madrid 5-1 in the final played in Rotterdam, Holland.

Of all the players it was John White who impressed me for skill and guile. I have seen him split defences wide open with one deceptive sway

344

of his hips before drilling the ball into the net. I came home from school one day in 1964 to see John White's face being shown on the TV news bulletin. They announced that he had been killed by lightning while playing golf. They found his gifted body in a ditch near a charred tree. I could scarcely speak. How could this be? He was only 27 years old. His ability to drift unnoticed into space on the field of play had earned him the nickname of 'The Ghost'. His story is told by his son, Rob, and the journalist Julie Welch in their 2011 *The Ghost of White Hart Lane – In Search of my Father the Football Legend.*

If I admired John White for his skills, it was the indomitable Dave Mackay who truly won my heart for his bustling, fearless, all-action style of play. He had finesse and sureness of touch on the ball but was also a ferocious tackler. Opponents tried to keep out of his way. Yet off the field he was a quiet, mild-mannered, gracious man. In 1982 Thames Television ran a competition to mark the centenary of the Spurs club. I entered by writing 50 words on my favourite player, Dave Mackay, and won a volume of photographs and historical narratives, which I still have, called *And the Spurs Go Marching On* (Hamlyn, 1982). Our third child is named John David, John after the writer of the fourth Gospel and David after Dave Mackay! When he retired, Mackay owned a factory manufacturing men's neckties. Many a Salvationist wears his ties. They carry the 'Mackay' label on the back. When several of my fellow Salvationists who were Arsenal fans (and thus felt nothing but antipathy toward my team) were told of this, they could not wait to get home to cut the labels from their ties! Such is football's rivalry! I laughed about that.

Helen and I often went to games together. She too was an ardent fan. Spurs were the first major English club to sign players from overseas. Manager Keith Burkinshaw brought in the famous Argentines, Osvaldo Ardiles and Ricardo Villa, after their national team had won the World Cup in 1978. Both became crowd favourites. I think of others in the array of talented players we have watched and urged on at White Hart Lane since the 'Double Team': Jimmy Greaves, legendary goalscorer for club and country; Alan Mullery, hard-tackling, indefatigable; Terry Venables, future manager of Spurs and England; the Scot, Alan Gilzean, all grace and poise, signed after the death of John White; Martin Chivers, peerless in the air, tall, robust; the Welsh international, Mike England, stylishly solid in defence; Pat Jennings, quietly spoken Northern Irishman with the safest hands of any goalkeeper; Garth Crooks, intelligent, tireless, now a TV pundit; Glenn Hoddle, a legend in midfield, perfectly balanced; Chris Hughton, aware, swift at left back; Ray Clemence, England's goalkeeper; Graham Roberts, like Dave Mackay reincarnate; Ralph Coates, Geordie winger for club and country; David Ginola, French, fast, a player with panache; Teddy Sheringham, shrewd, visionary, full of craft; Jürgen Klinsmann, German, with us for one season only but what skill; Paul Gascoigne, lavishly gifted but deeply flawed, the best player of his generation; Rafael van der Vaart, subtle, opportunistic; Aaron Lennon, too fast for any full back; Gareth Bale, young Welsh striker, awardee in 2013 of both the Young Player of the Year Award and the Footballer of the Year Award by the Professional Footballers' Association, crazily valued at £85 million and sold in 2013 to Real Madrid.

In November 2004 I went early one Sunday morning to the central London radio studios of the BBC to give a live radio interview. Major Richard Gaudion was with me. I put a suggestion to him: I would buy him breakfast if afterwards he would drive me to White Hart Lane and the Spurs stadium in Tottenham High Road. So it was that we made our way north through Stamford Hill and on toward the Spurs ground. Entrance was free. Only the section near Paxton Road was open. The famous manager of the 'Double Team', Bill Nicholson, had died aged 85 and now a memorial service was to be held for him in the stadium. We went in and joined the thousands who had also come to honour Bill's memory. The club chaplain, a Methodist minister, led the service from a platform built over the penalty spot. She did well. We sang and prayed and listened to tributes by players from the 1960s. Mrs Nicholson and her family were there. At the end doves were released from the centre circle to the prolonged applause of the crowd. Gratitude, dignity and lasting memories of great sporting achievements under Bill's guiding hand.

Our elder son, Matt, wanted to be a goalkeeper. He would plunge himself uninhibitedly to left and right as I took shots at him in the improvised goal in the local park. He had good anticipation and handling skills, being about eight years old in those days. His younger brother, John, began to receive coaching when aged only six. We lived in Middlesbrough. The coaches had these tiny lads playing 11-a-side on full-sized pitches and taught them how to tackle in a manner hard but fair. I did my bit in our garden as John came in to tackle me, taking the ball off my toes or by-passing me to the left or right with a flick of his foot. On reaching Boston, USA, when he was eight John was able to sign up for the local version of kids' football called 'soccer'. They played on reduced-size pitches with only six-a-side. No tackling was allowed (oh dear…). When he reached New Zealand, aged 15, he was able to play normal football again and developed into a hard-tackling, composed centre back coached by a former professional player from Falkirk in Scotland. He played for his school and also a local club, holding his own with composure even when competing against grown men.

One of the great pleasures of my life is to go to White Hart Lane and watch the Spurs play, with Matt and John seated either side of me, the crowd roaring support, and Spurs in form with their traditionally skilled game built on rapid, short passing of the ball. Style, all style. Better to go down to defeat in style than to eke out a dull draw playing the long ball drearily forward in the vain hope of a chance goal.

So Spurs remain dear to my heart. I am a shareholder in Tottenham Hotspur plc which makes me eligible to attend and vote at shareholder meetings, a right I have yet to exercise!

By way of a passing footnote I should mention lowly Carlisle United in the far north of England. Often Helen and I saw them play at Brunton Park during our holiday visits to Cumbria's Lake District. On one occasion we sat near a radio commentator who was relaying reports of the game for local hospital radio. 'I have two Spurs fans next to me,' he told his listeners, 'but tonight they are cheering for Carlisle!' Nice.

Sport in Boston, USA

Our two short years in Boston, Massachusetts, instilled into us a strong attachment to the city's famous baseball team, the Boston Red Sox. There is an old saying: 'Don't get involved with the Red Sox for they'll only break your heart!' Our first experience of Fenway Park, home of the Red Sox, was in July 1995 soon after arriving in the States. The visiting team, the Texas Rangers, seemed to do well that Saturday evening. It was a low-scoring game over nine innings and, as newcomers not yet educated in the finer points of baseball, we went home thinking it all a bit dull. However, as time ticked by our grasp of the game improved and we became committed Red Sox fans, seizing every opportunity to obtain tickets or to watch the game live on TV.

The club had an illustrious past and had won the so-called 'World Series' several times until selling the famous Babe Ruth to their arch-rivals, the New York Yankees, in 1920. Thereafter many decades went by without further 'World Series' success. Those of a superstitious mind believed the Red Sox to be cursed and that they would never win the 'World Series' again, but in 2004 they came back from a 0-3 best-of-seven games deficit to defeat the New York Yankees and win the American League Championship. They then went on to overcome the St Louis Cardinals and to win the 'World Series'. Next day the sports headlines announced that the dreaded curse had been lifted! All very silly, but great fun. As I write, news is to hand of the Red Sox winning the 2013 World Series!

When Matt and Jen came to Boston to visit us in August 1996 we went as a family of five to Fenway Park to see our team take on, but lose to, the Seattle Mariners. We were in the cheap seats in the uncovered stands, the 'bleachers', when just a few minutes before the game was due to start a public announcement told the capacity crowd to abandon their seats forthwith and take cover down below under the seating areas. A violent thunder and lightning storm was about to hit Boston. Rapidly the crowd evacuated the seated areas and huddled under cover among the food outlets. For two hours we waited out the storm. Many simply went home, but we were 'real' fans and stayed to see the whole game. It ended at 1 am the next morning. Helen spent the final hour asleep with her head on my shoulder. We wanted mid-game snacks, but found that all the outlets had been stripped of every single drink and food commodity during the storm!

Each year the Red Sox feature a 'Salvation Army Night'. The fans would bring cans or packets of food, handing them to Army staff manning tables near the turnstiles. An Army vocal group in uniform would start the evening's events by singing 'The Star-Spangled Banner' from the centre of the playing area. On these occasions we would be given several complimentary tickets for the game, a nice bonus. Even now we still keep an eye out for the Red Sox results.

Pakistani sporting passions

If you do not understand cricket you will never quite grasp the strong passion of Pakistanis for this once-gracious game characterised by sportsmanship and courtesy but which today is played with large sums of money at stake and with the once-honourable rules stretched to the limit. The old adage, 'But that's not cricket!', once an appeal to transparency and fairness, has lost its meaning.

Pakistanis play cricket everywhere: on street corners; on every piece of waste ground; in the parks; and of course in the purpose-built stadia. Even territorial headquarters in Lahore has its own cricket pitch where the staff and their children play long into the lighter evenings using an ordinary tennis ball covered in insulating tape to give it added weight, a 'tape-ball'.

On the day we first landed at Lahore airport (see Essay 6) the skies were dark and heavy. Rain fell for hours. As we drove through the city with the flooding rain water washing over the front of the car, still the impromptu games of cricket continued on every hand. John, aged 10, was delighted. Things were looking up! Perhaps leaving Boston behind would not be so bad after all.

The Pakistan Test team were renowned for their formidable skill and passion. It was in late 2000 that the England team came to face them. Helen, John and I went to see them play a warm-up game against a local Lahore team in Lawrence Gardens. John toured the boundary rope gathering players' autographs, even following the team bus at the close of play in late afternoon back to the rather grand Pearl Continental Hotel. There he hung around the elevators. Eventually the famous England pace bowler, Darren Gough, emerged from his room. This bluff Yorkshireman happily provided an autograph and asked John what he was doing in Lahore. 'I am here with my parents who work for The Salvation Army.' 'Ah, yes, they do good work,' said Gough. John's day was complete.

A few months later the McDonalds chain of fast food outlets, then recently established in Lahore, brought another Yorkshire and England cricketing legend to Pakistan to promote their brand. This was the famous Geoffrey Boycott. On 8 February 2001 John and I went to McDonalds for the great man's appearance. All the customers had miniature cricket bats awaiting his autograph. After some delay suddenly there he was, elegantly tailored in tropical beige, complexion tanned, the strong jaw immediately noticeable. He was less tall than I had imagined. This was one of the greatest batsmen the game had ever seen and here we were in Lahore about to meet him on a hot, humid night. We lined up for his signature with six mini bats to be signed. We were the only non-Pakistanis in the crowd. Geoff saw us coming and grinned. 'Eh, fancy seeing you 'ere. What are you doing 'ere?' The Yorkshire accent was unmistakeable. As he signed our bats I spoke of our work and of the Army. 'I like that,' said Geoff, 'yes, I do admire that.' I told him, 'I've often seen you play when I was young and it was wonderful.' Amicably he shook our hands. With that we merged into the crowd and headed home to Helen with our autographed trophies. The signed bats became gifts for our family's men folk the next time we took homeland furlough. How pleased we were to give one to my Dad, a Yorkshireman and for long an admirer of Boycott's sporting prowess.

Late in 1998 the mighty Australian cricket team came to Lahore. They faced Pakistan at the huge Gaddafi Stadium in a one-day game, each side batting for just 50 overs. Thinking this would be a day/night event beginning in mid-afternoon I promised John I would collect him when school was over and we would head for the stadium. Imagine my puzzlement when Rudy Moore, my private secretary, told me at 11 am that the game had already begun. Hastily he connected me by phone to the Lahore American School, where the school secretary took my call. 'I need to come and collect my son,' I told her. 'What is the reason, Mr Clifton? Does he have a medical appointment?' 'No.' 'Is it for a family emergency?' 'No.' 'Then please tell me the reason, Mr Clifton.' 'Well, I need to get him to Gaddafi Stadium because the game has started already.' 'Oh yes, of course, you should have said so right away. We'll have him standing ready for you.' This was Lahore, not London! She understood! Wonderful! That day we were again the only white faces in the vast crowd. Each team hit over 300 runs, a record at that time for a one-day game. Australia won, but the Pakistani fans, often so ardent, laughed it off and offered respectful applause in a sporting spirit.

It was in Lahore that we first encountered the sport of polo (see Appendix A). It was played regularly at Racecourse Park. Although the rules normally allowed for six chukkas (six periods of 15 minutes) with a fresh pony used in each chukka, these games would comprise only four chukkas. The players were mostly Pakistani military officers or young, aspiring Argentine riders signed up for the season. As we picked up the finer points of polo our interest grew. It was a pleasant way to spend an afternoon when we were not travelling at the weekend. No charge was made for admission. We would simply turn up and be seated in the stand where refreshments were at once offered, usually sponsored by either Pepsi-Cola or Nescafé. On getting home to England one summer we found our way to Cowdray Park in Surrey to watch professionals play over six chukkas. Everything was done at lightning speed and with great seriousness. It seems the prize money was considerable.

The mighty All Blacks

If you live in New Zealand and fail to take an interest in the famous All Blacks rugby union team you will soon find yourself out of touch with most New Zealanders. This legendary national team is still feared by all who encounter them. Their weekend success or failure can set the national mood on Monday mornings!

In June 2003 the England team came to Wellington to face the All Blacks at the Westpac Stadium ('The Cake Tin') located on the banks of the wonderfully scenic harbour. England were seen as the old colonial masters but who, when in New Zealand, had never beaten the All Blacks (a name accorded to the New Zealanders a century earlier by an English sports journalist when the touring Kiwis lost their green kit and turned out in borrowed black shirts and black shorts). Helen, John and I planned to watch the big match at home on TV. Tickets were as rare as gold dust. The day before the game I was at my desk in Cuba Street when a call came in from one of our well-connected advisory board members in Christchurch. 'Shaw, if you get down straightaway to the offices of New Zealand Rugby Union there are two tickets awaiting you for tomorrow's game.' There was no time to lose. Things in the office would just have to wait! At once Helen drove me across town and dropped me off. A smartly dressed lady led me through innumerable security doors to the ticket office. I was reminded of the Bank of England's vaults! As she handed me the precious tickets she paused, holding them in mid-air to ask, 'Is that an English accent I detect? Who will you be cheering for at the game?' I smiled and replied, 'Not the All Blacks, but thanks very much for the tickets!' Hurriedly, I relieved her of the envelope and left.

The game was a cliffhanger. The wind swirled around the circular stadium that night taking the ball this way and that. Boldly John held aloft his England flag amid the baying, partisan crowd. England refused to be beaten and won narrowly by 15-13. We stayed in our seats to savour the victory as the crowd filed out. Noticing John's flag, an All Blacks fan paused in the exit aisle beside him to say, 'Well done, son, your team played well tonight.' A moment of sporting generosity, still remembered gratefully.

That England team went on to play Australia a week later, winning there by 25-12. A few months later they lifted the Rugby World Cup in November, defeating Australia again by the narrow margin of 20-17. Who can forget Jonny Wilkinson's dramatic drop goal with the last kick of the game?

Despite these stunning southern hemisphere victories for England, today the All Blacks are still the team easiest to admire and hardest to beat. I have two grandsons born and bred in New Zealand. Both Hudson and Lincoln are growing up as devotees of rugby and, of course, as ardent fans of the mighty All Blacks. I know what it is, as a boy, to form a lasting attachment to a team and to stick with them through all the years, come failure or success.

EPILOGUE

I WANT the final words of this volume to speak of the God who made me and who gave me Jesus. So let me adapt verses first penned in the 17th century by Paulus Gerhardt and which, translated by John Wesley, appear as Song 721 in our 1986 *Song Book*:

I give the winds my fears,
I hope and am not dismayed,
God hears my sighs and counts my tears,
And shall lift up my head.

Through waves and clouds and storms
He gently clears my way;
I wait his time, so shall this night
Soon end in joyous day.

Far, far above my thought
His counsel shall appear,
When fully he the work has wrought
That caused my needless fear.

Let me in life, in death,
His steadfast truth declare,
And publish with my latest breath
His love and guardian care.

Soli Deo gloria

APPENDICES

಄

A) POETRY
B) OFFICER APPOINTMENTS
C) INTERNATIONAL TRAVEL

APPENDIX A
POETRY

IT WAS 1979 and Christmas Eve, our first in Africa. We lived in a small but pleasant bungalow on the campus of The Salvation Army's Mazowe Secondary School. Just as I was about to take gifts to place at the foot of the beds of our sleeping children, Matt and Jen, Matt emerged from his bedroom! He was two-and-a-half years old. So here is my poem about that night (with apologies to Clement Clarke Moore and his famous poem 'The Night Before Christmas', also known as 'A Visit From St Nicholas'):

A Christmas Memory

'Twas the night before Christmas when all through the quarters
Not a creature was stirring, not sons and not daughters.
We had one of each then, they snoozed in their beds
With dreams of old Santa Claus filling their heads.
We'd sorted the presents, so crept t'wards their door
When we heard little footsteps come crossing the floor!
Dad dived for the cupboard; his face looked quite manic –
'Intercept him! Intercept him!' he hissed in wild panic.
Small Matthew emerged from his bedroom and said:
'I thought I heard Santa, so got out of bed.'

By now Mum was helpless with ill-suppressed glee
To see Dad reduced by a child of just three
To a state of such terror and paranoid fear,
'Just tell me,' he croaked, 'when the coast will be clear!'
Mum swept up the toddler before he could glimpse
His father come staggering out with a wince
To lean on the wall, giving mother a wave,
As he gasped in relief, 'Phew, what a close shave!'
Mum plied poor old Dad with some nice ginger wine
And told him that everything soon would be fine.

We still have a laugh when at Christmas we creep
To see if our brood have gone right off to sleep.
Old Santa still visits on late Christmas Eve
But now has a trick or two more up his sleeve:
He tries to avoid old floorboards that wiggle,
Resisting temptations to whisper or giggle,
And we dimly remember that when we were small
We used to hear rustlings out in the hall
And hardly dared ask, as we heard the soft pad
Of large slippered feet, 'Is that Santa – or Dad?'

'Bumhudzo' ('Place of Rest') was The Salvation Army's home in Rhodesia for stateless persons in Braeside, Salisbury. Still today it houses and nurses 110 older persons. One day an elderly male resident spoke of his gratitude for the centre and its personnel. He referred repeatedly to 'mapillo' which symbolised the help he had been given. 'Mapillo' was his word for 'my pillow', a symbol of luxury compared with what he had been accustomed to in his earlier years. Helen wrote the following:

Mapillo / My pillow

'Bumhudzo', place of rest, the sign
Engraved upon the door,
A place of rest for weary feet
When working days are o'er.

The tropic sun beats fiercely down
But here in gentle shade
The lonely traveller finds a home,
His head on pillow laid.

For any aged, homeless one
A welcome here is found;
'Come in,' the Major said to us
And proudly showed us round.

The residents were gathered in
The courtyard cool and green
And on their faces patient, dark
A gentle peace was seen.

Who knows the miles their feet have trod,
The sorrows of their life,
The labouring days in mine or farm
In days of peace or strife?

But now, too old to work, and with
Their families lost or dead,
They seek only a friendly home,
A place to lay their head.

'Sing up,' the Major calls, and so
They raise a lively hymn,
Voices still strong and firm belie
The age of bone or limb.

'And now a testimony please.'
At once a number rise,
Their voices sound in fervent praise
And shining are their eyes.

'Mapillo, Lord, this is the thing
That I most thank you for.'
''Til they came here,' the Major said,
'They slept upon the floor.

'They toiled all day and then at night
They lay down on the ground,
The hard-baked floor of wooden hut
The only bed they found.'

I thought of one who, though a King,
Became a helpless babe;
No palace room, no clean white bed,
But in a manger laid.

I thought of him whose parents trod
The rough and dusty road,
Searched for a kindly roof to house
Their small and precious load.

Then one threw wide an open door
With just a stable bed
And there the Lord himself was born,
No pillow for his head.

God bless all those whose call it is
To shelter those in need.
Who gives a home to homeless ones
Will serve the Lord indeed.

On 14 February 2001, St Valentine's Day, I wrote a poem for Helen. We had been watching polo during the tournament for the Basant Polo Cup in Lahore, Pakistan:

Polo

At a canter here they come,
There's a chukka to be won,
Four in all, with handicaps,
All the players such fine chaps.

Helmet hard and burnished boot
Cover riders head to foot;
Manly muscles stretch and strain,
Right hand stick and left hand rein.

Ball put in, they scramble so,
Hard to tell which way they'll go;
Then they're off and chasing hard,
Eating up each grassy yard.

Gaping goalmouths seem to say,
'Strike the ball across this way!'
Ponies pounding, nostrils flared,
Feats of glory to be dared.

Coloured shirt and swirling stick
Stand out in the mêlée thick;
Riding off or marking foe,
All a part of fine polo.

Umpires wearing white and black;
No horse here is just a hack;
Oh so fast they sprint and charge;
It's against the rules to barge.

Grandstand packed with knowing fans,
For both teams we clap our hands.
Padded fetlocks, saddles, bits,
Loudest cheers for mighty hits.

Ponies black, chestnut or gray
Have no time or breath to neigh;
Sleekly groomed, four to a string,
Swift obedience is the thing.

As we watch we clap and cheer
Every rider free from fear.
Polo is a rich man's game,
But we like it all the same.

In the winter of 2001 General John Gowans asked me to travel from Lahore to London to chair a study group charged with the task of revising and updating the Officer Undertakings, the document signed by candidates and cadets prior to being commissioned as Salvation Army officers (see Essay 6). Here is a light-hearted piece I wrote on the flight to London on board Pakistan International Airways (PIA – jokingly known among Pakistani travellers as 'Perhaps I'll Arrive'!):

On PIA

On PIA
I fly away
Lahore left far behind
It's time to go
In search of snow
The forecast said I'd find

P for 'Perhaps'
Seatbelt on laps
My place is near the aisle
With *Expos. Times*
And natty rhymes
I'll relish every mile

With I for 'I'll'
We'll go in style
There's duty to be done
The General's call
Is over all
It's actually quite fun

A for 'Arrive'
No need to strive
The crew does all the chores
I'll just lean back

I've learned the knack
No sweat in these here pores

No open door
The engines roar
We're on our way at last
The pilot's skilled
We're all just thrilled
The runway flashes past

'No smoking' signs
Banned heady wines
This is a Moslem plane
I do not mind
For to my kind
Booze / baccy are a bane

So what's on screen
All to be seen
By flyers large and small
I scan the lists
Too many fists
Do not this chap enthral

And so I go
To audio
It is the music channel
Schubert and strings
With other things
Like this nice soft warm flannel

That low French horn
Sounds quite forlorn
But now it's Mantovani
I take a drink

Just as I think
In Urdu water's 'pani'

The deep string bass
Throbs out the pace
The orchestra's just fine
Hostess with wheels
For midday meals
Time now to choose what's mine

There's quite a choice
So I give voice
And say I'll have the fish
Not murgh mughlai
That's chicken fry
Hot curry in the dish

Mutton pulao
Don't ask me how
The sheep goes with the rice
There's lots of food
They'll think me rude
If I don't find it nice

The chocolate mousse
Has one sole use
And that's to make you slurp
It's deep dark brown
With cherried crown
My neighbour gives a burp

Can there be more
Yes 'petit fours'
One sleeper makes a grunt
Oh woe is me

For can't you see
I've dropped it down my front

Lunch okey doke
With diet Coke
Chicken Manchurian
Look down below
I see deep snow
It is Uzbekistan

North is Tashkent
The hills are rent
With valleys deep and wide
It's Samarkand
Now close at hand
The air's so cold outside

Deep haze of blue
Is in my view
A colour I just love
The 'plane dips west
Must get some rest
No reading light above

I know this tune
It's 'Clair de Lune'
My headphones tell me so
Debussy's themes
Give way to dreams
Two thousand miles to go

And when I wake
They'll bring me cake
Washed down by strange green tea
No ice-cream cone

In this time zone
Just sandwiches and ghee

Who will be there
To stand and stare
To meet me as I come
Heathrow awaits
So clear the plates
And every single crumb

Both Lynne and Matt
Have promised that
They'll eat a meal with me
I'm pleased by this
For how we miss
Them back at home for tea

For Helen's Ma
And too her Da
Their anniversary
Is just this week
So I can speak
Two loving words or three

Safe in my case
As on we race
New clothing for them all
I hope they fit
I'll feel a twit
If they turn out too small

Marcus and Jen
Can't know just when
Old Dad hits London town
In Ohio

To prayer they'll go
To ask a smooth touchdown

Why do I roam
So far from home
Leaving my Love behind
Because you see
It is for me
New O and R to find

The Army's rules
We are no fools
Need modernising now
West Wickham Kent
Where I've been sent
Is where we'll try somehow

The group convenes
From diverse scenes
Its special task to do
I'm asked to lead
Ah Lord give heed
For I'll be needing you

And when I can
Of Pakistan
I'll think and feel homesick
To our front door
On the third floor
I'll get back double quick

To Helen haste
And John whose taste
Is all for Hula Hoops
Time to return

Let's rubber burn
Don't crash or we'll go 'Whoops'

We've done our best
It was a test
But helped by short tea breakings
We have set down
Oh please don't frown
Some brand new Undertakings

To John my pal
Helen my gal
I'll go and will not stray
No more to roam
I'll be back home
God bless ol' PIA

We lived in Lahore for five years. I allowed the following poem to appear in *The Officer* magazine some years later in mid-2008. It seeks to convey the manifold impressions that crowd in upon you as a newcomer there:

Lahore

Noise that won't abate
Smells that suffocate
Streets all in a mess
Cars inducing stress
Kerbstones chipped and cracked
Gossip short on fact
Chickens dripping blood
Monsoons bringing flood
Men with facial hair
Girls so dark but fair
Clothes that mask the face
Styles all charm and grace
Mosques that scream in prayer
Churches here and there
Heat to make you die
Humidity too high
Camels stomping past
Rickshaws moving fast
Kites that float and fly
Haze to cloak the sky
People stand and stare
Beggars everywhere
Police demanding cash
Prickly heat with rash
Children all brown-eyed
Motorbikes to ride
Bishops coming late
Armed guards at the gate

Shoeshine very cheap
Addicts deep in sleep
Hotels large and small
Shopping in The Mall
Donkeys carting loads
Potholes in the roads
Cloth in the bizarre
Sunblinds on our car
Saleem at the wheel
Ghulam cooks the meal
Perveen mops the floor
Dust comes more and more
Time to end my theme
Is it all a dream?
No it's real enough
Smooth or tough and rough
Tabla-drum and song
Here's where we belong

Many people, because of reports of violence, get a distorted image of Pakistan. We found it a vibrant, fascinating country. Once the capital city, Lahore in the end wins your affections. The people are hospitable and kindly. It is a city of some sophistication, with 80 higher education institutions which have earned it the title of 'the Athens of Pakistan'.

In the same issue of *The Officer* I shared the only poem I have ever written which in my view might be worthy of being called 'a poem'. Even though I like poems to rhyme, this one doesn't. As mentioned above, I was chairing a group which met in West Wickham, Kent. Jetlag woke me early. The poem came from seeing the results of a mindless act of vandalism, infant trees killed by forcing them over to snap against their own protective fencing. It shocked me, and reminded me that wanton, mindless violence is not confined to faraway places:

Morning Walk

In England briefly now
No longer in Lahore's hot cauldron sun
I wake too early
Cold morning pre-dawn beckons to my soul
With scarf still new and more worn gloves
I step into a chilled moonlit arena
Kent's countryside
My feet stride out
I follow feeling blessed
To know the cold of winter morning air
Stars over me and over field
I come to where they gather for the games
White football posts like wizened apparitions
Near my path
Then broken saplings
Nine in all
Snapped clean in half by callous killer mind
They lie beyond recovery
To kiss the dampened earth

Skin glowing live in dawn's caress
But inwardly my spirit seared by ice
How could a hand be brutal striking so
In downing wantonly
Nine living trees
The gardener had intended for our good
And then to my own children turns my mind
What hand goes out to break them bend them low
Until they snap beyond endurance point
I give them back to God there in the park
Good Father tender saplings stand and fall
Grant that my young might grow on straight and tall

After receiving my poems composed during the flight and at the West Wickham Retreat Centre, Helen replied as follows:

I Am Awake

I am awake and drinking tea
You are asleep and far from me
Still your email makes you near
And your poems bring good cheer
Glad the journey went okay
Wish you weren't so far away
Never mind we're staying cool
John's another week off school
We've moved the sofa, packed the tree
Watched two movies – make that three
To start the week imagine this
We're watching *Pride and Prejudice*
The mosques are wailing, morning's here
The night was somewhat short I fear
Never mind I can survive
'Til four o'clock or even five
After which I'll make more tea
And miss you sitting next to me
Sharing news about your day
And all the things the people say
Meanwhile amid the cars and kites
I'll try and watch the traffic lights
We'll pray for you 'til you come home
Perhaps you'll bring another poem!
We're sure we will not feel forsaken
If only you remember bacon!
Wrapped in newsprint, insulated
Frozen hard it won't get dated
Good to meet with Lynne and Matt
Time to sit and have a chat

Give our love to England fair
Breathe the lovely cold fresh air
Greet my parents on their day
Wish we weren't so far away
Now I'd better close in time
Or I'll talk all day in rhyme
We send our love and kisses too
And don't forget we're missing you!

In May 2004 we flew from Wellington, New Zealand to attend the International Conference of Leaders in New Jersey, USA, known as the Garden State. Jetlag kept me awake and the following was the result:

Sleepless in New Jersey

Garden State
Can't sleep late
Wide awake
Choice to make
Options few
So what's new?
Watch TV?
Can barely see
Get up now
Dress somehow
Before dawn
Stifled yawn
Hotel clerk
Thinks I'm a jerk
Lobby bare
Cool night air
Parking lot
Deserted spot
Then I hear
Birdsong near
Now I see
The blossom tree
Soft and pink
It makes me think
That even here
At hour drear
On every hand
Just where I stand
The signs are clear
That He is near

In late May 2004 we left New Zealand to take up new leadership roles in London. The following simple verses were written during the second leg of the journey, Los Angeles to London:

LA – London

Lofting like the eagle high
Homeward through the sky we fly
Ocean blue left in the west
California comes to rest

Thirty thousand feet high up
As I drink the pre-meal cup
Far below the desert drear
LA fades far to the rear

Rocky Mountains up ahead
I can see a riverbed
All dried up in sand and grit
Roads through barren passes fit

Oh the view the vista bright
God's rich world all bathed in light
Clouds break free to smile at me
I grin back my spirit free

Land of long white cloud recedes
We have tried to tend her needs
But right now we're on the move
God's good plan again to prove

John is in New Zealand still
This for him is 'Perfect Will'
Matt and Lynne and Hannah wait
Just beyond the airport gate

Big bright 'plane roars on and on
All we've done, well that's now gone
Salt Lake City off port side
On this panoramic ride

Snow-topped peaks look up to see
Jumbo jet Helen and me
Soon we'll be in Wyoming
Oh good Lord now there's a thing!

Greenland Iceland yet to come
Then we make the final run
Dublin Windsor Heathrow too
Vic and Rich to welcome you

'Are you in it, Lord?' we cry
As the UK draws us nigh
'Never doubt that,' comes the word
As we fly in silver bird

'Can we do it?' still we fret
'You are there, Lord, but...and yet...'
'Hush now, I'll be there to bless
Cast aside all strain and stress.'

APPENDIX B
OFFICER APPOINTMENTS

Date	Location
5 July 1973	Burnt Oak Corps, UK
4 October 1973	Attached to Overseas Department, IHQ
24 July 1974	Literary Department, IHQ
20 January 1975	Mazowe School, Rhodesia
10 November 1975	Vice-Principal, Mazowe School, Rhodesia
2 May 1977	Bulawayo Citadel Corps, Rhodesia
11 January 1979	Enfield Citadel Corps, UK
20 May 1982	Legal and Parliamentary Secretary, IHQ
1 June 1989	Bromley Temple Corps, UK
28 May 1992	Divisional Commander, Durham and Tees Division, UK
1 June 1995	Divisional Commander, Massachusetts Division, USA
1 August 1997	Territorial Commander, Pakistan
1 March 2002	Territorial Commander, New Zealand
1 June 2004	Territorial Commander, UK
2 April 2006	General, IHQ
1 April 2011	Entered retirement

APPENDIX C
INTERNATIONAL TRAVEL

RECORDED here are my international assignments as a Salvation Army officer. Journeys when Helen did not accompany me are marked with an asterisk (*).

SECTION ONE
JANUARY 1975 – MARCH 2006

Date	Destination and Purpose
3 January 1975	Sailed from Southampton, UK, to Cape Town, South Africa, then via train to Salisbury, Rhodesia, and Mazowe School
	Arrived Mazowe 20 January
28-30 April 1975 *	Johannesburg: South Africa
	Northern Divisional Youth Councils
25 November 1978	London: UK, via Johannesburg and Brussels
	New appointment in home territory
28-30 July 1982 *	Madrid: Spain
	Legal matters
10-13 September 1982 *	Barcelona, Valencia, Madrid: Spain
	Legal matters
29, 30 September 1982 *	Madrid: Spain
	Legal matters
13-15 April 1983 *	Madrid: Spain
	Legal matters
29 April-9 May 1983 *	Århus, Kolding, Copenhagen: Denmark
	Evangelical meetings
3-19 April 1985	St John's: Canada
	Holy week and Easter meetings
	and

3-19 April 1985 (continued)	Halifax: Canada Visit to Salvation Army Grace Hospital re medical ethics issues
17 October-8 November 1986 *	East-west, coast-to-coast tour of Canada Tour leader with Enfield Citadel Band *and* New York: USA Archival researches for doctoral studies
24, 25 March 1987 *	Chantilly: France Europe Zonal Conference
27-29 August 1987 *	Basel: Switzerland European School for Officer Training, legal constitution consultations
2-9 October 1987 *	Århus, Aalborg, Kolding, Valby, Copenhagen: Denmark Evangelical meetings
15 October 1987 *	Lunteren: The Netherlands Social work conference
22, 23 October 1987 *	Basel: Switzerland European School for Officer Training, ethics lectures
12 January 1988 *	Basel: Switzerland School for Officer Training, legal matters
19 February-1 March 1988 *	Winnipeg: Canada Catherine Booth Bible College, ethics lectures *and* Chicago: USA School for Officer Training, ethics lectures
7-11 May 1988 *	Helsinki: Finland Officers' refresher course (Series I)

12, 13 June 1988 *	Basel: Switzerland European School for Officer Training, Annual General Meeting of General Assembly
28 June 1988 *	Amsterdam: The Netherlands Legal and constitutional matters
19, 20 July 1988 *	Mexico City: Mexico Legal matters
21, 22 July 1988 *	San Salvador: El Salvador Legal matters
22-25 July 1988 *	Bogota: Colombia Legal matters and worship meetings
2-7 September 1988	St John's: Canada Camp meetings at Camp Starrigan
10-15 October 1988 *	Harare, Mazowe: Zimbabwe Legal matters
6-10 May 1989 *	Helsinki: Finland Officers' refresher course (Series II)
17-22 May 1989 *	Guelph: Canada United Divisional Youth Councils
21 September-8 October 1989	Sydney: Australia National Brengle Institute
4-11 March 1991	Copenhagen: Denmark Evangelical meetings
22-27 April 1991 *	Jeløy: Norway Ethics lectures
1-3 June 1991 *	Basel: Switzerland Territorial Youth Councils, seminar leader
8-12 April 1993	Århus: Denmark Evangelical meetings
15-22 August 1993 *	De Bron: The Netherlands European Youth Congress, plenary Bible studies
22-26 June 1994	Berne, Brienz: Switzerland Officiated at wedding

23-25 September 1994 *	Berne: Switzerland Territorial League of Mercy conference, medical ethics seminars
5-23 January 1995	Aizawl: India Inaugural Territorial Brengle Institute
21-24 April 1995	Århus: Denmark Evangelical meetings and seminars
31 May 1995	Boston: USA New appointments as divisional leaders, Massachusetts Division, USA Eastern Territory
1-4 October 1996	Grand Rapids: USA Divisional officers' retreat, USA Central Territory
7-10 November 1996 *	Winnipeg: Canada Catherine Booth Bible College, lectures
8-11 January 1997 *	Pittsburgh: USA Divisional officers' retreat, USA Eastern Territory *and* Alexandria: USA Committee meetings at NHQ
21-27 March 1997 *	London: UK Spiritual Life Commission meeting in Sydenham
17 April-3 May 1997	London: UK Homeland furlough
30 July 1997	London: UK Meeting of Spiritual Life Commission en route to Pakistan
12 August 1997	Lahore: Pakistan New appointments as territorial leaders
10-24 March 1998	Melbourne: Australia International Conference of Leaders (including South Asia Zonal Conference)

1 July-6 August 1998	London: UK Homeland furlough
26 January-3 February 1999	Colombo: Sri Lanka South Asia Zonal Conference
28 April-20 May 1999 *	Sunbury-on-Thames: UK 1999 High Council (Helen attended the later stages)
19 June-22 August 1999	London: UK Homeland furlough; family wedding
18 June-2 July 2000	Atlanta: USA International Conference of Leaders; Millennium Congress
3-10 July 2000	Sidney: USA En route to UK for homeland furlough
11 July-1 August 2000	London: UK Homeland furlough
2-15 August 2000 *	Melbourne: Australia Divisional Congress
27 September-11 October 2000	Wellington: New Zealand Territorial Writers' Conference; Territorial Congress
6-12 January 2001 *	West Wickham: UK Officer Undertakings study group
30 April-6 May 2001	Dhaka: Bangladesh Command officers' retreat
19 May-22 July 2001	London: UK Homeland furlough
20 October-4 November 2001	Toronto: Canada Social Services Conference; Training college lectures
16-25 January 2002 *	London: UK General's Consultative Council
27 February 2002	Wellington: New Zealand New appointments as territorial leaders
28 March-1 April 2002	Nuku'alofa: Tonga Easter meetings

10-13 May 2002 *	Nadi, Suva: Fiji
	Evangelical meetings
16-20 August 2002	Sidney: USA
	Furlough
21 August-12 September 2002	Sunbury-on-Thames: UK
	General's Consultative Council;
	2002 High Council
5-9 December 2002	Suva: Fiji
	Commissioning of cadets
20 December 2002-8 January 2003	Sidney: USA
	Dedication ceremony
9-19 January 2003	London: UK
	Homeland furlough
30 July-6 August 2003	Sydney: Australia
	Coutts Memorial Lecture
	and
	Collaroy: Australia
	Men's Camp
17-20 October 2003 *	Suva: Fiji
	Men's Camp and visit of the
	international secretary
27-31 October 2003	Geelong: Australia
	Tri-Territorial Conference
1-10 November 2003 *	London: UK
	General's Consultative Council
4-8 December 2003	Suva: Fiji
	Training college lectures
16-31 December 2003	Sidney: USA
	En route to London
1-27 January 2004	London: UK
	Homeland furlough
5-10 February 2004	Nuku'alofa: Tonga
	Opening of new regional
	headquarters
28 April-8 May 2004	New York: USA
	General's Consultative Council
	plenary session

23 May 2004	London: UK
	New appointments as territorial leaders
3-10 August 2004	Old Orchard Beach: USA
	Evangelical meetings
7-11 October 2004	Pasadena: USA
	Corps retreat
29 March-5 April 2005	Madrid: Spain
	Europe Zonal Conference
24-27 May 2005	Hanover: Germany
	Visits to Red Shield centres and
	to UK military authorities
31 May-6 June 2005	Moscow: Russia
	Territorial Brengle Institute
10-13 March 2006	Paris: France
	Territorial officers' councils
	(as General-elect)

SECTION TWO
AS THE GENERAL

Date	Destination and Purpose
10-13 May 2006	New York: USA
	Installation of National leaders
22-26 June 2006	Oslo: Norway
	Territorial Congress
1 July 2006	Sheffield: UK
	Officers' retirement meeting
7-15 August 2006	Johannesburg: South Africa
	Theology Symposium;
	Officers' meetings
30 August-4 September 2006	St Petersburg: Russia
	15th anniversary celebrations
14-17 September 2006	Copenhagen: Denmark
	Territorial Congress

27 September-2 October 2006	Colombo: Sri Lanka Territorial Congress
12-21 October 2006	Dallas: USA Pan-American Conference
18 November 2006	Singapore Consultations with territorial leaders
20-27 November 2006	Port Moresby: Papua New Guinea 50th anniversary celebrations
30 November-14 December 2006	Wellington: New Zealand Commissioning of cadets
24-31 January 2007	New Delhi, Amritsar, Gurdaspur, Kolkata: India Territorial Congress, India Northern Territory
1-6 February 2007	Aizawl: India Territorial Congress, India Eastern Territory
25 March-1 April 2007	Rome: Italy Europe Zonal Conference; Meeting with Vatican officials
5-8 April 2007	Boscombe: UK Easter Convention
24-30 April 2007	Winnipeg: Canada William and Catherine Booth College 25th anniversary *and* Toronto: Canada Consultations at THQ
16-21 May 2007	Berne: Switzerland Territorial Congress
5-12 June 2007	Hershey: USA Territorial Congress and Commissioning of cadets, USA Eastern Territory
28 June-2 July 2007	Stockholm: Sweden Territorial Congress
11-16 July 2007	Tokyo: Japan Territorial meetings

30 July-7 August 2007	Uruguay, Paraguay, Argentina Regional rallies in South America East Territory
8-12 August 2007	San José: Costa Rica Territorial Congress, Latin America North Territory
13-17 August 2007	Havana: Cuba Divisional meetings; consultation with Communist Party officials
8-10 October 2007	Oslo: Norway Funeral meetings for Colonel Bo Brekke
17, 18 November 2007	Torquay: UK Divisional Congress
17 June 2008	Sunbury-on-Thames: UK Brengle Institute
15-24 August 2008	Asheville: USA USA Southern Territorial Bible Convention and welcome to cadets at Camp Junaluska
25-27 August 2008	New York: USA Opening of building for International Social Justice Commission
4-8 September 2008	Helsinki: Finland Territorial Congress
12-14 September 2008	Aberdeen: UK Opening of refurbished Aberdeen Citadel hall
28 September-6 October 2008	Seoul: Korea Territorial Centenary Congress
29 October-5 November 2008	Accra: Ghana Territorial Congress
28 November-3 December 2008	Lahore: Pakistan Territorial Congress
4-7 December 2008	Dhaka: Bangladesh Territorial Congress and Commissioning of cadets

8-30 December 2008	Wellington, Nelson, Motueka: New Zealand Meetings; furlough
27-30 March 2009	Brussels: Belgium Officers' meetings and Soldiers' Rally
31 March-2 April 2009	Paris: France Officers' meetings and Soldiers' Rally
3-6 April 2009	Rome: Italy Officers' meetings; Meeting with Vatican officials
19 April 2009	Folkestone: UK Conduct Sunday meetings
10 May 2009	Enfield: UK Conduct Sunday meetings
28 July-5 August 2009	Old Orchard Beach: USA Camp meetings *and* New York: USA Visit to United Nations and meeting with Secretary-General Ban Ki-moon
5 September 2009	Reading: UK Conduct wedding
16-21 September 2009	Lusaka, Chikankata: Zambia Territorial Congress
22-29 September 2009	Harare, Mazowe: Zimbabwe Territorial Congress
8-11 October 2009	Madrid: Spain Command Congress
12-16 October 2009	Atlanta: USA Evangelical meeting *and* Dallas: USA Soldiers' Rally
17-29 October 2009	Sao Paulo, Porto Alegre, Recife: Brazil Pan-American Conference and regional rallies

17-22 November 2009	Santiago: Chile
	South America West Territorial
	Congress
23-25 November 2009	Kingston: Jamaica, Caribbean
	Consultations at THQ,
	Soldiers' Rally
26-30 November 2009	Port au Prince: Haiti
	Caribbean Territorial Congress
12 December 2009	Wellingborough: UK
	Officers' retirement meeting
6-12 January 2010	Boston: USA
	Samuel Logan Brengle 125th
	Anniversary Holiness Convention
10-15 February 2010	Brazzaville: Republic of Congo
	Territorial Congress
8-12 March 2010	Asbury: USA
	Visit to Asbury College
	and
	Alexandria: USA
	Visit to National Headquarters
30, 31 March 2010	Paris: France
	Europe Zonal Conference
1-4 April 2010	Kassel: Germany
	Territorial Congress
7-10 May 2010	Jersey, Alderney, Guernsey: UK
	Tour of Channel Islands corps
16 May 2010	Downham Market: UK
	Soldier enrolment
2-6 June 2010	New York: USA
	Commissioning of cadets and
	retirement of territorial leaders,
	USA Eastern Territory
7-9 June 2010	Dallas: USA
	Meetings with major donors
10-13 June 2010	Chicago: USA
	Territorial Congress and Commissioning
	of cadets, USA Central Territory

14-22 June 2010	St John's: Canada
	Territorial Congress and Commissioning
	of cadets, Canada and Bermuda Territory
7 July 2010	Sunbury-on-Thames: UK
	Pre-commissioning Covenant Day
10 July 2010	London: UK
	Commissioning of cadets
14-19 July 2010	Stockholm: Sweden
	World Youth Convention
21-26 July 2010	Seoul: Korea
	Dedication of centennial centre

SUMMARY OF ACTIVITIES
AS THE GENERAL

Number of countries visited: 41 (for 52 campaigns)
Air miles travelled: 297,226
Official speaking engagements in the United Kingdom: 10
Speaking engagements at the International College for Officers: 50
Other public speaking engagements: 650

INDEX

Notes on the Index

1. References to Shaw Clifton may also include references to Helen Clifton, and vice versa.

2. Many place names also refer to the Salvation Army corps found in those locations.

3. Ranks of Salvation Army personnel, and leaders within the Church and other organisations, have been omitted.

4. Page numbers in italics refer to photographs to be found in the photo pages sections, using the convention *p1-1* etc to indicate section 1, page 1.

393

CREST BOOKS

Salvation Army National Headquarters
Alexandria, VA, USA

Crest Books, a division of The Salvation Army's National Publications Department, was established in 1997 so contemporary Salvationist voices could be captured and bound in enduring form for future generations, to serve as witnesses to the continuing force and mission of the Army.

Stephen Banfield and Donna Leedom, *Say Something*

Judith L. Brown and Christine Poff, eds., *No Longer Missing: Compelling True Stories from The Salvation Army's Missing Persons Ministry*

Terry Camsey, *Slightly Off Center! Growth Principles to Thaw Frozen Paradigms*

Marlene Chase, *Pictures from the Word; Beside Still Waters: Great Prayers of the Bible for Today; Our God Comes: And Will Not Be Silent*

John Cheydleur and Ed Forster, eds., *Every Sober Day Is a Miracle*

Helen Clifton, *From Her Heart: Selections from the Preaching and Teaching of Helen Clifton*

Shaw Clifton, *Never the Same Again: Encouragement for New and Not–So–New Christians; Who Are These Salvationists? An Analysis for the 21st Century; Selected Writings, Vol. 1: 1974-1999 and Vol. 2: 2000-2010*

Christmas Through the Years: A War Cry Treasury

Stephen Court and Joe Noland, eds., *Tsunami of the Spirit*

Frank Duracher, *Smoky Mountain High*

Easter Through the Years: A War Cry Treasury
Ken Elliott, *The Girl Who Invaded America: The Odyssey Of Eliza Shirley*

412

Ed Forster, *101 Everyday Sayings From the Bible*

William Francis, *Celebrate the Feasts of the Lord: The Christian Heritage of the Sacred Jewish Festivals*

Henry Gariepy, *Israel L. Gaither: Man with a Mission; A Salvationist Treasury: 365 Devotional Meditations from the Classics to the Contemporary; Andy Miller: A Legend and a Legacy*

Henry Gariepy and Stephen Court, *Hallmarks of The Salvation Army*

Roger J. Green, *The Life & Ministry of William Booth* (with Abingdon Press, Nashville)

How I Met The Salvation Army

Carroll Ferguson Hunt, *If Two Shall Agree* (with Beacon Hill Press, Kansas City)

John C. Izzard, *Pen of Flame: The Life and Poetry of Catherine Baird*

David Laeger, *Shadow and Substance: The Tabernacle of the Human Heart*

John Larsson, *Inside a High Council; Saying Yes to Life*

Living Portraits Speaking Still: A Collection of Bible Studies

Herbert Luhn, *Holy Living: The Mindset of Jesus*

Philip Needham, *He Who Laughed First: Delighting in a Holy God*, (with Beacon Hill Press, Kansas City); *When God Becomes Small*

R.G. Moyles, *I Knew William Booth; Come Join Our Army; William Booth in America: Six Visits 1886 - 1907; Farewell to the Founder*

413

Joe Noland, *A Little Greatness*

Quotes of the Past & Present

Lyell M. Rader, *Romance & Dynamite: Essays on Science & the Nature of Faith*

R. David Rightmire, *Sanctified Sanity: The Life and Teaching of Samuel Logan Brengle*

Allen Satterlee, *Turning Points: How The Salvation Army Found a Different Path; Determined to Conquer: The History of The Salvation Army Caribbean Territory; In the Balance: Christ Weighs the Hearts of 7 Churches*

Harry Williams, *An Army Needs An Ambulance Corps: A History of The Salvation Army's Medical Services*

A. Kenneth Wilson, *Fractured Parables: And Other Tales to Lighten the Heart and Quicken the Spirit; The First Dysfunctional Family: A Modern Guide to the Book of Genesis, It Seemed Like a Good Idea at the Time: Some of the Best and Worst Decisions in the Bible*

A Word in Season: A Collection of Short Stories

Check Yee, *Good Morning China*

Chick Yuill, *Leadership on the Axis of Change*